IRISH AMERICA

REGINALD BYRON

CLARENDON PRESS · OXFORD

OXFORD

UNIVERSITY PRESS

Great Clarendon Street, Oxford OX2 6DP

Oxford University Press is a department of the University of Oxford.
It furthers the University's objective of excellence in research, scholarship,
and education by publishing worldwide in

Oxford New York

Athens Auckland Bangkok Bogotá Buenos Aires Calcutta
Cape Town Chennai Dar es Salaam Delhi Florence Hong Kong Istanbul
Karachi Kuala Lumpur Madrid Melbourne Mexico City Mumbai
Nairobi Paris São Paulo Singapore Taipei Tokyo Toronto Warsaw

with associated companies in Berlin Ibadan

Oxford is a registered trade mark of Oxford University Press
in the UK and in certain other countries

Published in the United States
by Oxford University Press Inc., New York

British Library Cataloguing in Publication Data

Data available

Library of Congress Cataloging-in-Publication Data

Byron, Reginald.
Irish America / Reginald Byron.
(Oxford studies in social and cultural
anthropology)
Includes bibliographical references and index.
1. Irish Americans—Ethnic identity. 2. Irish Americans—Cultural
assimilation. I. Title. II. Series.
E184.I6B97 1999   305.891'62073—dc21   99–19343

ISBN 0–19–823356–6
ISBN 0–19–823355–8 (pbk.)

1 3 5 7 9 10 8 6 4 2

Typeset in Ehrhardt
by Cambrian Typesetters, Frimley, Surrey
Printed in Great Britain
on acid-free paper by
Biddles Ltd,
Guildford and King's Lynn

In memory of my maternal grandfather,

ARTHUR CHARLES POUND
(1884–1966),

journalist, newspaper editor, essayist, biographer, historian,
and sometime Keeper of the Archives and official Historian
of the State of New York, who taught me that the past is
always with us, for better or worse.

PREFACE

It is the duty of social scientists to take nothing for granted, but to question our commonplace understandings about the social worlds we inhabit. By exploring the realities of Irish-Americanness today, this book questions the idea of Irish America and how we have come to imagine it. It takes as its point of departure an observation made by the American sociologist Herbert Gans in 1979, that as the generations have passed since their immigrant ancestors arrived in America, the ethnic identities of their descendants have been transformed by the nature of the social milieux which have nourished their expression.[1] As assimilation and intermarriage have proceeded over the generations, the hard edges of ethnicity have gradually worn away. While people may still be identified as ethnics by others on the basis of their surnames or physical appearance, the everyday lived experience that once went with being ethnic has largely disappeared, allowing individuals the latitude to decide when, how, and in what degree—if at all—to express their attachment to their ancestry. As the pedigrees of individuals have become mixed and complicated through intermarriage with people of other ancestral backgrounds, their ethnic identity has become increasingly indeterminate. The boundaries of belonging overlap, lose their definition, and melt away. Identity with one's ancestral origins becomes optional, a matter of personal inclination and interpretation.

For the later-generation descendants of European immigrants, Gans's hypothesis has been largely borne out by subsequent research. The American sociologists Richard Alba, Stanley Lieberson, and Mary Waters have shown that in terms of concrete social action, if not also in the ways that people think of themselves, distinctive differences associated with their old-country origins have dimmed and disappeared in everyday social experience as the generations have passed. It is now clear that what constitutes a sense of ethnic identity among these Americans varies greatly in quality and quantity from one individual to another. Moreover, free intermarriage across ancestral lines over the generations has had the result that most people of European origin are nowadays of mixed descent: *which* of their European origins they might identify with, if any,

---

[1] H. Gans, 'Symbolic Ethnicity: The Future of Ethnic Groups and Cultures in America' *Ethnic and Racial Studies*, 2 (1979), 1–20.

the analyst cannot presume to know in advance. Thus neither the social distribution nor the cultural contents of ethnicity can any longer be taken for granted, but must be established empirically.

In the same paper, Gans noted that ethnicity is determined not only by what goes on among the ethnics, but also by developments in the larger society, a remark which echoed the point made by Max Weber in 1921, that the appearance and persistence of ethnic identification is related to its political context.[2] Until the 1970s, the prevailing political ideology in America was that of the melting-pot: immigrants' children were officially described as native-born Americans who were expected to have largely sloughed off their parents' old-country loyalties, and it was widely assumed that by the third generation their grandchildren would be completely assimilated, unethnic Americans. For millions of people of European origin, this was not merely a political ideology buttressed by a scholarly theory (that of 'straight-line' assimilation): it was a moral project, a fundamental civic value of Americanness in which they were brought up to believe. Over the generations, they strove to make their children the same as their neighbours' children: unethnic, unhyphenated, unlabelled, and undifferent. That a high degree of assimilation was largely achieved, at least for the later-generation descendants of people of European origin if not for other Americans, is broadly supported by the findings of recent sociological research. Yet, paradoxically, as the lived-and-felt experience of ethnicity has been transformed by generational distance and complicated by intermarriage, a new political arena—that of multiculturalism—has emerged since the 1970s. New *ethnies* have been created, and moribund ones revitalized and reinvented just at a moment in American history when they had all but vanished for the descendants of mid-nineteenth century European immigrants. As it has come to be widely accepted—so gradually that the truly profound nature of this ideological shift has perhaps received less recognition than it ought—that everyone in America should now have 'an ethnic identity' and that every newly invented or reinvented *ethnie* should be furnished with 'a culture' and 'a history', Weber's observation now seems more applicable to American society than ever before: *ethnies* are not to be understood as things in themselves, but only in relation to the other *ethnies* by which they are defined. In exploring contemporary Irish-Americanness, then, this book also raises questions about the societal circumstances in which ideas of Irishness have been created and re-created.

---

[2] M. Weber, *Economy and Society*, i, G. Roth and C. Wittisch (eds.), 389–95.

The following chapters are the product of many minds and hands. This book could not have been written without the kindness and forbearance of more than 500 people in Albany, New York, who allowed us into their homes and let us talk to them about their Irish immigrant ancestors, their family traditions, and their feelings about being of Irish descent in contemporary America. To all, I owe a debt of gratitude. Nor could it have been written without the generous support of the Economic and Research Council, who funded this project for three years from 1991 to 1993. I am also grateful to my colleagues, former colleagues, and professional acquaintances who have in one way or another, knowingly or not, contributed ideas to this book including, at Swansea, C. C. Harris, Richard Jenkins, John Parker, and Marie Gillespie; in Albany, Richard Alba, George and Sharon Gmelch, and John McEneny; in other places Orvar Löfgren and Konrad Köstlin; and, anonymously, the reviewers and audiences of papers written and presented during the years when the ideas embodied in this book were in the making. I was also helped by the staff of the McKinney Library of the Albany Institute of History and Art, the library of the State University of New York at Albany, and the Albany County Hall of Records. To my former research assistants, Brenda McAteer and Eamonn McKeown, I am especially grateful. As my eyes and ears for nearly three years, Brenda and Eamonn conducted most of the interviews and collected much of the other raw material upon which this book is based. During those three years their thoughts merged with mine and mine with theirs, and they will find some of these ideas and perhaps even a few of their words from their case-file write-ups in this book. None the less, it needs to be emphasized that neither Brenda nor Eamonn was involved in the writing of this book; I take sole responsibility for the way the material they collected has been interpreted. Since some of those whom Brenda and Eamonn interviewed, often at length and on several occasions, will read this book, I would not like it thought that any infelicities in the way their words and feelings have been represented, or how they have been fitted into the argument, are Brenda or Eamonn's fault in any way. Finally, I should like to thank my wife, Caroline, and my two sons for their understanding of my absent-mindedness and obliviousness to all and everything around me during the sabbatical semester in which this book was written.

Swansea
January 1998

CONTENTS

LIST OF TABLES

1

Prologue

I

Irish America is an amalgam of images drawn from Irish and American history and popular culture, the product of two worlds in two centuries: Irish nation-building in the old world in the nineteenth century, and American pluralism and multiculturalism in the new world in the twentieth century. Interpretations of the past have merged into the present and have come to colour our understandings of social memory, self-image, and ethnic identity among the current generations of Americans who are descended from Irish immigrant ancestors.

Most Irish emigrants to America left their native country at a time of agrarian upheaval and economic depression. The causes of Ireland's condition generated passionate debate, which joined with other eighteenth- and nineteenth-century intellectual currents eventually to produce in literature and political rhetoric the idea of an Irish *ethnie*, a people with a history and culture distinctively different from those of their neighbours. The development of a cultural politics was not unique to Ireland, and as elsewhere in Europe crystallized into a nationalist movement whose proponents believed that it was the natural destiny of culture and polity to have the same boundaries. Nationalist sentiment in Ireland had a chequered history during the nineteenth century: sometimes rising to the surface, then falling out of public interest. Only at the very end of the century, and the beginning of the twentieth, did public sympathy with the nationalists' cause become widespread, and in the parliamentary general election of 1918 gather enough votes to give a popular mandate to the establishment of an independent Irish republic, so provoking a series of dramatic events that led to constitutional crisis and the dissolution of the Union with Great Britain in 1921.

Yet, today, Ireland is stereotypically portrayed as being constantly on the brink of revolution throughout the nineteenth century. It seems nowadays to be assumed that every immigrant from Ireland worthy of being regarded as truly and properly Irish was the embodiment of a distinctive, idealized national culture or ethnic type; that each was the innocent victim of deliberate oppression; and that all left Ireland against their will. The temptation to use exaggerated, overgeneralizing, and morally charged ideas of this kind to explain the nature of emigration and the character of Irish emigrants to America, and to interpret the ethnic identity of their descendants, has proved irresistible to scholars and popular writers on the Irish in America. These images of Irishness influence what research is done, where it is done, and how it is done. While much has been written recently about the 'Irish-American immigrant experience' and the 'culture', 'ethnicity', and 'identity' of the current generations of Americans of Irish descent, remarkably few writers have looked beyond the nineteenth-century ethnic enclaves of New York, Boston, Philadelphia, or Chicago; or have asked how the notion of a distinctive Irish-American ethnic culture in contemporary America can be reconciled with four, five, or six generations of intermarriage and assimilation over the last century and a half.

This study aims to discover in what senses and in what degrees the present-day descendants of nineteenth-century Irish immigrants possess distinctive beliefs and social practices, a goal which has influenced the research methods that were used, what pieces of evidence have been included in this book, and how they have been analysed. The significance of this evidence is assessed by a kind of methodological triangulation, using historical, sociological, and anthropological ideas and procedures. Most of this evidence was collected in a field study set in Albany, New York. The people whom we interviewed were the fourth-, fifth-, and sixth-generation descendants of people who left Ireland and came to America in the mid-nineteenth century.

Like the people this book concerns, I am a fourth-generation American, the descendant of mid-nineteenth-century immigrants. My family name is one that occurs in Ireland. The great-grandfather who bore this name emigrated to America from the north-east of England where the family had been settled for generations, and the nature of the connection with Ireland is now distant and uncertain. The family name might have been taken to England by an Irish migrant, or brought to Ireland by an English settler, in an earlier century. My other great-grandparents were crofters and fisherfolk from the west coast of Scotland, many of whom were forced off their smallholdings by agrarian reform and then tried to make a living in the highly unstable inshore fishery; another branch of the family were people of farming stock from rural Wiltshire who could not find enough land in their crowded native villages. Another set of great-grandparents were immigrants from Silesia, a former German-speaking province east of the Oder River (now in Poland) which was at the centre of territory disputed by Prussia, Austria, and Russia; speaking the wrong language or professing the wrong religion for whatever *ethnie* was proclaimed to be the correct one in the place where they had lived for generations, they moved west by degrees across Europe and then emigrated to the United States. Some of my ancestors were Catholics, and some were Protestants. They settled all over the country, and like most American families, moved around quite a lot. My mother's family moved from Michigan in 1922 to live on a farm just south of Albany, a place that is still connected with the family, and nowadays, after thirty years of living abroad, it is my home away from home.

Since 1970, I have lived in the British Isles, first as a graduate student in London, and then a teacher of social anthropology. Fifteen of these years were spent in Ireland, where my children were born; it is a place I know well and for which I have a great fondness. After a twenty-year absence, pursuing research interests unconnected with North America, on a brief visit to Albany in 1989 I was struck by its Irishness, something that I had never before really noticed. As a child and young person growing up in America, I had never been conscious of my ancestral background, nor that of those around me. While my friends had names like Herlihy, Holtermann, Maitrejean, Renzetti, Axelsson, and Greenberg, they were just like me. Their homes, and what went on inside them, were as familiar to me as my own. I do not think I even knew which of my friends were Catholic and which were Protestant, although I was aware that one or two were Jewish because they kept different religious holidays. On St Patrick's Day, I wore something green to school, like everyone else. It was merely something that we did without asking why, like exchanging cards on St Valentine's Day.

My years of living in a divided part of Ireland, where people were extremely sensitive to cultural and political nuance and varieties of Irishness, and where Irishness itself was a concept contested in the streets with flags, banners, parades, stones, bullets, and bombs, brought home to me the significance of ethnic difference and the sometimes tragic consequences of nationalist passion in ways that I had never experienced in America. And when those of my students who had spent summers working in Atlantic City, New Jersey in the late 1980s asked me, as an American, why people they had met in America said they were Irish too, even though it was clear that these people had been Americans for generations, I began to be intrigued. At first, I intended only to write a lecture or two about this phenomenon. I soon discovered, much to my surprise, that there was little scholarly literature upon which I could base a lecture. What academically respectable literature I was able to unearth in Ireland by Irish and American authors concerned nineteenth-century Irish immigration to America and was largely historical. Anthropological and sociological accounts of contemporary Irishness in America were scarce, patchy, fragmentary, and entirely restricted to the ethnic enclaves of the big industrial cities. It became clear that if I wanted to learn about Irishness in contemporary America beyond the big-city ghettos, I would have to go there and find out for myself. This connected, by chance, with a visit to relatives in Albany, and my rediscovery that it was one of the most Irish places in America and had been so for a century and a half.

Albany is a relatively small city of 100,000 people, yet it has a history which has felt the effect of virtually every rise and fall in the tide of trans-Atlantic immigration over more than three centuries. The livelihood of its people has reflected all the major shifts in the American economy, from colonial mercantilism to steam-age industry to the white-collar revolution of the postwar era. Its history and present-day social characteristics make it uniquely 'Irish' for a city of its size. While across America as a whole, between 55 and 61 per cent of those descended from Irish immigrant ancestors are not Roman Catholic, Albany is as markedly a Catholic city as Ireland is a markedly Catholic country. As a site of research, and a laboratory in which to test a number of taken-for-granted ideas about Irish America, Albany not only ought to show all of the features of Irishness we might expect to encounter outside the big-city ethnic enclaves, but to display them in as full a measure as we are likely to find anywhere in the United States.

The way I chose to design this project, and to present its results in this book, calls for a word of explanation. It has become the vogue in anthropology—especially the kind of cultural anthropology practised in the United States, if not also to a lesser extent in British social anthropology—to refer to the 'interpretive turn', to speak of the people about whom one writes as 'the Other', and to attempt to represent the cognitive worlds that they inhabit through one's writing. It has been a very odd and at times distinctly uncomfortable feeling, doing anthropological research among my own kind; the sort of people among whom I grew up. Try as I might, I have been unable to think of them as 'the Other': they are me, and I am them. Nor have I been able to recognize myself, as a fourth-generation American who can claim attachment to any of three or four 'diasporic cultures' which have no practical and scarcely any symbolic meaning to me (in fact I was almost completely unaware that I belonged to some of them before beginning to write this book), in what is now being imputed about the nature of my 'ethnicity' and 'identity' by my scholarly colleagues. Did the social worlds of people like me really change during my twenty-year absence from the United States, such that they are now more ethnic than they used to be, and have clearer senses of how their social identities are connected with their immigrant ancestors' origins? Or have the scholarly theories and modes of ethnographic and historiographic representation which have come to prevail over other paradigms during that interval had the unintended and unseen effect of inflating what few small and vestigial differences remain: in order, perhaps, to fill the voids newly created by the politics of multiculturalism? It seems important to try to resolve this question, and I have chosen to do so by taking an approach that owes little to recent theoretical fashion. In assigning primacy to systems of meaning that, it is claimed, are *shared* among the people concerned (as they must be if they are to constitute vital aspects of their 'culture') the interpretivist approach prejudges fundamental sociological and historical questions, and makes it difficult or impossible to ask *whether* culture—thus understood—actually matters: to whom, in what degree, and why. Rather than starting from a point which assumes that every 'member of the culture' is its bearer and shares its implicit meanings, as an interpretivist would, I take a broadly organizational approach in this book, asking how those qualities that are commonly regarded as being diacritical of Irishness, and which can be measured, are distributed among people who are descended from Irish immigrant ancestors. This approach, it seems to me, at least has the advantage of inviting inspection of the evidence for the general validity of what is being argued, and of being open to verification or dispute in ways that much contemporary anthropological writing is not.

Because of my experience of the contested nature of Irishness in Ireland, I was careful to make no a priori assumptions about what constituted the Irishness I might find in Albany, or who might qualify as 'Irish', things which most of the writers on the Irish in America that I had read did not seem to regard as being at all problematic. I therefore designed the data-gathering procedures for this piece of research to capture a broad sampling of people of Irish ancestry, which included anyone who claimed that any part of their ancestry was Irish, predominantly or not; regardless of their religion, social class, length of residence in Albany, or their interest in their ancestry. Over 500 people were interviewed, and 252 self-completion questionnaires were collected. These data were extended by a broad range of other materials, including data derived from participant observation, statistical material abstracted from our own surveys and the US Census, primary and secondary historical sources, and the recent sociological literature on the rapidly changing forms and processes of European ethnicities in the United States.

II

The research upon which this book is based was carried out between January 1991 and April 1997. The main part of the research was done between March 1991 and September 1993, and was supported by a grant from the Economic and Social Research Council in the United Kingdom. This award was based on an application that I submitted in March 1990 while a member of the Department of Social Anthropology at the Queen's University of Belfast, where I had been teaching since 1976. The project, as I had designed it, provided for the employment of two full-time salaried research assistants to carry out most of the fieldwork in Albany, and to help me with the organization of the data. Two recent graduates in social anthropology, Brenda McAteer and Eamonn McKeown, were employed on the project's funds and lived in Albany for fifteen months, collecting the bulk of the interview, participant observational, and questionnaire material. I joined them in the field during the university vacations, spending six months in Albany during the lifetime of the grant, and after Brenda and Eamonn's employment had ended, making further research visits over the following four years. The research design aimed to overcome some of the problems of single-handed anthropological research in urban milieux, especially those associated with the restricted range of data available to the lone anthropologist using participant observation as the chief research tool. Small numbers of key informants, resulting in narrowly focused datasets, present risks of over-interpretation and overgeneralization at the analytical stage; thus the replicability of single-handed studies is frequently questionable. As well as making possible a broader, systematic sampling of our target population to generate a more reliable basis for generalization, the research design also provided a framework for critical collaboration, in which, as long as the project funding lasted, the interpretations of each of its members were subject to continued testing as the ideas were formulated and applied to the data.

Three series of interviews were carried out in two phases of fieldwork. The Kent Street area of the city, or the Inner Brick, as it was identified in the 1980 US Census Neighborhood Statistics Program, was chosen as the site of our initial sample because the proportion of people who stated their ancestry as Irish in response to a question in the 1980 Census matched that for the city as a whole. It was chosen also because it is predominantly composed of modest detached houses, mostly built between 1910 and 1940, and possessed sociographic characteristics which reflected median values for the city as a whole in terms of household income levels, educational and occupational patterns, and so on. As a pre-war neighbourhood, the Inner Brick was thought likely to demonstrate the effects of postwar demographic change to better advantage than either an older or newer area of the city. In view of the resources available to the project, I aimed initially for a sample of 200 interviews, randomly chosen from this neighbourhood. After identifying the addresses from street directories, a list was compiled of the names of the occupants of every second house in each street in the sample neighbourhood. Initially, the plan was that Brenda and Eamonn, my research assistants, would knock on doors, explain who they were, present their university credentials, and try to set up a time to come back and conduct the interview. It took only a few days to find that their credentials as Irish university researchers did not impress people, and this sort of cold approach, even in the evenings when people were at home, was not going to be a satisfactory way of obtaining the required number of interviews. Of the first thirty or so addresses, only four residents agreed to be interviewed. State Assemblyman Richard Conners, a very well-known and popular local Irish-American politician, then came to our aid with a letter of introduction explaining that Brenda and Eamonn were lodging with him, and giving some details about the project. The letter from Mr Conners, requesting his 'fellow Albanians' to help us, was posted along with a copy of a *Times Union* newspaper article about the project (which was illustrated with a photograph of Brenda and Eamonn) to each of the names on the sample list. The letter was followed up by a telephone call requesting an interview.

Without this change in strategy it is unlikely that it would have been possible to have reached the target of 200 interviews in this neighbourhood. Potential informants were already aware of who they were when the interviewers contacted them by telephone and had had time to decide whether or not they wished to be interviewed. Despite a much improved rate of success in securing cooperation, there was still a significant number of refusals, and it was necessary to expand the limits of the sample neighbourhood from the Inner Brick to take in several surrounding streets in

order to make up the target number of interviews. The prime purpose of
this initial random sample was to give us a sense of proportion. From the
outset, I felt there was a risk that unless we did this, there was a high
degree of probability that we might find ourselves talking to a largely self-
selected sample of people who were especially conscious of their Irishness
and wanted to talk to us about it. Moreover, we would have no way of
knowing how representative they were of people of Irish ancestry generally, or whether there was any significant difference between the way
people of Irish ancestry thought about themselves in ethnic terms, as
compared with people of other European ancestries. As the research
proceeded and our network of contacts expanded, it was planned that as
opportunities arose for interviewing other people, we would take advantage of any prospects that came our way. An initial target was set of a
further 200 interviews to be obtained by this means. We started by interviewing some of the people with whom we had made contact in our first
few weeks in Albany. At the conclusion of each interview we asked the
informant if he or she knew of anyone else who might be willing to be
interviewed. As names were suggested, they were telephoned and asked if
they wished to take part in the project. If they agreed, then they were in
turn asked if they knew of anyone else who might agree to be interviewed.
Networking in this way was a successful strategy for obtaining willing
informants.

Unlike the respondents in the sample area, however, the networked
informants had, without exception, at least some Irish ancestry.
Sometimes names were suggested because it was known that these people
had shown an interest in their Irish background at some stage in the past.
Those with the best recommendations were not necessarily those who
were the keenest to agree to an interview nor were they especially know-
ledgeable or enthusiastic about their ancestry. There was a significant
number who expressed doubt that they could be of any help to us but
agreed to be interviewed anyway. Among the networked sample, we sought
to include people who were involved in various local organizations, institutions, and political parties. Members of the Ancient Order of
Hibernians (AOH) and the Irish Northern Aid Committee (Noraid), for
example, were contacted particularly; as were several prominent politicians, including the mayor of Albany, a former governor of New York
State, and some politicians, now retired, who had been a part of the Albany
Democratic machine in its heyday in the 1930s, 1940s, and 1950s. There
were also a number of chance interviews with people of Irish ancestry with
whom we came into contact during the course of our fieldwork.

The interviews were tape-recorded. As they were transcribed, the interview materials were entered into the project's database. During this phase of the project, we collected skeletal biographical information about each informant, dwelling particularly upon topics such as the family history, neighbourhood and schooling, courtship and marriage, entry into employment, religious practice, and attitudes about politics: questions which were designed to invite our informants to talk about their ancestry and to allow us to gauge the qualities of their ethnicity. During the first year of the project, the volume of data generated by the project surpassed expectations by a considerable margin. Data accumulated at a rate that sometimes exceeded our capacity to process them as the project progressed. We did not, however, regard this as a problem. Quite to the contrary, it was seen as evidence that the project was succeeding in its own terms, and that the original research proposal was conservative in its estimates of the productivity of the methods employed. On the interviewers' return to base at the end of November 1991, time was taken (as it was intended to be) for catching up, taking stock, and laying plans for the next phase of fieldwork.

The second phase of fieldwork, from March to September 1992, was devoted to two series of more intensive, in-depth interviews. A non-random, stratified sample was drawn from the first-series sample of 400 people who had been interviewed in the previous year. Eighty people were selected for two further rounds of interviews on the basis of their age, gender, social class, degree of Irishness (strong or weak), and general performance as informants. All those included in this stratified sample had at least some Irish ancestry. The second round of interviews was designed to elicit more detailed information about the informant's interest in and knowledge of family history, the experience of emigration and the establishment of the family in the United States, and their perceived connections with Ireland. The spine of the interview was the classic anthropological tool of taking genealogies, systematically tracing out the family tree, and testing the informant's knowledge about each relative. Details about each relative's known social and ethnic background were recorded. Some informants produced documents and photographs, which were also noted. These interviews were open-ended, and ranged in length between two and eight hours.

The third series of interviews sought to explore, in greater depth, the symbolic and cognitive dimensions of Irishness. As the working relationship between the interviewer and informant developed through earlier rounds of discussion, more sensitive and subtly-nuanced questions could be asked about the ways that being of Irish ancestry mattered to them (or not), how they thought other people perceived them, and whether and how these notions about themselves translated into social action in the choice of friendships, engagement in cultural activities, religious practice, political support, and so on. These interviews were also open-ended and tape-recorded. During the second phase of the fieldwork, the case studies of the institutions which have been particularly closely associated with the Albany Irish continued. These included parish churches, schools, old-country associations, cultural events such as concerts of Irish music and Irish theme days, and Democratic Party politics.

Early in the project, it was apparent that the idea of employing two young Irish people to do the bulk of the interviewing and participant observation was working well in practice. Brenda and Eamonn were the objects of a good deal of friendly interest, and found that their national-ity opened doors to them that might otherwise have remained closed. For example, both were formally initiated into the Ancient Order of Hibernians, and took part in its activities as fully incorporated, regular members. They were also involved as Democratic Party volunteer campaign workers in local elections. As anticipated in the original research design, their cultural connections proved to be a good way of getting people to talk about the nature of their Irishness. People in Albany were surprised, for example, that neither of the interviewers, although both were of impeccable cultural credentials in contemporary Ireland, could speak Irish, or sing what Americans considered to be traditional Irish songs. It was recognized, of course, that the Irish backgrounds of the interviewers could encourage our informants to overstress their own Irishness. Potentially this was a drawback. On the other hand, given that, on the basis of recent published findings in the sociological literature, we did not initially expect to find a high degree of ethnicity among the fourth-, fifth-, or sixth-generation descendants of nineteenth-century Irish immigrants in Albany, it could be said that the Irishness of the inter-viewers offered the best possible chance for evidence of ethnicity to be manifested in our data if it was there to be found.

In October 1992, work started on the final part of the project, which was based in Swansea, where I had moved the year before. The transcrip-tion of all field-note files, case histories, and tape-recorded interviews (about 1,000 items in all) was planned to be completed by the end of February. The pressures caused by the weight of data had been building up for some months, and at that point I took the decision that some addi-tional information and a more systematic way of generating quantitative outputs would be highly desirable. Accordingly, I designed a self-completion questionnaire on the basis of our experience and assessment of what we most needed to have more systematic information about. An additional research visit to Albany was made in March to distribute and collect the questionnaires. The questionnaires were posted or delivered by hand to all those informants in our original, first-stage sample; of the 400 distributed, 252 (63 per cent) were returned. From April 1993, inputting and coding our data for analysis by computer continued. Inputting the questionnaire data for quantitative analysis was the priority to mid-June; following this each interview file was formatted and keyed for Ethnograph (a software package for qualitative analysis) and printed out for visual scanning and cross-checking. As time was becoming short, the interviews were prioritized: the best 200 were chosen for immediate coding; simultaneously, trial SPSS runs were made on the university's mainframe, and variables for cross-tabulation were identified and run shortly before the project's funding lapsed on 30 September 1993, and Brenda and Eamonn's contracts of employment came to an end. At that point, Brenda and Eamonn went on to other things: Brenda enrolled as a graduate student at Swansea and returned to Albany to do independent doctoral research on Albany politics; and Eamonn enrolled as a graduate student at Queen's, later completing a Ph.D. thesis based on fieldwork in highland New Guinea.

The remaining systematization of the data, reworking and refining of the Ethnograph variables, reworking the quantitative material on the basis of smaller, controlled samples of people schooled in Albany and identifying themselves as of Irish ancestry, and the analysis and interpretation of this data and the other materials collected during the project's funded lifetime, and garnered in my subsequent short periods of fieldwork in Albany, was done single-handedly, when time could be found from my administrative, teaching, and family obligations, over the next four years. In the following chapters, I use 'we' and 'our' in preference to the first person, both to acknowledge my debt to my former research assistants who collected the bulk of the interview material that I analyse, and to avoid clumsy circumlocution.

III

As so many of our ideas about Irish America are tied up with history—what happened in Ireland, why Irish people came to America, and how they were treated in the new country, circumstances which are said to inform their present-day ethnic identity—this book begins with a critical look at the past. The first half of Chapter 2 gives a view of Albany's history which synthesizes secondary sources to create a portrait of the development of its social organization and economic and political institutions which has the power to explain its attractiveness to the tens of thousands of Irish immigrants who chose to settle there. By 1855, the city had been transformed from a mainly Anglo-Dutch and Protestant settlement to one that was largely Irish, German, and Catholic. The second half of Chapter 2 focuses upon the event in Ireland which provoked a huge surge in Irish emigration to America between 1847 and 1854, and which accounted for 20 per cent of all Irish emigration to the United States in the nineteenth century: the Great Famine. I again draw upon a variety of secondary historical materials, relying mainly on the interpretations of contemporary Irish historians who are now trying to understand what happened, and why, during a period in Ireland's history that was soon to become mythologized, surrounded by public passion, polemic, and prejudice. Since the 1960s, Irish historians have made considerable progress in separating fact from fiction. The purpose of my synthesis of their findings, which privileges an on-the-ground view of what happened as it may have been apprehended by ordinary people over the high political drama that is often emphasized by historians, is to connect Albany's fate with that of Ireland's, for it was at that moment and by reason of the Famine that Albany became one of the most Irish places in America. I also argue that no account of Irish-Americanness that claims scholarly detachment can afford to ignore what these Irish historians have to say about the Famine.

I go on to examine the impact of the Famine on Albany and American society more generally in Chapter 3. In popular belief, the Famine immigrants got no farther than the nearest Irish ghetto at their port of entry where they met hostility at every turn from the nativists. I raise a number of questions about generalized representations of the past. I ask who the Famine immigrants were, where they went, what conditions they found in places beyond the big-city enclaves, how they were received, and to what extent they were held back by their Catholicism. I argue that far from being an underclass, in Albany their large numbers forced the Anglo-Dutch ascendancy to take notice of them and to turn their labour, voting power, and religion to their advantage. Those local institutions which were able successfully to incorporate the immigrants from Ireland prospered and rose to unrivalled and enduring power in Albany's affairs. With the patronage of these powerful institutions, the Irish soon began to climb the ladder of socio-economic success. By the 1880s, some had already entered the lace-curtain middle classes; by the First World War they had caught up with people of English surnames in employment patterns, and by the 1920s had surpassed them. The chapter concludes with a brief sketch of the socio-economic position of the Irish in Albany today as a prelude to the chapters which follow.

Chapter 4 gives voice to our informants. During our interviews, we repeatedly asked people about their Irish ancestry, approaching the topic from several different directions to gauge what they knew about their immigrant backgrounds in the nineteenth century, and in what kind of cultural terms and imagery their knowledge about their origins was cast. This chapter asks how Ireland and the experience of their ancestors' emigration is now recollected by their descendants. Four, five, or six generations have passed since the historical moment when the Famine-era Irish immigrants came to America, and none of our informants was within living memory of this event. While a few people knew quite a lot about their ancestry, the accounts that have been handed down to the present are for the most part blurred and truncated. Many of our informants were uncertain about where their ancestors came from in Ireland, or when they had left, or why. Some knew nothing at all about their Irish ancestors. A similar picture emerged in their general knowledge about Irish history. This chapter is composed of a representative selection of quotations from our interviews, covering the full spectrum of responses. There is no authorial commentary, apart from a few explanatory footnotes. What our informants said speaks for itself in the light of the preceding chapters, and the chapters which follow.

An extended analysis of some measurable dimensions of Irishness among our informants is given in Chapter 5. We sought to gauge, by various means, the degree of their active interest in their Irishness: how they had learned about their family history, what things they had done over their lives which in some way demonstrated their attachment to their ancestry, and what things they possessed that served to remind them of past generations. Names—family names, given names, and married names—are then considered as boundary-markers: what influence names have on those who bear them, what people read into names, and what conventions influence the bestowal of children's given names. The latter half of the chapter asks how the Irishness of our informants has been affected by the passage of the generations since the mid-nineteenth century. This involves an analysis of the ancestral backgrounds of our sample of Albany-born informants and their close relatives and spouses about whom they gave us information, which yielded 804 cases in which the ancestral backgrounds on individuals were complete enough to be tabulated, and 385 marriages that could be analysed to see what patterns might be revealed as the generations have passed. The analysis shows that our informants' ancestries were typically mixed not only by generation— that is, in previous generations people had taken spouses of Irish or part-Irish ancestry who had arrived in the United States before the Famine or much later—but that they have been marrying, at a steadily increasing rate over the generations, persons with no Irish ancestry. Those born since 1915 and identifying themselves as of Irish ancestry were, on average, less than 50 per cent Irish as a result of ancestral mixing. Of those born since 1945, 90 per cent were of mixed ancestry. I explore the social dynamics of intermixing by asking which other European ancestries the people of Irish backgrounds chose to marry, and why; and I conclude that the religious boundary still matters.

In Albany, being Irish, being Catholic, and being a Democrat are so firmly tied together in the popular imagination that they might as well be one thing rather than three. Chapter 6 teases this idea apart to see what kind of social glue holds these three things together. This is, again, as much a historical question as a sociological one, and I examine the patterns of residential and social mobility and ethnic succession in Albany for clues about the social organization of the city before going on to examine its institutional structures. I argue that because the Irish were English-speakers, they were never confined to ethnic neighbourhoods. Non-English-speakers tended to aggregate in space for a variety of practical reasons mainly connected with language. The Irish, in contrast, had extraordinarily high rates of residential mobility which had the effect of diminishing the significance of neighbourhood as an integrative institution. I argue that, instead, party politics and church membership were much more significant local-level institutions. Albany's political parties sought to capture the voting power of the new immigrants, and because they were English-speakers, the Irish were immediately recruited as party workers and early came to play a leading role in the development of a Democratic political machine, much like Tammany Hall in New York City, which dominated Albany politics for the best part of a century and was known far and wide for its practice of doling out municipal jobs, at all levels, to loyal party supporters with Irish names. Since they were Catholics, the Irish immigrants of the mid-nineteenth century also ensured that the institutions of the Catholic Church were greatly strengthened and came to play a highly influential role in civic life. The

Democratic Party and the Catholic Church, both of which relied on the support of the Irish, were the two most powerful institutions in Albany, and frequently collaborated to their mutual advantage. People of Irish ancestry likewise derived benefit from these social institutions, whose patronage—in return for their loyalty—was the foundation of their integration into American society and their social and economic advancement.

Chapter 7 considers how 'being Irish' was experienced by our informants, and to what degree they thought of themselves in these terms. Introducing the chapter is the narrative of Phyllis, a woman of third-generation Irish background, who recollects her childhood of the 1920s and 1930s: hearing her mother's stories of her grandparents, going to a Catholic school, comparing her experience of being of Irish background to the second-generation Italian and Polish children who were her playmates, speaking of her brothers and sisters—one of whom married a Protestant—and of her own children, her nieces and nephews, and reflecting on the way that attitudes have changed over her lifetime. This is followed by an edited transcript of an interview with Helen and Joe, a couple born after the Second World War, both of mixed backgrounds, whose sense of their Irishness was very different from Phyllis's. The contrast between these two accounts is explored, focusing especially on the way that having mixed ancestry heightens one's sensitivity to questions of ethnic identity; frequently provokes one to choose whether to be Irish, German, or English; and to articulate one's reasons for doing so. The chapter goes on to explore the extent to which our informants' feelings of their Irishness could be seen to emerge from family traditions, and looks closely at musicality, which is commonly taken to be a cultural trait of the Irish. Finally, Chapter 7 analyses our informants' responses to a set of questions about the traits of personality they saw in themselves and those nearest to them as attributable to their Irishness, as a means of testing some commonplace assertions about identity and self-image among Irish-Americans. The chapter concludes with the observation that although our informants were well aware of the stereotypes, few saw themselves and those close to them in terms of this kind; a finding which raises methodological as well as substantive questions.

The next chapter examines the public symbols and rituals of Irishness. Chapter 8 analyses recent controversies surrounding St Patrick's Day parades in Albany, Boston, and New York City, and what these social dramas have revealed about the meaning invested in the symbols displayed on these occasions. Because of its obvious association with the

Irish, the St Patrick's Day parade is conventionally understood as an expression of Irish ethnicity; as one of the many pieces in the American ethnic mosaic which cumulatively constitute American national culture. This chapter argues, contrarily, that St Patrick's Day in Albany, and perhaps other cities, has now become a quintessentially American institution that owes relatively little to Ireland and is Irish only in superficial ways. When, in 1993, Irish ethnic politics intruded into the organization of the parade in Albany, a crisis of confidence was created which nearly led to the abandonment of the event. I argue that being Irish in Albany on St Patrick's Day is best understood not as a manifestation of ethnic Irishness, but rather as a celebration of unethnic Americanness: to be 'Irish' on St Patrick's Day is to claim membership of the fully assimilated mainstream of middle Americans who have left the cultural baggage of their immigrant origins behind them.

The concluding chapter considers how scholarly and popular knowledge about Irish-Americanness has been produced, and why its conventional understandings do not fit the Albany case. That much scholarly and popular writing has focused on Irish enclaves in America's larger industrial cities has had far-reaching implications about the way we understand the immigrant experience, what is characteristic of Irishness, and the place occupied by the Irish in American society. I present sociographic evidence to show that there are things about big-city ghetto life which make it distinctively different from life elsewhere, but in the absence of much information about the far greater proportion of Irish immigrants who did not live in these big-city ghettos but scattered themselves across the smaller cities, towns, and rural areas all over America, the struggles of the Irish to be accepted in these large industrial cities is extended as a general view of the immigrant experience everywhere. These views may be of questionable typicality, and may have led us to hold ideas about Irish-Americans that exaggerate or misrepresent their characteristics, and thus have tended to reinforce the essentializing myths and stereotypical images of popular belief. I then attempt to describe a sociographic profile of the Irish in America beyond the ghettos, drawing upon analyses of the 1980 US Census (the first to ask an ancestry question), which offers a rather different picture of the dynamics of Irish ethnicity. Finally, I question the notion of Irish-Americanness itself, connecting this idea with contemporary American cultural politics and the commodification of 'heritage'. I argue that scholarly and popular writers have taken it as their task to discover what lies within the space defined by the idea of 'Irish-American ethnicity'. But if they have not questioned the legitimacy of the category by critically examining the nature of its boundaries, how they have been defined, by whom and for what purpose, and what happens at the boundary-zone and beyond, not infrequently they have merely brought into being that which they were looking for.

I hope that this probing at the taken-for-granted boundaries of the idea of Irish America will provoke others to do likewise, and to take our knowledge of who the Irish were and what they accomplished in America far beyond what I have been able to do here, for their achievements and triumphs in becoming Americans constitute a rich and vibrant human story that deserves fully to be told for its own sake, not just quoted selectively for partisan ends.

2

Colonists and Immigrants

Over 4 million people from Ireland settled in the United States in the nineteenth century. More than a million arrived in just seven years, from 1847 to 1854, nearly twice as many as had emigrated to the United States during the previous half-century. Their impact on American society was enormous, in some places transforming the previous social fabric in less than a decade. One of these places was Albany, New York. By 1855, a quarter of the city's population was Irish-born, and by 1875 this former Dutch colonial outpost and British garrison town had become one of the most Irish and Catholic places in the United States. Why so many Irish immigrants settled in Albany, and how they became integrated into American society has much to do with the circumstances of the city's historical development: what kind of social order the Irish encountered in the mid-nineteenth century, what economic conditions then prevailed, and how its political and religious institutions received them. Why Albany became Irish also has to do with what happened in Ireland in the mid-nineteenth century, and how the fates of Ireland and America came to be connected.

I

New York Bay and the great north river was surveyed in 1609 by the English navigator Henry Hudson, for the Dutch East India Company. Hudson sailed his ship *Halve Maen* up the river as far as present-day Albany, thus establishing that seagoing ships could penetrate deep into a region rich in furs. Hudson was followed by a Dutch mariner and fur trader, Hendrik Christiaensz, who made annual voyages to North America from 1610 to 1616. In 1614 Christiaensz established a small, temporary fortress far upriver on Castle Island, near Albany, which was named Fort Nassau and garrisoned by an agent of the East India Company and ten or a dozen soldiers. The purpose of this outpost, which consisted of a redoubt 50 feet square surrounding a single crude building made of logs, was to induce the local Indians to trade beaver pelts for wampum. By chance, the Dutch had chosen a place in the midst of contested territory roughly dividing two quite distinct native peoples: the Iroquian-speaking Mohawks to the west and the Algonquian-speaking Mahicans to the east. At least three Mahican villages were located on the west bank of the Hudson River to the north and south of the outpost. The nearest Mohawks were 20 or 30 miles further to the west, between present-day Schenectady and Canajoharie.[1] Reasonably good relations with both tribes were apparently established, even though the Mohawks and Mahicans were continually at odds with one another. For three years, a brisk trade was carried on in furs, including beaver, otter, fox, bear, mink, and wildcat. The land was said to be, by a contemporary visitor, 'excellent and agreeable, full of noble forest trees and grape vines, and nothing is wanted but the labour and industry of man to render it one of the finest and most fruitful lands in that part of the world'.[2] Unfortunately, Christiaensz was killed in a quarrel in 1616, and Fort Nassau seems to have been abandoned soon after this date.[3] All traces of it were eventually washed away by the spring floods.

With the English settled in Virginia and the French in Quebec, the Dutch were forced to consolidate their territorial claim in order to hold it against the French and English, and to continue to control the fur trade in their dominion. In 1612, the States General granted the charter of the West India Company, entrusting to the Chamber of Amsterdam the colonization of the New World. The Dutch possessions in North America, which included parts of present-day Connecticut, New York State, New Jersey, and Delaware, were given the name Nieuw Nederlandt and accorded the status of a royal province, with all legislative, judicial, and executive powers vested in the Company. To recruit settlers to their territories, the Company agreed to enable the colonists to 'settle honourably and prosperously' by providing transport, clothing, land, tools, animals, and seed; to sell the colonists household articles at the same prices as in Holland; guarantee Christian religious freedom and civil order; furnish a schoolmaster; maintain the poor but worthy; adjudicate disputes; and reward discoveries of precious minerals with one-tenth of their value over six years:[4]

---

[1] T. E. Burke, *Mohawk Frontier: The Dutch Community of Schenectady, New York, 1661–1710* (Ithaca, NY, 1991), 3.

[2] J. F. Jameson, *Narratives of New Netherland, 1609–1664* (New York, 1909), 48.

[3] A. C. Pound, *Johnson of the Mohawks* (New York, 1930), 18; C. Hislop, *Albany: Dutch, English and American* (Albany, NY, 1936), 35.

[4] A. C. Pound, *The Golden Earth* (New York, 1935), 21; A. van der Donck, *A Description of the New Netherland*, T. F. O'Donnell (ed.) (Syracuse, NY, 1968), 133 ff; O. A. Rink, *Holland on the Hudson: An Economic and Social History of Dutch New York* (Ithaca, NY, 1986), 77 ff. 'Notes on Non-English Immigration to New York in the Seventeenth Century', *New York History*, 62 (1981).

The farmer, being conveyed with his family over seas to New Netherland, was granted by the company for a term of six years a Bouwerie, which was partly cleared, and a good part of which was fit for the plough.

The company furnished the farmer a house, barn, farming implements and tools, together with four horses, four cows, sheep and pigs in proportion, the usufruct and enjoyment of which the husbandman should have during the six years, and on expiration thereof, return the number of cattle he received. The entire increase remained with the farmer. The farmer was bound to pay yearly one hundred guilders and eighty pounds of butter rent for the cleared land and Bouwerie.[5]

In return, colonists were required to render obedience to the Company and its officers; reside six years in whatever place might be assigned; plant and cultivate as directed; contribute labour, as required, to the service of the Company; sell no furs, livestock, crops, or handicrafts to any but the Company; give no information about the colony to strangers; and trade with no one except the Company on pain of expulsion.[6]

Thirty families of colonists, mainly French-speaking Walloons from Hainault, Namur, Luxembourg, and Liège, were assembled and a ship was loaded with all that they would require to establish a Dutch settlement in North America. The party sailed from Texel in 1624 in the ship *Nieuw Nederlandt*, under the command of Cornelius Jacobsz Mey.[7] Eight people were put ashore at Manhattan, to join the handful of Dutch traders already there. Others were landed at the mouths of the Delaware River and the Connecticut River in order to establish Dutch control of the fur trade in the regions upriver. The remainder of the party, eighteen families, continued north along the Hudson. The river runs for much of its length through a deep gorge; 120 miles from Manhattan, near the confluence with the Mohawk River which branches off to the west, seagoing ships reach their practical limit. Here the hilly, thickly wooded landscape opens out into a fertile flood-plain intersected by a network of creeks and streams rich in beaver, and offering good possibilities for agriculture. The remaining families and a dozen or sixteen soldiers landed on the west bank of the river at this promising and strategic spot, opposite Christiaensz's earlier encampment. There, Captain Mey ordered the carpenter and the ship's crew to construct a small fortification, to protect the colonists and to serve as an entrepôt for the trade in furs with the local

---

[5] E. B. O'Callaghan, *Documents Relative to the Colonial History of the State of New York*, 13 vols. (Albany, NY, 1853–87). i. 371.

[6] van der Donck, *Description of the New Netherlands*, appendix.

[7] Pound, *Golden Earth*, 23; Rink, *Holland on the Hudson*, 79.

Indian tribes. The settlement was later to be called called Beverswijck (Beverwyck), 'the place of beavers'. The redoubt, constructed of logs and armed with four or five cannon, was rather grandly named Fort Orange.

Two more ships arrived in the following year, carrying additional settlers, cattle, horses, seed, and other supplies. Yet things were not going well. Continual warfare between the Mohawks and the Mahicans eventually caused the settler families to be evacuated for their safety to Manhattan, leaving a garrison of about twenty-five fur traders and soldiers.[8] Several families had left Beverwyck before the rest were evacuated, finding life in the wilderness harsh, dangerous, and the company's monopolies excessively constraining. Few new recruits could be found in Holland. An attempt to make the terms less restrictive, by removing some of the Company's monopolies and allowing the colonists to sell and trade their produce, excepting only furs, met with limited success. The cost of each settler, transported, housed, equipped, and maintained at the Company's expense, was proving to be heavy and increasingly unpopular with the Chamber of Amsterdam.

An ingenious plan was then promoted by which large tracts of land were to be given as semi-feudal hereditary estates to those wealthy burghers of the Chamber of Amsterdam who sought to elevate themselves to the landed gentry. The colonization of Nieuw Nederlandt was thus put into private hands. In return for the grant of land and broad legal powers over any tenants they might recruit, the *patroons* were free to extract what profit they could from the new territories.[9] The application by Kiliaen Van Rensselaer—a prominent investor and director of the West India Company, and the principal promoter of the scheme—to the States General to make as his estate tracts of land on both sides of the Hudson River at Beverwyck, which was to amount to more than a million acres, was approved. It was a shrewd choice. The head of navigation of the Hudson River was entirely within his domain, and it had the protection of Fort Orange. The first party of Van Rensselaer's settlers arrived in 1630, to be followed by annual arrivals over the next fourteen years.[10] Of the 174 Rensselaerswyck settlers before 1644, roughly a third were family groups, but most were single men, farm labourers, and artisans.

---

[8] A. W. Trelease, *Indian Affairs in Colonial New York: The Seventeenth Century* (Ithaca, NY, 1960), 36.

[9] For a full account, see S. Nissenson, *The Patroon's Domain* (New York, 1937) and T. J. Condon, *New York Beginnings: The Commercial Origins of New Netherland* (New York, 1968); Jameson, *Narratives*, 90 ff., gives a contemporary account of the articles governing patroonship.

[10] Rink, 'People of New Netherland', 17–20; *Holland on the Hudson*, 146–7.

Not all were Dutch. Of those who sailed from Holland to settle in the Dutch territories in North America, almost half were Huguenots from adjacent parts of Germany, France, and Belgium.[11] Father Jogues, a French Catholic missionary who visited Rensselaerswyck in 1646 remarked that the colony was composed of about a hundred persons, who lived in twenty-five or thirty houses.[12] Ten years later, the population was about 230.[13] Over the next twenty years, several hundred free settlers, whom Van Rensselaer had not sponsored, also applied to take up residence in his domain. Most of these free settlers were of British stock.[14]

Albany in these years was surrounded by a succession of wars between the Dutch and French, English and French, and Mohawks and Mahicans, which were a constant threat to European settlement. Yet relations between the Europeans in Albany and the neighbouring native peoples, especially the Mohawks, were said to be comparatively good. The Indians were eager to trade pelts for European goods such as rifles, gunpowder, cloth, blankets, iron axe heads, and cooking-pots. Wampum—strings of trade beads—functioned as a local medium of exchange. Diplomatic comings and goings were frequent. The Iroquois sachems, or chiefs, met in council with the Europeans in Albany and a number of agreements on the terms of trade, territorial control, and sales of land were concluded. The crux of the relationship between the Dutch and the Mohawks was economic; the iron axes and guns which the Mohawks obtained by trading their furs gave them an advantage over their rivals, the Mahicans and Hurons. The Mohawks were alert to any threat to their leading position in the fur trade, and were willing to overlook minor abuses by the Dutch in order to maintain it.[15] Mutual pledges were made to punish European attacks on Indians and vice versa, promises which seem for the most part to have been carried out in reasonably good faith.[16] While there must have been a good deal of friction, the Europeans and Indians continued to live in close proximity and recognized good relations as being in their mutual interest. Serious cases of violence, theft, or fraud, according to the official

[11]   D. S. Cohen, 'How Dutch were the Dutch of New Netherland?', *New York History*, 62 (1981), 51.

[12]   Jameson, *Narratives*, 262. D. Merwick, *Possessing Albany, 1630–1710: The Dutch and English Experiences* (Cambridge, 1990), 9, estimates the population of Rensselaerswyck in 1643 as 'about two hundred men, women and children'. It is unclear whether Father Jogues's account (ibid.) refers to Rensselaerswyck only, or included the population of Beverwyck.

[13]   Burke, *Mohawk Frontier*, 18.

[14]   Rink, 'People of New Netherland', 41.

[15]   Burke, *Mohawk Frontier*, 26–32 *passim*.

[16]   Trelease, *Indian Affairs*, 225.

court records of the period, were relatively infrequent, and when they did occur, something approaching justice seems to have been done in most instances.[17]

The British took control of the Dutch possessions in North America in 1664. Nieuw Amsterdam was promptly renamed New York, and Beverwyck was called Albany, after James, Duke of York, Albany, and Ulster, whom Charles II had made proprietor of the former Dutch territories. After a protracted dispute with the Van Rensselaer family about the status of the lands as their private property or the property of the Dutch state, the County of Albany was chartered in 1683. Three years later the City of Albany was given its own charter and public lands by the governor, Colonel Thomas Dongan, empowering the establishment of municipal institutions and officers, including a mayor, a common council, a sheriff, and keepers of the peace, courts, and justices.[18] By 1686, Albany had become the chief fur-trading centre for the British colonies. The population easily exceeded a thousand,[19] predominantly Dutch, but including a number of English and Germans, with lesser numbers of Scots, Scandinavians, French, Portuguese, Irish, Croats, Blacks from Africa and the West Indies—both free and slaves—Iroquois of several nations, and persons of mixed blood.[20] The place was described as scarcely more than a crude village surrounded by wooden palisades and containing but few masonry buildings among the hundred or so log houses, a rowdy frontier trading and garrison town set on a muddy flood-plain.[21] Many of the dwellings were located at the lower end of State Street and Court Street (now Broadway). There were shops and stores in Chapel Street. There were a town hall, two churches, a guard house or barracks, and a market. At the river's edge were three landing stages, apparently of rather flimsy construction, for ships continued to stand out in the river to receive their loads from lighters until 1727, when the Common Council took steps to provide proper wharves.[22]

That such a small and rough place should be granted the status of a chartered city, one of the first in the colonies, was a reflection of its strategic value to British interests. Colonel Dongan, governor of New

[17] Ibid. 227.

[18] A. J. Parker (ed.), *Landmarks of Albany County, New York* (Syracuse, NY, 1897), 283.

[19] Merwick, *Possessing Albany*, 73, quotes a contemporary source as estimating the population at 1,100 in 1659.

[20] C. Wilcoxen, *Seventeenth Century Albany: A Dutch Profile* (Albany, NY, 1981), 6.

[21] A. Weise, *The History of the City of Albany, New York* (Albany, NY, 1884), 184.

[22] Parker, *Landmarks*, 289–90.

York, clearly regarded Albany as an important counter to the French presence to the north. Albany commanded the main route southward from French-held territory into New York, and one of the main portage routes to the west, along the Mohawk River, Lake Oneida, and the Oswego River to Lake Ontario, upper Canada, and the west. Albany's location was pivotal; Dongan's judgement of its strategic value was demonstrated on several occasions over the following decades, as the city served as a forward base in perpetual wars with the French. Albany was the object of several unsuccessful French attacks and the staging post for British forays into French territory in 1689–97 (King William's War), 1702–14 (Queen Anne's War), 1739–48 (King George's War), and the Seven Years' War, (1755–9) which in North America was called the French and Indian War.[23] As well as being palisaded by a 15-foot high fence, Albany was heavily fortified with a stockade and guns at Fort Frederick, which commanded the river, and from time to time the city accommodated large numbers of people from the surrounding countryside seeking refuge during the ebb and flow of war. Albany was the headquarters of the Northern Department of the British Army. The city served as a troop assembly point, provided winter quarters for troops, acted as a supply depot, and furnished behind-the-lines hospital facilities.[24]

Certainly the townspeople understood the devastation consequent upon war. The military commander would interdict grain leaving the city, arrest townspeople absconding from the city to support a family elsewhere, extort insupportable taxes, and quarter soldiers who would in turn burgle homes and bring disease like smallpox. Men would live with the expectation that a farm's value would be 'notably diminished' by 'war, fire or otherwise'. People would desert the region in large numbers; the court would be supplicated to help support the illegitimate children of English [*sic*] soldiers; the rich would become rich and the poor poorer.[25]

French colonial power in North America came to an end in 1759, with the British capture of Montréal. Albany's position as an inland frontier garrison that could be rapidly re-supplied by seagoing troop ships was a

---

[23] See e.g. Pound, *Johnson of the Mohawks*, for an account of the French and Indian wars in the neighbourhood of Albany.

[24] K. Birr, 'Merchants, Manufacturers and Bureaucrats', in A. Roberts and J. Van Dyk (eds.), *Experiencing Albany: Perspectives on a Grand City's Past* (Albany, NY, 1986), 44.

[25] Merwick, *Possessing Albany*, 264. Regiments of colonial troops were raised in Ireland, Scotland, and Wales as well as in England. Colonial troops were also recruited locally.

decisive advantage to the British. This same advantage was in turn used against the British in the Revolutionary War. General Burgoyne, landing at Quebec and advancing south towards New York with 8,000 British troops, including two Irish regiments and a regiment of Hessian mercenaries, met stiff resistance by the American volunteers garrisoned at Albany. The Albany garrison was quickly reinforced by large movements of men and supplies brought up the Hudson River until there were more than 17,000 American troops in Burgoyne's path. Battles raged round Saratoga, 20 miles north of Albany, for three weeks in September and October. Burgoyne, outnumbered more than two to one, stalled in his southward advance, his ranks demoralized and thinned by casualties, his supplies exhausted, finally surrendered his entire remaining army of 5,800 on 17 October 1777, turning the tide for the American republic.

Albany's strategic position was not only of military importance, but also of great commercial value. The city prospered as a river port, and the surrounding farmland continued to attract settlers. In 1737, there had been 10,681 European residents of Albany County; by 1771 the population had grown to 42,706.[26] After the Revolutionary War ended with the Treaty of Paris in 1783, a century of almost constant warfare and, most recently, seven years in a continuous state of siege, had come to an end. Albany soon became transformed from a frontier fur-trading outpost and a military headquarters into a thriving commercial centre. When the fur trade began to decline as the trappers and traders moved further to the west, the Albany merchants concentrated increasingly upon dealing in livestock, wheat, flour, and timber, drawn in from the upper Hudson area, and selling manufactured goods to the farmers and woodsmen. By 1774, Albany had over 400 buildings, stone quays at the river's edge, and early evidence of industrialization was beginning to appear that included tanning pits, asheries, brick and lumber yards, livestock pens, warehouses, and mill sites.[27]

Moreover, no longer did the place merely mark the northern limit of seagoing navigation along the Hudson, but its role as the gateway to the western territories began to assume an equal and gradually greater importance as the threat of Indian, French, and British attacks on westward travellers receded. Overland emigrants from the eastern seaboard states had to negotiate the great barrier of the Appalachian Mountains, which were a formidable impediment to westward expansion. The route westward from

[26] J. J. McEneny, *Albany: Capital City on the Hudson* (Woodland Hills, Calif., 1981), 12.

[27] S. Bielinski, 'A Middling Sort: Artisans and Tradesmen in Colonial Albany', *New York History*, 83 (1992), 267.

Albany, however, took advantage of the most practical gap in the mountain ranges, and was the most economical trade route to the west. Travel could be undertaken mostly by water to Lake Ontario and Lake Erie, along the Mohawk–Oneida–Oswego system, the 'Fort Stanwix Line', so-called because a line of forts, spaced a day's journey apart, had marked the limit of the British territorial defences and protected the route against attack by enemy forces, Indians, and brigands. Peace meant that travellers could now pass in safety, and the civilian traffic along the route soon began to increase dramatically.

Albany soon became an important centre of east–west trade and transport. By 1790, Albany was the new nation's sixth-largest city, with a population of about 3,500. The national origin stocks of Albany County were now about 50 per cent English, 20 per cent Dutch, 9 per cent Anglican or Presbyterian Irish, 8 per cent German, 5 per cent Scots, and 4 per cent Catholic Irish.[28] The city's streets were laid out in grids, and substantial stone and brick buildings had begun to appear. Albany was made capital of the State of New York in 1797; soon the city began to assume political as well as economic significance. The governor's office and meetings of the state assembly brought many dignitaries, officials, and civil servants to the city, prompting much new building. Major turnpikes radiated south to New York, east to Boston, north to Montréal, and west to Buffalo.

Traffic converged on Albany en route to the west. Tens of thousands of westward-bound emigrants passed through Albany during the 1790s, sometimes three or four hundred wagons or sleighs a day.[29] The business of feeding, lodging, and supplying them provided a livelihood for many of Albany's residents. Manufactories including iron foundries, spinning, lumber and paper mills, and agencies in manufactured goods also developed in Albany; once settled in their new homesteads in western New York and Ohio, the emigrants were followed by wagonloads of iron stoves, drawn wire and cut nails, seed and agricultural implements, tinware, lamp oil, cloth, paper, glass, and other necessities. The port of Albany continued to grow in importance, as river-boats disembarked their cargoes of emigrants brought north from New York to begin their westward transit into the interior of the country. Ships landed finished goods for onward dispatch, and supplied Albany's mills and factories with raw materials. In

[28] T. L. Purvis, 'The National Origins of New Yorkers in 1790', *New York History*, 67 (1986), 133–53.

[29] A. P. Kenney, 'The Transformation of the Albany Patricians, 1778–1860', *New York History*, 68 (1987), *passim*.

1803, traffic at the port was sufficient to justify the establishment of a Custom House, enabling seagoing vessels to arrive and depart directly to and from Albany, without clearing customs at the Port of New York.

Westward travel none the less remained arduous. Arthur Pound, in his history *Lake Ontario* (1945), describes the journey of Christopher Schultz, one of the first author-travellers to take a passage on Robert Fulton's new Hudson River steamboat, the *Clermont*, in 1807, as remarkably speedy. It took Schultz only fifteen days to reach Buffalo (see Table 2.1).

Schultz travelled by the fastest available means, spared no expense, and was not encumbered by much luggage. An emigrant family would have made much slower progress. If they travelled as much as possible by water, as Schultz did, it would probably have taken three or four weeks; if they travelled by wagon or sleigh, 10 miles a day over unmade roads would have been a good speed. By wagon road, the journey from New York to Buffalo would have taken ten to twelve weeks.

TABLE 2.1. Schultz's journey from New York to Buffalo

	Miles	Method	Days
New York to Albany	160	Steamboat	1.5
Albany to Schenectady	15	Turnpike	1.5
Schenectady to Utica	104	Keel boat	5
Utica to Oswego	104	Keel boat	3
Oswego to Lewiston	172	Sail boat	3
Lewiston to Buffalo	17	Road	1.5

Pressure was growing to improve the route to the west. The idea of a canal, eliminating the overland portages between the lengths of navigable natural waterway, had been officially proposed by Cadwallader Colden, the Surveyor General of New York, in 1724. The idea was raised again in 1777 by Gouverneur Morris. George Washington, in his youth a surveyor for the British Army, wrote in a letter of 12 October 1783:

I have lately made a tour through the Lakes George and Champlain, as far as Crown Point. Thence returning to Schenectady, I proceeded up the Mohawk River to Fort Schuyler (formerly Fort Stanwix), crossed over to Wood Creek, which empties into Oneida Lake, and affords water communication with Ontario. I then traversed the country to the head of the eastern branch of the Susquehanna, and viewed Lake Otsego, and the portage between that Lake and the Mohawk River at Canajoharie. Prompted by these actual observations, I could not help taking a more extensive view of the vast inland navigation of these United States, from maps and the information of others; and could not but be struck with the immense extent and importance of it, and with the goodness of that Providence which has dealt its favours to us with such profuse a hand. Would to God we may have wisdom enough to improve them. I shall not rest contented, till I have explored the western country, and traversed those lines, or a great part of them, which have given bounds to a new empire.[30]

A few years later, Benjamin Franklin engaged Elkanah Watson, who had a knowledge of European canals, to survey a canal route. Watson thought a canal to Lake Ontario perfectly feasible, and had gained sufficient financial backing by 1792 to establish the Western Inland Lock Navigation Company and to begin the ambitious task of opening a water route from the Mohawk River, near Albany, through to Lake Ontario via Lake Oneida, the Fort Stanwix route. Accounts differ as to whether the project extended beyond 5 or 6 miles of improved waterway near Wood Creek, bypassing the great waterfall where the Mohawk meets the Hudson. The project evidently did not prosper; the enterprise, however sound in principle, was simply much too large for a single private entrepreneur and the rudimentary banking and credit system of the day. After collecting tolls for a few years, the company went into decline and eventually sold its rights to the State of New York.[31]

The influential Clinton family, of Irish ancestry, next took a hand in the matter. Colonel Charles Clinton had traversed the region on a British campaign against the French presence on Lake Ontario in 1758; his son General James Clinton had gained experience of the Mohawk and Susquehanna Valleys in 1779. James's brother George, the first governor of New York under United States administration, was always a westerner in politics, favouring the development of the western hinterlands. James Clinton's son De Witt, twice governor of New York and a leading citizen of Albany, planned the even grander project of building a waterway not just to Lake Ontario, but across the entire state of New York to Lake Erie, and thence into lakes St Clair, Huron, Michigan, and Superior, making possible unbroken communication by water as far as Illinois and Minnesota. De Witt Clinton succeeded in persuading the New York State Assembly to give legal backing to the project as a public work, authorizing private contractors to raise capital to construct sections of the canal using the State of New York as a guarantor for their loans. Shares and

[30] A. C. Pound, *Lake Ontario* (Indianapolis, 1945), 202–3.
[31] N. Miller, *The Enterprise of a Free People: Aspects of Economic Development in New York State during the Canal Period, 1792–1838* (Ithaca, NY, 1962), 21.

bonds were issued to raise the capital for the venture, which was so effectively promoted that it attracted substantial amounts of foreign investment.[32] De Witt Clinton, as chairman of the Canal Commission, himself oversaw the project, which began ceremoniously on Independence Day, 1817.

For eight years an army of workers laboured in the rough country between the Hudson River and the Great Lakes. Many are believed to have been Irish, but it is not known how many came directly from Ireland, and how many were recruited from among the Irish labourers already resident in Montréal, Toronto, New York City, Boston, and Philadelphia. Towards the end of the canal's construction, when the numbers of labourers had reached a peak, huge Irish work gangs totalling perhaps 50,000 men were said to be scattered across upstate New York, with an Irish middle class of brewers, salt-makers, and merchants in the canal ports of Buffalo, Rochester, Syracuse, and Albany.[33] Before the Great Famine, Anglicans and Presbyterians from the northern, central, and eastern counties of Ireland, who composed about 25 per cent of Ireland's population, significantly outnumbered the Catholic migrants to North America.[34] That the Irish canallers were mixed, and that some individual contractors may have had preferences for either Protestant or Catholic labourers seems to be suggested by occasional reports of fighting, in which politics and religion were said to have played a part, between rival Irish work gangs.

The project covered 600 miles of territory, of which 360 miles lay through frontier wilderness. From Atlantic tidewater at Albany to Lake Erie, an elevation of 571 feet was gained through eighty-two locks. The canal was 40 feet wide and 4 feet deep. At two points, Little Falls and Lockport, the channel had to be blasted and hewn through solid limestone. In the marshlands at the head of Cayuga Lake, where the problem was too much water instead of too much rock, hundreds of labourers died of fever. Stone aqueducts carried the canal across Schoharie Creek and the gorge of the Genesee River at Rochester, for which skilled stonemasons were recruited in England, Scotland, France, and Germany. With great fanfare, as befitted the engineering marvel of the age, the largest

---

[32] Ibid. 70 ff.

[33] D. N. Doyle, 'The Irish in North America, 1776–1845', in W. E. Vaughan (ed.), *A New History of Ireland*, v, *Ireland under the Union, I, 1801–70* (Oxford, 1989), 702–3.

[34] D. H. Akenson, 'The Historiography of the Irish in the United States', in P. O'Sullivan (ed.), *The Irish World Wide*, ii, *The Irish in the New Communities* (Leicester, 1992), 105.

undertaken in the United States until that time, the Erie Canal was
opened on 26 October 1825.

The canal had an immediate and dramatic effect on western trade and
settlement. Rochester, a village of 331 people in 1816, by 1840 had
become a wheat-shipping and milling centre of 40,000.[35] But Rochester
and Buffalo were only waypoints along the emigrants' journeys to the
farmlands of Ohio, Michigan, Indiana, Illinois, Iowa, and the upper
Midwest. Millions of acres of cheap farmland had become accessible to
European immigrants by mid-century. Yet, despite the advent of the Erie
Canal, before the westward extension of the railways, the emigrants' journeys were still exhausting ordeals. Henry Lucas, the historian of the later
Dutch settlements in America, describes the journey of a group of
seventy Seceders, adherents to the Old Reformed faith who risked
imprisonment for their beliefs in their native Bentheim, on the German
side of the Dutch border:

They left Bentheim on March 23, 1847, and journeyed through Coevorden and
Hasselt by canal to Rotterdam, where, together with thirty-four emigrants from
Drenthe, they boarded the *Antoinette Marie* on April 4. After an uneventful
voyage of forty-nine days, they arrived in New York on May 23. Travelling by way
of the Hudson River to [Albany], and thence by the Erie Canal to Buffalo, they
sailed across lakes Erie, Huron and Michigan and finally, on June 20, landed [near
Holland, Michigan]. Thus an odyssey of seventy-seven days ended happily for
everyone.[36]

Another, larger group of Seceders emigrating to the Dutch settlements in
south-western Michigan a few months earlier had a more eventful and
sadder journey. They sailed from Hellevoetsluis on 14 October 1846 in
the *Isabella Bath*. The ship ran into a succession of gales and did not
arrive in New York until 19 December. Dazed by more than two months
of being pitched about in Atlantic storms and weakened by seasickness
and a lack of fresh food, the passengers disembarked on 22 December and
with one intermediate day in New York went on to Albany. It was a cold
winter. They decided to travel by the Hudson River Railroad, rather than
by sleigh, which meant getting themselves—including a number of weak
and sick adults and children—and all their baggage across the city
through the unfamiliar streets to the railway depot. They were so rushed
and anxious to keep the children and invalids together, along with all their

---

[35] Pound, *Lake Ontario*, 208.
[36] H. S. Lucas, *Netherlanders in America: Dutch Immigration to the United States and
Canada, 1789–1950* (Ann Arbor, 1955), 106.

belongings, that some neither slept nor ate for forty-eight hours and were so exhausted that one woman died only moments after boarding the train. On reaching Albany, weary from the long journey and prevented by illness and the severity of the winter weather from moving on to Buffalo, twenty-four of the group decided to spend the winter in Albany. They were assisted by Isaac Wyckoff, a local Dutch Reformed minister who frequently met groups of Hollanders passing through Albany, as well as by several townspeople. Nevertheless, within two weeks, the group was reduced by death to nineteen. Wyckoff helped the able-bodied to find work through the winter. In March, as soon as the Erie Canal was clear of ice, the fifteen remaining members of the group went on to Buffalo, and walked most of the rest of the way to western Michigan, arriving in May at the new settlement of Groningen in Ottawa County.[37]

In 1835, the Erie Canal was widened and deepened to cope with the traffic. By 1862, it had been enlarged several times, its dimensions nearly doubled to 70 feet wide and 7 feet deep. Albany continued to grow in size and importance as the traffic flowed westwards in inexorably increasing volume. Albany's piers and basins, with a capacity of over 1,000 canal boats and 50 paddle steamers in 1825, were soon overloaded. In the canal's first year, 12,856 boats passed through the basin. Within two years, Albany's wholesale business had quadrupled. In 1800, before the Erie Canal had opened, the city's population was 5,000; by 1830, it had grown to 30,000 and then doubled again in the next thirty years. Albany's merchants continued to prosper. Their profits and needs for credit turned Albany into an important banking and financial centre.

With the coming of the railway age, Albany's position as a principal gateway to the Midwest was further consolidated. The Delaware and Hudson Canal Company, later headquartered in Albany, built the first railway in America at Honesdale, Pennsylvania, in 1827, and imported America's first locomotives from England, the *Stourbridge Lion*, *America*, *Hudson*, and *Delaware* in 1829, the year of the Rainhill Trials on the Liverpool and Manchester Railway which were won by Robert Stephenson's *Rocket*. The Mohawk and Hudson Railway, which began operation in 1831, provided among the first railway passenger services in the country, connecting Albany and Schenectady. At the zenith of the railway age, Albany was a strategic junction: the centre of the Delaware and Hudson's railway operations north to Montréal and south-west to the Pennsylvania coalfields, and the western terminus of the Boston and

---

[37] Ibid. 110–11.

Albany Railroad. Albany was also an important point on the much larger New York Central system. The Central's modest beginnings as the Mohawk and Hudson had grown, under its entrepreneurial Albany directors, Erastus Corning and J. V. L. Pruyn, to include a number of smaller companies by 1853. Eventually the Central extended along both shores of the Hudson River from New York to Albany, then turned west approximately along the line of the Erie Canal to Buffalo, and on to Cleveland, Detroit, Chicago, and St Louis, directly linking Boston and New York City with the industrial cities of the Midwest. Until the 1950s, the New York Central and the Pennsylvania Railroad rivalled one another as among the largest and wealthiest transport undertakings in the United States.

The railways brought more industries and jobs to Albany. Extensive stockyards were built to feed and water the livestock brought by train from the west before their final transit to New York City, Boston, and other eastern markets. Some of the livestock was slaughtered at Albany. Albany was an important meat-packing centre for thirty years, until development of the railway refrigerator car, which allowed the shipment of dressed meat directly from Chicago. The Albany and Susquehanna Railroad (later the Delaware and Hudson) established their main workshops at Colonie, on the western outskirts of Albany. At West Albany, the New York Central also built extensive locomotive repair shops and car works, which alone employed two to three thousand people. Freight and passenger cars by the hundreds were built of wood in the railway companies' shops, with the ironwork and wheels supplied by local foundries. Selkirk, just south of the city on the New York Central's West Shore line, developed as the main marshalling yard for freight trains to points south, carrying such commodities as coal, sand and gravel, wood, bricks and cement, grain and other foodstuffs, machinery and finished goods. In nearby Schenectady, new locomotives were built in a factory that later (in 1901) became the main plant of the American Locomotive Company, which supplied not only the New York Central and the Delaware and Hudson, but grew to become the world's second-largest commercial manufacturer and exporter of railway locomotives.

Heavy traffic on the Hudson River continued to create jobs for warehouse and dock workers and bargees. The forests of the Adirondack Mountains supplied the raw material for the increasing number of sawmills producing sleepers or ties and bridge timbers for railroad-building; planing mills made finished structural lumber, mouldings, turnings, doors, shutters, and sash windows; box and barrel works made kegs, casks, and crates; furniture factories produced dressers, chests, tables, and chairs; wagons, carriages, and watercraft were also made in Albany. At one time, Albany was said to have the largest lumber yards and the greatest concentration of woodworking industries in the country. The grain from the farms in Albany's hinterland—said to have been of the highest quality available in the country at one time—supplied several brewers; as early as 1829, 42,000 barrels of beer were produced, most of it for shipment elsewhere. These and many other activities created thousands of additional jobs and stimulated much new building of factories, offices, and dwellings, which in turn drew in large numbers of carpenters, masons, and other skilled tradesmen. By 1880, Albany's population had reached 90,000. The city had now become a bustling, thriving industrial and commercial centre.

The construction of the canals and railways, and later their expanding operations, absorbed great quantities of immigrant labour throughout the nineteenth century. English, Scots, Welsh, German, Irish, Scandinavian, French-Canadian, Italian, Russian, Slovak, and Polish immigrants arriving at New York found work in Albany, only a couple of days' journey up the Hudson River, as did immigrants arriving at Montréal and at Boston, who migrated south and west in search of employment. Early in the nineteenth century, the numbers of immigrants began to rival the native-stock Dutch, English, Protestant Irish, and Scots residents of Albany. German Lutherans had been present in the city and in the surrounding farming townships in substantial if scattered numbers since colonial times. Lutherans are mentioned as living in Albany in 1644, and a church existed from 1674; by 1750 the Germans had had a church in rural Knox township for perhaps twenty or thirty years, and many other German Lutheran congregations were formed from about 1780.[38] The nineteenth century saw a great influx of Germans, including Evangelical Lutherans, Catholics, and Jews, and there were several German-speaking neighbourhoods in Albany clustered around their churches and synagogues, schools, restaurants, butchers, grocers' shops, and bakeries. Daily and weekly newspapers in German were published locally until the First World War.

By far the greatest number of European-born immigrants to settle in Albany, however, were from Ireland. Some had arrived in the 1780s or earlier. The majority were Anglicans or Presbyterians, with small numbers of Baptists, Methodists, and Quakers, but by 1798, there were

---

[38] Parker, *Landmarks, passim*; Wilcoxen, *Seventeenth Century Albany*, 84.

enough well-to-do Irish Catholics in Albany to sponsor the construction of a small Roman Catholic church, St Mary's, second in the state only to St Peter's in New York.[39] Initially the church seems to have served the needs of a few dozen people, which had risen to two or three hundred by 1820. After the completion of the Erie Canal, the congregation grew rapidly. The canal-diggers, some of whom were Catholic Irish, lived and laboured on the canals during the spring, summer, and autumn, but sought lodgings in boarding-houses in town in the winter. When the canal was completed, some drifted back to Albany to look for other work. Some fell on hard times. In December 1829, 40 of the 219 paupers in the Alms House were Irish immigrants,[40] and a traveller to Albany observed that 'the poor Irish have greatly increased in the streets'.[41] There were grumbles from a few anxious Protestants about the 'increase of Popery'.[42] By this time the term 'poor Irish', as it was used in the newspapers, plainly meant Catholics exclusively, of whom there were now somewhere between one and two thousand in the city, many of whom were likely to have been first-generation immigrants, born in Ireland.[43] The other Irish—the Anglicans, Presbyterians, Methodists, Baptists, and Quakers—of whom there must have been several times as many in Albany, were much more likely to be second or third generation: they seem to have preferred to be called 'native-born' or categorized as British, English, or Scottish rather than Irish, for the word 'Irish' was already coming to signify Roman Catholics only, just as it was in Ireland. The effort to distance themselves socially from the growing tide of poor Catholics would in time cause many of the descendants of non-Catholic Irish immigrants to lose completely their Irish ancestral identity.[44]

Nevertheless, the Catholic Irish who came to dig the Erie Canal, together with other pre-Famine arrivals, soon began to succeed in the rapidly industrializing city. They were not drunks and beggars, illiterate navvies, or living in fatherless families of twelve children in squalid tenements, as the exaggerated stereotypes of nativist demagogues were wont to convey. The 1830 Census indicates that the Irish were widely scattered, with substantial numbers in five of the six wards and the largest concen-

---

[39] J. J. Dillon, *The Historic Story of St. Mary's, Albany, N.Y.: First-Second-Third Church* (New York, 1933), *passim*.

[40] W. A. Rowley, 'Albany: A Tale of Two Cities, 1820–1880', Ph.D. thesis (Harvard University, 1967), 145–6.

[41] W. A. Rowley, 'The Irish Aristocracy of Albany, 1798–1878', *New York History*, 52 (1971), 280–1.   [42] Ibid. 282.

[43] Rowley, 'Tale', 256.

[44] Cf. Akenson, 'The Irish in the United States', 103.

trations in two South End wards. They were represented by two Irish Catholic aldermen on the Common Council. While there were still some unskilled labourers among them, and the majority were in the lower-paying jobs, by no means all were, and there were signs that they were already beginning to move up the occupational ladder. A number had evidently brought skills and, possibly, some capital with them from Ireland.[45] Numbers of immigrants were beginning to come to Albany directly from Ireland in the 1820s. They came from Leinster, Ulster, and Munster; they were mostly couples in their thirties with children; they were English-speaking, and Catholics predominated over Protestants by about three to one. The 1830 Census listed 63 Irishmen as labourers, 23 were in skilled building-trades jobs, 7 were carters and teamsters, and 30 were in skilled manufacturing jobs, in some cases in their own workshops. Twenty-nine were listed as grocers, and another 6, listed as peddlers, were probably on their way up to becoming grocers.[46] The established middle-class Catholic Irish included not only merchants and factory-owners, like the Cassidys, Mahers, Barrys, and Goughs, who were the benefactors of St Mary's, but also two physicians, at least one lawyer, several teachers including two at the Protestant Albany Academy, several other merchants, a steamboat captain and agent, a hotel proprietor, and a brewer. Over the next twenty-five years to 1855, which included the years of the Great Famine in Ireland in the 1840s, the number of Irish in the city would rise to 23,000, to comprise 40 per cent of the population. In 1855, more than 14,000 of Albany's residents—one in every four people living in the city—had been born in Ireland.[47] Another 12 per cent of the city's population were German, and altogether almost half the churchgoers of Albany were Roman Catholic.[48]

The Catholic congregation had already outgrown the original St Mary's by the mid-1820s. It was demolished in 1829 and a new church in Pine Street was consecrated in 1830. Still the congregation grew. In 1839, St Mary's parish was divided in two, and a new parish, St John's, served the southern part of the city from a reconsecrated Anglican church in South Ferry Street. In 1843, St Mary's parish was divided again: its northern part became St Joseph's, with a new church on North Pearl Street. In 1847, when the Diocese of Albany was set off from that of New York, John McCloskey became its first bishop, and St Mary's served as his

---

[45] K. Miller, *Emigrants and Exiles: Ireland and the Irish Exodus to North America* (New York, 1985), 195–6.
[46] Ibid. 149.
[47] Rowley, 'Aristocracy', 284.
[48] Rowley, 'Tale', 256.

seat for five years until the new Cathedral of the Immaculate Conception was completed on Eagle Street, once again subdividing St Mary's parish. Next, St Patrick's parish was formed in 1858, with a church on Central Avenue; St Ann's was created twelve years later with a new church on the corner of Fourth Avenue and Franklin Street; and finally the North Albany parish of the Sacred Heart of Jesus was formed in 1884, with a church in Walter Street. St Joseph's was replaced by a larger church in 1856, and St Mary's was again demolished and a larger church built upon the Pine Street site in 1867. As well as the Irish Catholic churches, in the nineteenth century there were three German Catholic churches in the city: Holy Cross, at Hamilton and Philip Streets (1849); Our Lady of Angels, Robin Street (1868); and Our Lady Help of Christians, on Second Avenue (1880). French Canadian Catholics had their own Church of the Assumption from 1869, at the corner of Dallius Street and Fourth Avenue.[49]

Irish Catholic institutions grew apace. For example, a Roman Catholic Sunday school was formed at St Mary's in 1828; in St Joseph's parish, Father Conroy established the Girls' Orphan Asylum on North Pearl Street, built a parochial residence, and established an elementary school for both boys and girls. Annual dinners of the St Patrick's Society, sponsored by the Irish bourgeoisie, social events that attracted prominent Protestant leaders, were already being held in the 1820s. The St Vincent's Female Orphan Asylum, opened in 1829, was described as 'one of the finest institutions of its kind in the state'.[50] In 1833, a Hibernian Provident Society was formed to help the poor fund sickness insurance.[51] An Irish Association of Hibernians was already in existence by 1836. St Ann's had a Sunday School Union, and chapters of the St Vincent de Paul's and Ladies' Aid societies. Bishop McCloskey founded the Convent and the Academy of the Sacred Heart to provide an education for young Catholic women, which was at first accommodated in the Westerlo mansion on North Pearl Street (1853–8), before eventually moving into new buildings on the Kenwood Estate. La Salle Orphanage was built to care for immigrant and homeless children. A secondary school for boys, Christian Brothers' Academy, was established in 1864. St Peter's Hospital, originally accommodated in the former mansion of Governor King which was purchased by the trustees of the estate of

---

[49] Parker, *Landmarks*, 350 ff.
[50] M. J. Louden (ed.), *Catholic Albany* (Albany, NY, 1895), 28.
[51] Rowley, 'Aristocracy', 284.

Peter Cagger, a prominent Irish Catholic lawyer, and given to the Sisters of Mercy, was opened in 1869. The hospital was attended by several Irish physicians as well as a number of other doctors and students of the Albany Medical College who gave their services in charity to the hospital.[52] There was a Catholic home for the aged, Catholic undertakers, and a separate Catholic cemetery. By 1875, a distinctive set of Catholic institutions had been created, largely under the direction or with the encouragement of Bishop McCloskey. Each of the twelve parishes in Albany had its own elementary school staffed by brothers and sisters of the teaching orders. More than 2,000 children now attended the city's Catholic elementary and secondary schools.[53] It was increasingly possible, and likely, that Albany's Irish would be born, schooled, cared for when ill and aged, and be buried, entirely within Irish Catholic institutions, whatever their social level.

Within fifty years, Albany had become a largely Catholic city. The reason for this transformation is not merely that jobs on the canals and railways attracted people from Ireland, for this fact alone does not explain why Irish immigrants chose to settle in Albany in such numbers rather than in other industrializing towns in New England or along the westward route. Much of the explanation must turn upon the forceful personality of John McCloskey, Bishop of the Diocese of Albany from 1847 to 1864, during the critical years of Irish immigration. Born in Brooklyn, New York, of parents who were natives of Derry, McCloskey proved to be an organizer, administrator, and diplomat of genius, as well as an orator and scholar of great ability. Under his direction, a number of vocational orders were introduced in the diocese, including the Jesuits, Franciscans, Augustinians, Sisters of Mercy, Ladies of the Sacred Heart, Sisters of Charity, and the Sisters of St Joseph. Parochial schools were organized in all twelve parishes in the city, two secondary schools were created, a theological seminary was established across the Hudson River in Troy, and the charitable work and social welfare institutions of the church were greatly strengthened. McCloskey did more for the Catholic community in Albany than any of his predecessors or his immediate successors, and he was instrumental in establishing the reputation of Albany, among Catholics in Ireland and in America, as a place where they were welcome, well provided for, and unlikely to be looked down upon. McCloskey invited Famine immigrants to come to Albany, and the charities he had organized helped the refugees to settle in. There

---

[52] Parker, *Landmarks*, 207–8.   [53] Rowley, 'Aristocracy', 297.

was even an emigrants' savings scheme, by which people in Ireland could send money to the church in Albany until the cost of their passage had been paid. Moreover, McCloskey could rely upon the generous patronage of a prosperous, well-established, pre-Famine Irish Catholic middle class who had good social connections with the Anglo-Dutch political ascendancy, and who could smooth the path for McCloskey's reforms and new developments. He charmed the English and Dutch gentry of Albany as he did the Pope and the Vatican Council in his visits to Rome, for he left Albany only to become Archbishop of New York, and shortly thereafter to be elevated as the first Roman Catholic cardinal in the United States.

The refugees from the Famine and its aftermath in Ireland did not find 'No Irish Need Apply' signs on the doors and windows of boarding-houses, workshops, and factories in Albany, as they did in Boston and other eastern-seaboard cities. Instead, they found a well-run system of Irish Catholic parish churches and schools, hospitals, orphanages, and institutes for the blind, deaf, and poor. Albany was as Catholic, and as Irish, as any city in the United States. Those who had taken the less-expensive passage to British North America, but found Toronto and Montréal to be the preserve of Scots or Ulster Presbyterians and fran-cophones, gravitated south in large numbers towards Albany and other American cities in search of greater civil and religious liberty. The non-Irish people of Albany—Dutch, English, and German—were sufficiently well disposed towards the Irish to elect Irish-born Michael Nolan as mayor in 1878, to re-elect him for two further two-year terms, and then to elect him to the United States Congress as their representative in Washington. Between 1840 and Michael Nolan's election in 1878 there were, however, momentous events that included the Potato Famine and a great influx of Famine refugees into Albany, which would fundamentally alter the composition of the city's population.

II

In Ireland, the population grew rapidly in the eighteenth century and into the nineteenth, a phenomenon that occurred in many other places in north-west Europe at much the same time. Unlike other European countries, however, Ireland lagged behind in industrialization and urbanization and thus in the ability of its economy to absorb people into spheres other than primary agricultural production and rural labour. The capacity of the economy to create wealth was low,[54] limited by its lack of natural resources such as coal, oil, iron ore, timber, or fish, coupled with its wet, maritime climate and its unfavourable location on the remote fringe of western Europe, conditions which continue to handicap Ireland's economy to this day. The population grew by 1.2 million in the twenty years from 1821 to 1841. This does not, of course, include those who emigrated: 1.5 million are thought to have emigrated permanently between 1801 and 1845; there were at least 400,000 pre-Famine Irish arrivals in North America in the twenty years before 1845, and an even greater number migrated to Scotland, England, and Wales.

Ireland's economy was heavily reliant upon agriculture, and its population was predominantly rural. Four-fifths of Ireland's 8 million people lived in rural areas or in hamlets or villages of less than twenty dwellings on the eve of the Famine. The majority had no secure hold upon land. They lived in dreadful conditions: 40 per cent of Irish dwellings were one-room mud cabins with earthen floors, no windows, and no chimney. Landless farm labourers were the largest single occupational category in the country: there were nearly 600,000 in 1841. They exchanged their labour for small and irregular wages and the temporary use of an acre (or less) of their employer's land upon which to erect a cabin and cultivate a potato patch under a traditional system known as conacre. These cottiers considerably outnumbered tenant smallholders, who themselves typically had less than 6 acres and relied on earnings from tillage, agricultural labour, or spinning or weaving to eke out a bare subsistence. The next group, small farmers, had between 6 and 15 acres, a cow or two, and employed a couple of labourers under the conacre system. There were over 400,000 smallholders and small farmers in 1841; very few had written tenancy agreements and could be evicted (along with their labourers) at any time. Finally, there were some 450,000 commercial farmers who held more than 15 acres, frequently rented on long leases from large landowners. Three-quarters of all farmers, including smallholders, had fewer than 30 acres but occupied less than 40 per cent of the land. The smallest holdings were concentrated in Connaught and Ulster. One-quarter of the farmers, those with 50 acres or more, occupied 60 per cent of the land, predominantly in the east and south of the country.[55] The poorest districts of Ireland lay to the west of a line drawn between Derry and Cork: nearly forty per cent of the houses (and in

[54] J. Mokyr, *Why Ireland Starved: A Quantitative and Analytical History of the Irish Economy, 1800–1850* (London, 1983), 275.
[55] M. Winstanley, *Ireland and the Land Question, 1800–1922* (London, 1984), 16.

some places over eighty per cent) were one-room mud cabins of the most primitive sort.[56] Where, today, there are fifty or sixty people to the square mile in these districts, in 1841 there were anything up to 300.[57]

The lower economic strata of Ireland's population, the cottiers and smallholders, subsisted almost entirely upon the potato. The potato was a reliable, highly nutritious, and efficient food crop, well adapted to Irish soils and climatic conditions. One acre of potatoes was, on average, sufficient to feed six people for a year.[58] According to expert estimates made at the time, roughly three million people—40 per cent of the population—had come to depend almost wholly upon the potato for food by the mid-1830s, and the fact that three times as many people could be supported per acre under a potato-planting regime than by grain or milk undoubtedly made a major contribution to the capacity of the Irish rural economy to absorb an expanding population, whether or not it was the cause of the increase.[59] The consequences of the increasing population were a more monotonous diet, the extension of cultivation to ever-less fertile land, and greater vulnerability to density-dependent contagious diseases, such as smallpox, cholera, and puerperal fever.[60] A third of the population was wretchedly poor, and there was much rural unrest, but there is nothing to suggest that the Irish were eating themselves out of house and home, or that in Ireland as a whole the capacity of the land available to the peasantry had reached the absolute limit of the population it could sustain under potato cultivation.[61] While there were local and seasonal scarcities, and in some places the size of individual landholdings had become too small to support the number of people dependent upon them, creating temporary shortages between the last potatoes of the old harvest and the first crop of the new, serious and widespread harvest failures directly resulting in large numbers of deaths by starvation were unknown in the hundred years to 1845. The 1841 census records only 117 cases of death by starvation during the previous ten years; most of these deaths were of homeless beggars and vagrants.[62] In Connaught, the poorest part of Ireland, the

[56] T. W. Freeman, 'Land and People, *c*.1841', in W. E. Vaughan (ed.), *A New History of Ireland*, v, *Ireland under the Union, I, 1801–70* (Oxford, 1989), 253.

[57] Ibid. 264.

[58] K. H. Connell, *The Population of Ireland, 1750–1845* (Oxford, 1950), 123.

[59] M. E. Daly, *The Famine in Ireland* (Dublin, 1986), 6.

[60] C. Ó Gráda, 'Poverty, Population, and Agriculture, 1801–45', in W. E. Vaughan (ed.), *A New History of Ireland*, v, *Ireland under the Union, I, 1801–70* (Oxford, 1989), 110.

[61] Mokyr, *Why Ireland Starved*, 269; C. Ó Gráda, *Ireland Before and After the Famine: Explorations in Economic History, 1800–1925* (Manchester, 1988), ch. 1.

[62] C. Ó Gráda, *The Great Irish Famine* (Dublin, 1989), 22.

summer hunger was most acute, distress was frequently reported, and some deaths undoubtedly occurred, but even in the poorest districts the supply of food available to individuals, occasionally supplemented by local arrangements for relief to those in most need during the summer months, seems to have been sufficient to ensure that starvation was rare, and was not a statistically significant cause of death. Recent research by Irish historians discounts emotive claims by popular writers and political polemicists that the Great Famine was simply the climax of centuries of actual or potential starvation, and that there had been a gradually escalating series of minor famines which ought to have alerted the government to an impending, widespread food crisis.[63] This is to read history backwards, exaggerating the difficulties of the pre–Famine economy.[64]

The food, at least in dietary terms, was quite adequate most of the time, because in the potato the poor had chosen 'the only single cheap food that can support human life when fed as a *sole* article of diet'. Moreover, although life expectancy was lower than in England, it was not significantly so. ... The Scandinavians and Dutch may have lived longer than the pre-Famine Irish, but the French or the Germans apparently did not, and the life expectancy in southern and eastern Europe was also probably lower.[65]

In the hundred years leading up to the Famine,

... as potatoes [became the staple foodstuff] of the bottom third of the population and made substantial inroads further up the social scale, the Irish population was abundantly fed, indeed well-fed. Pre-Famine diets were 'excellent, not merely when measured by the "recommended daily intake" of the nutritionist, but also when set against the historical reality of the later nineteenth century'. Except for short periods of dearth, [fertility trends] in pre-Famine Ireland [were] subject to none of the constraints that a chronically inadequate diet might impose.[66]

Disasters are usually well documented, but it is not easy to find detailed accounts of pre-1845 food crises in the Irish historical record.[67]

---

[63] L. A. Clarkson, 'Conclusion: Famine and Irish History', in E. M. Crawford (ed.), *Famine: The Irish Experience 900–1900* (Edinburgh, 1989), 220.

[64] Ó Gráda, 'Poverty, Population and Agriculture', 108.

[65] Ibid. 111. The quotation within this passage is from S. Davidson and R. Passmore, *Human Nutrition and Dietetics* (Baltimore, 1963), 285.

[66] L. Kennedy and L. A. Clarkson, 'Birth, Death and Exile: Irish Population History, 1700–1921', in B. J. Graham and L. J. Proudfoot (eds.), *An Historical Geography of Ireland* (London, 1993), 163. The quoted sentence within this passage is from L. A. Clarkson and E. M. Crawford, 'Dietary Directions: A Topographical Survey of Irish Diet, 1836', in R. Mitchison and P. Roebuck (eds.), *Economy and Society in Scotland and Ireland, 1500–1939* (Edinburgh, 1988), 191.

[67] Connell, *Population of Ireland*, 144.

The best-known case, the famine of 1740, was the result of damage done to the potato crop by freak weather conditions: an early, severe, and prolonged frost, which spoiled the crop before it could be lifted and froze the stored potatoes that had already been harvested. Because the rivers were choked by ice and the water-powered mills could not operate, extra grain could not be milled into flour to substitute for the shortage of potatoes. The winter and spring were unusually dry, and the famine, accompanied by an outbreak of cholera, continued into 1741. Estimates of the deaths are unreliable but there may have been about 100,000; nevertheless we can infer, from the events of a century later, that the greater number are likely to have died from the cholera epidemic which occurred at the same time. Of the other crop losses mentioned over the following century, most were caused by drought, frost, or excessively heavy rains, and were localized in their effects. These were normal hazards of intensive agriculture which were experienced in other unindustrialized European countries with much the same frequency and severity. Until the years following 1815, with the end of heightened demand for Irish agricultural produce during the Napoleonic Wars and the return of thousands of discharged soldiers, reliable reports of deaths from food shortage were exceedingly scarce.[68]

The post-1815 agricultural depression deprived many of Ireland's landless farm labourers of steady cash incomes, forcing them to migrate or to rely on their potato patches and little else for the whole of their livelihoods. Awareness of Ireland's worsening economic situation increased after the Act of Union with Great Britain in 1801, and a number of official inquiries were undertaken with the object of drawing up plans for the 'general improvement of Ireland', including the extension of the English Poor Law to Ireland, the most ambitious administrative reform to follow the Union, and one which would be relied upon heavily during the Famine.[69]

The Irish rural problem was not unique. In the western Highlands of Scotland ... there was what can properly be called a 'peasant society,' with the overwhelming majority of the inhabitants depending to a significant extent on smallholdings and tiny patches of land for subsistence. This population was to experience the potato blight of 1846–7 and suffer from its consequences, since the potato was central to its diet. And this area, like much of Ireland, was confronted with a crucial and alarming fact: its population growth, while not in itself a cause of social destitution, was in a kind of imbalance with its resources and its employment possibilities.

[68] Connell, *Population of Ireland* 145 ff.
[69] Ó Gráda, *The Great Irish Famine*, 31.

There was simply no alternative for the people except the precarious existence available to them from their simple diet and their small patches of land; none, that is, except emigration. Between 1815 and 1845 over a million inhabitants left Ireland; and one of the remedies frequently suggested for the Irish rural problem was state-assisted emigration rather than workhouse relief. But emigration in itself, while possibly a palliative, was not a cure, since the fundamental problem—that of a society in which most people did not have the money to buy alternative means of subsistence if their staple crop failed—remained untouched. What the inhabitants of peasant Ireland needed was greater employment opportunities, which mere emigration could not provide.[70]

The Irish Poor Law, introduced in 1838, brought a modern social welfare institution to Ireland, supplanting the semi-feudal, patrimonial custom by which landlords were expected to provide relief to their tenants, which in practice was highly variable in its effectiveness: some landlords were benign, and looked after their tenants well; others did not, and it was the general perception in London that Irish landholders were not taking sufficient responsibility for their tenants and labourers. With the Poor Law, Parliament accepted responsibility for the relief of poverty in Ireland, as it had done in England, Wales, and Scotland only four years earlier. No better or worse than similar arrangements being made at the time in other western European countries and in North America, the Poor Law was an attempt systematically to provide food and shelter to the indigent. It differed from the English Poor Law of 1834 in three important respects: the relief of destitution could be provided only to those admitted to the workhouse, there being no provision for 'outdoor' relief; no right of relief existed, so that when the workhouse became full, paupers could be turned away; and, finally, there was no test of local residence, so that the destitute were entitled to apply for admission to any workhouse in Ireland.[71] The Poor Law arrangements were intended to meet a long-term problem by concentrating only upon the very poorest: those too young, too old, or too sick to support themselves. Stringent tests of destitution were applied; otherwise it was feared that Ireland's taxpayers could not bear the cost of a poor relief system: 'A well-managed workhouse was one which deterred people from applying for relief, whilst those who did receive Poor Law relief, would not be encouraged to stay in the workhouse building for a protracted period'.[72] Ireland was divided into 130 local

---

[70] D. G. Boyce, *Nineteenth Century Ireland: The Search for Stability* (Dublin, 1990), 106.

[71] C. Kinealy, 'The Poor Law during the Great Famine: An Administration in Crisis', in E. M. Crawford (ed.), *Famine: The Irish Experience 900–1900* (Edinburgh, 1989), 158.

[72] Ibid. 159.

administrative units, or Poor Law Unions, each governed by a Board of Guardians who were charged with raising taxes in their localities to pay for the construction and operation of a workhouse, each of which was to have a capacity of 1,000 people; thus 130,000 places were to be made available across the country. The Unions were expected to be entirely self-supporting. These arrangements were implemented with impressive efficiency: by the summer of 1845, in the last weeks before the potato blight struck, 118 workhouses had been opened.

The immediate cause of the Great Famine was an entirely new phenomenon that had never before been experienced in Ireland or indeed anywhere in Europe: the fungal potato blight, *Phytopthera infestans*, which thrives in hot, damp weather and whose spores are carried by wind or mist. An entire field can be infected in a matter of hours. The spores can lie dormant during the winter months, to reappear the following season. The potato blight apparently came to Europe from South America, and was first seen in Belgium and the Netherlands in June 1845, where it caused widespread devastation, destroying two-thirds or more of the crop. It had spread to England, Wales, and Scotland within a month or two and by 13 September had reached eastern Ireland. Damage to the Irish potato crop in 1845 was restricted mainly to the eastern counties of Leinster, where its impact was mitigated by the larger farm sizes and greater prosperity of this region. For more than a year following the blight's appearance, matters seemed to be under control. On every occasion that local shortages of food appeared, the relief efforts and Poor Law arrangements were well able to cope, and were regarded as very successful both by contemporary observers and subsequently by most historians. There were no deaths attributable to starvation from the first appearance of the blight in 1845 through the spring and summer of 1846, prompting confidence in the capacity of the relief measures to deal adequately with the distress caused by the blight.[73] By October, however, as the autumn harvest season began, it became clear that much worse was in store. The warm, damp, windy summer of 1846 had provided ideal conditions for the spread of the blight, carrying it across the whole of the country, including the poorest districts of Connaught and Ulster, where the people had virtually nothing else to sustain them.[74] Eighty per cent of the harvest was destroyed. Confidence in the relief arrangements immediately evaporated.

[73] C. Kinealy, *This Great Calamity: The Irish Famine, 1845–52* (Dublin, 1994), 51.
[74] Daly, *The Famine in Ireland*, 52–3; P. Solar, 'The Great Famine was no Ordinary Subsistence Crisis', in Crawford (ed.), *Famine*, 112; P. M. A. Bourke, '*The Visitation of God'? The Potato and the Great Irish Famine*, J. Hill and C. Ó Gráda (eds.) (Dublin, 1993), ch. 7.

The final two months of 1846 were remarkable for a spiraling demand for relief in any guise, that is, in food, on the public works, or even in the workhouses. There was also an inability of the supply to keep up with demand. A mood of panic, despair and desperation was apparent within the country, amidst growing reports of starvation.[75]

Elsewhere in Europe where the potato blight had struck, the damage had been localized in its effects. No one had any reason to believe that Ireland would be affected any differently, and everyone, including the government, was caught unprepared for the nightmare of a general failure of the potato crop throughout Ireland. The sudden, extreme severity of the situation overwhelmed not only the capacity of rural social networks, but also the efforts of landlords, private charities, and the public authorities. The Poor Law arrangements and the workhouses had never been designed to cope with such a calamity. Public works projects were organized to make more cash earnings available, soup kitchens were set up in village streets, and 'outdoor' relief was very early in the crisis extended by Boards of Guardians throughout the country even though they were not empowered to do so under the Poor Law; Parliament in London responded by authorizing outdoor relief and giving the Boards of Guardians permission to spend more than their incomes, which over the Famine years eventually amounted to £7,132,268 in free grants and credit from the British exchequer,[76] by today's values equivalent to perhaps $1.5 billion. A further £8 million (or $2 billion, by today's standards) was raised locally in Ireland by increasing the Poor Rate levied on landholders, which in some localities rose to 10 shillings in the pound; a property tax rate of 50 per cent.[77] Through voluntary donations from Britain, Canada, and the United States, millions more flowed into the private charities such as the Society of Friends, the Irish Relief Association, and the General Central Relief Committee. Albany responded in a way that was typical of many American cities. The Albany Committee for the Relief of Ireland was organized on 15 February 1847, within three months collecting together over 250 tons of relief supplies including 2,000 barrels of wheat flour and corn meal, new and used clothing, and $16,000 in cash, shipped to the Society of Friends on the chartered British ships *Minerva* and *Malabar*, which arrived in Dublin and Cork in

---

[75] Kinealy, *This Great Calamity*, 79.

[76] Boyce, *Nineteenth Century Ireland*, 111; J. S. Donnelly, 'The Administration of Relief, 1847–51', in W. E. Vaughan (ed.), *A New History of Ireland*, v, *Ireland under the Union, I, 1801–70* (Oxford, 1989), 328.

[77] Ibid.

started work on 6 May. The Union infirmary was enlarged to 90 beds, fever sheds were erected in the workhouse grounds and even a large shed beside the General Hospital in Frederick Street, the old cholera buildings were put in service, the College Hospital in Barrack Street was re-opened, and tents were set up in the workhouse grounds and in the environs of the town. By July the weekly admissions were over 600 and the total 'institutionalised' was 2,118 in a spot census on 17 July. When the epidemic ended in November and the 'normal' admission rates resumed, there had been 13,469 cases of fever admitted, 1,836 of dysentery, and 325 of smallpox with nearly 2,500 deaths all in a population of some 100,000, i.e. one in six of the population were admitted with a case mortality of 17 percent. Add to that the countless hundreds who died outside the hospitals—in the streets, the fields, the hovels of the poor and the mansions of the rich—and extrapolate to Ireland as a whole and the enormity of the 1847 fever pandemic can be calculated if hardly credited.[83]

The extrapolation to Ireland as a whole produces 1,360,000 deaths. Since the epidemics were variably spread across the country, this figure is probably far too high. Yet the epidemics did not necessarily strike the rural population uniformly harder than city dwellers or the well-to-do. Solely by virtue of greater population density, the residents of Dublin, Belfast, and Cork were at greatest risk. Those who lived in the 'congested districts' of highest rural overcrowding were at much greater risk of contagion than those living in sparsely populated districts, whatever their diet. Contemporary accounts note the unexpected fact that relapsing fever was more likely to be fatal to more prosperous people. Now that this disease is better understood, it can be seen that their wealth allowed them to bathe and change their clothes frequently and to live in circumstances less likely to be infested by bedbugs, fleas, and lice; thus they had accumulated less immunity to the diseases carried by these insects. More than 20 per cent of the doctors and medical students tending to fever patients in Dublin between 1843 and 1848 died, a significantly greater rate of mortality than among their patients.[84] The death rate was also higher among magistrates, clergy, and others in comfortable circumstances who were attending to the hungry and poor.[85] Upper-class mortality was very high indeed; among those who caught the fever, 66 per cent in Cavan died, 70 per cent succumbed in the vicinity of Ballinrobe, and almost everywhere in Ireland death rates among the upper and middle classes

---

[83] P. Froggatt, 'The Response of the Medical Profession to the Great Famine', in Crawford (ed.), *Famine*, 143–4.

[84] Ibid. 148; see also Kinealy, *This Great Calamity*, 171–2.

[85] Daly, *The Famine in Ireland*, 105.

were reported to be much higher than among the poor.[86] Since there were far more poor people than prosperous ones, however, poor people died in vastly greater numbers. The very poorest were the most vulnerable to contagion because they were forced to endure conditions likely to expose them to the highest levels of risk. Overcrowding in the workhouses, hospitals, and hostels, and close contact at the soup kitchens and in the public-works labour gangs undoubtedly contributed to the spread of disease. Ironically, for no one could have known it at the time, as they were being fed and sheltered they were being infected with relapsing fever and other diseases. Not just once, but over and over and over again. That they did not all die must suggest that the pre-existing levels of immunity, although variable from one part of the country to another, were in general very high indeed among the poorest fraction of the population.

There were between 1,600,000 and 2 million fewer people in Ireland in 1851 than there were in 1841. Beyond this, little is certain. One million to 1,200,000 are thought to have emigrated. The best estimates of Famine mortality from all causes are therefore between 500,000 and 1 million.[87] Forty per cent of these deaths occurred in Connaught, 30 per cent in Munster, 20 per cent in Ulster, and 10 per cent in Leinster,[88] rates which are roughly proportional to the levels of poverty in these areas. The total number of fever deaths will never be known because so many of the dead were perfunctorily buried without any formalities, but Woodham Smith's estimate of 1962, that perhaps ten times as many people died of fever as of starvation—an estimate which was thought exaggerated at the time— now seems more plausible in the light of recent findings.[89] Even for the very poorest, their chances of death from typhus or relapsing fever were perhaps ten times greater than starving, and if they caught the disease there was a roughly one-in-five chance that they would be dead within ten or twelve days. Those who were not destitute, the majority of Ireland's population, were at no appreciable risk of starvation, but once infected stood an even greater chance of dying of fever than the very poorest.

After 150 years of advances in public health disease control and medical science, it is difficult for us to imagine the situation then. The

---

[86] C. Woodham Smith, *The Great Hunger* (New York, 1962), 204.

[87] Mokyr, *Why Ireland Starved*, 264–8. See also P. J. Blessing, *The Irish in America: A Guide to the Literature and the Manuscript Collections* (Washington, 1992), 289, 316–17; D. Akenson, *The Irish Diaspora: A Primer* (Streetsville, Ontario, 1993), 258.

[88] J. S. Donnelly, 'Excess Mortality and Emigration', in Vaughan (ed.), *A New History of Ireland*, v. 351.

[89] Ibid.

epidemics spread with astonishing speed. There were no effective sanitary or quarantine measures. People were dying of fever everywhere in Ireland, the rich with the poor, the well-fed with the starving. It must have been terrifying. No one knew what caused these diseases, and there were no cures. The common louse—even just inhaled dust from its desiccated droppings could cause infection—was not identified as the vector of relapsing fever until 1891, nor were bedbugs implicated until 1927. Fear of contagion provoked panic and desperation to get as far away from infection as possible. People abandoned their farms and villages and took to the roads. Those who could afford it left Ireland altogether. Healthy people sold their land, livestock, and household goods for whatever they could get and bought tickets to Britain, Canada, the United States, Australia, and New Zealand. The tide of human movement carried the vectors of disease aboard the emigrant ships and to their eventual destinations across the Irish Sea and the Atlantic. Tens of thousands of Irish immigrants, attempting to save their own lives and those of their children by escaping the fevers in Ireland, perished of fevers at sea, or weeks after their arrival in Liverpool, New York, and Montréal.

Had it not been for an acute lack of food in the first place, which triggered a chain of events, people never would have been exposed to the diseases which ultimately killed them in such staggering numbers. However they died, by fever or starvation, the Famine was one of the worst natural disasters in modern European history. Whether it was avoidable, and, in the light of the medical knowledge of the day, whether different official responses during the Famine would have altered the outcome a great deal, no one can say with certainty. When the Famine had ended, and what had been done had been done, perhaps 90,000 of the poorest 3 million had starved, and 900,000 people of all social classes, rich and poor, had died of fever. But no historian disputes that over a million had emigrated, nor that there were at least 6 million people left in Ireland who had survived the Famine. Ninety per cent of the pre-Famine population had survived a catastrophe of unprecedented magnitude. Yet the shock and tragedy of that great pestilence has continued to haunt Ireland to this day.

3

As Irish as any City in America

I

The arrival of large numbers of Famine immigrants in the United States in the middle of the nineteenth century had far-reaching consequences for the ethnic composition of many American cities, not least because the great preponderance of Famine immigrants were Catholic; they were the first Catholics to arrive in the United States in large numbers. Until then, the country remained predominantly Protestant. Among these Protestants were many people of Irish ancestry. Since the sixteenth century, between a fifth and a quarter of the population of Ireland has been Anglican, Methodist, Presbyterian, and Quaker, and today well over half of the 40 million Americans who trace their ancestry to Ireland are Protestant.[1] Much of the American South had been gradually settled by Irish immigrants in the century preceding the Great Famine. If, however, the Irish emigrated to the American South in anything like their religious proportions in Ireland, then many, if not a majority, must have been Catholic.[2] The pre-1815 Irish Catholic settlers in the southern states did not, apparently, remain Catholic for very long; rather, they mostly became Baptists or other kinds of Protestants. Until Catholic emancipation in Ireland and in the United States, Catholic worship was discouraged: no priests accompanied the emigrants to America, and there were no Irish Catholic churches, yet Irish migration to the American South had already been in full force for thirty or forty years, and British Army regiments raised in Ireland had been deployed in the American colonies for a hundred years or more. Since there is no reason to believe that these newcomers—ordinary farm labourers and soldiers—were particularly religious, or had left Ireland for religious reasons (unlike many other European emigrants, who came to America to found religious communities), they probably merged into the Protestant population, intermarrying

---

[1] D. H. Akenson, *The Irish Diaspora: A Primer* (Streetsville, Ontario, 1993), 219–20.

[2] See e.g. F. McDonald and G. McWhiney, 'The Celtic South' *History Today*, 30 (1980), 11–15.

with the Welsh, Scots, English, Germans, Dutch, and Scandinavians. This would have been more likely if they came mainly as single men rather than as family groups, which appears to have been largely the case. There were few Catholic women for them to marry, no clergy to look after their spiritual welfare, and no churches for them to attend. That they did not remain Catholic is unsurprising.

By 1847, when the refugees from the Great Famine in Ireland began to arrive in the United States in large numbers, the situation was changing. With the end of the Napoleonic Wars in 1815, immigrants from Ireland who were readily identifiable as Catholics began to arrive in the United States in substantial numbers. Most appear to have been family groups, and to have brought skills and capital; these were not the Gaelic-speaking landless poor from Connaught and Munster (who did not have assets to sell in order to pay for their passages, and those of their families, to America), but people from the more prosperous, English-speaking counties of Ireland.[3] Before the Great Famine in Ireland, steadily increasing numbers of Irish Catholic immigrants were settling in the United States, and Catholic churches and institutions had already begun to appear in some places. From 1820 to 1846, 450,000 Irish emigrants had arrived in the United States; by the early 1840s, arrivals had risen to more than 40,000 per year.

The Famine provoked the emigration of over a million people to America between 1847 and 1854. After 1854, the emergency was clearly over; the numbers arriving abruptly returned to their pre-Famine levels where they remained for a decade, before beginning to increase gradually after the Civil War. The Famine changed the social composition of the emigrant stream. Those who arrived between 1847 and 1854 were of two distinct kinds. First, there were those who were from the better-off counties of Ireland, mainly in Leinster, Ulster, and the eastern counties of Munster. They were predominantly Catholic, but there were numerous Anglicans and Presbyterians among them. Some were townspeople from Dublin, Belfast, and Cork; although, as Ireland was a heavily agrarian country, most were rural people: smallholders or small farmers, or their children. English was their first language; they had at least a primary-

---

[3]   The records filed in Albany in 1830 by those Irish immigrants registering an intention to become US citizens indicate that 59 per cent had been born in the midlands counties (Leinster and the adjoining counties of Cavan, Leitrim, Monaghan, Roscommon, Tipperary, and Waterford); 25 per cent had been born in Ulster (Antrim, Armagh, Derry, Donegal, Fermanagh, and Tyrone); 9 per cent had been born in the westernmost counties of Connaught (Clare, Galway, Mayo, and Sligo); and 7 per cent had been born in Cork, Kerry, and Limerick.

school education, and they could read and write. On the whole, they were from the middle and lower-middle strata of Irish society. They were neither rich nor poor, and brought with them enough skills and capital to make a start in America. Previous depressions in the Irish agricultural economy had, since 1815, provoked surges in immigration of people seeking a better future in America, just as such local depressions had triggered peaks in emigration from other parts of the British Isles and western Europe. The disastrous potato crop failures and spread of disease in 1846–7 through 1849 were far worse than anything that had previously been experienced in Ireland and impelled hundreds of thousands of people to leave Ireland—many of whom, given the emigration trends before the Famine, sooner or later would probably have left anyway. The Famine greatly accelerated the established pattern, and provoked many more to leave Ireland than might otherwise have been the case. Most of these people were not in any immediate danger of starvation; they were escaping a country where disease was epidemic, the economy was in a dreadfully distressed state, and where they saw no future for themselves and their children. They were able to pay for the passage to America, and on arrival joined relatives who had previously emigrated. They were essentially economic migrants, part of already-established chains across the Atlantic.

The second stream of immigrants was new and very different, and had not been seen in previous migrations from Ireland. They were the true refugees of the Great Famine, the rural poor mainly from Connaught and western Munster, the most remote and distressed parts of the country. Nearly all were Catholic and about half were Gaelic-speaking, though except for the very young and very old and those from the most isolated parts of the west of Ireland, they were probably also able to speak English with some degree of fluency, and if they had attended school in Ireland were more likely to read and write in English than in Gaelic. They were mainly cottiers and landless farm workers and their families, whose position within the Irish agarian economic and social order was very insecure. They eked out a precarious existence from casual rural labour, sometimes involving seasonal migration to other parts of Ireland, Scotland, and England. Their earnings in cash and kind were supplemented by potato patches which their employers allowed them to cultivate in return for their labour; the very poorest were squatters, who reclaimed their potato patches from the rocky and barren western seashores and fertilized them with seaweed. Their poverty made them Ireland's most vulnerable people, who were most immediately threatened with the spectres of starvation and eviction as well as disease. Very few could afford to emigrate during the Famine years and many were unable to leave Ireland until the 1850s. When they arrived, they were often in bad health and without savings. They came as unaccompanied children and single women and in family groups which sometimes, through death, lacked husband or wife. Many had no relatives to join and nowhere to go, and soon would have found themselves in desperate straits had it not been for the Catholic charitable institutions which had already begun to develop in a few places like Albany. There are suggestions that these refugees were invited to Albany in considerable numbers and gravitated to Albany from other cities in the region because of the reputation for pastoral care that its church and civic authorities provided, helping them to weather their first few months and assisting them to find their feet in the new country.

By 1855, when the influx of Famine immigrants had peaked, 25 per cent of Albany's population was Irish-born. Albany was transformed from an Anglo–Dutch, exclusively Protestant settlement before the American Revolution to a largely Irish and Catholic city a century later. Most of this transformation occurred in just twenty-five years, from 1850 to 1875. How were these immigrants incorporated into Albany society? To begin, let us dispose of a pervasive myth. There is a widely held view that as the first large group of Catholic immigrants to arrive in the United States, the Irish were marginalized and alienated by the discrimination they suffered at the hands of the working-class Yankee nativists with whom they competed in urban labour markets in New York, Boston, and other big cities; their rise to social acceptance, in consequence, was slowed, and their solidarity as an ethnic group was consolidated and reinforced by this historical experience.

The expression 'No Irish Need Apply' has passed into folklore as if anti-Irish prejudice were found everywhere the Irish went, and this aphorism is nowadays frequently repeated by ordinary Americans of Irish descent to encapsulate their understanding of the experience of nineteenth-century Irish immigrants in general.[4] Yet the experience of the Famine-era Irish Catholic immigrants in New York, Boston, and other big cities does not tell the whole story of the Irish in the United States, or even more than a small part of it. We know, for example, that of the 1.8

---

[4] The Bibliography at the end of this book gives a sampling of works which give varied interpretations of the social conditions which were met in American cities by Irish Catholic immigrants in the nineteenth century; in this literature, there are numerous variations on a theme that imputes Irish-American identity, ethnicity, or sense of community to a reaction to British oppression in Ireland, or to nativism in the United States, or both.

million immigrants who landed at the Port of New York during the Famine years, 848,000 were Irish (the rest were mainly German); but only 134,000 Irish-born people were resident in New York City when the census of 1850 was taken.[5]

This is a most remarkable fact. Even at the height of the Famine migration, 85 per cent of those arriving from Ireland used New York only as a stepping-stone. The statistics make it plain that eight or nine out of every ten Irish immigrants had no wish to remain in New York City if they had any prospects elsewhere. Those who had relatives to join, or the promise of a job, or who knew where to look for work—evidently the huge majority of those who arrived at the Port of New York—immediately headed west, scattering themselves across New York state and the rest of the country, and within a generation had merged into American society as their children married into families from other religious or ancestral backgrounds. Beyond the big cities, their numbers in most places would have been insufficient to form a pool of potential marriage partners and thus encourage cultural or even religious endogamy, and for the most part they created no lasting ethnic institutions based upon old-country ties and thus left few traces in the localities in which they initially settled. Yet it could be argued that these people, whose histories have scarcely begun to be written, were the real heroes and heroines of the Irish diaspora. They were enormously successful in integrating into American society; so successful that they almost immediately vanished into the social and economic landscape of a rapidly industrializing America.

To generalize from the experience of those 10 or 15 per cent who stayed behind in Boston, New York, or Philadelphia gives a heavily biased and quite certainly inaccurate view of the Irish in America. It is a view which enormously exaggerates the difficulties the Famine-era immigrants encountered, the prejudice and social marginalization they suffered, the importance of their religious piety, their sense of exile in a foreign land, the significance of their participation in labour unions and political parties, the extent of their support for Home Rule and Irish independence, the centrality of Irish ethnic associations, and the maintenance of distinctively Irish cultural forms. All of these things are, one suspects, processes and products of the specific economic and social situations in which a small minority of Irish immigrants found themselves in

---

[5] H. Diner, ' "The Most Irish City in the Union": The Era of the Great Migration, 1844–1877', in R. H. Bayor and T. J. Meagher (eds.), *The New York Irish* (Baltimore, 1996), 91.

the big cities. These situations could not have typified the experience of most Irish immigrants, the vast majority of whom were never—even for a single generation—part of the big-city, working-class ethnic enclaves that have provided the focus of much American historical scholarship and have informed the folklore of Irish America. A history of Irish America which seeks to represent the other 85 per cent will not be discovered in big cities, but in hundreds of smaller cities, towns, villages, and rural communities scattered across the United States. If the history of those who went west to find industrial employment, to set up in business, or to farm has not yet been written because these Irish men and women left so few traces in the documentary record, then we must look to other places which can give us clues to the way the Famine immigrants were received: places like Albany, where the new immigrants from Ireland probably never saw a sign saying 'No Irish Need Apply'.

Any discussion of the Irish in nineteenth-century America is fraught with difficulty for the social scientist, since so much folklore and deeply felt emotion pervades not only popular sentiment but also much scholarly writing on the Famine and its consequences. One single voice from the past has carried far more weight in American interpretations of the Great Famine than any other: the writings of John Mitchel (1815–75), a journalist, pamphleteer, demagogue, and radical Young Irelander. It is to Mitchel's mid-nineteenth century oratory and polemical tracts that we can trace the politicization of the Great Famine, and the emotive claim that the Great Famine was, if not deliberately planned and provoked by the English, then simply allowed to happen while the British government did nothing, a charge that was subsequently incorporated into nationalist rhetoric and eventually into twentieth-century Irish-American folklore. Echoes of Mitchel's claim that the English starved the Irish out of their homeland by malign intent or culpable inactivity can still be found in recent American historiography of the Irish in America. Yet, remarkably, such sentiments are largely if not entirely absent from most recent accounts of the Great Famine by Irish historians.

In Ireland, the struggle for independence and, with it, self-conscious attempts to create a national identity, coincided with the great outflowing of people from the 1820s to the 1920s. The nineteenth-century national project was, inevitably, intimately intertwined with interpretations of emigration, which was, and is, frequently portrayed as the culmination of seven centuries of British oppression. A reconstructive ideology looked back to the millennium, a mythical golden age before the English conquest of the twelfth century, when Irish native traditions are said not yet to have become polluted by the unwelcome importations of the English. The English were held to be the cause of Ireland's cultural decline. They are said to have ruthlessly imposed foreign notions of capitalism, class, and hierarchy, as well as their language and religion, destroying the harmonious wholeness of Irish culture and a well-adjusted pre-industrial economy, so causing the social and economic havoc which eventually led to starvation and mass exodus.

Nation-building inspired much passionate philosophizing and psychologizing about the putative mentality and character of the Irish, playing upon centuries-old political animosities. The cultural differences between the Irish and the other peoples of the British Isles were exaggerated in an effort to construct a distinctive national identity which distanced the Irish from their nearest neighbours, with whom, ironically, they shared much of their culture and many of their historical experiences. Catholicism—the religion of the people throughout the British Isles—was also suppressed in England, Wales, and Scotland. Because of its remoteness, Ireland escaped many of the earliest and worst excesses of the Reformers, who persecuted priests, burnt monasteries, and wantonly destroyed Catholic images the length and breadth of Britain. Anglicization also encroached upon the ancient Britannic languages of Cornwall, Wales, the Isle of Man, and Scotland; the Norse language of the Northern Isles, and the Norman French of Jersey and Guernsey. Enclosures of common land and clearances of the peasantry occurred throughout the British Isles as an inexorable tide of mercantilism, industrialization, and economic and social change advanced across western Europe, leaving no region completely unaffected. The transformation of the European agrarian system from a condition of patrimonialism to one that was fully monetized at the same historical moment that there was a dramatic growth in the rural population throughout Europe provoked crisis and mass emigration from many parts of the continent. Apart from the tragedy of the Famine, what happened to Ireland was in many ways unexceptional in this broader context. Yet these supranational processes are rarely given their full due in explanations of Irish emigration. Instead, attention is usually drawn to a purely parochial matter, the governance of Ireland, which perennially raises the same, unanswerable question: did the British interfere too much in the management of the Irish economy, or did they interfere too little?

The demonization of others as the enemy within or without in order to create and reinforce an ideology of 'us' and 'them' is a common way of fashioning group solidarity, seen in nationalist movements the world over, then as now. John Mitchel was remarkably successful in creating, in the image of the English, a folk devil which could be vilified and blamed for Ireland's plight. It could easily have been otherwise. In common with other Irish nationalists of his time, Mitchel refused to exploit religious sectarianism, another obvious source of folk devils, as a mobilizing principle of national identity (Mitchel was himself a Protestant, as were many other Irish nationalists at mid-century): had his own religion been different, Mitchel might have demonized Protestants rather than the English; had he done so, his ideas would now be forgotten. But by coincidence or design he chose the same folk demon that sustained the American national origin myth, and the same folk devil that personified the Know-Nothings who attempted in some American cities to prevent the Famine flood of poor, mostly Catholic Irish from taking the jobs of native-born Protestant Americans. In the poor American Irish of New York City, living in the slum tenements of Hell's Kitchen and doing dirty and menial jobs, Mitchel found an eager audience for his hate-filled harangues. His catalogue of putative English injustices against Ireland, combined with appeals to American republicanism, made for a heady brew of moral outrage, a struggle of epic proportions against an eternal, primordial enemy. It is of such stuff that enduring myths are made.

Among Irish-Americans, some of these myths have now become accepted as normative or prescriptive, defining certain characteristics of the Irish self which people believe one is supposed to have if one is to consider one's self to be correctly and self-consciously Irish. One such characteristic is the presumption that to be properly Irish entails hostility towards the English, and that this hostility is 'inherited' or 'in the blood'. In America, much more than in contemporary Ireland, most popular and some scholarly writers still appear content to demonize 'the English', and to assert that the Irish are naturally anglophobic, in doing so demonstrating an uncritical acceptance of grossly stereotypical psychologisms and 'racial' essentialisms of a sort that have been long since discredited in the social sciences. Indeed, a great deal of historical and sociological evidence has accumulated which suggests something quite different and immensely more subtle. From the late eighteenth century, English was the language of choice in Ireland among parents who were, understandably enough, more ambitious for the economic and social advancement of their children in the social order which then prevailed in Ireland than they were mindful of the cultural sensibilities of backward-looking poets and antiquarians who regretted the encroachment of industrial society, the passing of the old language, and the loss of cultural innocence.[6] Except for a brief period of seventy years (1850–1920) when England was overtaken by the United States, England was, and has since continued to be, the principal destination of Irish migrants seeking a better future, despite the exhortations of nation-builders that emigration to England was, and is, a cause of Ireland's economic stagnation and cultural decline. And, in Albany, Irish–English marriage was once one of the most prevalent varieties of mixed-ancestry marriage; such marriages were, and are, exceedingly common across the United States, just as they were, and are, in England itself.

What, then, is one to make of the disjunction between purported anglophobia and the empirical reality that the Irish, as individuals, chose to speak English, to live in England if they had to live abroad, and to marry the English in great numbers? Are these tens of millions of Irish men and women to be peremptorily dismissed as 'soupers',[7] dupes, traitors, or the pitiable victims of false consciousness? Clearly, there is a variety of possible explanations, but sooner or later the persuasiveness of any must be measured against a great deal of empirical evidence, drawn from a wide range of societies, that residential patterns, language choice, and intermarriage are normally the most reliable measures of cultural proximity, acculturation, and social assimilation. The views from within by the antiquarians and nation-builders cannot be simply ignored, for the legacy of these ideas, transformed into contemporary mythology and folklore, may have a significant effect upon the way people come to regard themselves; but neither can these views be taken at face value by social scientists, however attractive these emotive and sentimental conjectures about the distinctive qualities of the Irish mentality or character may be.

II

Despite the enduring, emotive image of impoverished Irish immigrants cast out from their beloved homeland, tearfully taking their leave of Mother Ireland at Cork or Sligo for a hellish voyage to New York, the general pattern of mid-nineteenth century emigration from Ireland was

---

[6] See O. MacDonagh, *States of Mind: A Study of Anglo-Irish Conflict 1780–1980* (London, 1983), ch. 7; K. P. Corrigan, ' "I gcuntas Dé múin Béarla do na leanbháin': eisimirce agus an Ghaeilge sa naoú aois déag" ', in P. O'Sullivan (ed.), *The Irish World Wide*, ii, *The Irish in the New Communities* (Leicester, 1992), 144, 149–53.

[7] 'Soupers' was a pejorative term applied to people who, it was claimed, had converted to Anglicanism merely to gain economic advantage from the British in colonial Ireland.

much less dramatic and far more complicated. For most of Ireland's poorest, who could afford only the cheapest tickets, their port of entry on the American continent was in Canada, at Halifax or Montréal. Since, at that time, there were no immigration controls at the border, the new arrivals from Ireland were free to enter the United States as they wished, or had the resources to do so. On the American side, no one recorded their names, or even so much as counted them. Large numbers of Famine refugees apparently gravitated southward from their ports of entry in Canada, looking for work in English-speaking towns and cities which were not hostile to Catholics. Albany was among the obvious places that people migrating to the south from Montréal might have stopped, at least temporarily, just as it was one of the first places on the route to the west that might have tempted the better-off Irish migrants who landed at New York or Boston. Of course, those immigrants whose fares were paid by relatives already living in the United States would also have landed at New York and Boston, proceeding directly to Albany or other places to join their relatives for at least as long as it took them to find their bearings and make their own way in the new country.

Mid-nineteenth century Irish immigrants were part of a process of staged (or 'step') migration. Often they came to North America only indirectly, and then moved on to the west from their places of initial arrival or settlement. Most people leaving Ireland went first to Glasgow or Liverpool, the ferry ports just across the Irish Sea. The Irish Sea crossing took less than a day and the fare for a deck passenger was only a shilling or two, sometimes only a few pence. Movement across the Irish Sea had been well established since the eighteenth century, even for Ireland's poorest people. Throughout the nineteenth century, there was a regular pattern of seasonal migrations of farm workers from parts of Ireland to Britain to pick apples and harvest field crops. In summer and autumn every year, the decks of the cross-channel packets were crowded with men, women, and children from all parts of Ireland, including the most remote counties of Kerry and Donegal, as people went east to seasonal jobs in England and Scotland, or returned homeward with the cash to pay their rents.[8] England was also familiar to the hundreds of thousands of young men from Ireland who had joined or had been impressed into military service. Irishmen volunteered for the Royal Navy and British Army regiments in the eighteenth and nineteenth centuries

---

[8]　T. Coleman, Passage to America: *A History of Emigrants from Great Britain and Ireland to America in the Mid-Nineteenth Century* (London, 1972).

and saw service in all parts of the Empire, including the American colonies before (and during) the War of Independence; as a route offering escape from impoverished circumstances, and adventure, it had its own attractions. A wide variety of other Irish people, from construction labourers to skilled workers to middle-class professionals, spent periods in Britain, which at that time had a much more highly developed economy than Ireland did. The ports of Glasgow, London, Cardiff, and Liverpool were thus familiar waypoints to Irish migrants, and it was from Liverpool, not Ireland, that most of the transatlantic ships carrying Irish immigrants departed.[9]

People in Ireland were aware that there were more jobs and opportunities in Scotland, England, and Wales than there were at home, and that wages were higher. Then, as now, there were no barriers to the free movement of labour within the British Isles, and Irish people were probably more footloose than is nowadays appreciated. Large numbers of Irish people of all social classes moved to Britain looking for a better life. They came as single people and as families and stayed for anything from a few weeks to several generations. The censuses of Scotland, England, and Wales, from 1841 onwards, enumerated Irish-born people in every part of Britain and in virtually every walk of life. Some married in Britain (not necessarily to other Irish people) and had children. Only later did they, or their children, decide to emigrate to the United States, Canada, Australia, or New Zealand once they had acquired the resources to do so, initially joining relatives who were already established overseas.[10]

These step-migrants were intermingled among a large outflowing of emigrants from the British Isles generally; they sailed on the same ships as people from Wales, England, and Scotland who wanted farms of their own, or better lives than Britain's crowded industrial cities could offer them; they shared the same kind of second-class, third-class, or steerage accommodation on board, ate the same food, and had much the same hopes and dreams. Our informants' genealogies suggest that there must have been many Irish-born immigrants with histories like this, economic migrants from rural backgrounds who had spent substantial periods in Britain before emigrating overseas; some had children born in Britain as well as Ireland; some had non-Irish spouses. We will never know how

---

[9] Sixty-seven per cent of those who signed affidavits in Albany giving notice of their intention to become US citizens between 1854 and 1856, and who had been born in Ireland, recorded their point of departure from the British Isles as Liverpool; less than 6 per cent departed from Cork, Sligo, or Galway.

[10] G. Davis, *The Irish in Britain, 1815–1914* (Dublin, 1991).

many there were, because their nativity as 'Irish-born', as given in censuses and other official documents after they had arrived in the United States, does not tell us whether or not they came directly to America; nor do the census takers' descriptions of them as wage labourers in New York City or Albany tell us whether they had hopes to set themselves up as, say, respectable independent farmers in Ohio or Oregon; nor about their eventual success, or lack of it, in realizing their dreams of having a place of their own.

Most Irish immigrants were English-speaking, or bilingual in English and Irish. The 1861 Census of Ireland recorded 98 per cent of the population of Ireland as English monoglots or as bilingual. While there are acknowledged problems with the census figures, there is ample evidence that, by mid-century, the monoglot Irish-speaking population was already mainly restricted to the older generations in the farthest reaches of the west and south.[11] More than 80 per cent of Albany's Famine refugees came from counties where English was said to be the majority language; of these, nearly 90 per cent came from counties where Irish was apparently spoken by less than 10 per cent of the population. This questions Kerby Miller's gloss that at least half the Famine emigrants to the United States were Irish-speakers;[12] Miller gives scant attention to the prevalence of bilingualism in pre-Famine Ireland. An unknown number of those he describes as Irish-speakers are likely to have been more-or-less proficient bilinguals. A recent, major collection, Ihde's *The Irish Language in the United States* (1994), sheds no further light on the problem: Irish immigrants are for the most part treated as speakers of either Irish or English; the significance of bilingualism for the rapid assimilation of Irish immigrants into American society receives no extended discussion. In Albany, a remembered family tradition of spoken Irish in ancestral generations is negligible.[13] That first-generation Irish immigrants were competent in English (whether or not it was their first language in Ireland) is also consistent with the observation that the Irish moved up the occupational, educational, and property-owning ladders in Albany much more rapidly than other European immigrants who came to the United States without a good command of English.

The mid-nineteenth-century immigrants who settled in Albany had

---

[11] See Corrigan, ' "I gcuntas Dé múin Béarla do na leanbháin" ', 144.

[12] K. Miller, *Emigrants and Exiles: Ireland and the Irish Exodus to North America* (New York, 1985), 297.

[13] R. D. Alba, *Ethnic Identity: The Transformation of White America* (New Haven, 1990), 94. See also this volume, Chapter 5.

been born in every county of Ireland. A sampling of the naturalization records for the peak post-Famine years of 1850 to 1860 gave the place of birth of the majority (62 per cent) of Irish immigrants as the midlands counties of Leinster, and the adjoining counties of Cavan, Leitrim, Monaghan, Roscommon, Tipperary, and Waterford—the most prosperous and most English-speaking parts of Ireland—and there were also substantial numbers from Limerick and Cork (17 per cent); in contrast, less than 5 per cent came from the poorest, westernmost counties of Kerry, Mayo, and Donegal. Many had probably come to Albany to join relatives who were already established there. The poorest immigrants— the true Famine refugees, many of whom had landed at Montréal— stopped in Albany because they were looking for work. Their immediate, overriding need was for some way to earn enough to keep themselves and their families for their first few seasons. They had heard that there was work for the Irish in Albany, or their arrival had been arranged by Bishop McCloskey's charities, or else the city was as far as they were able to reach before their small savings were exhausted or their strength failed them. Many were sickly on their arrival and could not immediately work. Even those who appeared healthy had been weakened by bouts of fever. They were not acclimatized to the bitterly cold winters and hot, steamy summers. Young men working at heavy labouring jobs in their first winter or summer risked death through overexertion in the extreme heat or cold of the unaccustomed climate. Summer was as great a danger as winter: the Albany *Argus* recorded numerous cases of death by heatstroke among Irish immigrant workmen in their twenties, presumably clad in the clothes in which they had arrived, thick woollens suitable for the mild, year-round Irish climate of 40 to 60 degrees Fahrenheit, but lethal in temperatures of 90.[14] Albany's almshouse and hospitals were filled with weak and sickly Irish immigrants. The spectre of the fevers the Famine refugees brought with them, as well as their desperate poverty, were a real worry to the townspeople of Albany.

Many unwary immigrants arrived in Albany only to be immediately fleeced of what little they had by Irish 'runners' who bullied and even beat them into parting with their money, promising to arrange jobs or accommodation, or selling them worthless tickets to the west, vanishing as soon as the money had changed hands. Albany's Irish poor at first lived in miserable tenements and shanties in the slums or in shacks on the city's

---

[14] W. A. Rowley, 'Albany: A Tale of Two Cities, 1820–1880', Ph.D. thesis (Harvard University, 1967), *passim*.

outskirts. The orphanages and prisons, as well as the almshouse and hospitals, were filled with Irish. There were begging in the streets, thievery, drunkenness, and fighting. Bishop McCloskey's charities were overstretched, mediating between the newcomers and the city authorities, finding lost sons and daughters for their parents in Ireland, distributing food, clothing, and fuel, and arranging for the arrival and settlement of still more newcomers. Yet even as they were beginning to establish themselves (within ten years, by 1855, more than half the Irish were in skilled jobs and 20 per cent owned property), exaggerated stories of the burdens they were said to impose on the city's charity still filled the newspapers and, for the first time, American nativism began to gain ground. The nativist or 'Know-Nothing' movement, a phenomenon seen in many other American cities, was a reaction against the floods of immigrants, especially the Irish, whose Catholicism and presumed loyalty to the Pope, a 'foreign power', made their loyalty to American ideals doubly suspect. The arrival of huge numbers of Famine immigrants had shaken the native-born working class. Yet, for the most part, the middle-class Anglo-Dutch entrepreneurs and politicians, who dominated the city's affairs, tried to ease the immigrants' arrival in the city, and to protect them from the grasping runners who beset them on the docks and at the railroad stations, and to shelter and feed them until they found their bearings.[15] Not even the nativists were willing to condone the maltreatment of the immigrants. The *Express*, the main nativist paper in Albany, said (if with a barb) in 1854: 'In almost every case, they are robbed, swindled, overcharged, cheated, deceived, forcibly detained, and even beaten with fists and clubs, *by their own countrymen.*'[16]

Yet the nativist reaction was not so strong as it was elsewhere. At the peak of their influence in the 1850s, the nativists were able to rally only 3,000 votes in Albany, far short of the majority needed to give control of the Common Council and to reverse the city's policies of encouraging and aiding continued Irish immigration. None of the prominent Anglo-Dutch leaders was inclined to give nativism any credence, not least because the Irish now formed a very large proportion of the electorate. Whether through generosity of spirit or an eye to practical advantage, the city's gentry and the ruling Democrats continued to press for the protection of the newcomers, setting up an Emigrants' Society to combat fraud. When the immigrants, swindled out of their money, wandered penniless

---

[15] W. A. Rowley, 'Albany: A Tale of Two Cities, 1820–1880', 312.
[16] Ibid.; my italics.

in the streets, the city put them up overnight and fed them at police stations or the almshouse. Many immigrants were given food and fuel relief for their first few months in Albany. The Common Council was not ungenerous, although they sought reimbursement for these expenditures from the state, and occasionally sent back groups of immigrants who were suspected of having been dumped on Albany's well-known charity by other cities.[17]

The Irish newcomers were a strain on the city's finances, and there were other things which increasingly tried the patience of the townspeople. Irish names predominated in the police reports, a fact seized upon by the *Express* and the nativist demagogues. Charges of vote rigging—that votes were bought for money and cast by 'unnaturalized foreigners' were repeated endlessly: this was probably true enough, for Irish ward bosses had been turning out the vote for the Democrats, by whatever means was effective, since the early 1840s. It was also said that the presence of so many Irish threatened the job security of native workers, thousands of whom, it was claimed, were being forced out of work by immigrants taking lower pay. The nativist outcry reached a pitch in the mid-1850s, but by then, ironically, the 'aliens'—the Irish and German immigrants— were no longer in a minority in the city, but constituted at least one-half of the population.[18] None the less, nativism continued to simmer in Albany politics for another twenty years.

The Fenian movement, and the development of labour movements of various shades of militancy, presented challenges to the conservative leadership of the Democrats in the 1860s and 1870s. The Irish Republican Brotherhood was first seen in the United States in 1857.[19] The society sought the independence of Ireland through armed force, and the Fenians' cause found some support in Albany. The true extent of genuine sympathy for the Fenians is difficult to gauge. While the leaders of the Catholic Church were actively involved in charitable works for Ireland, they opposed revolutionary republicanism. Bishop McCloskey described the Fenians' activities as 'mischief' that could only 'incite ... the anger and distrust of the American people against us'.[20] Nevertheless, Irish nationalism caught the public imagination, and a number of prominent members of the Irish bourgeoisie, especially those with political

[17] Ibid. 314.   [18] Ibid. 317.
[19] B. Greenberg, *Worker and Community: Response to Industrialization in a Nineteenth-Century American City, Albany, New York, 1850–1884* (Albany, NY, 1985), 136.
[20] Ibid. 137.

aspirations, lent highly visible support to the nationalist cause. Colonel
Terence Quinn, for instance, organized a mass rally in support of Irish
nationalism in 1870; it is perhaps not entirely coincidental that Quinn was
elected to Congress soon after this. William Cassidy, editor of the *Argus*,
which generally supported the conservative line of the Democratic Party
and was considered to be the voice of respectable Irish Catholic opinion,
moderated his initial opposition to the Fenian movement as it progressed,
eventually giving it lukewarm endorsement. Being seen to support Irish
nationalism was clearly expedient politics.[21] However, there was a big
difference between the popular enthusiasm for Irish independence, which
involved nothing more than crowd-pleasing rhetoric and waving the Irish
tricolour, and committed Fenianism. After six months of sponsored balls,
lectures, and rallies, from January to June 1866, in support of a planned
invasion of Canada to force Britain to free Ireland, events which thousands of people are said to have attended, less than 150 (0.5 per cent) of
Albany's 30,000 Irish actually turned up on the appointed day to march
on Canada. Nevertheless, Irish independence remained a popular, vote-
catching issue, and even the most patrician leaders of the Democratic
Party were forced to bend to popular sentiment by taking public notice of
specifically Irish issues and aspirations.

The party thus took on a more populist character, and was soon to
become increasingly opportunistic in its pursuit of Irish votes. By the
1870s, the chiefs of the police and fire departments, and many of the rank
and file policemen and firemen, were Irish.[22] By 1902, when the Albany
Police Service published a memoir listing the place of birth of each police
officer currently on the force, and the religion of all those above the grade
of sergeant, 3 of the 5 captains were second- or third-generation Irish, as
were 17 of the 21 detectives and sergeants. Sixty-four of the 141 ordinary
police officers, all men, were Irish, of whom 49 had been born in
Albany.[23] In 1910, 30 per cent of the teachers in Albany's schools were
second- or third-generation Irish women. The stereotype of the Irish
policeman and the Irish schoolmistress who owed his or her job to the
influence of the Democratic Party, probably not entirely divorced from
reality, persisted until the imposition of federal fair employment legislation in the 1960s. The party's patronage, bestowed upon individuals
through its control of municipal jobs, helped to ensure a certain level of
loyalty. Yet the party had no clear policies on labour matters, and seemed

---

[21] Greenberg, *Worker and Community*, 137.
[22] Rowley, 'Tale', 485.
[23] W. H. Paddock, *History of the Police Service of Albany* (Albany, NY, 1902), 75–137.

able adroitly to avoid class-based issues whenever they arose. The party remained a curious but durable coalition of the Anglo-Dutch gentry, bourgeois business interests, and immigrants. Democratic dominance was strengthened by Irish votes, and by their growing economic power.[24] By 1875, 32 per cent of the 5,968 Irish families in Albany owned property, usually their own homes, compared with 20 per cent in 1855. Yet the valuations show that more Irish families were moving into better housing in more respectable parts of town. Where, in 1855, the property owned might amount to a flimsy wooden house worth only a few hundred dollars, twenty years later some had bought substantial brick houses worth $5,000 to $20,000. Those at the top end of the social scale were living in the best areas, as neighbours of the Anglo-Dutch gentry. Their rising prosperity was founded upon substantial changes in occupational patterns: the number employed in skilled jobs and the professions, as a proportion of their numbers, had doubled in twenty years.[25] Irish names such as Keegan, Coyle, Brennan, Hogan, O'Connor, Reilly, and many others—the children of the Famine immigrants—were beginning to be seen in significant numbers in the class lists of the Albany Law School, the Albany Medical College, and the State Normal College.[26] A number of Irish lawyers had been admitted to the Bar, and some were rising to the Bench.

From 1869–70, the State Assembly included a number of elected Albany representatives with Irish names, such as Murphy, Lenahan, Ronan, O'Brien, Kelly, Curran, Delahanty, Murray, and Gorman. Michael Nolan, a successful Irish-born businessman and proprietor of the Beverwyck Brewing Company, was elected mayor in 1878 as the Democratic Party's official candidate. The preceding year, his business partner Terence Quinn had been elected Member of Congress. After serving three terms as mayor, Nolan was to follow Quinn to the House of Representatives in Washington. The elections of Nolan and Quinn brought nativism to an end in Albany, and further bound the loyalty of the Irish to the Democrats. The Irish could no longer be marginalized or treated as a minority, but had now asserted their power as the largest single voting bloc in Albany politics. No future major political candidate in Albany would succeed without carrying the Irish.

[24]   Rowley, 'Tale', 384, 386.
[25]   Ibid.
[26]   R. T. Beebe, *Albany Medical College and Albany Hospital: A History, 1839–1982* (Albany, NY, 1983), *passim*; A. J. Parker (ed.), *Landmarks of Albany County, New York* (Syracuse, NY, 1897), *passim*.

Albany's rate of growth began to slow after 1880, as the economy began to change. The railways took over from the canals and the centres of manufacturing moved further west. Albany's lumber industry waned as the great forests of Adirondack pine were exhausted. Lumbering became concentrated in upper Michigan and the Pacific north-west, and had largely disappeared as a major industry in Albany by the First World War. The Albany stockyards and meat-packing plants became redundant as Chicago took over most of the industry from the 1880s. Albany's iron foundries declined as the Bessemer process for making steel progressed, and as new specialized industries developed along the southern shores of the Great Lakes, nearer cheaper supplies of iron ore brought south from northern Minnesota by Great Lakes steamers. As the railway network expanded, Buffalo, Cleveland, Detroit, Chicago, and St Louis came to enjoy the locational advantages that Albany had possessed earlier in the century; these places soon became transportation centres and industrial cities in their own right. While in 1870 40 per cent of Albany's workforce had been employed in manufacturing, by 1900 only 26 per cent remained, a proportion that would continue to decline gradually over the next ninety years.

As the earlier Famine immigrants settled into Albany, they were frequently joined, over the next decade or two, by their brothers and sisters, parents, and cousins; in later generations by their grand-nieces and grand-nephews, second cousins, and more distant relatives. Somewhere between 30–50,000 post-Famine immigrants from Ireland arrived in Albany from the 1860s to the 1920s. Although, in Ireland, economic conditions had improved after the Famine, the country remained largely rural and unindustrialized. As time went on, the prospect of a better life elsewhere exerted a stronger pull and it took less and less to push an emigrant from Ireland. From 1855 to 1899, more than 2 million people left Ireland for the United States as economic migrants; more than 70 per cent of them after 1870, long past the time when any individual's immediate circumstances could have been directly affected by the Famine. The impact of their departure on the Irish economy was far-reaching. With fewer people to feed, and millions of overseas emigrants sending money to their relatives back home, the Irish economy began to strengthen. Emigrants' remittances were important, but did not wholly account for improving conditions: much more significant was the marked increase in wages after 1850, largely the result of continued emigration which prevented the accumulation of the excesses of surplus labour which had formerly driven wages down. Housing conditions and general standards of living improved, and there was a substantial increase in the consumption of luxury goods such as tea, sugar, and tobacco, indicating that incomes had risen well above subsistence levels even in the most marginal areas of the country.[27] Nevertheless, hopes of a better life than they could expect in Ireland meant that Britain, Canada, Australia, and the United States continued to exert a strong pull for the younger generations, and the attraction of emigration was a major factor in the rapid Anglicization of the remaining Irish-speaking areas in Connaught and Munster: monoglot parents, ambitious for their children, made sure they learned English, and demanded English-language schooling for their children.[28]

There was no contemporary consensus on the merits and demerits of [continued] emigration. 'We can understand', wrote a contributor to the London *Economist* in 1863, 'that the Irish poet whose fancy is stronger than his reason, should lament over shiploads of Celts leaving their native land'. The poets were plentiful. But economists such as Nassau Senior and Neilson Hancock, little concerned with poets or patriots or the old people left behind, argued that emigration from a low wage to a high wage area benefited those who left and those who stayed. '*Go bhfóire Dia ar na Sean daoine, ni fhanfaidh éinne len iad a chur ar an bhfuadar atá fen saol*' (God help the old folk, there will be nobody left to bury them, with all this restlessness), complained Muiris O Suilleabhain's father in *Fiche Blain ag Fas*. But economists have always been a rather unsentimental bunch, and the disagreement is in part one of sentiment. In retrospect, though, the emigration must be seen as inevitable, Famine or no Famine, a by-product of the Industrial Revolution and the breaking up of the 'antiquated system of society', rather than the result of a deliberate British policy of extermination. As Karl Marx put it in one of his contributions to the New York *Tribune*: 'Society is undergoing a silent revolution, which must be submitted to … [T]he classes and the races, too weak to master the new conditions of life, must give way'. The same was happening in rural areas throughout Europe, and nearer home in parts of Scotland and Wales, places removed from the raw material sources linked with modern industry. The availability of temperate zones for emigration made the adjustment of labour supply to demand much easier in the nineteenth century. Not without trauma, to be sure, but compare present-day labour surplus economies![29]

After the Famine had passed, immigration to Albany from Ireland resumed a pattern that had begun in the mid-1830s. In the twenty years

---

[27] C. Ó Gráda, 'Irish Emigration to the United States in the Nineteenth Century', in D. N. Doyle and O. D. Edwards (eds.), *America and Ireland: 1776–1976: The American Identity and the Irish Connection* (Westport, Conn., 1980), 101.

[28] Ibid.; see also Corrigan, ' "I gcuntas Dé múin Béarla do na leanbháin" ', 149–53.

[29] Ó Gráda, 'Irish Emigration to the United States', 102.

to 1875, there were another 9,000 arrivals, or an average of about 450 per year. The flow increased to 6–700 a year in the 1880s, which were years of economic depression in Ireland, and then gradually declined over the decades to less than 200 per year by the 1920s.

Post-Famine emigrant streams were dominated by single, young people, mainly the surplus sons and daughters of farmers and labourers. ... By contrast with emigration from other European societies, this was not a male-dominated exodus. In most years there was a rough equality of the sexes, though in the later nineteenth century women emigrants came to outnumber the men. This youthful and largely gender-neutral process, as well as the orderly and self-perpetuating nature of Irish emigration, suggest that, while the role of emigrant was filled by the *individual*, the traffic overseas was governed by group decisions originating with the *family* and its various kin extensions. ... [As] sons and daughters reached adulthood, they were shuttled along kinship networks from the Old to the New World. Emigrants' remittances flowed in the reverse direction.

There is no doubt that material well-being improved in post-Famine Ireland and that the country could have sustained a larger population. But this would have been at the cost of *per capita* living standards. The Irish were advantaged—self-indulgent notions of exile notwithstanding—by ready access to the two great labour markets of the industrialising world: North America and Britain. The prospect of employment abroad, and higher earning power, persuaded many people of the benefits of mobility. Those who remained were also convinced, as uneconomic household members departed and emigrants' remittances took their place. In this deliberate and orderly efflux, the encouraging hands of earlier emigrants, stretching metaphorically across the seas to Ireland, gave tangible evidence to the notion of pull factors.[30]

As the rate of new arrivals slowed, as earlier arrivals moved west, and as the newcomers' children—the second generation—were born in America, by 1900 only 19 per cent of Albany's population were first-generation immigrants. The effect of the influx of Famine refugees from Ireland at mid-century receded. As Albany's manufacturing industries declined, other places became more attractive to the new waves of immigrants from other parts of Europe, and population growth fell away dramatically. At the turn of the century, Albany had already taken on

---

[30] L. Kennedy and L. A. Clarkson, 'Birth, Death and Exile: Irish Population History 1700–1921', in B. J. Graham and L. J. Proudfoot (eds.), *An Historical Geography of Ireland* (London, 1993), 176–7. The advantages included, of course, the emigrants' proficiency in English as well as having relatives who could help them settle in and who reinforced this linguistic advantage by speaking English at home. Their possession of English as their natal language eliminated a major problem faced by immigrants from continental Europe: in general, only in the second generation did the children of these non-English-speaking immigrants attain a level of fluency which was equal to that of the first-generation Irish.

much of its present character: a city with a fairly static population, in which nearly 75 per cent of the workforce were already in service or professional occupations.[31] The children and grandchildren of the Famine immigrants and the canallers who still remained in Albany, by choice or circumstance resisting the tide of westward movement to the growing industrial and commercial cities of the Midwest and far west, had now moved into more skilled and specialized jobs. With each succeeding generation, there was a steady progression up the educational and occupational hierarchy. The daughters and granddaughters of domestic servants and seamstresses were secretaries, bookkeepers, nurses, and teachers. The sons and grandsons of unskilled labourers and factory workers became mechanics and machinists, railroad conductors and loco-motive engineers, building contractors, salesmen, business proprietors, accountants, and civil servants. There was no longer as much scope for new immigrants from southern and eastern Europe, lacking fluency in English and arriving at a time when unskilled work and manufacturing jobs were already in decline, to move as swiftly into the mainstream of Albany's economy as the first-generation Irish had done at mid-century.

The children and grandchildren of the Famine immigrants were well served by the parochial school system and the network of community institutions provided by the Catholic Church and the City of Albany. The second generation, those born between 1855 and 1884, were well equipped to make rapid progress up the social scale as they entered the labour market. By the 1890s, despite the continued immigration of considerable numbers of mostly unskilled young people from Ireland, the Albany Irish had begun to rival the old-stock English, Scots, and Welsh surname categories in employment patterns. While, in 1887, about two-thirds of those of British ancestry were in skilled or white-collar occupa-tions, only 40 per cent of the Irish held such jobs; but by the eve of the First World War in 1916–17, the Irish had caught up: two-thirds of the Irish were in skilled and white-collar jobs, the same proportion as those with British surnames. There was, at the same time, a dramatic decline in the number of Irish in unskilled labouring jobs, from 25 per cent in 1887 down to 6 per cent in 1916–17, and the combined figures for unskilled and semi-skilled employment were virtually the same for the Irish and British surnames, at about 30 per cent. A decade later, as the third gener-ation became established in the labour market, by 1928 those of Irish

[31] M. E. Conners, 'Their Own Kind: Family and Community Life in Albany, New York, 1850–1915', Ph.D. thesis (Harvard University, 1975).

surnames surpassed the British in higher-status jobs: fully 75 per cent were in skilled trades or in clerical, administrative, managerial, or professional occupations as against 70 per cent for those of British ancestry, and there were fewer people of Irish than British surnames in manual or semi-skilled jobs.[32] Especially notable is the success of women of Irish ancestry in entering skilled and white-collar occupations, including nursing, teaching, and secretarial work: in 1928, one-third of all those of Irish ancestry employed in such occupations were women, a significantly higher proportion than among those with British surnames.

As they moved up the occupational ladder, the second- and third-generation Irish also moved out of the older parts of the city down by the Hudson River. New housing was thrown up as fast as it could be built along the streetcar lines extending to the west: a mile from City Hall, two miles, and then three miles by the time of the First World War and the advent of the motor car. Modest three-bedroom houses with driveways and garages on quarter-acre plots filled in much of the remaining open space within the city limits, and soon spilled over into adjacent townships. As the streetcar and the automobile took the Irish further out, the church followed. New parishes were established and churches built. Additional church elementary schools were opened in the parishes of Blessed Sacrament (1916), St Vincent de Paul (1917), St Margaret Mary (1921), St James (1926), St Teresa (1927), and St Catherine (1954). In addition, churches and parish schools were provided for the Polish community (St Casimir's, 1903), the Italian community (St Anthony's, 1912), and the Lithuanian colony (St George's, 1917). Several new secondary schools were opened as the children and grandchildren of Catholic immigrants came of age and as Catholic families moved into new neighbourhoods. As well as Sacred Heart Convent and Christian Brothers' Academy, the new secondary schools included Notre Dame (later Holy Names), 1881; St Joseph's, 1889; Cathedral, 1890; St John's, 1895; Holy Cross, 1900; St Ann's, 1909; and the Vincentian Institute, 1921. The College of St Rose, a university-level institution for women, was opened in 1920; Siena College, for men, was established in 1937. In

---

[32]   This analysis is approximate, and is derived from the *Albany Directory*, sampled for the years 1830, 1842, 1854, 1871, 1887, 1902, 1917, and 1928. The Irish surnames counted were Kelly, Murphy, and Ryan; the British surnames counted were Jones and Johnson. There are greater problems with British-stock surnames than Irish: first, in finding suitable numbers of people bearing these names to make comparisons, and secondly, in their ancestral integrity, since many British surnames, including the two chosen, were taken by people of African origin, and additionally as an Americanization of Scandinavian names such as Jonsson and Johannsson.

1930, more than 22,500 children and young people were attending the 28 elementary, secondary, and college-level Catholic educational institutions in the City of Albany, eventually rising to a peak of nearly 30,000 at the height of the post-Second World War baby boom in 1955.[33]

By the 1930s, Albany's status as the state capital began to play an increasingly important part in the city's economy as its industrial base continued to crumble. That Albany had been state capital since 1797 had always had some effect: a greater than average number of lawyers, clerks, secretaries, and civil servants; more hotels and restaurants; and demand for good-quality housing and schools by state legislators and their families. Building work on the magnificent state capital building consumed thirty years, from 1867 to 1897, employing hundreds of tradesmen, including stonemasons and decorative artists especially recruited from Italy. Under Franklin Delano Roosevelt's governorship of the State of New York from 1928 to 1932, the business of government in Albany grew substantially. Roosevelt introduced measures to regulate public utilities more closely, created an agency to develop hydroelectric power from the St Lawrence River, modernized the state prison system, established old-age pensions, simplified the court system, and put in place extensive programmes for farm relief, reforestation, and land management. When the Depression began, Roosevelt established the first state system of unemployment benefit. With Roosevelt's election as president in 1932, the New Deal legislation of 1933–6 created dozens of new offices and agencies at state level to carry out federal mandates. Albany benefited doubly; not only did it have the seat of state government in the city, but many of the new federal agencies also opened their own offices in the principal state capitals. Hundreds, then thousands of additional state and federal office workers were employed. Municipal administration grew in step. Government and administration—federal, state, and municipal—became the leading employers in Albany. Those who had clerical skills or college degrees moved into secure, well-paid, white-collar jobs in large numbers at a time when the Great Depression was causing havoc elsewhere in the economy of the industrial north-east. This trend continued through the 1940s and 1950s. By 1960, 89 per cent of all jobs were in the tertiary sector; 18 per cent of all employees in Albany County and 20 per cent of all employees in the city of Albany—over 14,000 people—were government workers.

[33] Sister M. A. Leary, *The History of Catholic Education in the Diocese of Albany* (Washington, 1957), 326.

Employment in municipal, state, and federal administration entered into a period of renewed expansion in the 1960s. Under the governorship of Nelson Rockefeller, which occurred during the presidencies of John Kennedy and Lyndon Johnson, a great increase in the number of federal and state programmes coincided with worsening city-centre decay. Several neighbourhoods, run down but redolent with history, were swept away in urban renewal projects, including the old immigrant neighbourhood around the Erie Canal basin, where housing was demolished to make way for a shopping and commercial centre. In the South End, another old immigrant neighbourhood, hundreds of small row houses were replaced by high-rise apartment buildings that provided 2,300 units of public housing. Rockefeller's grandest project, however, was the Empire State Plaza: a huge, showplace complex of modern public buildings covering several acres in downtown Albany, adjoining the capital building. When it was completed, the Plaza incorporated many new civic amenities including a concert hall, museum, and library as well as legislative offices, a justice building, and six office buildings housing various state agencies, all built upon a huge platform of concrete with four stories of parking beneath. By 1980, the Plaza provided accommodation for no less than 11,000 of the 20,000 state workers in Albany.

Several immigrant neighbourhoods and landmarks were demolished to make way for the Plaza. The entire French Canadian neighbourhood was torn down, including the Church of the Assumption. Substantial parts of Little Italy and the Greek quarter vanished, and even Bishop McCloskey's chancery—the administrative headquarters of the Albany diocese—disappeared along with Cardinal McCloskey High School, which had amalgamated the secondary schools of St Ann's, St John's, St Joseph's, and the Cathedral and had been opened only a few years previously. The State Normal College, which by then had been renamed as the State College for Teachers, was transformed into the State University of New York at Albany. An extensive new campus was built on a greenfield site on the western edge of the city, adjacent to the State Office Building Campus, itself an extensive complex of buildings accommodating agencies such as the departments of transportation, taxation, and employment. Downtown urban renewal, which had eliminated hundreds of residential units, together with the relocation of many jobs to the city's western edge, created new housing pressures during the 1960s. The late 1950s and the 1960s also saw a substantial increase in the black population in most north-eastern cities, and Albany was no exception. Families displaced from the old European immigrant neighbourhoods by urban renewal and black immigration sought housing further to the west, driving up prices. In turn, those who sold their houses in the more westerly parts of Albany moved out of the city into new developments in the surrounding townships of Guilderland, Bethlehem, and Colonie.

As the ethnic composition of Albany's neighbourhoods changed, the Catholic parish schools gradually began to close. Declining recruitment into the teaching orders and the increasing necessity to hire lay teachers at salaries comparable to the public school system also created difficulties. Of the eighteen parochial elementary schools still operating in 1954–5, only six remained by 1993–4: Blessed Sacrament, Holy Cross, St Casimir's, St James's, St Catherine's, and St Teresa's. Four secondary schools merged to form Cardinal McCloskey High School in 1957, which in turn was replaced by Bishop Maginn High School. The Vincentian Institute was closed in 1977, and the Academy of the Sacred Heart, locally known as the Kenwood Academy, was merged with the Anglican girls' school, St Agnes. Holy Names and the Christian Brothers' Academy, alone of the nine Catholic secondary schools in the city in 1955, survived intact into the 1990s. The Irish, the Italians, the Catholic Germans, and the Poles dispersed as they moved out into the suburbs beyond the city limits, mixing indiscriminately with one another and the English, Scots, Jews, Dutch, and the Protestant Irish and Germans. No new ethnic neighbourhoods formed in the suburbs. Only in four places were there sufficient concentrations of interested Catholic parents to make the establishment or maintenance of parochial elementary schools worthwhile: Westmere, Delmar, Latham, and Loudonville. These schools catered for only a few hundred of the tens of thousands of elementary-school-aged children in the surrounding townships, at least half of whom were from Catholic families. The rest of these children attended the public schools, as did nearly all of those of high-school age.

Demographic change had reduced the Irish population of the city to 26 per cent by the 1980s. As well as the parochial schools, some of the parish churches were threatened with closure as their congregations continued to dwindle. While the Irish population of the city has declined, their numbers in the surrounding townships have grown. According to the 1990 Census, nearly 40 per cent of the residents of Albany County gave their ancestry as Irish. Despite demographic change, the Irish remain, as they have since 1855, the largest ancestral category in the Albany area (see Table 3.1).

By 1990, when these census figures on ancestry were collected, nearly 150 years had elapsed since the Famine immigrants came to Albany. The

TABLE 3.1. Ancestry totals, Albany County, US Census, 1990

Ancestry	Total	% of County
Irish	116,435	39.79
German	79,986	27.34
Italian	71,543	24.45
English	44,337	15.15
French	40,458	13.83
Polish	30,929	10.57
Black	24,702	8.44
Dutch	17,772	6.07
Russian	10,456	3.57
Scottish	7,662	2.62

canal diggers had arrived a generation earlier. At a conservative estimate, taking the length of a generation at an average of forty years and counting the original immigrants as the first generation, today's children of Irish ancestry are fifth-generation descendants of the Famine immigrants. A twenty-five year average reproductive interval gives seven generations. For the descendants, now children, of those Irish men and women who came at the time of the building of the Erie Canal in 1815, the corresponding figures are six to eight generations.

III

Those born in the 1940s are the fourth- and fifth-generation descendants of the young adults who came to America between 1847 and 1854. Since then, another full generation has passed, and the children of the 1940s are now moving into grandparenthood. How will their grandchildren, the sixth generation, remember Ireland and the experiences of their ancestors?

There is almost certainly no one left alive today who could have known a grandparent or a great-grandparent who would have been old enough to have remembered Ireland before coming to America between 1847 and 1854. It is still possible, but only just possible, that for a handful of people born before 1910, their early childhoods might have overlapped with a septugenarian great-grandparent born in Ireland before 1847. Most people, however, are no longer within living memory of the momentous events which brought the Famine immigrants to Albany, and have not been within living memory of these events for two generations or more. This break with the past, as the past could be remembered by those with first-hand experience of the calamities and conditions of the mid-nineteenth century which provoked millions of people to leave their native country, now makes the Irish an old-stock ancestral category who are no longer able to touch the past through living links.

This chapter, and the last, described something of Albany's history and how Irish immigrants came to play an important part in it. The circumstances which gave rise to Irish emigration to North America are well documented, and there have been a number of studies that describe the way that the first-generation Irish immigrants settled into their new lives in the larger cities of the United States.[34] Those who were born in Ireland brought with them world-views which were products of their personal histories in the old country. Though nearly all came to America voluntarily, and very few Irish emigrants ever returned to Ireland, themes of homesickness are said to have pervaded their letters to their relatives back home.[35] The homesick, Irish-born immigrants of whom Kerby Miller and other social historians have written were the great-grandparents or even great-great-great-grandparents of today's living generations.

To what extent is Ireland still remembered by the descendants of these nineteenth-century immigrants? The purpose of this question is to explore a critical dimension of ethnicity. Ethnic categorizations are usually the results of historical contingencies. Stories about what happened in the past are common features of groups with strongly marked senses of themselves as being distinct from other groups. A sense of 'us' as opposed to 'them' presupposes classificatory or categorical differentiae, some means of drawing contrasts, some notion of how and why 'we' are not the same as 'them'. In strong forms of ethnicity, the boundaries between groups are rigid, obvious, and clear-cut, marked by objective cultural features which might include physical appearance, endogamy, language, religion, eating habits, and residential segregation. Such groups may have a high degree of corporateness and organizational coherence, with closely knit institutions which coincide with the ethnic boundary. Economic and political competition between these groups may be intense, and an awareness of one's ethnic difference is a significant part of every encounter with a non-member of the group. In its weaker forms, the boundary may be much more subtle and fluid. The members of such

---

[34] See Bibliography.   [35] Miller, *Emigrants and Exiles.*

groups may lack any obvious physical markers or cultural differences which set them apart from the others with whom they interact. In most situations, ethnicity does not matter. The boundary may be unseen and without significance for much of the time and becomes relevant only upon occasion, in certain situations. Ethnicity in its weak form may have little content apart from individual self-ascription and a more-or-less standardized notion of the cultural distinctiveness of the group. It is up to the individual to decide upon the relevance and significance of this self-knowledge in any given social encounter.

Some cultural stuff, however minimal, is an operational essential of ethnicity. Without it, there can be no concept of ethnicity, for the idea must mean sharing *something* with somebody. This something may be an ideology of shared ancestry, some knowledge about putative primordial origins, an interpretation of history, or some other kind of intersubjective symbolic capital. Ideas about the past, and notions of shared origins, are usually crucial for ethnic identity, and interpretations of history are important to ideologies seeking to fashion, strengthen, and maintain ethnic identities.[36] To ask how, and to what extent, Ireland is still remembered by the present-day descendants of nineteenth-century immigrants is, thus, to measure a critical dimension of ethnicity. Yet the possible answers to this question depend upon what is meant by 'remembered' and 'descendants'. One could ask what people know in a general way about Ireland's past; why, in general terms, the Irish emigrated; and how, in general, the Irish found life in America. The answers will be largely unspecific and mostly in the nature of beliefs, legends, and myths, the stuff of folklore and what has recently been called 'social memory'. And, one could ask these questions only of people whose ancestry is known to be uncomplicated by the passage of too many generations; or by excessive social, economic, and geographical mobility; or by a great deal of interethnic and interreligious marriage. Further questions then arise about the representativeness of such carefully restricted samples, and whether what is said about them can be taken to apply to the tens of millions of other people of Irish ancestry in the United States whose descent is not so pure and who have not remained rooted in the same place for several generations.

Largely for these reasons, our data-gathering procedures sought to capture a broad sampling of people of Irish ancestry in Albany, which

---

[36] T. H. Erikson, *Ethnicity and Nationalism: Anthropological Perspectives* (London, 1993), 59.

included anyone (limited only by the numbers of people our methods and resources could cope with) who claimed that any part of their ancestry was Irish, predominantly or not, regardless of their religion, their length of residence in Albany, or their interest in their ancestry. Each of our 507 informants was invited to tell us about their ancestors and the specific circumstances of their ancestors' emigration. About one-third were able to give us a complete account of their grandparents, including their two grandmothers' maiden names, where their four grandparents were born, where they settled in the United States, and what their occupations, levels of education, religions, and natal languages were. A generation further back, our informants' knowledge about their eight great-grandparents declined markedly. Most had only sketchy knowledge, if any knowledge at all, of their eight great-grandparents or of the next ascending generation, their sixteen great-great-grandparents: when they did, it was usually the result of recent, deliberate genealogical enquiry; seldom was it family knowledge that had been handed down by the informant's parents or grandparents.

A number of people possessed documents about their ancestors. The most common was a genealogical chart prepared by a member of the family, giving names, but frequently omitting essential details such as dates of birth, marriage and death, and places of origin and residence. Other forms of documents were rare: some people said they had probably been thrown away when an elderly relative's house had been cleared, or that another relative had a box of old letters and photographs. The ramification of family trees over the last century and a half has meant that what few letters and other vital documents such as naturalization papers and birth and marriage certificates have survived from the earlier part of the century are widely dispersed among their descendants who themselves are now scattered all over the United States. Relatives more than two generations removed have frequently lost touch, and no longer have the means of finding out anything more about their common ancestor beyond, perhaps, just a name.

Where our informants knew about the circumstances of their ancestors' emigration, the normal reasons were that they were escaping the Famine, or that they hoped they could do better for themselves and their families in America. The latter was the same reason given by the descendants of German, English, Scottish, Polish, Italian, and Swedish immigrants, and it is the same reason that Irish emigrants give today. How the Famine came to happen, or how young Irish people came to feel that they could do better somewhere else may be a question that exercises historians and political economists, but ultimately cannot satisfactorily explain why some individuals left their native country and others did not. Perhaps because their ancestors' reasons for leaving were so obvious and commonplace at a time when millions of Europeans were emigrating for much the same reasons, their reasons were unremarkable and are no longer remembered by their descendants. By and large, our informants' recollections of their family histories do not extend back to Ireland, but begin only in America. In the small number of cases where a story about Ireland had been handed down, it was much more likely to concern some memorable personal attribute or achievement of the emigrant, or matters of marriage and inheritance, than broader matters of culture and history.

Our data show that there has been a great deal of mobility among our informants. This mobility has been occupational, social, and geographical. Seldom could our informants confidently trace their Irish ancestry back to the 1850s or before. Many of the original Famine immigrants who came to Albany seem to have moved out of the city, once they had established themselves and accumulated some savings. They pushed on further west, following the westward tide of the nation's industrialization; or, two or three generations later, their descendants moved to the scattered suburbs beyond the city limits. Most of the people of Irish ancestry captured by our sample had moved to Albany within the last generation or two, after having initially settled elsewhere in the industrial north-east, or had ancestors who were post-Famine arrivals.

The excerpts given in the next chapter are quoted from our tape-recorded interviews or from the essays our informants were invited to write, in the self-completion questionnaire, about the circumstances of their ancestors' emigration from Ireland and arrival in America. In most cases the passages are quoted virtually verbatim and at full length, although repetition and obvious digressions have been deleted. The colloquialisms and tangled syntax sometimes characteristic of speech have been edited slightly to make the passages more readable and to save embarrassment to our informants, most of whom were well-educated people who would not like to see their words and punctuation left completely unpolished. We have striven to give as representative a sampling as possible, balancing the shades of opinion, knowledge, and circumstance that were expressed to us. However, the accounts given below are not, in their relative numbers, representative of the full range of replies. Eighty per cent of our informants had no definite knowledge of the circumstances of their ancestors' emigration. It would be extremely tedious to the reader to give proportionate space to a large but empty category. Our attempt to give a representative sampling, then, is mostly limited to the 20 per cent who did possess some information about their ancestors who emigrated to America.

As these excerpts suggest, there was a considerable range of variation between our informants in the extent and depth of knowledge about their family history and the circumstances of their ancestors' emigration. There were cases in which virtually nothing was known of the grandparents, and those where an extensive knowledge of ancestry going back several generations could be quoted. The majority fell between these two extremes. During the interviews, a number of people consulted family records and keepsakes such as family bibles, letters, naturalization papers, birth certificates, newspaper obituaries, photographs, and family trees. In some cases, these documents were brought out especially for the interview and had not been examined in much detail before. A few people interrupted the interview to telephone a relative, often their mother or a sister, to ask about a grandfather's occupation or the like. The majority, however, did not produce any documents or make any telephone calls and replied to our questions unaided.

We asked our informants to start on their mother's side of the family and to work back as far as they could go, and to identify which ancestral generation had emigrated. An informant might know, for example, that her maternal grandfather's parents had both been born in Ireland, but know only that her grandmother was of Dutch and English origin and have no knowledge of the original emigrants on that side of the family, or when they came to the United States. Another might say that his maternal grandmother had been born in Germany, know the area of Germany where she had been born, when she came to America, why she came, who she came with; and that his grandfather was 'a third-generation Irish-American', his forbears having emigrated at about the time of the Famine. The number of permutations in our sample relating to the degree of knowledge, the national origin, the number of generations resident in the United States, and the subsequent history for each strand of ancestry was extensive. Some people had lost track after only one ascending generation (i.e. beyond their parents), while others could speak knowledgeably about their grandparents' grandparents (the fourth ascending generation). Much seemed serendipitous and dependent upon personal circumstance: whether, for whatever reason, informants had taken some interest in their background, or whether in youth and adulthood they had had much contact with grandparents and great-grandparents were the reasons most commonly given in explanation for the extent of knowledge about their ancestry.

As well as exploring our informants' knowledge of the particular circumstances of their ancestors' emigration from Ireland, we invited them to talk about their general understandings of the shape and substance of Irish history, as a way of gauging their knowledge of, and interest in, the broad context of their ancestors' emigration. Some had heard family stories passed down the generations. Only most exceptionally did these stories relate to the general circumstances of emigration and Ireland's past as described in the standard scholarly histories: the English conquest, the suppression of Catholicism, the plantation of the North, the Battle of the Boyne, landlordism and clearances of the peasantry, the Famine, the Land League, the Republican Brotherhood, the Easter Rising, the establishment of the Irish Free State, or more recent events. Indeed, only one-third of our informants of Irish ancestry felt confident in naming two major events in Irish history, and were able to do so more-or-less correctly; nearly half had no knowledge at all of any Irish historical event, including the Great Famine.

Our interviews testify to the frailty of 'social memory' of the Famine and other events in Ireland's past, which are commonly said to inform the ethnic identity of contemporary Irish-Americans. For the great majority of our informants, the links with the past had been broken, and no family traditions of Irish history or stories of the circumstances of their ancestors' emigration have been passed down to the present generations. Two-thirds had an incomplete knowledge of their grandparents' origins, occupations, or religions. Fewer still possessed details of their great-grandparentage. Eighty per cent did not have any definite information about the circumstances of their ancestors' emigration. Of those who were able to give a reason for their ancestors' emigration, the majority (nearly 60 per cent) cited economic conditions: lack of opportunity in Ireland, poverty, or the effects of the Famine. A few suggested, tantalizingly, that mixed marriages or the risk of a mixed marriage provoked emigration. A small but significant minority mentioned politics: that their ancestor had been involved in the Land League or the Republican Brotherhood, or had been forced to leave Ireland involuntarily because of his political beliefs or activities. If homesickness was characteristic of the first generation, as Kerby Miller has claimed, little of it has passed down the generations. What few mentions of exile can be seen in our informants' accounts of their ancestors are more than balanced by other views: that an escape from poverty was positively welcomed, that they did not look back, and that they had no desire to return to Ireland. None the less, Ireland still continues to exert a strong emotional attraction for their descendants, many of whom have 'gone over' to visit the country of their origins, or have read books about it. In the following chapter, our informants tell their own stories about the past.

4

The Past in the Present

I

Recollections of the Pre-famine Years

Q: Do you know any of the reasons why your great-grandmother or great-grandfather left Ireland?

A: I think it was the Famine, I guess, or they were really poverty-stricken over there, and a lot of people got out. It wasn't like they all came over in families, in fact my great-grandmother and great-grandfather came over without family and later their families met them. Her sisters and brothers would eventually have come over. Some stayed there in Ireland. That is really all I know about the legacy.

(Informant 565)

A: [It was] my mother's great-grandmother who came over from Ireland. I don't know the history. My grandmother's parents were from Ireland, so she always talked about them and where they came from and all that stuff. At that time we were too young and didn't care and thought she was [just] babbling.

(Informant 253)

Q: So your great-grandparents on both sides came over with their children, your grandparents?

A: They came over in the Potato Famine, you know, about 1840. Both sides, but they didn't know each other in Ireland. They met in Rochester. They came [through] New York. In the basement I have the trunk that would have been my great-grandmother's. She came on the White Star Line, and the trunk is marked. It is about this big, a little tin trunk, that [contained] all her possessions.[1]

(Informant 185)

All surnames, some distinctive given names, and a few other details mentioned in these accounts have been altered to preserve the anonymity of our informants. Place-names, however, remain as our informants gave them.

[1] The White Star Line's first passenger service to New York was made in 1871, with the maiden voyage of the new SS *Oceanic*. With its three sister ships, the *Oceanic* when new

My mother's mother was Hopkins and her father was Irish. I don't know what part of Ireland he was from. She married a fellow named Duffy. That's my grandfather. He had an interesting family story. My grandfather's father emigrated directly from Ireland; I believe it was from the southern part of Ireland. He was thirteen when he emigrated [and] had lost a number of his brothers and sisters to some type of disease. He got a job in the Brooklyn Navy Yard and I guess over time got interested in the law and eventually was able to pass the Bar exam and became a lawyer. He eventually became a judge on the New York State Supreme Court, which is an appointed position. He didn't marry for a long time and I guess he had a brother or a sister who also emigrated [and later] died. He took care of the kids and the story goes that he used to take them away every summer to a place in Monroe, New York, which is down in Orange County. I guess he got to about the age of 60 and still went to the farm, and the farmer had a daughter who was about 18. Well, he asked her to marry him and she accepts and they then have four kids of which my grandfather was the youngest. I think when my grandfather was born his father was almost 70 years old. My grandfather died five years ago and I think he was 70, so I'd say [his father] emigrated in the mid-1800s.

(Informant 544)

My mother is [a quarter] Irish. My grandfather's mother was all Irish. Her parents came over during the Potato Famine. Her father was from County Cork and her name was Gallagher. They may have married over here. They settled in [rural] Washington County. A lot of Irish who came over in the Potato Famine settled there. Most of my mother's family kept marrying into the Irish. My grandfather did not marry Irish but he was the exception. There is some English, some Scottish, some French Canadian in [my mother]. Great-great-grandfather married someone English whose family went way back to the 1620s. Then their son was the one who married my great-grandmother who was the Irish Catholic. And so my grandfather was half Irish and he married a woman who was Scottish and English. Some of my grandmother's family may have come out of [the north

was among the fastest and most luxurious ships in the transatlantic passenger trade. As the informant is probably not mistaken about the White Star label on the tin trunk, either it did not belong to her great-grandmother or her great-grandmother left Ireland at least twenty years after the Famine and, even in third or emigrant class, she would have travelled in relative comfort.

of] Ireland about the 1700s. [Her] name was McAllister which some say [is from the north of] Ireland.

My [paternal] grandfather came to this country [from Co. Londonderry] at the age of 21, by himself, because he was the youngest son and had no land to work, so he came to earn money to buy a farm here. He worked for many years as a hired farm worker [in Washington County] before he saved enough to buy a farm. He had two sisters here when he came. My grandmother came with her sister a few years later from County Tyrone; she was one of a family of twelve, and her father was a tenant farmer. My grandfather and grandmother had known each other in Ireland and that is what brought her here. She worked as a maid and a dressmaker before she and my grandfather married. She and her sister arrived here broke and sent word for my grandfather to meet them at the train station.

(Informant 180)

And so all I really know is that my grandmother's grandfather would probably have been born in the mid to early 1800s and I think he came over at 30 or something like that. Actually the only [reason] that I know he came from Ireland [was because] they used to imitate him talking with an Irish accent. See, the thing is that my father's side of the family is Catholic and my mom's side of the family was always Anglican and I remember them telling stories [about] how he would just go on and on about the bloody Papists and I used to think oh God, how embarrassing.

(Informant 538)

I know a little about my family. I have one family member who is trying to trace things back. As far as we know, both my mother's and father's parents were born in this country. We think that their parents four generations ago came from Ireland about the same time. [There is some association] with the Erie Canal. My father's family we think came through New York but we are not sure. I have no idea who they came to. I don't know which counties they came from. Both families settled in Troy and Watervliet. A lot of the canal people settled in the Watervliet–Cohoes area and then moved to Troy. We have been in Watervliet [four] generations now.

(Informant 462)

A: My mother's side is very easy. My mother came from Scotland in 1950. She came to Albany. She met my father during the war so I guess she [wanted] to see what America was like. She is still here. She is from the Edinburgh area. I guess [her family] came from Skye originally, but one of her cousins traced the family back to Fife in 1700.

Q: What about your father's side, then?

A: My father's mother was a Kelly. One of my uncles traced her side of the family back to New Orleans [but could not trace further back]. He could not figure out where to start looking over in Ireland. She was Hazel or Mary Kelly. She was born and baptized a Catholic but because her parents died she was taken in by an aunt or something. One of my father's aunts told my mother that they called her Mary but her real name was Hazel. They are a very strange family. One of the reasons I don't know much about them is because none of them talk to each other. My father was nine when she died. He was not of an age to ask [her] questions, and then his father died when he was about 22 [or] 23. The family fought over my grandfather's estate, so as a result we were cut off from the older brothers and sisters who might have been able to tell us things about my grandmother.

Q: What about your grandfather's side?

A: Grandfather Mahon was born in Albany as far as I know. His father lived in Albany and his [father's] father was born in the 1850s or something like that, [of] parents [who] came from Ireland during one of the famines. [Great-grandfather Mahon] had fifteen brothers and sisters and some of them were born in Ireland and some of them were born in America.

Q: Do you know which part of Ireland?

A: It depends on which day you're asking. My father apparently did have some interest in the family. He used to talk to his grandfather and used to ask him questions, and he began to notice a pattern. Depending on the day [he] asked [his] grandpa which part of Ireland [we] came from, you got a different answer.

(Informant 586)

Q: My mother came over from a town in Germany called Kassel, I guess somewhere around 1910. She was 3 years old when she came here. Moved into Queen's, New York, Ridgewood section, where she and her six siblings were raised. Her father preceded the family, came over here as a carpenter, worked, brought the rest of the family over.

Q: Your father's side, then?

A: I have to admit that I don't know as much about the history of my father's side because it goes back a little bit further. I don't know about the part of the history starting in Ireland. I believe it was my great-grandfather who came over to this country. I heard my grandfather talk about the Potato Famine in the 1800s that drove him over here. My grandfather was prone to a little bit of exaggeration, if I could be kind about it. He always said that his father was involved in this uprising or that uprising. It got grander and more exciting [the more he retold] it. As kids we loved it, we loved to hear the stories about it.

Q: Do you know what part of Ireland your great-grandfather came from?

A: No, but I'm sure my brother does. I think my grandfather's parents [settled] in New York City, but as a young boy he ran away and worked on the railroad, the [Union] Pacific Railroad across the country, which I understand [employed] a lot of Irish labour and it was kind of an adventurous thing. He was 16, and wound up in San Francisco [where] he met my grandmother, who was a recent immigrant from Australia—of Irish descent originally. [They] married, when my grandmother was 15 years old and he was 18. We never even found out about that until they died. They were there for the Great Earthquake and Fire, and then they moved back to New York and started a family. My grandmother's parents ... had a difference of opinion about this country and my great grandfather returned to Australia and left his wife and his daughter. [They] lived in [New York City] for a while and then moved up north to the Highland Falls area and lived on an apple farm. I don't think he was very successful. They moved back down to the city and he became a trolleycar operator. He later graduated to bus driver and supervisor.

(Informant 590)

Well, my father's people came here around 1840. They were from Newton Forbes in County Longford. My great-grandfather was a farrier on Lord Longford's estate. And somebody, I don't know the details, tipped him off that he was going to be deported to [Australia]. So he picked up his family and came to America, and landed in New York. But he felt the immigrants and the Irish were being exploited in New York. So whether he had relatives or friends in Albany, I don't know, but he came to Albany. He had a brother who was in Montréal. He walked from Albany to Montréal, and he found that his brother was a paymaster in the British Army. So he turned on his heel and walked back again. He would have nothing to do with him, naturally. So he arrived at a little town called St Johnsville, and they needed a blacksmith, so he got the job. Then he brought his family there and there was some kind of an epidemic, I had no idea what it was, but some of the children died. And a minister's wife came to them and said they would bury the children in their cemetery if they'd go to their church. So my grandfather packed the poor little children in a wagon and brought his family back to Albany and buried [them] in St Mary's cemetery. Then the railroad started up in Rensselaer and then when the [New York Central] shops opened up here in [West] Albany he moved back to Albany and bought a house on Washington Avenue. His sister lived next door to them. My sister and I are the last of that branch of the family in Albany. There are more in Ohio, but here we're the end.

(Informants 573 and 382)

Most of my family is Irish. My maiden name is Finnegan and I have traced my father's family back to Massachusetts in 1832. I have discharge papers for my great-great-grandfather from the Civil War. [Beyond that, we have] run into an absolute blank. Maybe he was not born in Lowell, but he was evidently born in America. Whether his parents were born in Ireland I do not know. I understand Finnegan is a Longford name. But on the other hand, when I went to a place outside Dublin there were a lot of Finnegans buried there. I understand that there are [also] a lot of Finnegans from Waterford, so I don't really know where [my great-great-grandfather's people] came from. My paternal grandmother's name is Daly. Her father, I believe, was born in Ireland, but [again] I do not know where. When I was growing up nobody talked much about it. I used to say to my father, 'Where did we come from in Ireland?' and he used to say, 'We do not talk much about it. We were run out for horse thieving', and I am beginning to think that it was no joke. The thing is that he did not know his own father very well. His father was in the Spanish-American War and got malaria and died at the age of 32. His father was supposedly one of fourteen children, according to the New York City census, but we only know of one sister. So whether they all died as children, we do not really know. I just know that his family was Irish.

(Informant 176)

I am not really sure if there is Irish on both sides of my family, but I know both my maternal and paternal sides of the family have been in America for, on my father's side I am at least the six or seventh generation American, and it is almost the same on my mother's side, maybe they came a little later. There is also some German in my mother's side. My mother's mother's name was Cunningham. I think it is [an] English [name]. My maternal grandmother was from the Albany area. [My father's] mother's maiden name was Kenny, my [paternal] grandfather's was O'Herlihy, so there was a lot more Irish on my father's side than my mother's side. I don't know why [my maternal grandfather] settled here.

(Informant 615)

My grandfather's grandfather came to the US in 1822. He was orphaned in Ireland and did not get along with his guardians, so he sailed to the US. My mother's father came to the US to avoid military service in Germany. Why the families settled in Albany I do not know. Having seen California and the Hawaiian Islands, I do not know why anyone would settle here, [but] of course these two places were almost unknown to the European emigrants.

(Informant 103)

My paternal great-grandparents came to the US during the Potato Famine. [Their] three sons all settled in different areas of the [country]. Most married non-Irish.

(Informant 82)

One of my great-great-grandfathers, Thomas McDowell, [was] born in Ballycastle, County Antrim, in 1805, but lost his wife Catherine in 1846. Somehow or other he came to Ticonderoga, New York, to prepare a new life for his children. The two oldest boys came with him in 1850. He had cousins or brothers already established in Ticonderoga (I am researching that now). Anyway, the remaining four children came over together, my great-grandmother, Mary Catherine, among them. Their father Thomas supposedly was on the docks to meet them. Stories of the boat trip came down through the years to me and I remember various tales of typhus, seasickness, etc., etc. [The] other three great-grandparents on my father's side also came from Ireland: County Cavan, County Fermanagh. And my great-grandfather John White who married Mary Catherine McDowell came from Ireland but I don't know where. He fought in the Civil War and was a Union prisoner at the renowned prison camp, Andersonville. All four great-grandparents on my mother's side came from England with one exception. She was born in Canada. The three came from Devonshire, England (2) and Cornwall, England (1).

(Informant 10)

Most of my mother's and father's families settled in the countryside near Monticello, New York: Hartwood, Glen Wild, Port Jervis, etc. There were tanneries in the area, and jobs were plentiful. Most of the men worked at tanning, lumbering, farming, and servicing the canals. Some were 'canallers' who lived on the canal boats with their wives and children. Children were tethered to the boats so they would not fall off. The owners of the tanneries also owned the 'company store' so nobody could really get ahead financially. My great-grandmother (Margaret Fitzpatrick Lynch—married to James J. Lynch—immigrant ancestors who came to the USA in 1853) was a 'mantle maker' or seamstress. She also drove the horse and wagon 25 miles to Port Jervis, bought groceries (wholesale?), and sold them from her home to make a few pennies. Most of the farming families who stayed in the area (the next generation) ran boarding houses, first for tuberculosis patients (the air was 'salubrious') and later for Jewish families who got out of the summer heat of New York City and came to Monticello for sunshine, fresh air, good food. They built large summer hotels and the name, Sullivan County, was jokingly called 'Solomon County'.

(Informant 99)

References in the family bible date back to the mid-1800s. Some relatives were born and died in Canada (Hamilton, Ontario), and others in Albany, NY. The Nolan name is prominent. All the writing is in a beautiful script, very easy to read. In the 1870s, there are a few references to Logan and Reilly, who married into the Joyce family. The bible belonged to John Joyce, Esq., Albany, NY, who was the father of Nellie Joyce, who married Francis Tracey [my paternal grandfather]. Those who left Ireland were glad to leave and never went back. They went to Guelph in Canada and thence to St Lawrence County in the Adirondacks and eventually to Albany. They were hard-working, prosperous individuals, who owned farms and paid taxes. They stressed education for both male and female [children]. They did not look back to where they came from but rather to where they were going.

(Informant 38)

Three of the children left the family farm at Blue Ball, King's County, in 1845 and settled in Albany. [One of them, John] was the first to build a house in what is now North Albany (Emmett Street). His brother, Joseph, was killed in a bar-room brawl in 1869 [and] his son Joseph jr., an infant at his father's death, died at age 29 of severe alcoholism. Bridget [the third sibling] married John Gray, and her grandson Patrick Gray was awarded a posthumous medal for heroism in World War One. A local landmark in Albany is named in his memory.

(Informant 331)

I have been successful in tracing some information on my great-grandfather and his wife. It is believed that James, then 18, and Winifred, then 22, left Liverpool on the *Ashburton* and arrived in New York on October 27, 1846. They were later joined by James's brother Thomas, his wife Anne from Limerick, and his mother and her sister, Brigid and Ann, from County Cavan. (Winifred was born in Roscommon). It would be a great pleasure to visit Ireland and attempt to trace the roots further.

(Informant 173)

I was always told that my Irish ancestors emigrated to the United States around the time of the Potato Famine. I do not know any further details as to dates or my ancestors' specific circumstances, unfortunately. I also do not know how or why they settled in Albany.

(Informant 161)

II

Recollections of the Later Nineteenth Century

Q: Can you tell me anything about your [mother's] ancestors, who they were, where they came from, and when they came to this country?

A: I lived with my grandmother in Brooklyn and she came to the United States in the blizzard of 1888. She was 13. Her father had insisted that she go to the United States. Her mother had not thought it a good plan. My grandmother, Elizabeth Sullivan, from County Meath, was the oldest of a number of children. I do not know how many. The plan to have Lizzie go to the United States divided the parents. The story is that there was a relative, not a very close relative, who had come here and who had made their way and had prospered and promised that if Lizzie came over she would get an education; they would send her to school. But when she got here they did not send her to school. She was put into domestic service for them and she lived in their attic and she took care of their children who were only a few years younger than she was. She read the dictionary and educated herself.

Q: Your father's side of the family, then?

A: My father's mother was a McMullan from Derry. She was the youngest child of a first marriage. Her mother died and her father remarried. The second wife did not welcome the daughters of the first marriage, [and so the] older sisters [emigrated] and brought her with them. I don't know that it was sad or anything.

(Informant 333)

A: I have some letters and that is as far back as I can go. They were sent to my great-grandmother from her mother who was still in Ireland [in 1874]. Another letter is from [my great-grandmother's] brother, several years later and is dated 1904, and sounds as if it [was sent from] Africa, Yanawanga or something,[2] and he talks about going for gold and a gold rush. [My great-grandmother's] name was Mary Corrigan. [She] married James Mulvaney, which is my maiden name. He was from Ireland. I have his citizenship papers. Several years ago, I tried to track down where he came from, but all [the documents] said was 'Ireland'. My father always said we were from Cork, but Mulvaney is not from Cork. If anything it is a Galway name, so I suspect they just left from Cork. Mary [Corrigan] was from Lisnaliggan, [a] little village which no longer exists in County Down.

Q: Where did your great-grandparents come to? Was it New York?

A: My great-grandparents came to New York. There was someone in Schenectady [whom] they knew. There was a reference to that in one of the letters and also my mother told me that at one time. My grandfather kept some old records in a box; [which are] the things that I have [now], the letters, the couple of pictures, naturalization papers, and cemetery records. My father located the box and gave it to me, because I have a greater sense of [heritage]. I treasure the letters. They are important to me. We were brought up with a sense that being Irish was important, but I think that it means more to me than to the rest of the family.

---

[2] The informant let us have a photocopy of the letter. It appears to have been sent from Yarrawonga, New South Wales, Australia. The place and date fit with gold prospecting in the eastern watershed of the Snowy Mountains. The writer says that he had 'taken up some land and was farming. When the last rush broke out I sold my land, went and like thousands more got broke. I suppose if I had married it might have been different but it is a lonely life on a farm in the bush and I was tired of it. Times have not been very good here these last few years. I often think it would have been better if I had went to America.'

Q: What about your mother's side of the family? What do you know
     about them?
A: My mother['s] mother was Irish and my grandmother's mother came
     here. A priest out in Binghamton did a family tree of my grand-
     mother's family. John O'Connor married Rose Murphy and that was
     [in Westmeath, Ireland] in 1855 and he died in 1866 leaving her with
     six children, one of [whom] was my great-grandmother.[3] My great-
     grandmother [Maggie Murphy] married Owen Cahill from
     Coxsackie. They had two children, John and Sarah, and Sarah was
     my grandmother. Sarah had one child, Janet, my mother.

                                                      (Informant 91)

My mother's mother, Catherine Fitzgerald Bryan, used to tell the
story to my mother when she was a little girl. She told of when she
was a little girl in Ballyhaunis, County Mayo, she and her mother,
Anna Fitzgerald, would meet with their cousins every year and walk
the seven miles to the Knock shrine pilgrimage. My father's sister,
aunt Charlotte Black Kramer, told me the story of her great-grandmother, Mary Ellen Kennedy, in County Kerry. The landlord's son
fell in love with Mary Ellen, as she was so beautiful and a young girl
of 18 years. When young Mary Ellen told her father of the boy's
intentions, the next day he went to the landlord, the boy's father—
they were Protestants—and struck [a] bargain with him. The next
week, Mary Ellen and the whole family had a passage to New York
City. My aunt said, 'Now wasn't that smart of your great-great-
grandfather to strike that bargain with the landlord?' I said, 'No,
wasn't it smart of young Mary Ellen to make the landlord's son fall
in love with her in the first place!'

                                                      (Informant 130)

The Irish [on] my father's side of the family left Ireland during the
Famine. Although Grandfather Delaney was born in Boston, Mass.,
the rest of his brothers and sisters were born in England, where his
parents met. Grandmother Delaney's family [also] emigrated from
Ireland to the US.

My mother's family came to the continent on the *Mayflower*.
Some followed on subsequent boats from England. My maternal

---

[3] The informant gave us a copy of the family history to which she refers. Rose
Murphy, the widow, had a half-brother, William, who had previously emigrated and settled
as a farmer in Coxsackie, New York, a few miles south of Albany. On learning of her
husband's death, William wrote to Rose offering to help her get started in America. William
met Rose and the children on the docks in New York.

grandparents were distant cousins. As Protestants, they opposed the marriage of my mother to my father, an Irish Catholic from the 'big city' of Boston. My parents eloped, were married in Albany, and settled in Vermont. Over the years, the families became more tolerant of the [difference in their] religious and ethnic [and] cultural backgrounds, but not entirely!

(Informant 33)

My maternal grandmother's grandparents were from [the north of] Ireland [and] were Protestant. My maternal grandfather's grandparents were from [the south of] Ireland and were Catholic. My grandparents grew up on adjoining estates in which both sets of their parents were servants. This was on Long Island, New York. It gave them both a lot of grief because of the difference in religions but their marriage survived. My mother and her sisters were raised Catholic [but] my grandmother worshipped at the Quaker meetinghouse because it was less stress than going to a Protestant church. My grandmother converted to Catholicism about eight years *after* my grandfather died, because she said that [only then] the decision was hers and not his family's!

(Informant 51)

My mother's grandfather Thomas Pierce was born in Dublin and came to America when he was 2 years old. It sticks in my mind that he might have been born in 1856, but I am not sure of the dates. His father was Patrick Pierce; his mother's name was Elizabeth Burke, we have that much. We know the [name of the ship] they came over on. My son is in the process of tracing this, but it is a long, arduous thing. My mother's mother's grandfather was James Douglas. He was born in Aberdeen, Scotland. His mother's name was Susannah McLean; she was the daughter of a Scotch Presbyterian minister. She married an Irishman named Francis Morrison, which is not a typical Irish name, so I wonder if he might have been Anglo-Irish, [but] he was a Catholic. When she married this Catholic, her father disowned her and told her she better get out of [the] country as quickly as she could. So they came and settled [near] Albany and they owned a stone quarry. And my great-grandfather and his brothers worked on the capital [building] here in Albany. He died in a smallpox epidemic that occurred when [the capital] was being built. My mother's family is kind of a hodgepodge but as far as I know my father's family is all Irish.

(Informant 176)

My mother's side was German. [On] my father's side, my grandmother's maiden name was Brown. Both of my grandparents were alive
on my dad's side when I was growing up, so I got to know them pretty
well. [Grandmother's] family emigrated from Glasgow, Scotland. They
came into the States through Hamilton, Ontario, and most of [her]
family still lives [there]. Interestingly, that is how my grandfather, who
came from Limerick, Ireland, came into the country as well; through
Canada. My grandmother was Protestant and my grandfather was
Catholic: that caused a certain amount of problems. [Grandmother]
ended up converting to Catholicism after she married my grandfather.
They moved [here] because they felt there was more economic opportunity here than existed in Ireland or in Scotland. My grandfather had
a variety of jobs [in Buffalo]: he worked for a while as an assistant in a
jewellery store; he had a job for a long time with the railroad; he worked
for a coal company; so he had a lot of different things that he worked
at, and actually they did [all right] during the Depression. I think my
grandmother took in some domestic work as well. [She] used to take in
boarders from [St Mary's] School for the Deaf. Taking it back a step
further, my grandmother's dad apparently was a nasty guy; he used to
beat his wife and beat the kids up and disappear for months on end. He
died a short time before I was born, but I don't think when he passed
away there was a tear shed in the family.

(Informant 583)

I don't know a lot about my mother's [side of the] family. Most of the
relatives were from Alsace-Lorraine [and from] Germany, and they
came in the 1840s. I know my great-grandmother could not read or
write but her husband was quite well educated. He was a surveyor
and cartographer. There was a large family up in [Lewis County], all
in farming, large farms. They still run some big farms today. [On]
my father's side, his grandmother and grandfather came from
County Cork. My grandfather and grandmother were born in this
country in the 1870s. My grandfather was a railroad man, fifty years
with the New York Central. He was also highly involved with politics. He was mayor and judge for many years in a little town in northern New York. They actually did quite well. My mother and [her
mother-in-law] didn't see eye-to-eye on a lot of stuff. My grandmother was quite upset because my mother married an Irishman
from the other side of the tracks. My mother's family were poor
farmers and the other side, my father's family, was more well off.

(Informant 531)

My father's parents came from Sligo; what town I don't know. They were married in Sligo. My grandmother's name was Mary Ryan. She was married to John Lavery. [He] came here first, I'd say about 1875. [Mary Ryan] was taken to the ship twice [but] the relatives and everybody made such a terrible fuss that she wouldn't come. My grandfather went to the parish priest, I suppose it was St Joseph's, and told him his problem. And [the priest] wrote and said your husband will die of loneliness. Anyway, she came. [On my mother's side,] my [maternal] grandfather had studied to be a priest in Ireland. He came from Claremorris in County Mayo. He got into a spot of trouble because I think he probably belonged to Sein Fein, I don't know. [He] wrote pamphlets in Gaelic [and] got in[to] trouble over it. When he came here to America he got a job from the priests, [teaching] in a small prep school called St Mary's down in Maryland. He [then] came to Albany and got a job on the old *Knickerbocker News*. He was a newspaperman the rest of his life.

(Informant 152)

A: My grandfather came from Ireland by way of England, and landed in Pennsylvania [in] 1898 [or] somewhere in there. He worked in the coalmines. His name was Thomas McCall. After he came up from Pennsylvania he married my grandmother who was born over here. She was Irish [and English]; [one of] her parents was from Cork and my grandfather was from Clare.

Q: Did your grandfather McCall talk much about Ireland?

A: Thomas tried very hard to assimilate, and because of his background and political affiliations in Ireland, Ireland was not spoken of. My grandfather came over for political reasons. He was forced out of Ireland for his political beliefs. I think that his heart was always in Ireland. There was that sadness he could never go back. And to be put out of a country that you feel very strongly about and never be able to return, I think that is very painful. The one thing he did do, he wrote a lot of poetry that was [never] published, but I have never come up with one piece of it.

(Informant 345)

Seven out of eight of my great-grandparents came from Ireland. The eighth was my father's grandfather on his mother's side who was mostly French-Canadian, but he claimed also to be part Irish, part English, and part Scotch, but he was mostly French-Canadian.

On my father's side of the family, my great-grandfather, William Laughlin, came from a village called Anglesborough, County Limerick, just outside of Mitchelstown, County Cork. He came [to America] in the late 1870s [or] early 1880s. He was the eldest child and as such was expected to go and pave the way for his siblings to follow. I know he left about the time of the first troubles, when the Land League was being formed, something like that. Mitchelstown was a hotbed of Land League activity. My uncle maintains that one of the reasons my great-grandfather left may have [been] something to do with the troubles because he was the oldest in the family, so rightfully the family farm would have been his. Apparently there were people from his home area over here. He came to New York and [then] to New Haven, Connecticut, where he worked as a stonemason and married Margaret Quinn, [whose family] was also from Anglesborough. I know very little about her. I don't know the circumstances of her emigration [or] where she was born. A couple of my grandfather's siblings were born [in New Haven]. Due to discrimination against the Irish and other Catholic immigrants in New Haven, he was unable to secure enough work to sustain his family. Around 1900 the family moved to Albany where my great-grandfather worked on the New York State capital building. The family were apparently too poor to keep [my grandfather], so he actually went to live in the parish rectory house with the priests that was up in St Patrick's church on Central Avenue. He lived there for a while, [but] apparently got into some sort of trouble. He got himself thrown out [of the Christian Brothers' Academy] at 15 and went to work for the railroads. He ended up starting his own business here in Albany which my father eventually took over.

(Informant 74)

My roots are Irish, French, and German. The Irish and German come in on my father's side and the French is on my mother's. We don't know too much about the Irish side. We assume that we are from the Galway area, probably because there are so many Sheas from that area. My father has visited there, as I have. My grandfather on my father's side would not speak of Ireland or what he knew of it. Whether this was because he knew nothing or he just wanted to forget because of hard times I do not know. My father would tell stories, but they would all be about his [own] childhood.

(Informant 404)

My grandfather came to this country [in 1885] at the age of 21 because he was the youngest son and had no land to work, so he came to work to earn money to buy a farm here. He worked for many years as a hired farm worker before he saved enough money to buy a farm. He had two sisters here when he came. My grandmother came with her sister a few years later because my grandfather was here. She worked as a maid and dressmaker to earn money before she and my grandfather married. She and her sister arrived here broke and sent word for my grandfather to meet them at the train station.

(Informant 180)

A: My people came over between 1880 and 1890.

Q: From where?

A: My mother came from County Mayo, my father came from Roscommon. I don't know [anything] about them except that they were all settled in the same vicinity in Troy. They met through relations, got married, and had seven children, two of [whom] died in infancy. They're all passed on. I'm the only survivor. I'm 87. All I have is a couple of nephews and a couple of nieces.

Q: When your family came over here—your mother and father—do you know what they worked at? Did they have relatives here to help them get started?

A: They had relatives here but they were all in the same boat. They were poor people. I don't know, you probably know about Mayo, the people are all kind of poor. My father worked as a labourer; dollar-fifty a day. That amounted to eight dollars and twenty-five cents a week because of a half a day on Saturday. With five children, it was pretty tough going.

(Informant 587)

Q: Were your father's parents born in America?

A: My grandfather and grandmother were both born in Boston. My grandmother Donnelly's parents were born in Ireland and moved from Ireland to England and lived in Kensington [London]. They were married [there]. All of their children [were born] in England except for my grandfather, [who] was born in Boston.

Q: Do you know anything about the reasons why your great-grandparents emigrated?

A: Well, of course they [had already] left Ireland for England. They left for economic reasons. I don't know what my great-grandfather did, [but he] came to this country to make a better living.

Q: Would you know the exact date?

A: I am sure I could find it. [Returns with papers.] This census was done in 1880 and that was when he was 38 years old. He was born in Ireland, so he had to come over some time before 1880.

Q: Where did you get this information?

A: This is from the census reports from the genealogical library in Salt Lake City, Utah. Actually, according to this, my great-grandmother was born in England. It was her parents who came from Ireland. I was not able to go back any further.

(Informant 33)

A: My father's mother's parents came from Tyrone. O'Connor [was] their name. My father's father's parents came from Galway. His wife's name was Lodge. So it was Michael O'Connor and Mary Lodge who came to the United States. They are [my paternal] great-grandparents. I think they married before leaving Ireland.

Q: Do you know why they left Ireland?

A: I never really heard why my great-grandparents left Ireland. Conditions might have been rough, and they would have come here in search of a better life or maybe just for survival. My great-grandfather must have come about 1870, I think. My grandfather O'Connor was born about ten years after that, in 1880 or so. They missed the Famine.

Q: Your mother's side, then?

A: My mother's side I don't know that much about because her parents died when she was young. She is from a mixed background. She has Irish ancestry as well as Scotch and German. I honestly don't know who in her family was of Irish descent and who is of German and Scottish. Her maiden name was Tierney; her mother's maiden name was Wagner. The Wagners were the German and the English, Tierney was the Irish and Scotch. I would really like to know more about that side my background, but she was an only child [and] I have nobody to ask. People have tried to find out more but [have] failed.

(Informant 521)

A: My father's mother is a Powers, and she was born in Leeds, England. I guess after the Potato Famine, her father and mother moved to England. Then the whole family came over [to America]. They went to [a place] near Attleboro [in Massachusetts].

Q: Did they have any relatives there already?

A: Of that I have no idea.

Q: Do you know what your great-grandfather's occupation was?

A: I don't know. My grandmother was probably [in her] early sixties when I was born, and they were in Massachusetts, so I didn't see a terrible lot of her. My grandfather died before I was born.

Q: What about your grandfather Regan?

A: His family was all from Ireland. Someone said that it was Tipperary, but we don't really have [anything definite].

(Informant 186)

I am third-generation Irish-American and three of my grandparents came from Ireland; from Cork and Kerry. They came over in the latter part of the last century, that is as close as I can come to. I never endeavoured to find out too much about them in Ireland because [my] relatives [over there] have a way of saying, 'Oh, we will do this tomorrow, and we will do that', so I never delved too deeply into it. [My grandfather's] whole family were pavers, they paved roads in Ireland and when they came over here they were fortunate enough to get the same work.

(Informant 223)

We were supposedly from Roscommon. It was my great-grandparents who came over with my grandfather who was born there but came over with them. Grandpa died real young, so I heard more from Grandma Mulcahy. She was Irish-German; her [maiden] name was Wieshofer. My great-grandparents came to Baltimore. [My grandfather] hadn't graduated from high school and was hanging around playing football, sandlot football. He was a pretty good athlete. He got lucky and a guy picks him up and puts him into prep school and into Villanova [University], where he played football for six years, and that is how he got his education. He became a civil engineer. [There were a lot of] other Mulcahys. He had a brother who was a dentist. We never kept up the connections after Grandma Mulcahy died.

(Informant 120)

A: My mother's side is mostly English and Dutch. On my father's side, his parents, my grandparents, came from Roscommon and Leitrim and they died when [my father] was about 14.

Q: Do you know when they came over, and did they come over separately or together?

A: I believe [they] came together. I could be wrong, but I don't know for sure. He didn't talk much about that, when they came here. [And] I don't know for sure which one came from where. I think my father was the eldest and he had a sister and a brother. There [were] the three of them. Other than that I can't tell you an awful lot about the heritage or the family tree.

(Informant 44)

A: My father was German. They lived down near Second Avenue. His parents were born in Albany. His grandfather [was] born somewhere in Bavaria in the 1820s. My mother's mother, her father [was] named Maguire. [He and his wife] were born in Ireland, as far as I know in a town called Listowel in County Kerry. They came here in the 1870s, somewhere in that era.

Q: Do you know why they left Ireland?

A: I don't know anything about that.

Q: Do you know who they came over with?

A: I don't know. I'm not even sure if they were married here or not. I know they came to Brooklyn for a short time and then came up to Albany. They lived on Sheridan Avenue.

Q: Do you know why they came to Albany?

A: I'm not really sure but it must have been because they had friends or possibly cousins in this area.

Q: What sort of neighbourhood was Sheridan Avenue?

A: Sheridan Avenue was a very working-class area. Poor people, I would say. My grandfather, what [little] I know about him because he died when I was 2 or 3 years old, was a grave-digger at one time, in St Agnes's Cemetery. I remember my mother telling me that she used to [take] his lunch up to him on the horse car. My grandmother had quite a few children. She might have had as many as eight or nine children. Only four of them survived.

(Informant 106)

A: My great-grandmother came from Waterford. She originally came over to be a maid on my great-great-grandfather's estate out here in Albany. My great-grandfather's family were big in the judicial system [and] very wealthy. My great-grandfather fell in love with her and they got married. My great-grandfather's family [was English] on his father's side; his mother's side of the family came from either Belfast or Cork—I am not sure. I have no idea why they came here [originally], but I know my mother would have all the answers.

Q: Have you asked her about all this?

A: My mother gets all caught up in her Irish ancestry. She is very strong about her family and her roots.

Q: About both the English and Irish parts?

A: She disowned the English part for whatever reason. If she is asked, nine times out of ten she will say she is Irish and neglect the English part. My grandfather was very proud of his Irish roots, as was my mother. How the English and Irish got together I will never know, to be quite honest. In my house, growing up, if you [wanted] to keep the peace you had to disown [your] English heritage. You had to be Irish.

(Informant 508)

When my grandmother Molly left Ireland as a young teenager, she swore never to return, as she said life was very poor and life wasn't very good. As many times as we asked her to come to Ireland for a visit [or a] vacation, she refused. [She] never went back and had no desire to do so.

(Informant 254)

III

Recollections of Twentieth-Century Migration

My grandfather Madden left Ireland as a young man (in his twenties) because of poverty [and because] his brother got the family farm in 1900, when he emigrated. He came with his uncle Joseph who was in his forties and single. He never spoke of 'home' or a desire to go back until later years [but] when it came time something happened and he never went. When I went to Ireland and met his nieces and nephews, one [of them] told me how [my grandfather] used to send money home, but he was bitter over 'having to leave'. My dad (his son) went back at the age of 72 on a tour but never had the opportunity to meet his cousins. I think grandpa's [refusal to speak of Ireland] greatly influenced my dad until he went back; [now] he hopes he'll live long enough to go back again, but I don't know if he will. My maternal grandmother [Mary Elizabeth Wiley] went back many times with her sister Bridget, who emigrated with her. Unfortunately we haven't connected with the Mooneys of County Mayo [my father's mother's family].

(Informant 16)

My grandmother and her sisters emigrated from Ireland around the turn of the century. Her oldest sister married and settled in East Greenbush [near Albany]. Her younger sister contracted consumption and returned to Ireland with my grandmother. The sister unfortunately infected several other family members. As a result, the sister, along with others, succumbed to the disease at an early age. My grandmother stayed on and married my grandfather, who was about thirteen years older. They had six children, including two sets of twins in eighteen months. My grandmother died at 47, having young children. My grandfather died four years later. All of the children emigrated to America in their teens and were cared for by relatives already living here.

(Informant 140)

[My father] came over to this country when he was 17. He had two brothers here. One was in Boston and the other was in Schenectady. And I think he came over with his father and mother and sister because there were four in the family. My grandfather was arrested when he was in England and he had a choice of going to jail or going into the army. So he went into the British Army. [He] served in India in the 1880s. His oldest son was 15 years older than the next one and that is how I know he was in India a long time. They came over here in 1910. I have no relatives left in Ireland that I know of.[4]

(Informant 568)

I think my father came in 1922. My father was Joseph Francis O'Rourke. When we were over in Ireland, my uncle had just died, and it said in the paper that my father fled to the United States so that he would not have to face the firing squad. I think [he] went to Canada and then came down here, but my father never really talked that much. He was a real IRA man of the old IRA and he had plenty of fights, and he would occasionally talk to people about the uprising and stuff, but generally he was not that talkative about Ireland. He only went back once, in 1952, [when] my grandfather died. My mother [Mary Bailey] came over in 1925. She had an aunt [in New York] who was supposed to put her up but didn't. There were other relatives up here [and] she settled down around St Ann's church. My

---

[4] Large numbers of Irishmen volunteered for service in British regiments in the eighteenth, nineteenth, and twentieth centuries. While impressment into the army or navy for a fixed period was sometimes given by magistrates as an alternative to a prison sentence, in this informant's account the grandfather is thought to have served for a lengthy period, which would appear to have required voluntary re-enlistments.

mother went back [to Ireland] in 1930 after she got her citizenship and I think she planned on staying there, [but] after [she had] lived in this country for a while it [was] too hard, [and] her family did not get along. Her own father died when she was six months old and her mother remarried and there [was] a brother and sister from that marriage. [My mother and father] met at the Hibernian Hall in 1940, at a dance. They were married in 1942.

(Informant 332)

There were four sisters over here [from County Kerry]. I guess [my mother] came over at the tail-end of World War One because she had to leave from Liverpool [and] the Germans were attacking [British ships]. She had three sisters already here. She came to Chicopee, Massachusetts, where there [were] quite a few Irish people, and I think it was an uncle of my father's who sponsored her. My mother [lived] with [a sister] for a while, and then [moved to] Holyoke. She worked in a mill and then as a maid. She met my father in Holyoke. My father was not born in Ireland, but his parents were. They got married in 1923. He died young, though, when I was 8. There was no Social Security then. She came to Albany to work as a chambermaid. [When she came to America, she] thought the streets were paved with gold. She thought [life] was going to be easier [than in Ireland]. [When she was a girl, back home] her father used to go and collect her [wages]. She never went back and we never understood it. She was afraid to fly and she would never take the boat again.

(Informant 368)

Both my parents came from Ireland in the 1920s, joining cousins in New York City. Their memories of Ireland were mixed—generally fond recollections of relatives and friends and harsh memories of rural poverty, growing up in large families and small farms. My father did not get along with his father, who treated him sternly and perhaps beat him. He was sent at a young age to live with a grandmother. In total, three of my mother's sisters came to New York. They were all close throughout their lives, and two remained in Ireland. In my father's family, one brother came to New York and two remained at home. My siblings and I maintain close relations with our first cousins in Ireland. Most of my Irish first cousins came to New York State for the wedding of my niece last September.

(Informant 86)

In March 1926, a letter came from America asking me to come out, that it would be nice for my aunt whose sister had just died. I thought, 'I'm free now. I'm off to America!' Fifteen years old and a half. I'll be my own boss now, nobody to bother me, nobody to tell me what to do or where to go, just freedom at last! My mother said yes [and] my father said yes. There were eleven children already in the family, [so] it seemed like a fairly good idea.

My grandmother once said, your mother will never be happy until the last one [of you children] is out of the house. [Q: Why was that?] Because it seems as though that was your heritage. You grew up and when you grew up you went to America. At that point in time it seemed to be the thing to do. Everybody seemed to go when they grew up. There was really nothing for them around there. The [oldest] usually got the farm and the rest went off. You were fortunate not [to be the daughter] they swopped; it was really kind of bad.[5]

My grandmother took me down to apply for my passport and I suppose an appointment with the American Consul in Dublin. It was on the thirteenth of May, 1926, etched in my memory. I sailed in July for America. I felt like I was really very important because I was going to America. Not all my friends were going, not at that age. [Q: How did you feel leaving everybody, your family and friends?] I wasn't a bit disturbed by that. There were two older girls with me and both their mothers were dead. So, I never even cried. I said I'll be back in a year [and] I'll be a big Yank with lots of money. I didn't really think there was too much to cry about. It was an adventure! We sailed on Sunday morning. And that wasn't an adventure. [I] was sick, sick, sick. I remember we were all on deck walking around and all of a sudden it seemed as if the whole thing was going around in a circle. All you could do was sit down before you fell down. I never went to dinner or anything I think till Thursday. [But then I felt better and] went out and danced—there was a beautiful ballroom. I had my

---

[5] The informant seems to be referring to an arranged, dowered marriage, a customary practice in rural Ireland by which brides brought property ('fortune') to the union, usually in the form of a dower field. Clearly it would be in her father's interest to avoid settling property on more than one daughter, or indeed any daughters at all, if this could be done without a loss of esteem among his peers. The son would also benefit by inheriting a larger farm than would otherwise have been the case. Exporting daughters to relatives abroad might have been one way to achieve the advantage of consolidating or expanding the family's landholding, but it had the unfortunate consequence of draining the pool of potential wives for the inheriting sons. This was one of the contributory reasons for the high incidence of male bachelorhood in rural Ireland.

hair cut in bangs. I did the whole bit. I started living big, the big life. My aunt met me in New York before I got off the ship. And I got 45 dollars a month [and] had to pay [my aunt] back 25 dollars a month [for the 300 dollars my passage had cost].

Do you want me to tell you what I did nights? I went to bed and cried. And I thought just as soon as I have paid my passage back, I'll be home. And of course next day I'd rip up [the letter I'd written] and put it in the waste basket. I would never [admit] that I was lonesome.

(Informant 567)

My father left County Mayo at 14 years of age and went to Liverpool to work. His sisters, Celia, Rose, and Nell worked as domestics for a family in Philadelphia. They brought my grandmother over for a visit. My father had [emigrated from Liverpool to Canada, and] ended up in Detroit. [He] decided to [go to see his mother and sisters]. From Detroit he took a taxicab to Philadelphia. My father never told me this story—my aunt Nell told me. According to her, 'He threw in his bags like he was [only] coming around the corner, and we each had to borrow three months' [wages] to pay for the taxi!'

(Informant 92)

I was born in Ireland. [In] 1957 my father and my mother and my brother and I flew from London to Albany. We had left Ireland, Tralee, County Kerry, in 1955 and spent two years in England. I was 6, going on 7. My mother had two brothers working in Albany, so while [my parents] were living away from home anyway they decided we may as well be in America seeking our fame and fortune. [We] got here before they had [anti-]discrimination laws on age and what have you. [My dad] was 36, [and] they would not hire him. He was too old for the telephone company here in America. That [had been] his job at home. So he had to go and seek employment somewhere else. Eventually, after one or two moves [he] ended up with a meat-packing firm here in Albany.

We came to my uncle Paddy, who had sent some money to help with the fare. My parents eventually paid [him] back. We stayed for six weeks with uncle Paddy and my aunt Mary, who had six children of their own, so that was a major inconvenience at the time. We eventually got a three-room apartment down on Lancaster Street, which at the time was going downhill. I don't know how long we were there [before someone] said, 'Mrs O'Grady, I don't know how to tell you this, but you know the ladies who live upstairs from you—well, they ain't no ladies'. When my father came home she told him, 'Here we are in this foreign land. Saints preserve us, we have to get out of this neighbourhood!'

So they moved to another apartment which was a little bit better. We spent a year or two there and eventually moved to Northern Boulevard which was a lovely apartment. In '62 they bought their own home on Pennsylvania Avenue, and then when I was 16 they bought a home out in Colonie, which they are still in.

(Informant 527)

It took a long time before I discovered what exactly my parents had accomplished by coming to this great country. Being first-generation, I always felt that I was different from other people who were born here. We did not realize as children how hard our parents had to work to get us to be responsible adults. I can't say we had an easy time growing up. There were times of great financial difficulty, but we were always loved and felt wanted. Both I and my sister share an immense feeling of pride having survived these times. I hope my sons some day will share these same feelings. If I have learned anything from my parents, it is that family comes first and everything [else] is second. The Irish in this country have made great progress in the last fifty years. And all can be traced to people like my parents who had the moral fibre and fortitude to teach their children the difference between right and wrong.

(Informant 178)

IV

Lost Links with Ireland

My father's side was Irish and and my mother's side was English and Dutch. I don't really know when anybody came over and I have no idea what part of Ireland my father's family came from. I have often wanted to try to find out what generation it was [which] came over and to do my family tree, but I have not had the chance to do it yet. Nobody in the family has ever done it either. My father and his father were both born in Albany. My father came from this neighbourhood, just a few blocks up. His mother was a Mulhern. She was born here but of Irish descent. His father was a Flaherty. He worked on the railroad like my mother's father, but [my mother's father] had a better job because they had a better house and seemed more well off. My father was not well educated. Nobody on either side of the family was. Just grade school and maybe some high school. [My father's father] was a carpenter. I think he could have gone to college if he had had the money and the encouragement, for he was an intelligent man. [My father] was an only child.

(Informant 17)

I don't know the answer to why [my] relatives left Ireland, and I wonder why they ended up in Albany and Ballston Spa. On Orange Street [in Albany, where I grew up], many of the names were names from Leitrim, but I don't know the connection, as no one ever told me.

(Informant 2)

I am half Irish, half German. My father's parents were both dead before he married, so I honestly do not know if they were born here or if they came over. [His father] was the only boy and none of his sisters had children, so there is nobody to communicate with. I have an idea they came over and I know that his name was Keenan and his mother's name was Hart. And it was either County Cork or County Clare; I am not sure which, although I found a lot of Keenans in another part of Ireland. We went over to Ireland a couple of years ago. Our children gave us the gift of a trip to Ireland for Christmas, and it was wonderful. We enjoyed it immensely. But I am afraid that is as much as I know.

(Informant 603)

I would say that I am 99 per cent Irish, but nobody seems to know when [my ancestors] came over. I know my grandfather was the oldest of twelve or thirteen kids. His parents were already over here, so it might have been in the mid-1800s when they came over. My grandfather was too young for World War One and too old for World War Two. So exactly when they came over I am not sure. My grandfather was an Albany cop and an Albany Democrat. He lived on Albion Avenue, just off Delaware Avenue, up in St James parish. And during the Depression, the Albany Democratic machine used to drop packages off on the back step, just to make sure there was enough food for the family.

(Informant 458)

Q: Did your great-grandfather come from Ireland?

A: Yes, he came from Cork, my father always said we are from Cork, although he was born here. My grandfather was an engineer in the Albany Fire Department.

Q: Do you have any idea why your great-grandfather chose Albany?

A: No, that I don't know. In those sort of days they came, a lot of the Irish, and then they started working their way west. Now why he ever stopped here I don't know. He may have gotten some work which kept him here instead of shipping out on the railroad.

Q: What about your grandmother Sheehan?

A: Her maiden name was Finn. I have no idea whether her relatives carried on or not, but she was Irish. She must have been born here. [My grandparents] lived in the South End, down one of the streets [near] St Ann's church. There was a little pocket of Irish down in the South End of Albany. My grandfather was born in 1883 down on Myrtle Avenue. I was also born in that house.

(Informant 591)

The circumstances of my ancestral emigration are sadly lost; even my great-grandparents were all born in Albany and likely their parents as well. I guess that I, as the eldest, am more 'American-Irish' than 'Irish-American'.

(Informant 230)

[With] the passing of the older generation, my parents, the Irish identity, particularly from my father's side, slowly fades away, leaving only half-remembered stories of family events and history. The absorption into the contemporary American culture is usually completed by the third generation, and only small vestiges, such as celebrating St Patrick's Day, listening to Irish music, or going to the Hibernian Hall, remain. If no living relatives maintain contact with the old country, interest and concern usually disappears.

(Informant 155)

V

Family Knowledge of Irish History

Q: Can you tell me about what you've been told about Ireland's past, or what you might have learned about it?

A: I like history, I'm a history buff, so I read all about it. And my mother, what little she knew, she told me. Mostly about her family. Of course, if you know history, you know the history of your kind. So her family [are] direct descendants of the O'Connor *dun*.[6] And that's how I knew about the family history and as far back as the history of Ireland goes. I go back to the Druids and the Normans and the Spaniards and the English and the way they treated [the Irish].

(Informant 382)

I am embarrassed by how little I know. My father used to tell us stuff about things, but I guess he held back a lot. I was 20 when he died. Had he lived, we would have discussed a lot more, because it is at that age that one becomes more political.

(Informant 187)

My father always blamed the English for the difficulties the Irish have among themselves. He always felt that if you looked back at England at that time when it all took place, they were conquering areas and islands, they were taking over areas in Africa and they were taking over Canada, Australia and they took over everything that they needed to benefit themselves, he always felt. Whatever they could get from a country they would take, and so he felt that they took what they could from Ireland. When it was depleted then they left it alone, but kept [their] stronghold in Northern Ireland because of the manufacturing [industries] that were there.

(Informant 44)

A: My uncle, who was an in-law, hated the British. But [he] was the only person that I ever heard who hated the British. We loved to hear him when he got really wound up about the British. His family in Connemara were driven [out], [he said]. I think that his family were starving and all that, so he had reason to hate them. But he really was funny because my husband was a real authority on English history and [his own] family. I have a book here about them, and they trace right back to near 800 in England. So it was really funny when my uncle Michael would come and visit with my husband. [I have read] *Trinity*,[7] but my husband was the one who was very interested in Irish history.

---

[6] O'Connor (or O'Conor) Don is a Roscommon landed family that claims descent from Rory O'Conor, the last High King of Ireland in the twelfth century; this informant thus seems to be claiming descent from the high kings of Ireland.

[7] A novel by Leon Uris, published in 1976.

Q: What general impression do you have of Ireland's past?

A: Well, I thought a lot of the things they did were extremely foolish. When we were in Ireland and we went to the Abbey Theatre, [we saw] a play about this man who was English and I believe he was in Parliament or something, and he really wanted to help the Irish, and of course I don't have to tell you that some fool shot him, and this is true, he thought he was doing a great thing for the Irish. And if only he had let the poor guy live he would have done much more for the Irish. And so it seemed to me that a lot of the things they did in history were stupid.

(Informant 185)

[My parents] talked about the Black and Tans and King George and Cromwell. My mother's brothers were in some of the activity [in the Civil War], I guess around 1921. My mother and father talked about different things. In fact they had some of their [old] schoolbooks and they used to look at [them], and we used to be impressed that they were so much more difficult than [American] textbooks. My mother had a geography and a literature book [which] I thought were [very] advanced for school ages.

(Informant 28)

My overall impression of Irish history is not unlike what my impression of Derry City was. It was sad. I think that Irish history has been very unfortunate. There has been a lot of needless bloodshed and destruction. I have the impression that the Irish, at least in some parts, were certainly very unsophisticated in a lot of ways, in their early history [especially]. I think the English just took advantage of that, and that is [what] in large part shaped the attitude [towards the English], at least as I perceive it from this country and reading about it. There was a period in Irish history when the Irish people were very, very poor and really did for the most part live very, very poorly. [They] were not educated and [were] really quite unsophisticated. Sometimes I am rather taken aback to be reminded that it was [not] all that many years ago, in terms of generations, when the Irish really were in large part peasants. I don't think it is true today, but I think it was like that. And I think they were mistreated by the English. I have always identified more with Ireland than I have with the English side of things.

(Informant 33)

Up until I did [our] genealogy and began to know about Ireland, we were too busy. I notice though in the [Hibernians']

Hall[8] when I went over to talk to a couple of women about what was in the paper, they said, oh it's just about Northern Ireland. And I said I was from the north of Ireland, and it is as if they kind of shun us. As far as I am concerned we are fighters, and I think [this] is [typically] Irish. My brothers were arguers. I was looking for a book and I was in the library doing research and they listed a book about the Famine, but that I do not want to read about.

(Informant 236)

I don't really know much about Ireland. When [my father] talked about Irish it was in the context of his father or grandfather doing eccentric things, associating those characteristics with being Irish. They don't really teach a lot about Ireland in school here.

(Informant 586)

The Irish books in this country could fill a thimble. I think I know more about the history of the Irish people in this country than the history of Ireland. I've read some novels and things, [such as] *Trinity* and *Thornbirds*. A lot of the history I know of Ireland is not too widely known, and that is what my grandfather told me about the Easter Uprising and the Potato Famine and what it was like living over there then. I think it's what he got from his grandfather. My grandfather kept in touch with people over in Ireland.

(Informant 590)

History was always a backdrop in our family. My grandfather named his dog Brian Boru, and there was always this sense of concepts and ideas [that] came at you from someplace. The nuns taught us no Irish history. I think my impression is that most Irish-Americans don't want to hear about the country. They are nostalgic but they don't really want to remember. I think most Americans have a view of Ireland with horses and carts and leprechauns.

(Informant 187)

VI

Other Sources of Knowledge about Irish History

Q: What impression does Ireland's past give you?

---

[8] The premises of the Albany Chapter of the Ancient Order of Hibernians, at the corner of Quail and Benson streets. The Hall is a social centre and the venue of lectures, musical events, etc. The chapter maintains a small library.

A: The antiquity of it, I mean, back to the bog. It fascinates me. I would probably be disappointed that it [has] changed so much. It is getting more and more modern all the time and too American. I like to hear about the old days, and [to] read about the old times. I can't bear reading about the Potato Famine and Cromwell and that kind of stuff. I have never been to a Hibernian Hall thing, though I have been to Irish lectures.[9]

Q: What kind of lectures?

A: About history or about Irish Catholic backgrounds or that sort of thing. Geographical. I love Irish maps and things like that.

(Informant 84)

Q: What are your impressions of Ireland's past?

A: I have watched programmes on it. I have read up on it and I would love to [go] there just to see what my father can't tell me. Maybe my father never asked any questions.

(Informant 375)

I took a course at the State University at Albany. I deliberately did it because I [wanted to] catch up. I have a general knowledge of Ireland's history. I do think that it is fascinating. It can be very emotional, however, because Ireland has had such a tragic history. I find myself thinking of the emigrants and of their strength in coming to this country and starting anew, and I ask myself if I could have done that.

(Informant 333)

My husband knew a lot about [Irish history] and he talked a lot about it. I can't say that I [know] a lot about it. My son, when he was at Harvard, took all the Irish courses available. So he knows quite a bit.

(Informant 176)

Q: This is not a test, but are there any major events in Irish history that spring to mind?

A: Gee, no. [Well], the Black and Tan wars, and that kind of thing.

Q: Do you [have] any general impression of Irish history?

A: Well, I get an impression that the people were mostly poor farming people and worked hard to eke out a living. That would be my impression.

(Informant 106)

---

[9]   As well as the lectures given from time to time in the Hibernians' Hall, public lectures on Irish themes organized by the Irish-American Cultural Institute, the State University, and other sponsors are occasionally given at other venues in Albany.

Q: Are there any major events in Irish history that spring to mind?
A: Probably not. No. I used to know [about] St Patrick chasing the snakes out of Ireland and all that, years ago as a little kid. I read *Trinity*.

(Informant 52)

I have read five or six books on the history of Ireland, all the way from Brian Boru to de Valera. I find that quite interesting, and the more I read the more I realize [what] I do not know. It's a very, very long history compared to ours.

(Informant 326)

We have several Irish books. The children always give them to us. If anything is in the paper, they will cut it out and send it to us.

(Informant 255)

Q: What impression does Ireland's past give you?
A: Are you trying to get me to give you an opinion on the Rebellion and war? I always just hate the way they're shooting each other. I don't know why they can't get along. I don't understand [the] Protestants [and] Catholics fighting. I guess that's British-oriented, is it? I remember as a little girl going to the movies and watching Clark Gable play Charles Parnell. I thought, Holy Moses, what are they doing all that for? But that was the beginning of the Irish uprising, wasn't it? Charles Parnell was a leader?

(Informant 10)

I can't really say that when we were growing up we covered [Irish history] in school. I think Ireland was [just] a paragraph in a book. Of course we [heard about] the Irish people emigrating to the United States because of the Potato Famine. They ran out of potatoes in Ireland and [they] all came over to America. That is about all we hear and that is all [we know].

(Informant 404)

I watch things on cable TV. I have read some books, but I would not say that I know that much about Ireland.

(Informant 90)

I just simply know that [the] first people that lived there were Celts. They were the original people. The priests were the Druids, and after a while I guess the Saxons invaded, and then the Angles [who] were Teutonic people, and they took over and subjugated the Irish. And then later the Vikings came in from the north, which is supposed to account for the bright red hair [of] some of the Irish people. And they mixed in. The Irish people are actually [a] very mixed race. Then the Reformation came in and the Irish Catholics turned Anglican, and they wanted the Irish land, and they persecuted the Catholics and sent a lot of them to the west of Ireland. They still speak Irish there in many places. And the best of the Irish land they took over, and they sent in their own people, the Scotch-Irish, [who] are largely in the north, which is one of the reasons why the north doesn't want to go back to the Free State because their loyalties are to England and a lot of them are Presbyterian people. They all look alike, but there's a vast difference mentally between them, and I don't think you will ever see them get together. But the south ... would be more or less where I belong, because my people lived in the south. They were Catholics, but if you were Catholic, for many, many years in Ireland—God help you. And then the Famine killed millions of them. It cut the population in half, and then the Irish turned on their own. The Anglo-Irish had corn and wheat, but they kept selling it out of the country and they did not release it to their own people. It was to their advantage, too, if they could get [rid] of some of the common Irish by hook or by crook. There was just too many of them around. A lot of them, of course, came out to this country, Australia and Canada. And then in 1916 there was the Rebellion. At least they were able to get the Free State. That's about as much as I know.

(Informant 95)

Q: Have you ever gone out of your way to learn about Irish history?
A: It grew on me. I think that I really got the impetus when I went over [to Ireland] in 1968, and I went to every county doing a graduate study, and I really became interested then. And I saw Vinegar Hill and these places that I had read about.

(Informant 223)

A: I have read *Trinity*, which helped give me some understanding about what goes on in Ireland. It is a real shame the way the Catholics and Protestants fight the way they do. It is difficult for us Americans to understand. That book helped to put the whole thing in a historical context and made me see how what happens now is a continuation of history.
Q: Could you identify any of the major events in Irish history?
A: I know about the Famine and the 1916 Revolution and things like that, but I am no expert.

(Informant 17)

Q: What impressions do you have about Ireland's past?
A: It was a struggle for the Free State to gain their independence in the twenties. And the waves of starvation they faced prior to that in the 1880s and 1890s. It's been a poor, long-suffering country.

(Informant 55)

Well, I usually try to watch programme[s] about Ireland on the television, depending on whether there is anything on, but there is so seldom anything on. And I very, very seldom go to movies now, but if an Irish movie came along, I always went.

(Informant 439)

Q: Have you ever read anything about Ireland's past?
A: We try to read as much of it as we can. We learn a lot by osmosis. We spend a great deal of time in Ireland, so I think we have an understanding of the country.
Q: What is your impression?
A: I would not want to have lived there over the last 300 years because of the way it has been treated by the whole of Europe. It was a very difficult place to live in.

(Informant 536)

I buy a lot of books, and on one of [my trips to Ireland] I went up to County Mayo. I sort of felt a magnetism there, since my grandparents [came from there]. You can't help but hate what the English did. When you learn that all that food [was] available, they were still exporting food during the Famine. And people were dying.

(Informant 157)

I don't know whether you have seen this in Ireland—what is the name of that wonderful TV show? 'The Irish R.M.'—I loved that, and I think it [was] based on quite a lot of facts. Years ago, I was visiting with these two women, and one was Boston Irish, and they were both former teachers at the State University and they [were] both of Irish extraction. I have a wonderful book called *The Great Hunger* about the Famine.[10] So I was mentioning about how sad it was that these Irish were so sick when they came here. These women were furious at me. They said you are misinformed, the Irish are very healthy people. Well sure I know they are healthy, but after living

---

[10] A non-fictional account of the Great Famine, by Cecil Woodham Smith, published in 1962.

[through] the Famine? I put in a good word for England, and I thought they were going to chop my head off.

(Informant 245)

My son, his name is Brendan, so I bought *The Brendan Voyage* for him to read. It is interesting. I think it was Conor MacNeasa who was a king around the time of Christ, and apparently the legend goes that the day Christ was crucified, in Ireland there was a great storm and MacNeasa had an intuitive vision of what was going on even though he could not possibly have known. And that legend has been passed down. Nineteen-sixteen of course everybody knows about. Nothing else comes to me readily.

(Informant 14)

I remember the Potato Famine, and the kinds of things that happened to people when they could not live off their land. Other than that. ...

(Informant 186)

There was a lot of prejudice in this country when they moved here after the Famine. 'No Irish Need Apply' was a famous saying.

(Informant 231)

I read a lot [about Ireland], but I take it as light reading. It does not stay in my head. It is like reading the history of Texas. It is nice, and interesting, but that is it.

(Informant 120)

I can't say I've done a lot of reading about Ireland. There's a book called *Tenant of Time*,[11] which is a study of Ireland which deals with the Irish Republican Army in the late nineteenth century, but I have not made an conscious effort. I guess I consider myself more American.

(Informant 544)

Q: What is your impression of Ireland's past?
A: My impression of Irish history is that for many, many years it [has been] a country which has been struggling with itself to be a country in its own right. That has to do with the English and not just the Northern Ireland portion, but the country's history as a whole is wrapped up in the effects of English domination. It has been struggling for other reasons as well. It had the Famine. But there are so many assets to the country. It has so much culture.

(Informant 521)

---

[11]   A novel about the land war, by the Irish-American author, Thomas Flanagan.

I won't say I [have] read tremendously, but I've got some background and I've tried to look into it a little bit, so I know about the Famine and some of the attempts at Irish nationalism. I think there was a lot of civilization in Ireland [before the English conquest]. The English involvement has stunted some of the potential for growth that existed in Ireland. I think that has had a great effect on people over there and how the people have evolved over time. It's almost like [Ireland is] waking out of a sleep. I know economically times are tough there, and I think a lot of that has to do with the fact that the country was stunted for a long time. It is exhausted, [with] all the struggles that it has gone through, [but] I don't think that is going to last. I think there is going to be another surge of Irish influence in the world.

(Informant 583)

Q: Have you ever gone out of your way to look into Ireland's past, or to find out why your ancestors came to America?
A: Not really, except what you would see on the television.
Q: Can you think of any major events in Irish history?
A: Well, I think a thing that bothered us was the [way] the English treated the Irish. Both times we were [over] there, [visiting Ireland], they never took us north. I think they were afraid. Somebody told me it is very beautiful up there.

(Informant 591)

A: Well I have books [on Ireland], but I am certainly not a student of [Ireland]. My brother gave me a whole set of Irish toasts and Irish sayings and things like that for my birthday. It is a four-volume set. I don't really know a lot. I just know there was a rebellion in 1922, or whatever. They seem to attach a great deal of significance to that. The main thing I think that my grandparents accepted was that Ireland was divided, that the northern part was Protestant and the southern part was Catholic.
Q: Did they ever talk about Irish politics, or Irish history?
A: No. American politics they talked, always. They had been over here so long.

(Informant 531)

Q: Did anything about Ireland's past come down through your family, or have you ever gone out of your way to learn anything about it?
A: No. The only thing I can say is that when I was pregnant with the children I did go and get an Irish name book and look for Irish

names, but a lot of them sounded so crazy to me that I didn't use any, you know I couldn't understand half of them. In high school we had to do a project to look into [our family backgrounds]. I did the Irish history and the family tree, and I [went to see] my grandmother and did a story on where she came from in Ireland, and where her mother came from.

Q: Are there any events in Irish history that spring to mind, that you could name?

A: No, I can't.

(Informant 253)

It saddens me that I know so little. My mother reads books on Ireland, but I don't think she is into the history that much. My sister has been to Ireland. There was a famine in Ireland at some stage, I do know that. It is agricultural and famous for its green fields.

(Informant 508)

All I [ever] knew about Ireland was that they were always arguing over it, whatever the north and south argue about. I guess it started out as a religious war, and then it got to be civil rights [or] whatever is going on. They're still arguing about that. People up [in] the north, and this is my personal opinion, the people up north who don't agree [with] what's going on, they should just vote with their feet and move out, stop arguing and stop fighting.

(Informant 417)

Q: Did anything about Ireland's past come down through your family, or have you ever gone out of your way to learn anything about it?

A: No. Only what we've heard.

(Informant 305)

Q: Did anything about Ireland's past come down through your family, or have you ever gone out of your way to learn anything about it?

A: No.

(Informant 340)

Q: Did anything about Ireland's past come down through your family, or have you ever gone out of your way to learn anything about it?

A: No, not really. Only what I learned when I was over in Ireland.

(Informant 603)

I am not much on history, but my husband is. I would follow the news from an American standpoint. My mother is a lot more interested, and my father was delighted and proud when I went to Ireland for the first time in 1977.

(Informant 91)

Q: Did anything about Ireland's past come down through your family, or have you ever gone out of your way to learn anything about it?

A: No. Just whatever I have heard, like the Famine.

(Informant 112)

Q: Did anything about Ireland's past come down through your family, or have you ever gone out of your way to learn anything about it?

A: I think growing up in this country you tend to become self-centred. Even [as] a history major in college, our world history course[s] skipped over much of Ireland itself.

(Informant 581)

Q: Did anything about Ireland's past come down through your family, or have you ever gone out of your way to learn anything about it?

A: Not too much. I really don't know that much.

(Informant 42)

I was just thinking today I heard something on television, some new president [of Ireland named] Robinson. That was the first I [had] heard of it. I didn't know that. I just happened to turn on a programme and she was on it. I had a friend [whose husband] was a dyed-in-the-wool Irishman. He loved all this Irish music and the Revolution or whatever it was. He seemed to know everything about the north against the south. To tell you the truth, I don't know who the good guys are and who the bad guys are. I have no idea. I know that somebody is fighting somebody else, [but] I am not quite sure what they are fighting about. They are killing each other and it has something to do with religion [and] it has something to do with the English.

(Informant 600)

5

Over the Generations

Of the 500 people whom we interviewed, only a handful, all in their sixties, seventies, and eighties had grandparents who had been born in Ireland before 1854. The rest of our informants were one, two, or three further generations removed from the Great Famine, the epochal event that brought many of their ancestors to Albany. After a century and a half, no one is any longer able to ask living relatives about their first impressions of America, or about their lives in the old country. Those who emigrated may have grown up in Ireland; a time and place they would never forget. Others might have been brought to America as infants or young children and have had no lasting memories of Ireland. The next generation knew only America from their own experience; but if they were curious, they might have known mid-nineteenth-century Ireland at second-hand, through their Irish-born parents. The third generation, born between 1885 and 1914, might have asked their Irish-born grandparents why they came to America and settled in places like Albany. The generation of the Great Famine has now been dead for a half-century or much longer. What legacy have they left to their descendants? How much of their Irishness has passed down to their grandchildren, great-grandchildren, great-great-grandchildren, and great-great-great-grandchildren of today? And, how can we measure this Irishness?

I

The degree of old-country language retention—or language loss—is one of the principal measures used by sociologists to evaluate the nature of ethnic social reproduction over the generations.[1] In Chapter 3, it was mentioned that the great majority of Albany's Famine-era immigrants were English-speakers who came chiefly from the better-off counties of

---

[1] See e.g. J. Fishman, V. Nahirny, J. Hoffman, and R. Hayden, *Language Loyalty in the United States* (The Hague, 1966).

the provinces of Leinster and Ulster. Most of those Irish immigrants who came from the poorer counties of Connaught and Munster, where Gaelic was most prevalent, arrived in the United States as economic migrants, well after the Famine. By then, English-medium National Schools had appeared in the furthest western and southern reaches of the country in response to parental demands that their children should be as well equipped to emigrate to Britain and America as those from Leinster and Ulster. By the end of the nineteenth century, immigrants from the west and south were almost universally bilingual: in Ireland, by 1891, there were only 38,121 monoglot Gaelic-speakers in a population of 4,704,750: a rate of less than 1 per cent. Those who came to America mainly as Gaelic-speakers, but bilingual, shifted to English quite rapidly, normally more-or-less immediately upon their arrival, and brought up their children as monoglot English-speakers.[2]

Of those of our informants who were born and raised in Albany, 96.6 per cent reported that there was no language other than English spoken in their households when they were growing up, nor in their grandparents' households. Only three of our informants had been exposed to any vernacular use of the Irish language; they remember parents or grandparents occasionally using Gaelic phrases and prayers. Significantly, in all three cases the parents or grandparents concerned were late nineteenth- or early twentieth-century immigrants from the west or south, and in none of these cases was the informant expected to understand or speak the Irish language beyond, perhaps, an isolated word. In most of our informants' families whose ancestry goes back to a point of arrival between 1847 and 1854, it would appear that Irish was seldom if ever used as an everyday language in the United States, even within the privacy of the home. The great majority of these emigrants were already monoglot English-speakers before they left Ireland, and the parts of Ireland from which most of them came had been thoroughly English-speaking for generations. None the less, some Anglicized words and expressions, or fragments of Anglo-Irish dialects (the 'brogue', of which there were— and are—a number of regional varieties) have survived to be passed down the generations in Albany families, and some stock words and phrases, many of them comical, have also passed into the common lexicon of Irish-American popular culture. Irish-language phrasebooks, and collections of Anglo-Irish stories, sayings, jokes, phrases, and words can be

---

[2] K. P. Corrigan, ' "I gcuntas Dé múin Béarla do na leanbháin': eisimirce agus an Ghaeilige sa naoú aois déag" ', in P. O'Sullivan (ed.), *The Irish World Wide*, ii, *The Irish in the New Communities* (Leicester, 1992), 149, 154.

bought in Albany's shops. For serious Hibernophiles, lessons in the Irish language are offered from time to time in Albany. The brogue, as it is now recognized and used, mainly in the 'sure and Begorrah' kind of Irish-American humour and storytelling, has now settled into a single, stylized music-hall idiom which anyone, of Irish ancestry or not, can immediately recognize as 'Irish'. In linguistic matters, things have gone full circle, as popular culture and efforts to relearn the lost language reinfuse Gaelic and Anglo-Irish words, expressions, and pronunciation into contemporary vernacular usage in ways that are now largely independent of family traditions.

Eating habits are another test of the strength of cultural loyalty; one has only to think of the kosher foods of Jews, and the Italians' elaborate and enduring cuisines. Richard Alba, in his capital region study, which was carried out in the Albany area, measured culinary preferences among people of different European backgrounds, and concluded that Irish food was one of the most limited in variety and regularity of consumption:

Irish food stands as an extreme case. Just a few foods, particularly corned beef and cabbage, are mentioned with any frequency. About 30 percent of the ancestry group consumes Irish dishes, but in many cases they do so only occasionally. Nearly half of those who eat Irish foods do so only a few times a year.[3]

Intriguing issues are raised by this finding. Just what is meant by, or perceived as, Irish food? Our informants of Irish ancestry gave us a wide variety of responses to our question, asked in a self-completion questionnaire, 'When you were growing up, were there any special ethnic food dishes eaten in your household that you associate with your parents' or grandparents' ancestral heritage?' Fifty-three per cent of our Albany-born informants answered by saying 'no'. The remainder listed the following foods that they associated with their Irish backgrounds:

ham
bacon
chicken
goose
roasts
blood sausage
lamb stew
beef stew

---

[3] R. D. Alba, *Ethnic Identity: The Transformation of White America* (New Haven, 1990), 87.

kidney stew
corned beef and cabbage
meat and potatoes
creamed cod
salmon
colcannon (cabbage and potatoes, boiled and mashed)
potatoes
potato cakes
carrots
turnips
onions
soda bread
brown bread
porter cake
biscuits
beer
tea

About three-quarters of our informants who mentioned any foods at all listed corned beef and cabbage, and about one-quarter mentioned soda bread. But in addition to these foods, widely regarded in the United States as typically Irish, a great variety of other foods had Irish associations for our informants, ranging from a grandmother's Christmas goose, remembered from a childhood fifty years earlier; to a monthly or weekly roast, stew, or meat-and-potatoes dish; to a daily afternoon tea break. One of our informants observed, wryly, 'I do not consider the food [we eat as] ethnic, [though] other people do'.

If we look beyond the statistical frequencies of certain foods, and accept as our definition of ethnic Irish food all those things which our informants say have Irish associations for them (even though these foods may be indistinguishable from those eaten by people who are not of Irish ancestry, and also those of Irish ancestry for whom these foods have no Irish associations), rather than restricting our definition to characteristically Irish-American foods like corned beef and cabbage and soda bread, then on this criterion a somewhat different picture emerges. Eighty per cent of those who ate dishes they regarded as Irish in their childhoods are still doing so later in life, or are cooking these dishes for their children. About 70 per cent ate these foods less often than once a week, but more often than just once or twice a year. In 85 per cent of cases, these dishes were prepared by the informant (if a woman) or her mother; or if a man, by his wife or mother. A third reported having these dishes on St Patrick's

Day, but most had them at other times of the year as well: for an occasional family Sunday dinner, on a birthday, at Easter, or Christmas. Overall, then, 43 per cent of our sample said that they ate, with some regularity, dishes that they had been taught to regard as Irish by their mothers and grandmothers, although only 14.6 per cent ate these dishes once a month or more frequently. Despite the paucity of dishes that could be regarded as distinctively Irish when compared with, say, Italian cuisine, the consumption of food that is considered to be Irish is not as negligible as might appear at first sight. Yet, compared with other ancestry-groups in the Albany area, such as the Italians, cuisine as a measure of the strength of Irishness does not score highly. More than 60 per cent of persons of Italian background ate Italian food at least once a week, according to Alba's study. At 14 or 15 per cent, the Irish score ranks low, within the range of those of Alba's respondents who said that their ancestral identity was unimportant to them.[4]

Of course, we also asked our informants about the importance of their ancestry, putting the question in a different way, in order to enquire about their degree of *interest* in their ancestral background, and following this up with two subsidiary lines of questioning, one exploring their interest in their ancestral country and the other their interest in the history of their family. The answers decisively demonstrate that the people of Irish background whom we interviewed had a strong interest in their origins, and that their ancestry was by no means unimportant to them. Of those who were born and brought up in Albany, 67.4 per cent said that they were 'very' interested in their backgrounds, and 32.5 per cent said that they had some interest. No one admitted having only a little, or no interest at all, in their ancestry. Since the responses to these questions could mean that our informants had nothing more than an awareness of their Irishness, and a passive interest in it (sufficient as this might be to their needs and wishes as individuals), we sought to gauge, by other means, the degree of our informants' active interest in their Irishness: in what they knew about the history of their own families (as contrasted with a general interest in Ireland), how they had learned about their family history, what things they had done over their lives which in some way demonstrated their attachment to their ancestry, and what things they possessed which served to remind them of past generations.

Chapter 3 has already mentioned some of our findings about our informants' knowledge of their ancestors, which they expressed in their own

---

[4] Alba, *Ethnic Identity*, 86–8.

words in Chapter 4. About two-thirds of our Albany-born sample (65.1 per cent) reported that they collected information about the ancestral generations in their family, or had gone out of their way to learn about them. A third said that they personally possessed no information of any kind, although another member of the family might do so, acting as a kind of family historian. For those two-thirds who had information about the past in their possession, about 80 per cent had photographs of their grandparents, great-grandparents, and other relatives. Just over 70 per cent had some papers or genealogical charts giving a few details of their family tree, mostly prepared by another member of the family (typically as a school project, in the wake of the 1980s television series, *Roots*); very few mentioned having themselves gone to public records offices or cemeteries to track down details of their ancestors. More than 40 per cent had old letters, and nearly 30 per cent had family bibles containing some genealogical information. A number of these people had information of several kinds about their ancestors. On the other hand, of the sample as a whole, only half had any photographs of their grandparents or the members of still-earlier generations; and fewer than half had any notes or papers giving the names or origins of their progenitors. What details they had were frequently fragmentary. For example, old photographs inherited from a parent or grandparent might not have been marked on the back with the subject's name, making these images unidentifiable a generation or two later; and *Roots*-type family trees drawn up by children usually lack maiden names or dates and places of birth and death, and only much later—perhaps after the death of a grandparent from whom the child had originally obtained oral information—does the rudimentary nature of these school projects, and their limited usefulness for further genealogical research, generally become apparent. Thus when we asked our informants for the names (and maiden names), countries of birth, occupations, and religions of their four grandparents, 37.6 per cent were able to supply all four of these details for each grandparent by referring to the information available to them, but 62.4 per cent were not.

This finding should not be interpreted as meaning that our informants' interest in the history of their families does not measure up to their wish to know about their ancestors, or that they responded to our question with misplaced zeal. Most of our informants were the fourth- and fifth-generation descendants of the emigrants of 1847 to 1854; a few were sixth-generation. When we asked them whether they were aware of any now-distant relatives living in Ireland, a very similar percentage—65.2 per cent—said that they were not, and moreover that they did not think that any of their relatives in America was aware of any relative now living in Ireland. For two-thirds of our informants, the genealogical links with the old country have been broken. For a not inconsiderable number of people, the branches of their families have been long enough in America—four to six generations—to have lost touch with one another, to say nothing of their distant relatives in Ireland. The sisters and brothers of one's four grandparents, and their spouses and children, and children's spouses and children are difficult enough for most people to keep track of; going back another generation doubles the number of potential relatives but halves their degree of relatedness; a further generation back doubles the number and halves their degree of relatedness yet again, but it is only at this point—five generations back—that the majority of our younger informants (those born between 1945 and 1974) had links with the Famine emigrants.

Tracing these links, or recovering them if essential details such as maiden names, and dates and places of birth and death have not been fully and accurately recorded in family documents or genealogical charts, can be tedious, time-consuming, frustrating, and expensive. Details for entire generations between the Great Famine and the present can be beyond recovery if such details were never written down and the knowledge of them was extinguished with the deaths of the people who knew them; or if family documents such as birth and marriage certificates, essential clues in the story, are dispersed among branches of the family who are no longer aware of one another's existence and do not have the means of discovering it.

Twenty-seven per cent of our informants had made visits to Ireland at least partly in the hope of re-establishing their genealogical connections in the old country, sometimes with some success if essential biographical details about their lineal ancestors were known, but if they lacked precise dates and places they had little real prospect of discovering anything further. Americans of Irish ancestry provide a steady clientele for genealogical bureaux in Ireland, more or less reputable, which nowadays supply the needs of increasing numbers of people who no longer have any other way to satisfy their curiosity about their origins; those bureaux which are reputable will tell clients who have no precise dates or places that there is nothing that they can do beyond pointing to a part of the country where the client's surname is especially common in the local telephone directories. Less scrupulous agencies will concoct entirely fictitious genealogies and heraldries, sometimes alleging the client's descent from the nobility of the pre-Conquest kingdoms of Ireland; fabrications related only to the client's ingenuousness and willingness to pay.

For the majority of our Albany-born informants (more than 60 per cent), a visit to Ireland had been part of their connection with the old country, a pilgrimage of communion with the past. Of these 60 per cent, about the same proportion had made the trip only once, and so, for them, seeing the land of their ancestors was a once-in-a-lifetime experience. Yet, about a quarter of the whole sample of Albany-born people of Irish descent had visited Ireland more than once. Ten per cent had been to Ireland twice; 7 per cent three times; 3 per cent four times; one person five times; one ten times, one more than fifteen times; and one had been to Ireland every summer since childhood. Compared with others in the capital region who trace their ancestries back to a European country, the proportion of our informants who had visited Ireland is extraordinarily high. Richard Alba found that, overall, only about 10 per cent of American-born descendants of European immigrants had made such visits.[5] Although Alba's statistics and ours may not be directly comparable, on the face of it our findings would appear to indicate that for most of those of our informants who expressed a strong interest in their ancestry, this interest had either been followed up with a visit to Ireland, or their visit to Ireland had provoked an interest in their ancestry.

None the less, there are complicating factors in comparisons with other European ancestries, which have mainly to do with generation and language. For other, non-English-speaking countries, as Alba points out, it tends to be members of the first or second generations who still speak the language and have active social relationships with reasonably close relatives who are the most likely to make visits—especially repeated visits—to the old country; among such people, roughly one in four in the capital region had visited their ancestral homeland. In the case of Ireland, however, language is not a limiting factor. Tourism, especially package tourism aimed towards Americans, is a major industry in Ireland, heavily promoted in the United States and Canada. A number of variations on the romantic 'Emerald Isle', 'Georgian Dublin', 'Land of Erin', or 'Celtic Ireland' themes can be bought from virtually any travel agency in the capital region, and probably from almost any travel agent in North America. Do-it-yourself bed-and-breakfast and self-drive holidays are also very popular, since for Americans in Ireland linguistic problems are very minor, and probably insignificant compared with getting accustomed

---

[5] Alba, *Ethnic Identity*, 157–8. Alba notes that although his respondents were asked whether they had made such a visit *in the previous five years*, some claimed this experience based on visits occurring more than five years previously. We asked our informants: 'Have you ever visited a country associated with your ancestry?'

to driving a car on the left-hand side of the road. Speaking the language is enormously important for a visitor's ability to appreciate more than just the look of a country's landscape and architecture or absorb more than interpreted-for-one, unconnected fragments of history, culture, and local customs. To be able to communicate freely with its people, and to feel at home even though one may no longer be aware of any living relatives there or even know what part of the country one's ancestors came from, makes a big difference to the way people perceive the relationship, in social distance and historical time, between themselves and the land of their ancestry. The common language is undoubtedly a major factor contributing to our informants' interest in their ancestry: it keeps open the possibility of going back to Ireland and finding out more about the past in ways that are denied to people who no longer speak the language of their ancestors' homeland.

A visit to Ireland, as a once-in-a-lifetime experience, is something to be remembered, making the ancestral connection with Ireland concrete, manifesting in personal experience something previously abstract and historically distant. For some, a trip to the old country is a way of satisfying their curiosity about where their ancestors came from. For others, who as children or young people may have had no special sense of any association with their Irish heritage, or with the past in general, a family vacation in Ireland might spark a life-long interest in their ancestral origins, or in Irish music or politics. For still others, a visit to Ireland is merely a more-or-less pleasant or diverting holiday without much immediate personal significance. But however important, or not, to the individual, a visit to Ireland is something to talk about, a part of one's biographical experience that one can share with others as the occasions arise; a source of conversation and anecdote, perhaps, with family, friends, and acquaintances.

Nearly all of our informants who had been to Ireland brought back souvenirs, objects with specific associations with Ireland which they frequently displayed in their homes, sometimes giving these objects pride of place in their living-rooms. More than just trinkets casually acquired on a vacation, these objects were often regarded as special treasures, symbolizing their connection with the land of their ancestors. These objects, seen and handled, are the material mnemonics of past generations, though they might not be more than a few years old and might have been bought in a Dublin department store, the duty-free shop at Shannon Airport, or even in an Irish curio shop in Albany. These objects include paintings and watercolours; sculptures in silver, bronze, and porcelain;

rosaries, crucifixes, and statues of the Virgin; crystal, china, and pottery; jewellery; linen tablecloths, runners, napkins, mats, doilies, antimacassars, and handkerchiefs; woollen blankets, hats, sweaters, coats, suits, skirts, sweaters, socks, scarves, ties, and tartans; blessings to hang on the wall, door knockers, shillelaghs, coats of arms, crests, banners, and flags; framed maps, coffee-table books of photographs, volumes of history and poetry; musical instruments, dancing costumes and shoes, CDs, records, and tapes of Irish music. While a small minority possessed veritable troves of such things, most had only a few.

Much more rarely did our informants possess any objects handed down over the generations since the Famine migration of 1847 to 1854. The reasons for this are not difficult to appreciate. Most of the Famine-era immigrants did not bring much with them beyond what could be packed in a single trunk, although one of our informants said that her great-grandmother had brought her iron cooking-stove from Ireland— ironically, as it turned out, because Albany was then one of the main centres of iron stove manufacturing in America.

To illustrate the principle of devolution down the generations, let us imagine that a woman who emigrated in 1850 had packed in her trunk a four-piece silver table service for eight people, and on her death left a will expressing the wish that her descendants should divide the thirty-two-piece set equally among them. If we assume that she had four children, each of whom again had four children, the resulting sixteen grandchildren would have two pieces each. If each grandchild again had four children, there would be enough pieces of the set for only half of the sixty-four great-grandchildren to have one piece each. Another generation further on, assuming again that each descendant had four children, her 256 descendants of the fourth descending generation (born 1945–74) would have no more than a 12.5 per cent chance of possessing a single piece of the original set. If the number of objects the immigrants brought remains fixed, but the number of their descendants doubles (in theory) with each generation, then the probability of inheriting anything the immigrants brought from the old country is halved with each passing generation. Thirty per cent of our sample of Albany-born informants possessed objects passed down from a grandparent or a still-earlier generation; in most cases, however, it was doubtful that these objects had come with an emigrant from Ireland; more likely they had been acquired in America by someone in the second or third generation and handed down to the fourth, fifth, or sixth. About half this number, 15 per cent, possessed undated and unmarked heirlooms which were thought to be quite old, including such things as rosaries and rings, which might, possibly, have belonged to an ancestor who emigrated between 1847 and 1854. But whatever the provenance of these objects, the devolution down the years of small treasures from the past is a way of giving material form to the continuity of the generations.

Yet, while 30 per cent possessed things that they regarded as family heirlooms, it is important to remember that 70 per cent did not. About a third of our informants possessed no objects, old or new, with any Irish associations. And, as we have seen, though 60 per cent had visited Ireland, 40 per cent had not and most of these felt no need or wish to do so. More than half did not eat anything that they regarded as Irish food, even on St Patrick's Day. Two-thirds, while interested in their ancestry, had less than a full knowledge of the essential details of their grandparents' biographies. Two-thirds had lost touch completely with their ancestors' relatives in Ireland. Ninety-seven per cent had not been exposed to any domestic use of Gaelic. While these findings help us to build up a rough, preliminary outline of some of the basic, measurable attributes of our informants' Irishness, there are many other qualities of Irishness still to be explored. The remainder of this chapter takes up two: names and naming practices, and the way that the generational and ancestral mixing of the generations has affected their Irish inheritance.

II

What's in a name? Over 90 per cent of the 252 informants from whom we collected systematic information thought they could recognize the ethnic ancestry of other people by their names with a reasonable degree of confidence. Because of their names, 80 per cent had had the experience of having been asked about their ancestral background, or had had their perceived ancestral background commented upon by other people; 37.8 per cent reported this as a frequent experience. Yet despite our informants' confidence in their ability to identify others' backgrounds by their names, 26 per cent said that their own ancestral attachment was sometimes, or always, mistaken by other people; two-thirds of this number were not especially concerned about this, and simply let these mistakes pass.

The names by which people might recognize ancestry are of three kinds: surnames, given names, and married names. In America, surnames, or family names, whatever the cultural conventions associated with their European origin, pass down through the patriline unaltered from one generation to the next, and in the same form regardless of the bearer's gender. Distinctive surnames are strong markers of presumed ancestral attachment: names like Mahoney, Schweigert, Van Gaasbeek, Le Roux, and Fiscarelli give clear indications that one is descended from an Irish, German, Dutch, French, or Italian immigrant. There are, however, complicating factors. People with (to American eyes and ears) surnames which were difficult to spell or pronounce sometimes changed them to make their lives easier; people also altered their surnames to fit in socially and to be more American; and after 1892 the immigration officials at Ellis Island are said frequently to have given people new surnames for both these reasons. Most people of Irish ancestry in Albany, however, did not alter their surnames, nor did later arrivals have them changed at Ellis Island, since most of their names were already widespread in America and familiar to anglophones.

None the less, some have names that are more distinctively Irish than others. A tabulation of the surnames of our Albany-born informants who identified themselves as Irish, together with their relatives of Irish ancestry, yielded 417 cases. Of these, 194 (46.5 per cent) were distinctively Irish, and could be mistaken for nothing else; they included such surnames as Brady, Carroll, Connors, Corrigan, Curran, Dennehey, Doyle, Feeney, Flanagan, Flynn, Higgins, Hogan, Joyce, Keegan, Kelly, Lanahan, Lynch, Maguire, McDermott, McGrath, Mulligan, Murphy, Nolan, O'Connell, O'Sullivan, Regan, Rooney, Ryan, Sheehan, and Walsh. One hundred and forty (33.6 per cent) were less distinctive surnames such as Andrews, Bradley, Brown, Hale, Harper, King, Knight, Leonard, Martin, Miller, Murray, Palmer, Pratt, Roberts, Savage, Smith, Turner, and White. These surnames are widely distributed within the British Isles; their bearers could be Scots, English, or Welsh as well as Irish. Not every immigrant from Ireland had a distinctively Irish patronymic on arrival in the United States. During penal times in Ireland, the spelling of Irish surnames was Anglicized and some people took (or were given) British surnames; moreover, by the nineteenth century, there had been 700 years of mixing and intermarriage with the Scots, English, and Welsh as people came and went in both directions between the neighbouring islands of Ireland and Britain. There was more intermarriage in America. In our sample, 20 per cent of those identifying themselves as Irish had surnames that suggested something other than an Irish or British background. Forty-three (10.3 per cent) of these informants' surnames were German, 15 (3.6 per cent) were Italian, 14 (3.4 per cent) were French, and 11 (2.6 per cent) were Polish or Russian. Some of these are accounted for by marriages in which, at some point along the line, a non-Irish man married into an Irish family; henceforth, no matter that each succeeding male married a woman of unmixed Irish ancestry, the children, although predominantly of Irish stock, would not have an Irish surname. Other cases are accounted for by the custom of the wife taking her husband's surname on marriage and dropping her own. Thus a woman of unmixed Irish descent might bear an Italian or Polish surname. Women who, in addition, did not have a markedly Irish given name to counteract some of the effect of the loss of their natal surname reported that other people usually misperceived their ancestry.

Given or Christian names, on the other hand, are chosen by parents rather than inherited or acquired on marriage. In Irish families in America, an old custom—widespread throughout the British Isles and parts of continental Europe—lived on, bridging the generations, linking ancestors to their descendants, as the following extracts from our interviews illustrate.

I was named after my father, and usually kids in our family would be named after aunts or uncles. Most of the names are family names, [like] James and John and Robert and Joseph, which I always thought of as more American names as opposed to [names like] Liam and Sean, which sound more Irish. Some of my nephews have those names. My mother was Anne, my sisters are Anne-Marie and Mary Ellen. The first-born male was not necessarily named after the father. Quite often it was after an uncle. [There was] no strict tradition [in my family]. [But] there was always a general attempt to pick a name that would relate back to some relative, whether it was your first or middle name. My middle name is Stephen because my grandfather's middle name was Stephen.

(Informant 558)

My father's [given names] are James Ryan, my brother is James Ryan junior and I think my grandfather was James Ryan also. My great-grandfather was Patrick. I don't know where [the] James came from, but [Patrick] had fifteen brothers and sisters [and] it is possible that it came from somewhere.

(Informant 586)

My sons are named after my father and my wife's father. My grandfather's middle name was Patrick and my middle name is Patrick, but I don't think there is anything that is real structured. But I think we like to have remembrance for people in our family, so I think my middle name Patrick had to do with my grandfather. My sister is named Patricia. And in turn I used the middle name of my sons to remember their grandfathers. [On the German side of my family] there [was] some naming of people after parents or grandparents, but I don't think it was as strong.

(Informant 583)

My name is my aunt's name, my great aunt's, and my great-grandmother's.

(Informant 253)

I am named after my great-uncle. He was born in Ireland. My great-grandfather [was named] Roger, my grandfather [too], and it is my middle name. Mary is a very recurring name on my father's side.

(Informant 33)

Most of my brothers and sisters have traditional names: Christopher, Michael, Donald, Peter, Hugh, Thomas, Kevin, Brian, and Paul. The girls are Helen, Mary, Nancy, Susan, and Alexandra. Mainly Catholic names as much as Irish. Hugh, my brother, is named after my father. My grandmother was Helen, my sister was Helen, and my mother was Helen. Sometimes the middle name is the maiden name of the grandmother or mother, just to keep the name in there somewhere.

(Informant 521)

My brother Tom is named after his grandfather. My name is Catherine Julia. I was named for my grandmothers on both sides. [One of my daughters] is named Anne Marie for both her grandmothers, [and my other daughter] Bridget [Catherine] is named for her great-great-grandmother and great-grandmother.

(Informant 92)

When I met [my future wife] my mother couldn't believe there was going to be another Mary Ellen [in the family].

(Informant 75)

Thomas, William, and Patrick seem to be the [names] that run around [in our family]. Its interesting that we've got two cousins who have named their children Brian and Daniel [although] Brian and Daniel were never names in our family.

(Informant 528)

We had seven [children]. All [the boys] have my father's second name for their second name, except my last one [who has] my grandfather's name.

(Informant 603)

My name is Patricia. My first name is [really] Elizabeth, but nobody uses that. My mother's name is Patricia. I have a sister Mary and an aunt Mary. My grandfather was Joseph Bernard and [my] uncle is Joseph Bernard. My brother is Joseph Bernard, and my uncle's son is Joseph Bernard. My youngest sister's name is Margaret Grace and nobody likes [it], but I have a grandmother who hadn't [had] anyone named for her yet. It's an old tradition that [has] carried over.

(Informant 462)

In my husband's family everyone seems to have the same name. It is so confusing. [My husband's name] is Timothy Patrick. I have one son who is Timothy Patrick junior. His two grandfathers were Patrick. My mother-in-law is Mary. Her brothers were Timothy, Maurice, Michael, and John. The first son was named after his father and the second son after his [mother's] father. I gather that is the Irish way. Names keep recurring. There are about six names that rotate among ninety [people in his family].

(Informant 176)

I said, we can't keep naming them Mary. Meet my sister Mary and my other sister Mary. [It was] ridiculous.

(Informant 237)

I originally had four first names. My grandfather on my mother's side was James Joseph. So my mother just naturally assumed that I'd be James Joseph. [My father's] idea was that I'd be Walter Harold [after his father]. And they fought over it. For a while they were calling me James Joseph Walter Harold. [They] finally settled on Walter Joseph.

(Informant 581)

I don't know if we were named for anyone. We were all named after saints. We had middle names that reflected the day we were born. They looked at the calendar and saw what saint was close to that day, or something of that nature. I wanted to name [our son] Joseph [because of that tradition, but] my wife wanted to name him Stephen and we couldn't agree, so we came up with a third name.

(Informant 404)

[I named] my son after my father, but I wouldn't say there is any strong pattern [in my family].

(Informant 547)

My [first two] children are named after family members. The first child was named after my mother. The first son was named after his father and grandfather. It is a very old name: he is the third William Joseph Devlin. Devlin was his [great-]grandmother's maiden name. Then we had four boys not named after family members. They were given names that had cultural connections: Peter Michael, Daniel Patrick, Stephen Vincent, and Andrew Thomas. Then a little girl was born, and she was named after my husband's stepmother.

(Informant 333)

I don't know where they got Judith. I really don't. There were five kids in my kindergarten class with the same name. I think it must have been after Judy Garland or something. I asked my mother once. She said, 'We were going to name you Helen, after your grandmother, but then we named you Judith'. I said, 'Why?' 'I don't know why' [she said].

(Informant 52)

I liked the Gaelic names, the ones that [don't] have an English translation. But [on] their middle names we compromised and named [our children] after relatives. Up until our generation, both sides of the family named the first-born male after the grandfather on the father's side. The second male was [named after] the grandfather on the mother's side.

(Informant 135)

I'm named after after my father's sister. My oldest brother is named after my father's father, and my second brother is named after my mother's father. That is very traditional. I [gave] my kids very Irish names. My oldest boy is Patrick James [Eamonn], Patrick James after his father [and] Eamonn is after a cousin in Ireland. And then my second son is Kevin Declan, and my third son is Dennis Patrick Brendan, and my fourth son is Sean Michael Cormac. Declan is after a cousin in Ireland, Brendan is after a cousin in Ireland, and Sean just wanted to be Cormac because he likes that name.

(Informant 305)

[The older generations] didn't really propagate the Irish names. All the poor young girls [who] were maids and everything were [called] Deirdre and Noreen and all that kind [of name]. In America, people wanted American names.

(Informant 152)

I named my daughter Kathleen because I wanted to keep some of that Irish concept.

(Informant 106)

My two daughters are Megan and Patricia. Both are Irish names.[6]
Patricia is my wife's name, and we liked Megan.

(Informant 58)

We have three children. We did not name them after anyone, but
they all sound very much Irish: Matthew, Colleen, and Megan. My
wife [who is mainly Polish] agreed to all of these; in fact she came up
with the names ... [but] my in-laws were not too happy.

(Informant 326)

I have a son named Sean. You know how the hell I spelled Sean? S-h-a-
w-n. Forgive me for that. Now the reason I did that, I tell all my friends,
[is that] I was married to a German girl. I started liking Irish music and
I would go off to Duffy's Tavern, and there was a whole bunch of
Irishmen [who were regulars]. Whether they were Irish or not, they
would talk like they were. They said [we] hear you have baby, and I said
yes. Good Irish name? I said his name was Sean. Oh good, and you
spelled it right, didn't you? And I said, no, as a matter of fact I didn't.
Jesus, Mary, and Joseph, what were you doing spelling it like that? And
I said, well, my wife is German and the alternative is Fritz! At least [his]
name sounds right. I was much more in my generation into an Irish
[-sounding] name for my child than either my father or grandfather.

(Informant 321)

We have three kids: Erin is 16, Kelly is 20 and Don junior is 22. With
a German last name, they had to have an Irish first name, just so that
their heritage should not be lost.

(Informant 332)

All of my son John's children [—he has six—] have Irish names like
Brigid and Maura and Kelly, Casey, John, and Michael. My son
Daniel has Caitlin and Megan and Sean and Daniel Patrick.

(Informant 164)

We named our children after no one. [Not] surprisingly, [they] came
out with Irish names, Noreen and Sean and Ciaran.

(Informant 29)

[We all had] family names. My children [do] not. They are all Irish
names I liked and I think it is good to [give] children their own
names. If you name them the same as grandpas and mothers and

---

[6] While both Megan and Patricia might be perceived by Americans as 'Celtic' names,
Megan is a Welsh name, and Patricia—while not unknown in Ireland—has never been
widely used as a given name, unlike Patrick.

everybody, there is confusion. I think names are supposed to distinguish individuals.

(Informant 28)

I named the [first] one Jimmy, after my brother. And then the other
one Brian; I didn't name him after anybody, I just liked Brian—it
was a real hot name at the time. Names run in circles, cycles: right
now, it's Jason and Jeremiah and Christopher, and every single kid
you find, including my grandson, is called Christopher. Christopher
[or] Megan. Megan is my granddaughter and every second little girl
[who is] about 5 or 6 years old [is called Megan]. You know where
that came from? The *Thornbirds*.

(Informant 95)

There were so many kids in our lineage that we have literally run out
of names. Names like Edward have been used for years and years,
generation [on] generation. John is another one. Thomas is another
one. Francis was used sporadically. That's in my immediate family.
In my wife's family, George is a big name; Peter was used very
commonly, as was John and Patrick. I have cousins [of] the same
names as everyone in our [immediate] family, and it really gets kind
of strained because at a family function, if someone says 'Where's
John Murphy?', eight guys might stand up. I think that [provoked]
my generation to get away from all of that. Like in the girls' names,
Mary Murphy or Margaret Murphy, fourteen would stand up. The
boys are now Timothy, Brendan, Peter, and Daniel. The girls are
Christine, Kelly, and Mary Frances. [In] my brother's family, it is
Edward again, Sean, and Terence and John is used again; the girls
are Erin and Nathea—which is a family name, although it is not
Irish. We have worn a lot of names out.

(Informant 385)

While some of our informants said that there was a pattern of recurring
names in their families, linking grandparent with grandchild, or parent
and child, the strength of this tradition varied within and between families, and it was by no means universal. Where it was the custom, it
provided important symbolic links with the past, inscribed and embodied
in present and future generations. People who bear the names of a grandparent or great-grandparent are, perhaps, more likely to have an awareness of, and an interest in, their ancestral namesake and possibly their
ancestors in general than might otherwise be the case. Nothing is more
personal than one's name; to have an ancestor's name is an intimate part

of one's social persona, firmly placing one in the history of the family's line of descent from its old-country origins. As the generations have passed, some families continue the tradition, but others have turned away from it. Why? By choosing names for their children which they perceive to be more Irish than their own, or their parents', are they—intentionally or inadvertently—loosening the bonds with earlier generations and lines of descent, replacing these specific attachments to real people and their biographies embodying first-person experiences of the past by a more generalized identification with a popular culture of Irishness in America, composed largely of modern myths and inventions? Or, as genealogies become more complex and the experiences and biographies of the immigrant generations have become forgotten as they recede into history, are they doing just the opposite: consciously attempting to hold on to the past, to recreate it, and to inscribe in the next generation the certainty of an Irishness which could formerly have been taken for granted, but is now slipping away as the earlier generations are lost in time and as intermarriage with people of other European backgrounds dilutes and reduces their Irishness? Or is it merely unreflective, meaningless fashion, a passing phase, as some of our informants' words suggest? Certainly, some of these Irish-sounding given names are now quite popular in general throughout the United States, and do not necessarily have any Irish associations to those who bestow them upon their children: names like Ryan and Shannon have become common among people who have no Irish ancestry at all. Indeed, such names may be just as frequent among people of non-Irish descent.[7]

What we can definitely say is that among our informants' families, Irish-sounding given names have more than doubled in frequency since the Second World War. An analysis of names given to children in Albany families of Irish ancestry during the period 1915 to 1944 reveals relatively few such names: for men, Vincent, Patrick, and Daniel; for women, Theresa, Noreen, Ellen, Patricia, Maureen, and Kathleen, although none of these names was restricted only to people of Irish ancestry. All the rest

---

[7] See S. Lieberson and E. Bell, 'Children's First Names: An Empirical Study of Social Taste', *American Journal of Sociology*, 98 (1992). The authors carried out an analysis of names given to children in New York State between 1973 and 1985. Among the fifty most popular names given to white girls were Kelly, Erin, Shannon, and Kathleen. For white boys, Brian, Daniel, Sean, Kevin, Timothy, Ryan, and Patrick were among the top fifty. The authors relate names to social class as measured by mothers' educational levels, but unfortunately do not attempt an analysis on the basis of mothers' stated ancestries. In Britain, in 1997, Shannon was among the top twenty girls' names; and among the top twenty boys' names were Daniel, Ryan, Connor, and Liam.

of the sixty names listed, such as Harry, Philip, Richard, Charles, Joseph, Mary, Joan, Faith, Elizabeth, Florence, and Alice were common Anglo-American names which were not in themselves specifically suggestive of either Irishness or Catholicism, though some, such as Michael, Joseph, Catherine, and Mary, were extraordinarily frequent in these families and might have suggested or reinforced Irishness or Catholicism when joined with a more-or-less Irish-sounding surname. A comparison with the names given to children in Albany families of Irish background fifty years later, from 1965 to 1994, shows a number of names popular a half-century earlier to have completely disappeared, and Irish-sounding names to have increased markedly, especially for girls. These names include Megan, Theresa, Ellen, Kathleen, Patricia, Shannon, Maureen, Brigid, Casey, Erin, Maura, Nora, Kerry, and Colleen; and for boys, Brendan, Daniel, Ryan, Sean, Declan, and Patrick. Some of these names are postwar innovations not seen in previous generations of Irish families in America. Erin, Megan, Patricia, Shannon, Ryan, Casey, and Kelly, as given names, though bestowed upon children because they are thought to be Irish, ironically do not commonly occur as given names in Ireland and would, more likely than not, make their bearers stand out as Americans were they to visit the old country. Of course, on marriage, girls are much more likely to lose their Irish surnames, if they have them to begin with, unless their partner is also of Irish ancestry. Nowadays, the probability that a woman of Irish ancestry in Albany who has married since 1965 will have an Irish married name is about 50 per cent.

III

Our sample of informants of Irish ancestry who were born and raised in Albany varied in age from 20 to 90. The dates of birth of their parents ranged from the 1870s to the 1940s, and that of their grandparents from the 1830s to the 1920s. One or two had Irish ancestors who had arrived in Albany before 1800, and a few were the children of 1950s Irish immigrants. The descendants of those Irish immigrants who came to America in the peak years of emigration, during and immediately after the Great Famine, are now of the third, fourth, fifth, and sixth generations. How has the Irishness of their descendants' ancestry been affected by the passage of the generations since the mid-nineteenth century?

The answers are at once simple and complex, and involve analysing the ancestral backgrounds of our informants, their progenitors, and their descendants. We invited nearly all our informants to tell us at length about their ancestry, and in a further series of interviews, we traced out the genealogies of 80 volunteers to the maximum extent of the information available to them about their lineal ancestors and collateral relatives. We also collected systematic data about the brothers, sisters, siblings' spouses, children, children's spouses, parents, and grandparents of 252 people, of whom 83 were of Irish descent, born and raised in Albany. The core sample, consisting of these 83 people and the information they gave us about their close relatives, produced 804 cases in which the ancestral backgrounds of individuals were complete enough to be tabulated, and 385 marriages that could be analysed to see what, if any, patterns might be revealed as the generations have passed.

The first difficulty is in defining what we mean by the much-used word 'generation', which in turn requires a reference point. This reference point might be a given individual: we would then have an ego-centred system of reckoning the generations. Our reference point, by this method, is always Generation Zero. We would count ego's parents as the first ascending generation, grandparents as the second, and so forth; and ego's children as the first descending generation, ego's grandchildren as the second descending generation, and so on. The main liability of this procedure is that a mother, daughter, and daughter's daughter are, from their own ego-centred points of view, all Generation Zero and there is no fixed reference point other than the individual herself. Another possibility, much more suitable for our purpose, is to define the reference point by some historically fixed event, such as the time of the immigrants' arrival. As we are interested in how the passage of the generations has affected our informants' ancestry since the Great Famine, the end of the surge in immigration provoked by the Famine—1854—would seem a natural reference point. Convenient as this may appear, reckoning the generations in this way detaches itself from the actualities of biological reproduction, which will vary from individual to individual and family to family. This is the way that most people use the term 'generation' with reference to themselves: third-generation equates to granddaughter or grandson, whatever the actual chronological span taken by these biological events. Yet for one family with a tendency to marry young, in which mother, daughter, and granddaughter each marries and has a child at the age of twenty, the birth of the first great-grandchild, initiating the fourth generation, would occur in sixty years. For another family with a propensity to marry late, say at the age of 35, it would take 105 years to reach the fourth generation. If the span taken by a generation varies with each family, we need a more-or-less arbitrary definition of the interval between an average individual's birth and his or her procreation of descendants, and hence the creation of a subsequent generation. For sake of argument, let us take this interval at thirty years, an age by which it can be assumed that most people will have had a child. This is conventionally referred to as the 'birth cohort': a set of people born within a chronological span; in this case, thirty years.

Of these individuals born within a span of thirty years, a few of the earliest-born may be marrying and having children within, say, twenty years of their birth; that is, before the youngest members of their thirty-year cohort have themselves been born. On the other hand, the youngest members of the cohort might leave having children rather late—to the age of 40 or so; the oldest members of the birth cohort might then be 70 or 80 years old by the time the last members of their same birth cohort have had their last child, and a line can finally be drawn under that generation. Thus at any given moment there will be, typically, a forty-year overlap between adjacent generations. The last members of Generation A yet to marry and have children will overlap not only with the members of Generation B (the children of earlier members of the cohort who have already married and had children), but also with Generation C, the grandchildren of the earliest-born members of Generation A. Clearly, reproductive intervals cannot, in themselves, adequately demarcate the generations. We need to add a further criterion.

One such criterion is place of birth. Conventionally, in immigration studies, the 'first generation' refers to those who emigrated: those who were born in the old country and took up residence in the new. Their children, born in the new country, are then counted as the second generation, their children's children as the third, and so on. Table 5.1 outlines a scheme for classifying the generations based on both birth cohort and the place of birth of earlier generations. We have added to this scheme the notion of 'marriage cohort', for reasons which will become evident later on. It is important to note that this scheme is an ideal type, which the genealogies of real individuals may approach in varying degrees. One of the obvious complicating factors here is that emigration from Ireland did not begin in 1847 nor cease in 1854. The genealogies of most of our informants mix the generations because some their ancestors arrived in the United States either earlier or later. The further back one travels over the generations, to eight, sixteen, or thirty-two ancestral lines, the more likely it is is that generational distance will become complicated by inter-marriage with the descendants of earlier or later arrivals from Ireland or other European countries.

One of our informants (67, born in 1945), for example, had six sets of great-great-grandparents (twelve persons of a possible sixteen) who were born in Ireland between 1814 and 1830 and came to Albany at the time of the Famine, but two great-grandparents who were born in Ireland after 1855 and came to the United States some years later. Although all the subsequent generations were born in America, by the scheme outlined in Table 5.1, Informant 67 is fifth generation on all but her mother's mother's side, where she is fourth generation. This is a relatively uncomplicated case: most of our informants' ancestral pedigrees, in terms of their generational distance from Ireland, are much more complex. Indeed, Informant 67's case is the least complicated of any fifth-generation descendant of Irish immigrants who arrived at the time of the Famine that we encountered; none of our other fifth-generation descendants had a number even remotely approaching Informant 67's twelve Famine-era Irish immigrant great-great-grandparents. The probabilities are heavily against there being many people of Irish ancestry in Albany, or elsewhere in the United States, who have perfect pedigrees extending back over four or more generations to the Famine immigrants of 1847 to 1854. Despite the common perception that today's generations of people of Irish ancestry are 'the children of the Famine', there has been so much generational mixing over the last 150 years that it is questionable how many people having some fifth-generation ancestry are even *preponderantly* the descendants of Famine immigrants, having eight or more great-great-grandparents (out of sixteen) who came to the United States between 1847 and 1854. In the next generation, the sixth, the prospects that a majority of anyone's thirty-two great-great-great grandparents having been Famine immigrants will be even more remote; the odds against it increase with each passing generation.

It is a curious paradox, made inevitable as the Famine recedes back in time while the generations move on inexorably, that while the numbers of people descended from the Famine immigrants increase—in theory geometrically, one Famine immigrant giving rise to two children, each producing two grandchildren, these four producing eight great-grandchildren, sixteen great-great-grandchildren, and so on—the proportion of their ancestral inheritance derived from this one original Famine immigrant decreases over the generations in inverse ratio, to a half, a quarter, an eighth, a sixteenth, and a thirty-secondth by the sixth generation. Meanwhile, as the generations have married, the ancestries of their potential spouses have been affected similarly, further complicated by random generational mixing as people have married the descendants of

TABLE 5.1. The descendants of the Famine-era immigrants from Ireland, 1847–54 by generation, birth, and marriage cohort

Generation	Born	Married
First	Before 1854 in Ireland	to 1894
Second	1855–84 in USA, of two parents born in Ireland before 1854	1875–1924
Third	1885–1914 in USA of two parents born in USA and four grandparents born in Ireland before 1854	1905–54
Fourth	1915–44 in USA of two parents born in USA and four grandparents born in USA and eight great-grandparents born in Ireland before 1854	1935–84
Fifth	1945–74 in USA of two parents born in USA and four grandparents born in USA and eight great-grandparents born in USA and sixteen great-great-grandparents born in Ireland before 1854	1965–2014
Sixth	1975–2004 in USA of two parents born in USA and four grandparents born in USA and eight great-grandparents born in USA and sixteen great-great-grandparents born in USA and thirty-two great-great-great-grandparents born in Ireland before 1854	1995–2044

Note: 'Generation' is the reproductive interval. The average length of this interval is taken here as thirty years. However, the average span of a marriage-cohort is taken as between twenty and forty years, since most marriages occur between these ages. Thus for any given generation there is a total span of seventy years between the birth of oldest members of the generation and the last marriages, forty years later, of the youngest of its members.

immigrants who arrived in America either before the Famine, or decades later. Putting the effect of this process at its most dramatic to demonstrate the point in the clearest possible terms, a member of the third generation who has one grandparent who emigrated between 1847 and 1854 is 25 per cent a child of the Famine; but a member of the sixth generation who has but one single great-great-great-grandparent who emigrated to the United States between 1847 and 1854 is 31/32—or 96.875 per cent—not a child of the Famine.

Our informants' ancestries were typically mixed not only by generation, but also by the national origin of their ancestors. Table 5.2 summarizes the results of our tabulation of the ancestral national-origin components of the ancestries of our informants and their close relatives. The first generation, born in Ireland, is taken for the purpose of this analysis to be of unmixed ancestry; this is an oversimplification, for as we saw in Chapters 3 and 4, some Irish migrants went first to Britain and came to America with English, Scottish, and Welsh spouses and children of mixed ancestry. The ancestry components were taken as they were given to us by our informants, and therefore may not be wholly accurate genealogically. If, for instance, an informant described himself as 'Irish-German-French', each component was taken at face value and counted once, although the informant may have had two Irish grandparents and one each of German and French. None the less, while this may distort the absolute numbers within each generational cohort, it should not affect the relative frequencies between cohorts. And the relationships between the generations are what is significant.

The figures show an unmistakable trend: the steady decline in the quantity of Irish ancestry over the generations: from about three-quarters in Generation 2, to roughly two-thirds in Generation 4, falling to approximately half in Generation 4, and substantially less than half in Generation 5. From the second generation onwards, the Irish were increasingly of mixed ancestry. The ancestries they were most likely to be mixed with, until the Second World War, were German and British. After the Second World War, the members of the fourth generation were somewhat less likely to have German ancestry, and rather more likely to be of mixed Irish, British, French Canadian, Italian, or Polish ancestry. Table 5.3 shows the ancestry components in more detail, and reveals a dramatic drop in the quantity of Irish ancestry among those born during the period 1915–29, in the first half of the fourth generation. To understand why people suddenly became so much less Irish, we need to consider what marriage choices the previous generations were making.

Surprisingly, perhaps, as Table 5.4 shows, one-quarter of the second-

TABLE 5.2. Ancestry components in sampled population by generation, 1860–1959 (percentages)

	Generation 1	Generation 2	Generation 3	Generation 4	Generation 5
Irish	100.0	72.2	69.3	48.0	42.7
German	–	13.5	12.2	15.4	8.7
British	–	6.2	10.1	12.4	11.8
French	–	4.9	3.5	7.3	10.0
Italian	–	–	1.4	3.4	8.0
Polish	–	–	0.8	4.0	5.6
Jewish	–	–	–	0.8	0.3
Other	–	3.1	6.5	8.6	12.8

TABLE 5.3. Ancestry components in sampled population, by informants' year of birth at half-generation intervals, 1860–1959

	1860–84		1885–99		1900–14		1915–29		1930–44		1945–59	
	n	%	n	%	n	%	n	%	n	%	n	%
Irish	117	72.2	97	66.4	78	72.2	123	47.1	123	47.1	123	42.7
German	22	13.5	18	12.3	13	12.0	24	15.9	39	14.2	25	8.7
British	10	6.2	12	8.2	13	12.0	22	14.6	27	10.3	34	11.8
French	8	4.9	6	4.1	3	2.8	7	4.6	26	10.0	29	10.1
Italian	0	–	4	2.7	0	–	4	2.6	11	4.2	23	8.0
Polish	0	–	1	0.7	1	0.9	7	4.6	9	3.4	16	5.6
Jewish	0	–	0	–	0	–	1	0.7	2	0.8	1	0.3
Other	5	3.1	8	5.5	8	7.4	12	7.9	24	9.2	37	12.8
Total ancestry components	162		146		108		151		261		288	
Total individuals sampled	154		125		94		109		170		152	
Average number of ancestry components per individual	1.05		1.17		1.15		1.39		1.53		2.19	

TABLE 5.4. In-marriage and out-marriage in sampled population, by marriage cohort

	Overlapping: both partners have Irish single or mixed ancestry %	Non-overlapping: only one partner has any Irish ancestry %
Generation 2: married 1875–1924	82.2	17.8
Generation 3: married 1905–54	72.7	27.3
Generation 4: married 1935–84	66.5	33.5
Generation 5: married 1965–2014	52.6	47.4
Generation 6:[a] married 1995–2044	–	–

Note: [a] Number of cases too small.

generation ancestors of our informants did not choose single-ancestry Irish spouses in a city in which it could not have been very difficult for either a man or woman to find a partner of unmixed Irish stock, since as many women as men arrived from Ireland as first-generation migrants (making the Irish rather different from, say, the Italian pattern of emigration, where male migrants predominated and there were not enough first-generation Italian women for them to marry). While over 80 per cent of second-generation Irish migrants married persons of Irish descent in the years between 1875 and 1924, over a quarter married second-generation partners whose Irish ancestry was partial—mixed with other European origins—or partners of any generation in America who had no Irish ancestry at all (details of this are given in Table 5.5). The most frequently intermarrying ancestries were northern European: German and British. The latter of these is the more interesting, for while large numbers of Germans were Roman Catholic, the old-stock British in Albany were exclusively Protestant, and nineteenth-century British emigrants were also overwhelmingly non-Catholic; however their religion of birth is now remembered—or misremembered—by their present-day descendants. A common language may have counted for more than a common religion, especially if neither partner was especially church-minded and had few relatives locally to pressure them into conformity, which is much more

TABLE 5.5. Ancestry components in marriage choices of sampled population by informants' year of birth, 1860–1959

	1860–84		1885–99		1900–14		1915–29		1930–44		1945–59	
	n	%	n	%	n	%	n	%	n	%	n	%
Complete overlap:												
Single Irish to single Irish	45	72.5	27	49.1	19	45.2	26	28.6	11	14.3	9	7.9
Partial overlap:												
Single/mixed Irish to mixed Irish	9	9.7	11	20.0	13	31.0	43	47.3	33	42.8	51	44.7
No overlap:												
Single or mixed Irish to other single ancestry:												
German	5	8.1	11	20.0	2	4.8	1	1.1	3	3.9	4	3.5
British	4	6.5	2	3.6	0	–	5	5.5	5	6.5	5	4.4
French	1	1.6	0	–	1	2.4	3	3.3	2	2.6	2	1.8
Italian	0	–	0	–	0	–	3	3.3	7	9.1	20	17.5
Polish	0	–	1	1.8	0	–	6	6.6	5	6.5	3	2.6
Jewish	0	–	0	–	0	–	1	1.1	2	2.6	5	4.4
Other	1	1.6	0	–	1	2.4	1	1.1	2	2.6	3	2.6
No overlap:												
Single or mixed Irish to other mixed ancestries	0	–	3	5.4	6	14.3	2	2.2	7	9.1	12	10.5
Marriages counted	62		55		42		91		77		114	

likely to have been the case in earlier than later generations. That people of the second generation preferred other second-generation (or later) people as marriage partners is a reflection of the social distance between them, and the worlds in which they moved as children and young adults: they went to the same kinds of schools, had much the same experience of life, and had overlapping backgrounds which made it much more probable that they would eventually marry one another than someone from a distant country with a very different set of life experiences, even if this was the same country from which their parents had come a generation earlier.

By the third generation, those born between 1885 and 1914 and marrying between 1905 and 1954, we see the effects of the continuing decline of the Irish-born of marriageable age in the population, together with the effects of out-marriage in the previous generation which has reduced the proportion of single-ancestry persons in the pool of potential marriage partners. Marriages in which both partners are of unmixed Irish stock now account for only half of all marriages; another 25 per cent of marriages were between persons of mixed Irish ancestry. Much more significant, however, was a large increase in out-marriage, and especially Irish-German unions between 1905 and 1940: remarkably, one in every five people of Irish descent married a German who had no other ancestry. While in the second generation, there was little difference in preference between the Germans and the British as marriage partners, from 1905 to 1940 a huge gap had opened up between them: the preference was six-to-one in favour of German ancestry. Intermarriage with British-stock partners dropped by half, while it rose two-and-a-half times with partners of German descent.

Three factors might help to explain this phenomenon. The first is that by the turn of the century, Albany's Roman Catholic institutions, including its churches and elementary and secondary schools, were reaching their peak of development, consolidation, and influence. Most Catholic families were now fully incorporated into the orbit of these institutions, and there was strong pressure from the church, inscribed in its ordinances, for them to marry within the faith. The development of the church school system, and the church's success in drawing most Catholic children into it, had the further effect of separating Catholics from non-Catholics, reducing the opportunities for social mixing and thus the likelihood that Catholics would marry out of the faith later in life. Finally, by the third generation, most people of Irish stock now had nearby grandparents, second cousins, aunts, uncles, and first cousins as well as parents and siblings, which would have constituted a further set of social conditions encouraging marriage with similar sorts of people; if not with someone of Irish stock, 'like us', then with someone nearly like us. The Germans, now also into the third generation, being English-speaking (though some would still have been bilingual), Catholic (considerable numbers of them, at any rate), and northern European, were obvious candidates. The predominant non-Catholicism of the British, in contrast, had under these early-twentieth-century conditions become a measurably greater impediment to free intermarriage.

The preference for the Germans, as those most nearly like the Irish, was not to last beyond the fourth decade of the century. The Second World War was a watershed in Irish-stock marriage patterns. Anti-German sentiment during the war touched everyone of German descent, no matter that most had lived in Albany for a century and, through previous generations of intermarriage, large numbers of people of Irish descent in Albany had a German parent, grandparent, or great-grand-parent, a German aunt or uncle by marriage, and half-German cousins. The German language vanished virtually overnight from Albany's streets, schools, and churches, and so, evidently, did the acceptability of German-stock spouses to those members of the third and fourth generations marrying between 1940 and 1955. Irish-German marriages practically disappeared, plummeting from one in five between 1905 and 1940 to one in a hundred during the war and the following decade. Only with the fifth generation, those marrying from the 1960s onwards, did intermarriage with people of German stock begin to return to its former, pre-war level. In her classic note on marriage patterns in New Haven over the years 1870 to 1950, Ruby Jo Reeves Kennedy describes much the same phenomenon.[8] Until the 1940s, the Germans were preferred over the Italians and Poles, despite being less numerous in New Haven than either of the latter two Catholic ancestries. From the 1940s, however, the relationship became reversed, with the Italians superseding the Germans as the most frequently chosen partners.

In Albany, as in New Haven, marriages with Italians and Poles increased significantly during the war years, continuing into the post war period. In our informants' accounts, there are suggestions that despite their Catholicism, before the war there was a good deal of antipathy towards the Italians. William Foote Whyte, in his classic study, *Street*

---

[8] R. J. R. Kennedy, 'Single or Triple Melting Pot? Intermarriage in New Haven, 1870–1950', *American Journal of Sociology*, 58 (1952).

Corner Society, notes that in Boston, Irish priests regarded the Italians' showy celebrations of saints' days as next to pagan, and Irish parents warned their courting children to stay away from Italians; we found evidence of this in Albany too. The Italians, arriving a full generation or more after the Irish, were mostly first or second generation in the 1930s, while the Irish were already third or fourth generation. Second-generation Italians seem to have been, on the whole, much more torn between the culture of old country and that of America than the second-generation Irish—whose parents were English-speakers—had ever been. Italian parents wanted their children to speak Italian and behave in ways that were familiar to them, since many regarded their sojourn in the United States as temporary; they intended to return to Italy when they had saved enough to buy a respectable piece of farmland or set up in business back home. In the 1930s, a very large number of first-generation Italians had, for this reason, not yet taken American citizenship, although they were entitled to do so. The Irish, in contrast, had applied for naturalization as soon as they had arrived in the United States. The Irish, then, regarded the later-arriving Italians and their children as distinctly more foreign than the Germans, and hence less suitable as marriage partners for their own children.

During the 1930s, as Richard Alba notes in his study of Italian-Americans,[9] Mussolini's nationalist government inspired a certain amount of pride among the Italians in America. When Mussolini signed a pact with Hitler, and the United States was gradually drawn towards war, Italian nationalism became increasingly suspicious. On the outbreak of war, those Italian immigrants who had not taken American citizenship were required to register as enemy aliens. When war came, second-generation Italians from places like Albany and Boston's North End volunteered, or were drafted, in their hundreds of thousands. For the college boys, as William Foote Whyte described them, their route out of the ghetto had been higher education. For the corner boys, as Richard Alba observes, it was the Second World War, and three or four years in the army or the navy. It had much the same effect. A substantial part of the second generation of Italian-Americans was drawn out of the immigrant neighbourhoods like Albany's South End. Many of them never went back: across the United States, the postwar economic boom created

---

[9] R. D. Alba, *Italian Americans: Into the Twilight of Ethnicity* (Englewood Cliffs, NJ, 1985), see esp. ch. 4; see also R. Alba, 'The Twilight of Ethnicity among Americans of European Ancestry: The Case of Italians', *Ethnic and Racial Studies*, 8 (1985), 134–58.

millions of new jobs and new suburban houses; large-scale structural mobility produced social change on a massive scale. These conditions allowed a much larger proportion of second-generation Italians to move up the social ladder than would otherwise have been the case. By the time the educational, occupational, and residential achievements of the third generation (the Cornerville boys' children born during and after the Second World War) began to find their way into the population statistics in the 1960s, 1970s, and 1980s, a convergence between the Italians and older-stock Europeans like the Irish and Germans had taken hold in earnest.

If Whyte had gone back to interview his Boston sample twenty-five or thirty years later, he would have found that a surprisingly high proportion of the corner boys, who had seemed destined for lives of manual labour, had merged with the college boys: they had earned trade-school diplomas or college degrees under the GI Bill, were employed in skilled or white-collar jobs, and lived in suburban houses they had bought with loans from the Federal Housing Administration. And, Whyte would have found that about half of his second-generation Italian–American boys from Cornerville had wives who were not themselves of Italian ancestry, but were Irish, Polish, or German. He would have heard little Italian spoken in these homes. He also would have found that the majority of the Cornerville boys now expected to send their children to college, or were actually doing so. When the Cornerville boys packed their bags to go off to war or to college, for many it was the end of their use of Italian as an everyday language. They spoke English in the army, in college, in the workplace, to their suburban neighbours, to their Irish wives, and to their Irish–Italian children. Perhaps to their parents, but only to their parents, might the corner boys still speak Italian dialect: to their brothers and sisters they would probably speak English. It was also the end of their distinctively anti-clerical Mezzogiorno Catholicism. A few, to the distress of their mothers, but under pressure from their wives, might have become Protestants; and many would have stopped going to church altogether, except for the odd high day or family occasion. In Albany, most continued to be practising Catholics, but either in their spouse's Irish Catholic church or an anodyne suburban Catholic church without much in the way of saints and shrines. St Anthony's, Albany's only Italian Catholic parish church, was closed for lack of a viable congregation in June 1972.

Among the Irish, by the 1970s the combined rate of in-marriage among people of Irish single and mixed ancestry had declined to about 50 per cent. Marriages between persons of single Irish ancestry were now less than 10 per cent, reflecting the ancestral mixing of the population. Similarly, members of the fifth generation marrying after 1965 made fewer unions with persons of German, British, and French single ancestry, since they too were now predominantly of mixed ancestry and there were fewer of them in the marriage pool than in earlier generations. Marriages with single-ancestry Italians, Poles, and Jews, however, increased in both absolute and relative numbers: they were clearly becoming more acceptable marriage partners. People of these ancestries, as a result of the war and the postwar boom, had moved up the social ladder to become more 'like us', while old prejudices broke down in the wake of Vatican II, the flight to the suburbs, and the decline of the segregated Roman Catholic school system.

The members of the fifth generation—the latter half of the current marriage cohort—are still choosing their spouses, and will continue to do so until 2014. The members of the sixth generation were beginning to choose their partners in the mid-1990s. The rate of Irish-stock in-marriage is now at a level that is, little by little, declining towards the overall percentage of people of Irish ancestry in Albany County as a whole. According to the 1990 US Census, over three-quarters of people of Irish stock in the population of Albany County were of mixed ancestry (Table 5.6). Of those in our sample of the fifth generation born between 1945 and 1959, the proportion is even higher: 90 per cent were of mixed ancestry, a level that has now reached parity with the oldest-stock, most assimilated ancestries in Albany County, the English and Dutch. The US Census of 2020 is likely to show that Irish-Irish marriages, whether single-ancestry or mixed, are no longer statistically significant. Indeed, such marriages may have declined to that point already.

Unfortunately, the census figures on ancestry, as given in Table 5.6, cannot be used to determine whether there is any longer a detectable preference for in-marriage. The published details of the 1990 US Census collapse ancestry into only three categories: single ancestry, first mixed ancestry-component, and second mixed ancestry-component. While this would adequately cover a population made up exclusively of first- and second-generation Americans, it is a woefully ineffective way to treat the ancestries of the third, fourth, fifth, and sixth generations, who may have—in theory—four, eight, or sixteen ancestries in their backgrounds. Any ancestry-component beyond the second is omitted in the census figures. Thus a person who is part-German, part-English, and part-Irish could be represented, variously, as German-English, English-Irish, or

TABLE 5.6. Ancestry, Albany County, US Census, 1990

| | Total | Percentage of county | Single ancestry | | Mixed ancestry | | | |
| | | | | | first component | | second component | |
			n	%	n	%	n	%
Irish	116,435	39.79	26,871	23.08	51,932	44.60	37,632	32.32
German	79,986	27.43	16,120	20.15	44,232	55.30	19,634	24.55
British[1]	54,267	18.55	9,656	17.79	25,091	46.23	19,460	35.85
French	40,458	13.83	8,443	20.87	20,761	51.31	11,254	27.82
Italian	71,543	24.45	22,827	31.91	37,873	52.94	10,843	15.16
Polish	30,929	10.57	8,107	26.21	15,450	49.95	7,372	23.84
Russian[2]	10,456	3.57	2,873	27.48	5,357	51.23	2,226	21.29
Dutch	17,772	6.07	2,475	13.93	7,201	40.52	8,096	45.55

Notes:

[1] Includes English, Scottish, and Welsh, since these categories were frequently not accurately differentiated by our informants.

[2] The US Census cannot use a religious category to delineate ancestry; 'Jewish' therefore does not appear. Russian is thus taken in its place as a rough approximation of the Jewish population, which came predominantly from Russia and Germany.

Irish-German; the third element is discarded, but which of these ancestries is discarded there is apparently no way of predicting. In Albany, taking the Irish as our point of reference, there are only seven main ancestry-groups with which the Irish intermarry, so the idea that there could be persons of sixteen non-overlapping ancestral lines of descent is never likely to be found in practice. However, among our sample was at least one case in which seven of the eight great-grandparents were of different ancestral origins: Irish, Italian, Armenian, German, English, Scottish, and French. Of our sample of the ancestry of the children of fifty-four couples, in which at least one of the partners identified himself or herself as of Irish ancestry and was born between 1945 and 1959 and raised in Albany, two sets of children (3.7 per cent) were of single Irish ancestry, sixteen (29.6 per cent) had two European ancestries, seventeen (31.5 per cent) had three, ten (18.5 per cent) had four, seven (13.0 per cent) had five, one (1.9 per cent) had six, and one (1.9 per cent) had seven different European origins. Yet their ancestry, as it appeared in the 1990 census, is accurately represented only for the eighteen sets of children who were of single Irish ancestry or mixed with one other ancestry. For the other thirty-six sets of children, two-thirds of the sample, their ancestries as recorded in the US Census are so misleading as to be quite useless for any scholarly purpose. The omission of individuals' ancestry-components beyond the second element makes *all* the census data on mixed ancestry gravely suspect. Researchers interested in determining the precise levels and mixture of ancestries in any given population containing old-stock Europeans cannot rely on the Census, but must employ their own sampling methods and collect the information themselves.

This, more than anything else one could say, throws into sharp relief the complexities of dealing with later-generation ancestries and the amorphous, boundary-less nature of the subject-matter. If our subject-matter were a set of discrete, conveniently demarcated groups, the statisticians of the United States Department of the Census would, presumably, have had no difficulty in devising effective criteria to identify them. Rather, our subject-matter consists not in groups but in individual human agents, whose ancestries are endlessly overlapping, ramifying over the generations as people become more distant from their ancestors' immigrant origins, and as they freely marry people of other mixtures of generation and old-country backgrounds, so resisting and defying simple classification and generalization.

In 1994, Michael Hout and Joshua Goldstein contributed an article to the *American Sociological Review* entitled, 'How 4.5 Million Irish

Immigrants became 40 Million Irish Americans'.[10] Hout and Goldstein's procedure was to count people identifying themselves in the 1980 US Census as being of Irish ancestral origin as Irish-Americans. Since a minimum of 74 per cent of those of Irish ancestry across the United States were of *mixed* Irish ancestry in 1980,[11] at least 74 per cent of these same 40 million persons were simultaneously something else: German-American, English-American, French-American, Italian-American, and so on, in addition to being Irish-American. Any such individual, depending upon his or her ancestral mixture, could be a number of these things at the same time. The 40 million Irish-Americans referred to by Hout and Goldstein are thus not to be confused with whole persons who form a neatly bounded group; rather they were, at least 74 per cent of the time, fractional identities of widely varying degree, components of the ancestries of persons having mixed, complex pedigrees of national origin.

IV

By 1990, more than three-quarters of people of Irish ancestry in the Albany area were mixed with other national-origin ancestries. Of those of Generation 5, 90 per cent were of mixed Irish ancestry, and any residual preference for Irish-Irish marriages is declining towards a point where it is difficult to detect in the data. There is still the possibility, however, that even though the Irish may not be selecting for partners of the same national origin, they may be choosing spouses of the same religion. Recent studies have shown that intermarriage among people of European backgrounds in America is crossing over religious boundaries, just as it has over national-ancestry boundaries. In his study of Italian-Americans, Richard Alba found that 80 per cent of second-generation Italian

---

[10] M. Hout and J. Goldstein, 'How 4.5 Million Irish Immigrants became 40 Million Irish Americans: Demographic and Subjective Aspects of the Ethnic Composition of White Americans', *American Sociological Review*, 59 (Feb. 1994), 64–82.

[11] S. Lieberson and M. Waters, *From Many Strands: Ethnic and Racial Groups in Contemporary America* (New York, 1988), 45. The actual figure for mixed ancestry may be higher than this, since the authors note that respondents to the 1980 Census were encouraged to give *the* ancestry group with which he or she identifies, which may have served to depress the number of people reporting mixed, complex pedigrees. The authors also note a tendency for some people of complex or indeterminate ancestries to simplify their pedigrees by applying just one catch-all label to themselves, making it appear that they are of single ancestry when in fact they are not.

Catholics married other Catholics (though, of course, not necessarily Italian Catholics).[12] But only half, or slightly less, of the third and later generations married Catholics. This percentage is continuing to decline because, since the 1950s and 1960s, there has been an exodus from the central parts of most American cities, which were well served by Catholic schools, to the more distant suburbs where such schools are less common. The children of the fourth and later generations are going to public schools, which means that they are mixing with non-Catholics much more than children did in the past. In his capital region study, Alba mentions that, nationally, by the 1980s the level of out-marriage for young Catholics had already reached 50 per cent. In the Albany area, his sample of the married population was 56 per cent Catholic, 40 per cent Protestant, and a little less than 3 per cent Jewish:

This above average religious diversity makes for a fairly high occurrence of inter-religious marriage, although interreligious marriage is still not as prevalent as interethnic marriage. In terms of religious origin rather than current affiliation, almost 40 percent of marriages cross religious lines, with the rate of intermarriage highest among the smaller groups (Jews and Protestants) and lower among the largest (Catholics). Since there is a tendency for one partner in a religious inter-marriage to convert formally or informally to the religion of the other, the degree of religious exogamy looks smaller when it is measured in terms of current religion—not quite 30 percent are intermarried by this criterion. It appears that about 40 percent of marriages between individuals of different religious origins become endogamous through conversion. While recent marriages are mixed in here and thus this figure may become higher over time, it is surprisingly low and thus may serve as a measure of the widespread acceptability of interreligious marriage.[13]

Alba's sample covered all the main European ancestries in the capital region; the Catholics enumerated presumably included Poles, Italians, Germans, Irish, French Canadians, American Indians, and Lithuanians. Also enumerated would have been small numbers of predominantly non-Catholic ancestries including Dutch, Swedes, English, Scots, Welsh, and others who, if they had not themselves converted to Catholicism, were descended from persons who had probably converted in an earlier generation or whose non-Catholicism is nowadays not remembered and are counted by their descendants as having been Catholic. Since the Catholic population of the capital region is 56 per

---

[12] Alba, *Italian Americans*, 149.
[13] Alba, *Ethnic Identity: The Transformation of White America*, 174–5.

cent, this is the level of in-marriage that could be anticipated were potential spouses paying no attention at all to one another's religion. Alba hints that it is higher than this, which means that somewhat fewer of Albany's Catholics marry out of their faith than they do nationally, but he does not put any exact figures on it either for Albany's Catholics as a whole, or for any of its national-origin constituents.

Our findings on this question are summarized in Table 5.7. Our sample covers 470 marriages between 1860 and 1959 in which the confessionals of both spouses could be identified, as contained in the information given to us by our 83 core informants, born and raised in Albany and identifying themselves as of Irish ancestry, about their own marriages, their children's, those of their brothers and sisters, parents, and grandparents.[14] These figures, if accurate, are very different from those which might have been anticipated on the basis of Alba's earlier findings for the Italians, and his estimates of the rates of in- and out-marriage for Albany's Catholics as a whole. If our figures are even roughly indicative, they demonstrate an extraordinarily low rate of out-marriage among our sample of Irish Catholics who live in the city of Albany. They also suggest, if they are right, that since the Irish represent about 40 per cent of the Catholics in the capital region, non-Irish Catholics—who represent 60 per cent—are marrying out of their confessional at a rate that is above the overall average. Since Alba appears to suggest that the overall out-marriage rate for Catholics is lower than the general rate of religious out-marriage (40 per cent), for non-Irish Catholics this rate would need to be somewhat higher in order to compensate for the marked propensity of those Irish who live within the city limits to marry within their confessional.

---

[14] There is a special problem with this dataset. Informants who gave details about grandparents or sons- or daughters-in-law were sometimes uncertain about their confessional. Where this was noted, the datum was not counted. However it is possible that a number of inaccurate guesses may have found their way into the tabulations. Further, informants did not always know whether a grandparent or an in-law had converted. Where a conversion was noted, the subject's confessional before marriage was tabulated, and the fact that he or she had converted was discarded. None the less, some inaccurate guesses as to the subject's religion may have been counted. As the author worked through the responses given to the survey questions about the religions of our informants' relatives, he was struck by a number of cases where the stated confessional did not match the most common confessional(s) of old-country background(s) of the person concerned: either there was a conversion to Catholicism in an earlier, unknown generation, or the informant was guessing and filling in the blanks with what was, to them, the most common kind of religion in their experience if they had no particular reason to think of the subject as having any other sort of religion. Thus some of these genealogical details—most strikingly with respect to religion—may have been adjusted in the light of contemporary social realities, a phenomenon that anthropologists have frequently noted.

TABLE 5.7. Marriage choices in sampled population, by generation, birth cohort, and religion, 1860–1959

| | Roman Catholic to Roman Catholic | | Roman Catholic to another faith | |
	n	%	n	%
Generation 2:				
born 1860–84	62	88.6	8	11.4
Generation 3:				
born 1885–99	51	89.5	6	10.5
born 1900–14	45	91.8	4	8.2
Generation 4:				
born 1915–29	67	91.8	6	8.2
born 1930–44	83	92.2	7	7.8
Generation 5:				
born 1945–59	108	82.4	23	17.6

These figures demonstrate a sharp divide between the preferences of people of Irish descent who live within the city limits and all other Catholics. Our sample shows a remarkably low rate of religious out-marriage. Even though it has increased significantly among those of the youngest cohort for which a tabulation could be made, the first half of Generation 5, it still has a long way to go until it reaches parity with other Catholics. Yet the sharp rise in out-marriage among those of Generation 5 who have already married (Table 5.7) suggests the beginnings of a sea-change in attitudes. Those born after the Second World War, between 1945 and 1959, and who married between 1965 and 1999, made their marriage choices in the more open religious climate which followed Vatican II and the increasingly individualistic social world of the 1970s and 1980s, in which the preferences and prejudices of the parental generation counted for less. Our sample was mainly restricted to people who were still living within the Albany city limits, yet our figures nevertheless show a 125 per cent increase in interreligious marriage from 1965 onwards. This increase must therefore be counted as occurring largely independently of the process of suburbanization.

For those whose parents moved to the suburbs beginning in the 1960s, at least half of this generational cohort, as children, had already been through the city's parochial elementary schools and perhaps through all twelve grades in the Catholic school system by the time their parents moved beyond the city limits. Of our sample of people of Irish

Catholic ancestry, born between 1945 and 1959 and raised within the city limits, 89.7 per cent had been sent by their parents to a Catholic elementary school, and 76.3 per cent had gone to a Catholic secondary school. Of those born from 1960 to 1974, 63.6 per cent had had a Catholic elementary schooling, and 49.4 per cent had attended a Catholic secondary school. Only the second half of Generation 5, those born since 1960 and whose parents moved to the suburbs in the 1960s, is likely to show the full effect of suburban secular schooling. For these suburban children who have been marrying since 1980, we have no intermarriage statistics, since most of the people in our sample lived in the city rather than the suburbs. If and when these figures become available, and they are compared with religious intermarriage rates within the city limits, significant differences may become apparent. It is likely that for those Irish Catholics brought up in the suburbs, who will have attended secular schools exclusively, marriage across religious boundaries will be as ubiquitous as it is for people of other ancestries. In contrast, for those brought up within the city limits, roughly half of whom will have attended Catholic schools, interreligious marriage is likely to be measurably lower, demonstrating that people of Irish ancestry who continue to live within the city limits and send their children to Catholic schools are substantially more 'ethnic' than those who live in the suburbs.[15]

For non-Irish Catholics as a whole, an out-marriage rate of 40 per cent which, conversely, is an in-marriage rate of 60 per cent, means that no significant preference for Catholic partners can be detected in the current data. If 56 per cent of the population of the capital region is Catholic, and the in-marriage rate for non-Irish Catholics is about 60 per cent, the difference cannot be counted as significant in terms of these two figures, each of which has been produced in a different way. Non-Irish Catholics, it would seem, might as well be choosing their marriage partners without any regard at all to their confessional: if their choices were entirely random, or their spouses' religion was completely unknown to them, the result would not be any different. This is, however, not the case with the Albany Irish; or at least not yet, even though things are changing.

Why have Irish Catholics been so endogamous in the city of Albany? What were, and are, the connections between being Irish and being

---

[15] Cf. R. D. Alba, J. Logan, and K. Crowder, 'White Ethnic Neighborhoods and Assimilation: The Greater New York Region, 1980–1990', *Social Forces*, 75 (1997), 883–909.

Catholic? What was the nature of the social glue which bound these things so tightly together over the generations? Why is this glue losing its grip? Some of the answers lie in history, far and near: in the development of Albany's political and religious institutions, and in the part the Irish played in them. The following chapter discusses some of these historical and social conditions.

6

Irish-Catholic-Democrat

Isn't everybody who is Irish Catholic a Democrat?

(Informant 92)

In the rank-order of American cities, Albany was second only to Boston in the proportion of the population reporting themselves to be of Irish ancestry in the 1980 US Census.[1] Nearly all those people to whom we spoke in Albany, and who identified themselves as Irish, said that they were Roman Catholics, despite the care we took in our methodological procedures to guard against any bias in our assumptions about what might constitute Irishness in Albany. This makes Albany an atypical place, since across the country as a whole, only 33 per cent of the Irish-ancestry population are Roman Catholic. Albany also has a history of ward politics and clientelism that is very reminiscent of Boston and New York. Albany thus shares, in some measure, the main institutional characteristics of Irish America that have been derived from studies of large industrial cities; characteristics which are said to have created and sustained an Irish-American ethnic identity. As a smaller city but with some similar features, Albany invites comparison with these images. As this and the following chapters will show, however, the differences are more telling than the likenesses, and call into question the generality of a number of taken-for-granted ideas about Irish America.

Most people in Albany say that Irish, Catholic, and Democrat are connected. Indeed, the phrase 'Irish-Catholic-Democrat' is a local stereotype: given the first of these attributes in respect of an individual, people say half-jokingly, and the other two can be predicted. It is objectively the case that most people in Albany are Democrats, and more people are of Irish descent and are Roman Catholic than any other single ancestral category and religious faith. But there is obviously more to be said, for this does not tell us how these three things came to be connected in the popular imagination, or why. Most anthropologists and historians who have approached a question of this kind have treated it as a matter of 'culture',

[1] See below, Chapter 9.

and offer explanations which trace these phenomena back to Ireland, positing the existence of a set of deep-seated psychological predispositions or cultural values that the immigrants brought with them to America. It would be easy enough to offer such an explanation for Albany, and it would be tempting to do so. There is good reason to believe that clientelism was well established in the nineteenth-century Irish political process, just as it is today,[2] and no one disputes that Catholic pietism was a powerful force in Ireland, at least in the latter part of the nineteenth century.

Yet primordialist explanations of these phenomena are fundamentally flawed. They give scant attention to the mechanisms by which this political acumen and religious piety were carried across the sea and, above all, by whom. Most of those who left Ireland were young single people or families from the lower-middle strata of Irish society who were actively seeking better lives than were available to them in Ireland, and who were willing to turn away from the lives they had known and to take some risks to find what they were looking for in a far-away country. These facts suggest, at a minimum, that their commitment to local politics or church life were not strong enough to persuade them to stay in Ireland. Their youth also militates against the supposition that they had had much practical involvement in the formal institutions of local parliamentary government in Ireland. Their footloose youthfulness further argues against the assumption that they were especially pious; it is clear that earlier waves of young, Catholic immigrants to America did not remain Catholic when and where there were no churches to claim their loyalty. More likely than not, those who came to America were among the least bound by their 'culture', and so would have been rather poor candidates to have been the agents of the transatlantic importation of these Irish institutions. To explain the connection between Irishness, Catholicism, and active involvement in a particular form of politics in Albany by saying that it was a part of the cultural baggage the mid-nineteenth-century immigrants brought with them would be speculation, about which sound historical evidence is unlikely to be found. It is, however, unnecessary to speculate about their cultural predilections in Ireland, or their psychological propensities for politics and churchgoing. There is a more parsimonious explanation much closer to hand: the Irish were Democrats, and Catholics, because that is the way Albany was organized. The relationship

---

[2] See e.g. Mart Bax, *Harpstrings and Confessions: Machine-Style Politics in the Irish Republic* (Assen, 1976).

between the Irish and the political parties and the Church was an instrumental one, which benefited both the immigrants and the indigenous institutions which incorporated them.

I

Looking back over the generations, there is a temptation to try to capture the essence of 'the immigrant experience' and so to generalize beyond empirically discoverable facts. There is, for example, an almost irresistible compulsion for writers on the Irish in America to speak of immigrants of the same geographical origins as forming a 'community' or as having communal identities which were derived from the social milieux in which they found themselves in Ireland, the United States, or both. This is connected with an implicit propensity to contrast the flux, individualization, and indeterminacy of modern social life with a time when people were thought to be more rooted in space, more involved with their neighbours, and more certain of who they were as a collectivity. Ethnic historians point to the immigrant neighbourhoods of the past and find them full of significance. Most studies of the Irish in America have, however, been carried out in big cities, not in small ones or rural areas, and a careful reader might notice that the sociological and anthropological terms 'ethnic', 'culture', 'identity', and 'community', are frequently employed, but are rarely treated as requiring much validation. A typical procedure is that people who are identified by the researcher as having some characteristic in common—Irish birth, for example—are imputed to be 'a community' or 'a culture'. Individuals are then said to derive a sense of 'identity' from their membership of this putative collectivity. Such a statement draws an abstraction from another abstraction, and thus is at least one step removed from validating evidence; it is, in the end, nothing more than conjecture.

Consider how 'Irish' might be defined for the purpose of delineating a community, in Albany or elsewhere. The geographical origin of individuals is clear from documentary records, which is material evidence, but unless living individuals are available to interrogate, or have left letters or other testaments or traces in the historical record to tell us more about who they thought they were, their place of birth is about as much as one can know about their Irishness. It is a long way from knowing about their geographical origins in Ireland to say, or imply, that such individuals were Irish in the sense of having a consciousness of being of the Irish nation and as having personal attributes, thoughts, and feelings which distinguish them from people of other nations or ancestries. Or, for example, to take for granted that since the nation-building project was going on around them in the mid-nineteenth century, any self-respecting person of Irish origin must have known about, been interested in, and attached importance to the idea of Irish nationhood and being of Irish nationality. In fact, while there is plenty of documentary evidence about what the literary and political élites—the antiquarians and nation-builders— thought and felt about these issues a century and a half ago, there is, by contrast, relatively little material evidence that these things were of equal significance to ordinary people, and that despite substantial differences of religion and piety, age and gender, social and economic class, urbanity and rurality, literacy and skills, and language and dialect, their identification with the notion of 'Irish' could be taken as being the same, without significant variation from one individual to another. Mid-nineteenth-century Irish immigrants may well have thought of themselves in as many ways as it is possible to imagine that ordinary, everyday people anywhere and at any historical moment might have thought of themselves. As individuals, they are likely to have had widely differing reasons for emigrating from Ireland, and different ambitions, plans, and expectations for their new lives in America. If they were occasionally called upon to give some thought to their self-categorization in terms of their place of origin, they may well have mainly thought of themselves as belonging to particular localities, rather than to an Irish nation in the abstract. Indeed, since the island of Ireland was a part of the United Kingdom from 1801 to 1920, some recorded their place of birth as Tipperary or Limerick, but their nationality as British. This was not a problem for them, any more than it is for most modern-day English, Welsh, or Scottish people; but it is a problem for us if we insist upon reading history backwards from a modern partisan position, cherishing the idea that people from Ireland *ought*, in the light of events that had not yet happened or of moralizing interpretations of these events propounded by other people decades later, to have thought of themselves first and foremost as Irish, and not as something else.

We could also create community by conveniently leaving non-Catholics out of the picture, even though historically they made up a fifth to a quarter of the population of Ireland, and were overrepresented in emigration to America before the Famine. Non-Catholics are a troublesome problem only if we are anxious to limit who or what qualifies as Irish. And, we could focus our attention on a particular social stratum: the urban industrial proletariat or those who stayed behind in the big cities, perhaps; ignoring the 'lace-curtain Irish' and the vast numbers of Irish immigrants who were geographically, economically, and socially mobile. Thus delimited, a community emerges, but at the cost of excluding every Irish-born person who does not fit the stereotype, and the stereotype may, on closer inspection, turn out to fit only a small minority of those who had Irish origins. For the great majority of Irish immigrants, if they paused at all in New York City, Boston, or Philadelphia, it was only for long enough to gather up some resources before moving on to find better lives than they had known in Ireland. The Irish immigrant populations in eastern-seaboard cities of the United States are likely to have been far more heterogeneous and transient than we are conventionally given to understand.

In Albany, it would be tempting, but ultimately misleading, to describe the city's immigrant neighbourhoods as communities. To describe them as *ethnic* communities would be to compound the difficulty, raising a further set of methodological questions. It would be misleading to use these terms because there is a sense in which the word 'community' ordinarily implies stable, perduring sets of social relationships and values among the people who live in a given place. If anything characterized Albany's neighbourhoods, however, it was their extreme fluidity. The census records and street directories tell a story that challenges the rose-tinted, nostalgic idea that in the past people were more rooted in space, more involved with their neighbours, and more certain of who they were as a collectivity than they are nowadays. That is, that they formed communities in a social and cultural sense now lost to us in an age of individualism and anonymous suburbanity.

To begin, let us examine a typical street in Albany's South End: the forty-six houses and shops along both sides of Broad Street, between Arch Street and Schuyler Street. In 1876, 47 per cent of the names associated with these houses were identifiably Irish; the rest were predominantly English, with a scattering of Dutch and German names. Only one of these names had been associated with Broad Street the best part of a generation earlier, in 1854. There had been a 95 per cent turnover of population in twenty-two years. A generation later, in 1902, four family names recur: one widow and three sets of sons involved in family businesses. In the twenty-six years between 1876 and 1902, there was a further 91 per cent turnover in population. Another generation on, in 1928, the street had become 25 per cent Italian, 15 per cent German, and only 11 per cent Irish; or, to put it another way, 89 per cent non-Irish.

Nevertheless, in Albany folklore, the South End is spoken of as an 'Irish community', from which is said to have arisen, in 1919, Daniel P. O'Connell's Democratic Party machine. By that time, the earlier generations of Irish immigrants had largely moved out of the South End, their places taken by a succession of later arrivals: other new Irish, German, English, Russian, Polish, and Italian immigrants.

As residential development proceeded in the western parts of the city, Broad Street and the South End became progressively more dilapidated, eventually becoming a district of cheap rented rooms and flats which were the new immigrants' first rung on the socio-economic ladder in Albany. Few stayed any longer than they had to, and nearly all succeeded in moving out of the South End, and up the social and economic scales, in less than a generation. It was a polyglot, footloose, here-today–gone-tomorrow population largely made up of young, single people and couples who had not yet established families, non-English-speaking newcomers without nearby relatives, and families with children who planned to move to more salubrious parts of town as soon as they could afford to do so. This is not a picture of a place where most people were putting down roots in the neighbourhood, and where lateral social linkages of friendship, marriage, and kinship were being forged and reproduced over the generations on a significant scale. Much the same pattern is evident in the other, older residential areas adjacent to the capital buildings and the central business district. For example, on Sheridan Avenue there was a 91 per cent turnover of population in the nineteen-year interval between 1917 and 1936; and along Jefferson Street, between Eagle and Swan, there was a 90 per cent replacement of population in the same period.

The South End and Sheridan Hollow were immigrant neighbourhoods *par excellence*, and it is not surprising that their populations were very fluid. What is more unexpected is that an extremely high degree of population turnover was the norm throughout the city, including the newer streets of owner-occupied houses. In Pine Hills, in 1917 at the western edge of residential development and, then as now, a highly desirable area of spacious family houses, there had been a 72.8 per cent replacement of the population along North and South Pine Avenues twenty years later. Along Morris Street, between Quail and Ontario, only nine of the fifty houses were occupied by people of the same family name from 1917 to 1936: 18 per cent were still there nineteen years later, but 82 per cent were not. Three-quarters of a mile to the north, on Benson Street, to the west of Quail, 90 per cent of the owner-occupiers had been replaced during this interval. In North Albany, a part of town affectionately called 'Limerick' because of its high proportion of people with Irish names, much the same picture can be seen. On Walter Street, twelve households of the same family name of the ninety-seven listed in 1936 had been there twenty years earlier: 88 per cent of the residents had been replaced. Eighty-six per cent of the residents of Lawn Avenue had come and gone. Along Bonheim Street, between Broadway and North Pearl (the houses to the west of North Pearl had not yet been built in 1917) only one of the thirty-four houses was still occupied by a household of the same family name twenty years later: a 97 per cent rate of turnover. These years included the upheavals of the First World War and the Great Depression, but they also included the boom years of the middle and late 1920s which provoked a great deal of speculative house-building, creating large numbers of new, empty houses for socially mobile people to move into. Even in less momentous decades, sampling the same streets in North Albany at succeeding twenty-year intervals confirms continued high rates of movement. Over the eighty years from 1917 to 1997, three-quarters of the population of the neighbourhood, on average, was replaced every twenty years; that is, in less than one full generation.

Everywhere one looks in Albany, people were on the move. They rarely stayed put in the same place for more than a generation. They moved into a neighbourhood to be near a desirable school for their children and perhaps the wife's mother or sisters for mutual aid when the children were young, and then moved out of the neighbourhood when most of the the children had grown up or had gone on to high school or college. Or, since distinctive Irish names frequently disappear altogether from the Albany street directories and census lists, we can infer that people were constantly moving on to other parts of New York State and the country beyond. Some neighbourhoods had, for longer or shorter periods, an association with the Irish, or Germans, or Russian Jews, French Canadians, Italians, Poles, or Lithuanians, and there was a variety of successional patterns as immigrant arrivals waxed and waned, and people moved up the social scales and into better-quality housing in other parts of the city, and as the immigrants' children married and made their own ways in the world. The Lithuanians, numbering about 400 families who arrived in Albany between 1905 and 1910, had only just managed to build a church, St George's in Arbor Hill, in which they could hold services when their names began to decline sharply along Livingston Avenue and the surrounding streets, to be replaced by Polish names. St George's church was only partially completed, and never finished as the architect intended.

Historians of nineteenth-century Albany have remarked that although Irish immigrants were more numerous in some wards than others, the first-generation Irish were widely dispersed throughout the city and were never restricted to certain neighbourhoods to the extent that the Germans, Italians, and Poles were. The limitations of social communication which constrained non-English speakers in their initial interactions with an English-speaking milieu were absent among the Irish. Non-English speakers coalesced in space for sound, practical reasons of linguistic convenience at least as much as for any 'natural' wish to stick together. If immigrants did not know English, it was to their advantage, at least at first, to live near other people who had the same problem, increasing the prospects of being able to cope with the business of daily life through the medium of their native language. The Irish, in contrast, were not limited in this way.

North Albany, made famous by William Kennedy's books, is locally regarded nowadays as the pre-eminent Irish neighbourhood. Yet, people with Irish surnames were constantly moving into and out of the neighbourhood and never constituted, even at a peak in the early 1950s, much more than 40 per cent of the population, at first sharing the same streets with people of English and German backgrounds, later with Italians, and now with people of African ancestry. Despite the neighbourhood's continued association with the Irish, its nickname 'Limerick, USA', and having its own St Patrick's Day parade, just over a quarter of its residents were of single-ancestry or mixed Irish descent in 1980, only marginally above the average for the city as a whole. By contrast, the more prosperous southern and western residential districts of Whitehall, Crestwood, Karlsfeld, Pine Hills, and the West End had proportions of people of Irish descent that were up to 50 per cent greater.[3] Limerick's Catholic parochial school closed in 1981, and few families of Irish ancestry with school-aged children remain in the neighbourhood. Most of its former residents of Irish descent, or their children and grandchildren, moved up the social scale to the middle-class, lace-curtain suburbs in the 1960s and 1970s, or earlier. Most of those of Irish descent who are left in Limerick are ageing, and are not being replaced by younger generations as they were at the zenith of the neighbourhood's Irishness in the 1930s, 1940s, and 1950s.

---

[3] US Census, Neighborhood Statistics Program, 1980.

II

The social organization of the city was, then, not based upon a set of urban villages characterized by lateral social linkages reproduced over the generations. There were, most certainly, neighbourhoods where people of the same European origins predominated but they tended, on the whole, not to last for more than a generation or two. As soon as the immigrant newcomers, or their children, had learned the language and American ways, they began to climb the social and economic ladder out of the areas where they had first settled. One by one, they moved out of the new-immigrant tenements to rented houses in blue-collar neighbourhoods, then to owner-occupied family houses in better districts, and ultimately to the western suburbs or new developments beyond the city limits. As each family climbed a rung up the ladder, geographically and socially, another family moved up from the next rung down. There were, of course, concentrations of people of certain European ancestries here and there in the city at various times. But overall the most striking feature of the city's demography was movement and fluidity, the relative absence of organic, structural boundaries between Albany's neighbourhoods and social classes which made it possible for immigrant families to climb the ladder of achievement, respectability, and assimilation, and the constantly shifting, kaleidoscopic patterns of the city's social composition.

Coherence and stability was created by Albany's political parties and churches. The city's segmentation by ward and parish were the building blocks of its social organization. The association between the Irish and ward-level politics was already becoming well established by the 1840s, as Albany's political parties sought to capture the voting power of the new immigrants pouring into the city. As native English speakers, and themselves new immigrants who were as close to the people as it was possible to get, the Irish were immediately recruited as party workers in the immigrant neighbourhoods. The ward leaders, the party representatives responsible for recruiting voters at the local level, made sure the new arrivals registered for naturalization, cultivated their loyalty to the party, and turned out the vote on election days. It is said that they handed out cash loans, delivered free coal and Christmas turkeys to people whose votes the party wanted to secure, and set themselves up as brokers between the various city departments controlled by the party and the people in the wards. If a resident wanted to appeal against a property tax assessment, or find out how to get a job as a janitor, clerk, nurse, or policeman, the ward leader offered to mediate. People were discouraged from making direct approaches to the city authorities, and told to see their ward leader, thus having to ask the party for a favour and being put under an obligation to it. The system relied on patronage, brokerage, and clientage. Machine politics was conspicuously successful in Albany, as it was in many other nineteenth-century American cities with large immigrant populations, for many of the same reasons. Having just arrived in America, sometimes with only a limited command of the language, with little knowledge of the workings of the labour market, or not much understanding of competing American political philosophies, new immigrants were more likely to be persuaded to exchange their votes for the promise of immediate, concrete rewards than for abstract ideals. Jobs in city government like the police and city engineer's department, relative to kinds of unskilled, seasonal, or unstable industrial jobs normally available to immigrants were, if not well paid, at least steady and secure, and, most importantly, might carry pensions and be used to obtain a mortgage to buy a house. Whatever party could be seen to deliver such rewards in the greatest numbers secured the loyalty of the new voters and their families.

Since they were English-speakers (or bilingual in English and Irish), the Irish-born had an advantage that amounted to a full generation's accommodation to an English-speaking economic and political system compared with other, non-English-speaking immigrants who arrived in Albany at about the same time. The Irish early established a dominance in the lower levels of party organization, elected office, and municipal employment, and they soon moved into higher-level positions in city hall. For example, by 1854, at least five of the twenty elected members of the city's Common Council had Irish names; the others had English and Dutch names; notably, there were no German names. By the late 1880s, the Irish had moved up in the ranks of municipal government to include the president of the Common Council and such prized political appointments as its chief clerk, the deputy city engineer and surveyor, two of the four excise commissioners, the inspector of weights and measures, all three police court judges, all three Board of Health inspectors, three of the ten fire captains, three of the five captains of police, five of the twelve police sergeants, four of the five detectives, and three of the four police court officers. Those names which were not Irish were mainly English, and there were still only a few German names, even though German immigrants in Albany were now very numerous. Once established in municipal politics and employment, the Irish predominance was further entrenched and perpetuated through party patronage and nepotism, which continued undisturbed under successive Democratic and Republican administrations. By the late 1920s, in the early days of the reign of the O'Connell Democratic Party organization, German names had begun to appear alongside a diminishing number of English and Dutch names in the list of city officers, but a majority of the names, at all levels, were distinctively Irish.

The machine was run by Daniel P. O'Connell, the party chairman, who never held elected office but engineered continued control of city hall and the government of Albany County for more than forty years; in that time, virtually every candidate backed by the party was voted into office. One of his chief allies, Erastus Corning II, of the old Anglo–Dutch mercantile aristocracy and a man of considerable charisma in his own right, remained mayor of Albany for forty-two years, the longest mayoral term of office in American history. Between them, these two men controlled politics in Albany from 1921 to 1983. Our informants mentioned that relatives had secured jobs at city or county level, or said they knew of people who had got jobs or had obtained contracts to supply goods and services through the influence of the party. Stories of the Democrats dispensing coal and food parcels at Christmas have become part of popular folklore in Albany and are often repeated. So are tales of corruption, including kickbacks, bribery, insider dealings, crooked bidding practices, the stuffing of ballot boxes, and other forms of venality, fraud, and electoral trickery which rewarded the party's clients and those who played by its rules. Certainly, indictments and convictions of public officials, or reprimands by state and federal investigative agencies, have been extraordinarily frequent in Albany politics.[4]

For every well-paid city or county officer whose name appeared in the official directories, and the highly visible, uniformed members of the police, sheriff's, and fire departments, there were scores, perhaps hundreds, of others in municipal employment whose positions might be owed, wholly or in part, to party patronage, among them lawyers, accountants, engineers, teachers, nurses, clerks, secretaries, chauffeurs, elevator operators, boilermen, labourers, gravediggers, cooks, cleaners, and caretakers. The budget estimates for the city included suspiciously large numbers of people on the municipal payroll. Low-level, poorly paid jobs were especially numerous, and are said to have been used by the party as a form of welfare. Having a large number of people on the payroll at

[4] Frank Robinson, *Albany's O'Connell Machine: An American Political Relic* (Albany, NY, 1973), *passim*.

meagre salaries could guarantee the loyalty of more people, and the votes of their families, than a smaller number at higher wages. If the salaries were low, formal selection procedures were often non-existent, job descriptions were vague, and supervision was lax, making it easy for city employees to hold another full-time job at the same time, thus provoking constant complaints by the state investigative commissions responsible for ensuring probity in local government affairs. For decades, Albany's newspapers ran regular stories critical of the party's persistence in providing an excessive number of jobs for the politically faithful. Even during the 1970s, the state Civil Service Commission continued to despair of the city's flagrant disregard of civil service employment procedures, which it held to be the worst in New York State.[5]

The party did not depend entirely upon dispensing jobs, contracts, and gifts to sustain its base; it maintained a hold over voters in other ways. People came to think that any dealing with a city department involved an element of favouritism, a belief encouraged by the party. A strong theme of our interviews was that it was generally felt to be a useful hedge to be a registered Democrat, and to be seen to vote a straight party ticket in local elections. The belief that property taxes were assessed according to party affiliation was widespread, and we encountered a number of cases in which people who had moved into a new neighbourhood were sent inflated property tax assessments; the expectation was that they would go to their ward leaders to ask to have them reduced. The party normally dispensed such favours. This way of creating a relationship of clientage was not very subtle, and new residents of Albany's wards were left in no doubt about the party and its local representatives to whom they owed an obligation. It was also alleged that if one's name did not appear on the party's registration list, a request for snow clearing or an extra rubbish collection might be inadvertently misplaced, or a building inspection might prove unexpectedly troublesome.

The belief that the Democrats are powerfully entrenched in local government, and that it is wise to be seen to be a Democrat, is still strong in Albany. Of the people whom we surveyed, 84 per cent said that they would normally vote for the Democratic Party in local elections. When asked whether they felt it important which party they were registered with, 60 per cent said that it was, and another 31 per cent stated that they thought it had been important in the past, but not any more. Thus over 90 per cent of our sample felt that the way one was registered as a voter

---

[5] Robinson, *Albany's O'Connell Machine*, 169–71.

was, or had been, important, and a solid majority thought that it still mattered. More than half were able to name their ward leader, who is a member of the Albany County Democratic Committee, and is not an elected public office-holder. Nearly a third of our informants said that they had at one time or another approached their ward leader for help. In most of these cases, it was to find a job for themselves or a relative with a municipal agency or a private contractor of goods or services to the city or county, or to seek a reduction in their property tax assessment. There is enough evidence of these practices in our informants' accounts to lend credence to the belief that the machine was in a position to dispense or withhold such favours on a significant scale throughout the 1960s and 1970s, and that people still, on occasion, sought favours from the party through their ward leaders into the 1980s and 1990s.

For most of the twentieth century, the Democratic Party has dominated the city's affairs, and the large number and prominence of the Irish names associated with it has contributed to the widespread, popular perception that people with an Irish name, or whose Irish ancestry is publicly expressed in some other way, are generally assumed to be Democrats. This stereotype has not always held in Albany. The Republican Party controlled the city from 1899 to 1921: it too relied on Irish votes, and Irish names in the list of city officers were just as numerous as under earlier Democratic administrations. Nor does the Irish-Democrat stereotype necessarily apply beyond the city limits, where the Republican Party, led by people with Irish names and supported by the votes of people of Irish ancestry, has held power in adjacent municipalities. In other eastern-seaboard cities with large populations of Irish immigrants and their descendants, Republican rule prospered for long periods. In Albany, although 84 per cent of our informants said they voted Democrat in local elections, substantially fewer voted for the Democrats on a national level. In the last four presidential elections, nearly a third consistently voted for the Republican candidate. About 25 per cent of our sample were registered locally as Democrats, but did not support the party in national elections.

The immortal sociologist Max Weber observed, at the turn of the century, that people who seek to be accepted in small-town America have a marked propensity to affiliate to local organizations merely for conventional, tactical reasons. Although Weber was writing about the membership of Baptist sects, his remarks can be applied equally to political parties or social clubs and fraternities, like the Masons, Shriners, Knights of Columbus, or the Ancient Order of Hibernians. People join in order to legitimate themselves in personal and social life; to gain an *entrée* into local society, forge bonds with potential allies, clients, and patrons, and obtain the advantage of being like everyone else (or at least those who matter); or to avoid being left out of favour and the social embarrassment of having continually to cope with and justify one's status as an outsider, perhaps at some real cost to one's business dealings and the welfare of one's family.[6] There is nothing inherently Irish about the policies and practices of the Democratic Party. Its Irishness is not mystical but sociological, and can be sufficiently explained by Max Weber's observation, together with a little history. In Albany, 'Irish' and 'Democrat' remain firmly tied together in the popular imagination, and people behave in a way that suggests, as Weber would have predicted, that it still pays to be seen, by one's neighbours and those in positions of parochial political power, to be a Democrat.

Albany was a strictly Democratic town. We voted Democrat. That had everything to do with who you were. Most of the people in Albany [who] were Irish would ascribe to that. They thought that they had a champion in the Irish Democratic party, and in a way of speaking they did with Mr O'Connell. He took care of his own and the people repaid him. They're still doing it. And it was something you lived by.

(Informant 152)

During the Depression years, I had many friends whose fathers and mothers did not have jobs and [were] on the dole. They would not admit to this day that Dan O'Connell saw to it every Thanksgiving, every Christmas, and every New Year that those trucks came round to all those people in the South End with baskets of food. They got turkeys, they got potatoes and vegetables, they had complete dinners. And when the winter came they had coal in their cellars for their furnace.

(Informant 236)

In return, they expected people to vote for them, and the people did. When my uncle died, [he] left my aunt [with] four kids, the youngest one 2 years old. The Democrats got her a job and that's how they were able to keep the family together.

(Informant 79)

---

[6] M. Weber, *From Max Weber: Essays in Sociology*, H. H. Gerth and C. Wright Mills (eds.), (London, 1948), 308 f.

My grandfather had a personal [dispute] with Dan O'Connell about garbage pick-up, or something like that. [They] had words. After that, the city raised the tax assessment on my grandfather's house. The intention was that if you wanted to set things right, you [would] have to go through your ward leader, apologize, and things would be sorted out.

(Informant 72)

My father was employed in what the Democratic machine gave him to do. He was a ward leader. He worked for the Parks Department. That was a purely patronage position. He would pay the guys who were given jobs by the machine to clean up the parks and streets. In return, the machine would pay him. That's the way the old guard took care of things. Everybody was on the payroll. If you were a loyal Democrat, you always had a job of some kind, be it raking leaves or mowing the grass.

(Informant 18)

In order to [be a teacher] in Albany, you had to be a Democrat, and you also had to be known. The only reason I got a job was because my father had just died, and he [had been involved in Democratic politics], and they kind of felt sorry for me.

(Informant 162)

When I was young, we went to the party [headquarters] so I could get a job at the Post Office at Christmastime. My father went to [our] ward leader.

(Informant 79)

When my two oldest children were looking for summer jobs one time, my father called up [the ward leader], [who] said, 'Yes, send the kids up', and the next day they had a job.

(Informant 44)

Our informants thought that Irishness is much less important now, and that today's politicians just happened to have Irish names rather than being 'Irish' politicians in the style of the O'Connell machine. Given the social composition of the city, there was every likelihood that Irish names would be common in any sphere of life. Yet most people saw the O'Connell organization as more than this: as an Irish hegemony:

Albany was run by O'Connell. They were all Irish.

(Informant 231)

[It was] like a Mafia, but it was run by Irish-Catholic-Democrats, and that's the way it was for years and years.

(Informant 44)

The O'Connell machine, you know, thrived for years. The interesting thing about Albany was [that] at one time [it was] 90 per cent
Irish Catholic.

(Informant 618)

I remember in senior year in high school having a conversation with
a guy who said that he was going to be a Republican poll-watcher in
the City of Albany, and I remember thinking that this was the first
Republican that I ever knew. Nobody was ever a Republican, you
know. It was kind of like being gay. When I was growing up [we]
were Irish-Catholic-Democrats.

(Informant 85)

When I went down to register for the first time I voted, I came back
[home] and my father said, 'How did you register? You registered
Democrat, didn't you? What do you mean, "I suppose so." Are you
telling me you didn't register as a Democrat? Do you want our taxes
to go up?' [I said,] 'Christ! Yes, yes, I registered Democrat, yes I
did!' Honest to God, you don't do that in Albany, or you didn't,
anyway. You vote any way you want, but you [had] better register
Democrat.

(Informant 242)

Q: Is there any tradition in your family as to the way you would vote?
A: Yeah. Democrat.
Q: Would you associate that with your Irish background?
A: Absolutely. That's Albany.

(Informant 215)

In William Kennedy's novels about Albany, stories about the Irish
ward bosses of the North Albany or South End neighbourhoods, who
stood on street corners on election days openly handing out five-dollar
bills to anyone who would vote for the party candidate, are not, many
people say, greatly exaggerated. The rise of the Irish to prominence
within the political arena was often explained by our informants in terms
of their beliefs that the Irish had an inborn flair for rhetoric ('the blar-
ney'), they were good at organizing people, and they had a natural apti-
tude for horse-trading, backroom dealings, and political shenanigans. But
above all, they were good at looking after themselves.

The Irish were not welcomed in every respect when they came here
and they had to organize and assert their rights, so if they didn't
come here with the skills they developed them. It worked very

successfully. In Albany it gave them a slice of power and they are not
about to give it up.

(Informant 150)

The connection between ancestry and party allegiance is not as important to the current generation of voters. Few of our informants said that
they would be influenced by the ancestral background of a politician.
Almost without exception, they said that it was the character of the
candidates and their policies which determined voting preference rather
than whether they happened to be Irish or German or of any other ancestry. Yet Irish names are still prominent in Albany politics, and the
Democratic Party continues to be firmly entrenched in Albany politics.

Well, in Albany I would say the majority of politicians are all of Irish
descent. I mean you look at the guys running today, the Democratic
committeemen. It's still considered by people outside the area as an
Irish town.

(Informant 155)

To this day, you would have to say that the people with power are
Irish Catholic. Now a lot of the Irish-Catholic-Democrats belong to
the Fort Orange Club as well. There was a time when they did not;
[this was] especially true when Corning was in power—there was an
accord reached between the WASP elements in the city, but only
with certain ones.

(Informant 72)

Q: Would the ancestral background of a candidate influence the way
 you would vote?
A: I wouldn't vote for someone just because they were Irish, if that's
 what you are getting at. But if there were two people in a primary
 and one was Irish and the other was, say, Italian, and with all else
 being equal, I would probably choose the Irish one.
Q: Would you vote for a Democrat just because he or she was a Democrat?
A: I think I've been doing that all my life!

(Informant 79)

Q: Would you associate voting Democrat with your Irish background?
A: I think years ago that was true. Not any more.

(Informant 55)

You recognize that [they are Irish, of course], but they are all politicians first. Years ago they weren't but they are now.

(Informant 231)

I don't think there is an Irish component in Albany politics any more.
They are all out for themselves.

(Informant 172)

I mean, if it wasn't a Democrat you were voting for in those days you
could lose your house and everything else. I think now that has eased
off a lot. [But] you [still] have to be a Democrat if you own your own
home.

(Informant 149)

You have to be [a Democrat] if you are smart. It is not as
outrageously strong as it was during the O'Connell regime. Fifty
years ago you voted the party line [with] no thought to it. Now I
think the voting population gives it more thought. But if you are
smart you still register as a Democrat just for taxes and things like
that.

(Informant 139)

It is to your benefit to register Democrat for your own peace of
mind, not that they are going to deliberately raise your taxes [any
longer, but] I am sure that [favouritism] still exists in certain ways. It
certainly doesn't hurt to be registered Democrat.

(Informant 242)

There are no longer charismatic leaders in the style of O'Connell and
Corning, but the Republicans have made few electoral inroads against
Democratic dominance. Politics, in Albany, is not a matter of competition between the Democrats and the Republicans, but a matter of
factionalism within the Democratic Party. Since Corning's death in
1983, rival groups within the party have struggled for control. Our informants were divided on the issue of how, and at what point, city politics
changed, if indeed they believed that politics had changed at all in the
last seventy years. A very large number mentioned 'the machine' when
discussing local politics, and they pointed to a number of things which
suggested, to them, that the city is still run by a machine. Yet others
interpret recent splits and factions within the party and the rise of independent Democratic challengers to the officially approved candidates as
being a sign that the machine, if not dead, is at least in decline. With the
demise of machine politics in other cities like New York, Philadelphia,
Boston, and Chicago, the term 'machine' itself has now become pejorative. Not surprisingly, the Democratic Party in Albany is anxious to
distance itself from the past and to present a new image of itself to the
electorate.

Today, I plan to run a real open and honest organization, and I use the word organization, not machine.[7]

(Leo O'Brien, chairman of the Albany County Democratic Party)

Obviously the machine is gone and that type of politics does not seem to work any more.

(Informant 326)

Albany has changed. I mean we had the bosses ruling Albany for decades, and now that has broken down a lot. Some new people are coming in, but there are still a few of the old guard in evidence yet.

(Informant 161)

[The new politicians] are smarter, not the crude, uneducated ward-dealers that they had years ago. They're better educated, they're okay. [The old crowd] were a pretty seedy bunch.

(Informant 152)

I have noticed a great difference since [Mayor Corning] died. I think politics has changed a lot. I think that things [which] could not have been said out loud are now [being discussed] in the newspapers, and a lot of the changes [have been] for the good. We are Democrats. Being registered Democrats is not as important now as it used to be. They can't really fiddle with your property taxes now, and hold your job over your head.

(Informant 175)

The new mayor, Tom Whalen, is slowly unravelling the machine and bringing Albany into the twentieth century. When we first came here, people were very careful about not offending the wrong people and though there is still an element of that, it is not as pervasive as it was.

(Informant 597)

Well, [the machine is] still there, but it isn't the situation that if you are not an Irish-Catholic-Democrat, or you are not part of that group, you'd be pushed aside. There is an opportunity now where there never would have been years ago.

(Informant 44)

The old-timers are dying out, dwindling. And the baby-boomers don't agree to this straight party vote, and most of them are a lot more educated than their predecessors, and they think about it.

(Informant 55)

[7] Quoted in the *Times-Union*, 26 June 1983.

Politically, things have changed quite a bit, although it is still over-whelmingly a Democratic city. It's opened up a lot with the passing of Dan O'Connell and Erastus Corning. City politics have changed a lot; there is no longer one strong figure. Also a generation have grown up who are less likely to have strong party affiliations. One of the reasons for that is the patronage system. City jobs or county jobs used to be coveted, [but] they are not any more. [The] people who were the backbone of the political machine, as their kids became more educated, they aspired to better jobs. There were no longer the jobs for loyalty-type transactions taking place.

(Informant 72)

The Albany machine no longer serves the instrumental purpose it once did. The historical circumstances which brought the Irish to Albany in such large numbers in the mid-nineteenth century, and the fact that they were English-speaking, meant that there was no linguistic barrier to their full participation in local politics and they had very few effective competitors at a time of enormous expansion in the municipal establish-ment. Their numbers made them a force which held the balance of power, and their votes could be harnessed immediately. They were recruited into the lower levels of a clientelistic system which rewarded their loyalty with public-sector jobs. Language, numbers, and the timing of their arrival made all the difference. The Germans, and later Russian Jews, Poles, and Italians, initially lacking fluency in English, were in the first generation restricted to forms of employment which did not involve communicating with the English-speaking public: for the Germans, this meant that their initial attachment in Albany society was mainly through German-speak-ing networks in the German neighbourhoods, which for linguistic reasons tended to be much more concentrated in Albany than Irish neighbour-hoods; for the Italians, local *padrones* exploited the labour of newcomers just as effectively as they did in other American cities. By the time the German immigrants, or their children, had become sufficiently fluent in English to participate fully in the labour market and the political process, or by the time later waves of immigrants from Italy and Poland arrived in Albany and had likewise accommodated themselves to the language and the American way of doing things, the Irish had long since monopolized party organization and public-sector employment.

Stephen Erie, writing of Irish-American urban machine politics, says that the Irish political machines of New York, Chicago, Philadelphia, and San Francisco ultimately did not do the Irish any favours. By recruiting the Irish into blue-collar municipal jobs in great numbers to secure their votes, the effect was to block or delay their upward social mobility into the middle classes.[8] While, for example, the second- and third-generation descendants of Irish immigrants were still content with poorly paid patronage jobs in the police or city engineer's departments, the children and grandchildren of German Jews had gone on to college and moved into the professional middle classes. Albany is different. The scale of the city is smaller, it is less industrial, and its status as capital of the state of New York has meant, since the 1930s, that an extraordinarily large number of people have been employed in public administration. In the middle and upper ranks, most of these jobs have demanded increasingly higher educational and professional qualifications. As the number and skill levels of state and federal jobs have grown in step with the increasing complexity of governmental functions and responsibilities, the descendants of Albany's Irish immigrants have been carried along in its mainstream. They are now highly trained specialists who have university degrees in such fields as economics, computer science, pharmacy, education, law, accounting, social welfare administration, criminology, and civil engineering. They work in air-conditioned offices and live in tree-lined suburban avenues. They have not been hindered or disadvantaged by the legacy of the O'Connell machine. On the contrary, they have become as much a part of the American Dream as anyone.

III

If the electoral ward was one of the building blocks of Albany's social organization, the other was the church parish. Until the Great Famine brought large numbers of Roman Catholics to Albany, the city's churches had been predominantly Anglican, Dutch Reformed, and Presbyterian, although there had been a gradual growth in the number of Catholic churches and institutions since the 1820s. With the arrival of thousands of Famine immigrants, the Catholic church was enormously strengthened and ramified. From 1854 to 1889, the city's population grew from 55,000 to 90,000, and the total number of its churches increased in close proportion, from forty-eight to seventy-one. The number of Catholic churches, however, rose at three times the average rate. By 1928, there were exactly as many Catholic parishes as electoral wards in Albany: nineteen. While ward and parish boundaries did not always correspond

---

[8] Stephen Erie, *Rainbow's End: Irish-Americans and the Dilemmas of Urban Machine Politics*, 1840–1985 (Berkeley, 1988), 5–9.

closely, and the aims and methods of church and party differed, there is much to suggest that they pursued parallel strategies in harnessing the loyalty of the immigrants and the human and economic capital that they represented.

Those refugees from the Great Famine in Ireland who arrived in Albany having suffered the deaths of loved ones, or who were orphaned, or who were ill or indigent, owed much to the comfort and practical help the church gave them. Later arrivals from Ireland found a highly elaborated system of Catholic institutions covering a wide range of human needs. Once recruited into the faith through birth or conversion, and once enrolled as a member of the parish, the church provided a network of social welfare services and means of economic advancement to its parishioners. These were important resources before the development of state and federally funded educational, health, pensions, and social welfare programmes, and the tithes people were called upon to pay to the church were a form of all-purpose social insurance. Looked at in purely instrumental terms, in return for their collection-plate contributions, the church provided its adherents with security in an uncertain world. This security went far beyond the moral and spiritual realm to deliver a cradle-to-grave array of benefits to new immigrants and their families in a way that was analogous and complementary to the practical benefits dispensed by the party in return for the immigrants' votes. If Albany's Democratic Party was a machine—a mode of organization designed to garner and maintain the loyalty of the immigrants and their descendants—so too, in many ways, was its Catholic diocese. And, if the party prospered because it succeeded in doing this, so too did the church.

Just as parties compete for votes, churches compete for adherents. European commentators have frequently remarked upon how wide-open the market for parishioners was, and is, in North America, compared with Europe. Max Weber, in 1904, noted that Americans seemed singularly free of concern about their antecedents' confessionals, and had a marked propensity to join churches and sects for reasons of social instrumentality. The United States has a secular constitution that privileges no church; censuses do not ask about one's religion, nor is one's confessional recorded on any governmental document. It is not impossible to imagine that many of those who went west, where there were few churches for them to attend, ceased to be Catholics within a generation. Over the generations, millions more married out of the Catholic Church, bringing up their children as non-Catholics. Elsewhere in the country, still millions more quietly dropped their Catholicism in the years up to John F.

Kennedy's inauguration in 1960, if their confessional proved to be an impediment to their social acceptance and professional careers. Nowadays, 55 per cent of those of Irish ancestral origin in America are not Catholics, despite the fact that about 75 per cent of the population of Ireland is, and has historically been, Catholic. Explanations for this phenomenon have commonly cited the earlier arrival of Irish Protestants and the effects of this on the number of ensuing generations, and hence the number of non-Catholic individuals, in the population.[9] Since, however, the religious affiliation of individuals has never been recorded by the US Census, this interpretation must remain speculative, and it is equally plausible that greater numbers of Irish men and women and their descendants have ceased to be Catholics than has heretofore been thought.

The ground laid by John McCloskey, Bishop of the Diocese of Albany from 1847 to 1864, created fertile conditions for the efflorescence of Catholic institutions. Together with the very large numbers of Irish Catholics who settled in Albany, some of them *because* of its Catholicity, by 1875 the Roman confessional claimed the loyalty of at least half of the city's residents. The other half was divided among eight Baptist, eight Anglican, ten Lutheran, eleven Presbyterian, six Dutch Reformed, six Methodist, and two Jewish congregations, and one each of Unitarians, Quakers, Christian Scientists, and Congregationalists. Roman Catholicism was far and away the single most common denomination, and there were fewer reasons for people to renounce their Catholicism for reasons of social instrumentality than in places where they were in a small minority. Indeed, in Albany, there are suggestions in our informants' family histories that the reverse was the case: that in mixed marriages, it was much more common that the non-Catholic partner converted to Catholicism, or agreed that the children should be brought up as Catholics, than otherwise. Where our informants did not know the confessional of an ancestor, or had no particular reason to be certain, their first response was that the ancestor must have been Catholic, even where the ancestor's name was English or German, because that is what our informants considered to be 'normal' in Albany.

By the 1930s, the church had organized an all-encompassing network

---

[9] Andrew Greeley, 'The Success and Assimilation of Irish Protestants and Irish Catholics in the United States', *Sociology and Social Research*, 72 (1988); Michael Hout and Joshua Goldstein, 'How 4.5 Million Irish Immigrants became 40 Million Irish Americans: Demographic and Subjective Aspects of the Ethnic Composition of White Americans', *American Sociological Review*, 59 (1994).

of institutions, and in the process had itself grown into a large and highly bureaucratized organization. Catholic children were brought into the world at St Peter's Hospital or the Maternity Hospital and Infants' Home. Orphans were looked after in the St Vincent's asylums, one for boys and one for girls; children were provided with a primary education in any of twenty parish schools by the Sisters of the Holy Names, the Sisters of Mercy, the Christian Brothers, the Sisters of Notre Dame, the Sisters of St Francis, the Sisters of St Joseph, and the Sisters of Charity; there was a Catholic Children's Vacation Villa, and for more difficult children, St Ann's School of Industry and Reformatory of the Good Shepherd. There were seven high schools: Sacred Heart, Christian Brothers', Cathedral Academy, St Joseph's, the Academy of the Holy Names, St Ann's, and the Vincentian Institute; and one university-level institution for women, the College of St Rose. On Sundays, boys and girls attended the Young Ladies' or Young Men's Sodalities in their parishes, while their parents attended meetings of the Society for St Vincent de Paul, the Rosary Society (women), and the Holy Names Society (men). Other Catholic societies included the Ancient Order of Hibernians (the old-country association, which required that members be practising Catholics), the Catholic Benevolent Legion, the Ladies' Catholic Benevolent Association, the Catholic Relief and Beneficiary Association, and the Knights of Columbus (a men's fraternal lodge and service club). There was an Albany Catholic Press Association, and an organization called the Catholic Charities of Albany, both run by Bishop Gibbons; a Catholic Association for Young Women; the Catholic Daughters of America; the Catholic Union of the City of Albany; and a Catholic Women's Service League. There were five convents in the city, some of which provided housing and nursing care for the old and sick. And, at the end of their lives, Catholics were laid to rest in St Agnes Cemetery.

It was possible, and for many Catholics likely, that their social and spiritual welfare throughout their lives would be provided for entirely within this enveloping network of institutions. The church dispensed moral teachings and practical help in virtually every sphere of social life, thereby cementing its parishioners' loyalty to the church and ensuring that they stayed within the fold. When, in the late nineteenth century, a fashion for social clubs and fraternal associations flourished, and it was *de rigeur* to belong to such associations, the church created its own parallel set of sodalities and sororities, removing the temptation for Catholic men to join the Masons, Elks, or Odd Fellows; or for women to join temperance associations, the Red Cross, or mothers' unions; young people were encouraged to participate in the Catholic equivalents of the YMCA and YWCA. Notably, however, the church was not successful in organizing parallel labour organizations. Catholic workers were active in local trades unions, craft guilds, and professional benevolent associations, including the police, firemen, printers, boilermen, railway engineers and craftsmen, bricklayers, cigarmakers, saloonkeepers, freight handlers, shirtcutters and garment makers, foundry workers, teamsters, and many others. Men with Irish names dominated the leadership of the Central Federation of Labor in Albany; and their prominent membership in the Ancient Order of United Workmen, with its Masonic-like ritual, was frowned upon by the Catholic hierarchy.[10] None the less, the church succeeded in capturing and maintaining the loyalty of most Catholics in Albany. This required a large, complex, and expensive apparatus with dozens of buildings and hundreds of functionaries. Such an apparatus could be supported only by voluntary contributions. Like a party machine, it could entice support with the promise of practical returns. Unlike a political party, the church could, in addition, offer the rewards of spiritual solace and heavenly grace. Or, when the occasion demanded, it could threaten recalcitrant adherents with eternal torment.

Of our non-random sample of 252 people from whom we collected statistical information about their degree of perceived Irishness, 86.5 per cent stated that they were of single-ancestry or mixed Irish descent (the remainder were mostly spouses of non-Irish ancestry); 87.2 per cent gave their religious denomination as Roman Catholic; 65 per cent had attended a Catholic primary school, and 57 per cent had been to a Catholic secondary school. Seventy-five per cent were married to Catholics. The majority of those in this sample were not born or schooled in Albany, but had moved to the city following marriage or for employment reasons.

To see whether there were any significant differences between those raised within the particular Catholic institutional milieu of Albany, as compared with other places, we controlled the sample for those identifying as Irish, omitting those not of Irish or mixed-Irish descent, and excluding all those who were not born and raised in Albany and did not attend Albany schools. There were seventy-four cases, and an even stronger set of trends does indeed emerge. All but two of our informants (97.3 per cent) said their religion was Roman Catholic; the two exceptions described their ancestry as, in one case, 'German-Scotch-Irish' and her

---

[10] Kendall Birr, 'The American Religious Experience', in A. Roberts and M. Cockrell (eds.), *Historic Albany: Its Churches and Synagogues* (Albany, NY, 1986), 43.

denomination as Methodist, in the other as 'Irish–German–English' and her confessional as Dutch Reformed. Fully 85 per cent of these Albany-schooled informants had attended a parochial school, a proportion that is more than 30 per cent greater than the sample as a whole. Eighty-five per cent also attended Catholic secondary school, proportionately nearly 50 per cent more than the sample as a whole. And, 93.8 per cent of our informants were married to Catholics, a figure which includes two cases in which a non-Catholic spouse had converted to Catholicism. There were only two cases of mixed marriages in which the spouse did not convert, a rate of 2.7 per cent.

A larger and more statistically sophisticated sample would probably give many of the same indications. It is objectively the case, for those born and brought up in Albany and identifying themselves as of Irish descent, that the likelihood that they are also Catholics is extraordinarily high. Being of Irish ancestry and being Catholic could hardly be more strongly associated. The Irish-Catholic stereotype, although it has become part of local folklore, is founded upon solid evidence. There is evidence, also, of the influence of Albany's Catholic institutions on the choices parents made about the schooling of their children during the 1960s and 1970s (when the youngest age cohort of our informants were schooled). These figures further testify to the effectiveness of this form of socialization in keeping Catholics within the fold: of those Albany-school respondents who went on to college, 50 per cent chose a Catholic institution despite a plethora of public and non-denominational universities and colleges in upstate New York; and nearly all those who married chose a Catholic spouse.

There is one other respect in which the data for the Albany-schooled show a significantly stronger trend than the sample as a whole. When asked if they thought that most people with the same ancestry as theirs had the same religion, 88.9 per cent agreed that they were nearly all, or mostly, of the same religion. For the sample as a whole, 76.5 per cent thought this was the case. Again, this demonstrates by another measure that for those born and raised in Albany, there is an extraordinarily strong association between being of Irish ancestry and being Catholic. In all other respects, there was little difference between the Albany-schooled and the sample as a whole. Eighty-five per cent of the Albany-schooled had parents who were both Roman Catholic, about the same as for the whole sample. Our sample captured eleven cases of mixed marriages among the parents of the Albany-schooled; in all of these cases, the informant and his or her siblings were brought up as Catholics, once again bearing out the institutional strength of Catholicism in Albany. Ninety per cent of our Albany-schooled informants said that they had attended Sunday school or religious instruction regularly throughout their childhoods. This early socialization has clearly remained with them later in life: 88.7 per cent of our sample said they were still churchgoers, and of this number 74.8 per cent reported that they attended mass on a daily or weekly basis. Eighty-two per cent thought that the personal importance of their religion had either remained much the same over their lifetimes, or had become more important to them as they had grown older. And, even though a substantial majority (70.7 per cent) thought that the church's teachings on mixed marriages had changed a great deal in the last twenty or thirty years, over half (54.1 per cent) still thought it important that husband and wife should be of the same confessional for the sake of harmony and stability within the family.

In our open-ended interviews, we asked about our informants' experience of religion; how they thought their experience differed from that of their parents' generation, and whether they saw any connection between their religion and ancestry. Revealingly, most of our Catholic informants framed their replies not in terms of their personal faith or belief in God, but in terms of the institutions and practices of their church: having, as children, said the rosary with their families, attended mass, or gone to a parochial school. Catholicism, as an organizational system and as an institutional milieu which ordered people's lives, has had a deep influence on the way our informants perceived their religiosity, as the following extracts from our interviews attest.

> We went to mass every Sunday. During Lent we went to mass every morning. We said the rosary every night when we did the dishes. The religious holidays were always observed. My father always went to mass; it did not matter how hung over he was, he went to mass. Christmas we always celebrated. My brothers were altar boys and I always sang in the choir.
>
> (Informant 215)

> We used to say the rosary. I remember when I was real young, we would go not just to mass but we would go to novenas. In those days they used to have novenas and stuff like that and we would go as a family. During Lent we would take and say the stations.
>
> (Informant 224)

> We always went to mass together. There was a period of time I can remember when we did the family rosary together at home.
>
> (Informant 90)

Well in our home it was definitely the thing to do on a Sunday for the kids to go to church. Not necessarily the parents, but the kids had to go. I was religious in the sense of a consistent churchgoer until I was in my mid-twenties. I don't think that was ever the case with my mother or my father.

(Informant 139)

My mother wanted to be sure we were brought up good Catholics because that is what our religion was. My father never went to mass.

(Informant 18)

My mother was a very religious woman. My father was religious in the sense that he went to church, but you know it's different [now]. Me and my brothers [are] religious in the sense that we go to mass and stuff like that but I think we're in a minority. [People are] not very conscientious about it. And the divorce rate is so high in this country at the minute. This whole block [has] gone mad. There's five or six families, kids and everything, Catholic too, all [getting] divorced.

(Informant 155)

The Church has disappointed me, so I have sort of fallen away. There was a school around the corner that my kids went to, and the priest that ran the parish didn't want to keep the school because it wasn't financially sound. We had always grown up with the idea that you provide your children with a Catholic education because we had it. Our parents had [it too], and that you sacrifice to pay the tuition and send your kids to the Catholic school. Well it is kind of tough to do it if they keep closing them. We tried very hard to keep that place open and we were fighting the pastor, and that is tough, that is a no-win battle, and when [the school closed] we all moved our kids to other schools, and now they are in public high school, and there really isn't any reason for us to [be involved in the parish any more].

(Informant 14)

I loved going to school. I look back more fondly on grade school than I do high school. We were a very close family and I had an aunt [who] was a nun and taught at grade school, so we were very, very involved in the parish, and we still are.

(Informant 238)

My parents' generation attended church more frequently. More than once a week. They prayed more often I think than our generation does. They fasted on Friday and no meat and all that stuff, they abided by that. Even the attire. Women had to wear hats or mantillas and dresses to church, you know. I don't know if it was a decree, but this is how they did it back then. I don't know if you ever attend church [in Albany]. Some of these people look like they're going to go rake the lawn or something, or clean the garage, the way they turn up at church. I think it's terrible, but that is just a reflection as to what they're all about. You know, I don't wear a shirt and tie to church. A pair of jeans and probably what you've got on, on certain occasions. But yes, it was tougher for [my parents' generation]. More strict. And I think they believed more fervently than this generation.

(Informant 55)

Religion was very important [to] my mother. My father went to church because he had to go to church. He would go and stand at the back of the church and if he could talk to the old men outside he would be perfectly happy with that. I remember in school we had to say the rosaries with our families. I said to my father 'Daddy, you have to say the rosary with me' and he said, 'Will you leave me alone?' So I went to school and the teacher asked who didn't say the rosary and I stuck my hand up and she said 'Why didn't you?' and I told her what he said and she was shocked. I was taught by nuns in what was really an Irish Catholic grade school. There were other nationalities, there were Italians but I do not remember them. There were Germans, but the German parish was down the street—they went to Our Lady of Angels. I went to Catholic High School. I went to [the] Vincentian Institute.

(Informant 92)

[In my parents' generation] you didn't marry a person because they were decent or hard-working or you loved them. You also had to think of ethnic background and religion. It was a very big factor and my father was more or less ostracized from his family because [my mother] was not Catholic, nor was she Irish and that was a big thing. So my contact with my relatives [on] his side are very, very [poor]. They had little to do with him and kind of pushed him out of the family because of it and he was an extremely stubborn man and if that's the way they wanted it that was fine with him and he would never cross this line. They did not like him marrying someone who was not Irish and not Catholic. Even though she converted it did not make a difference. For a long time [my father] stayed away from the church because of that problem, but I went to church. They always made sure I went to church.

(Informant 44)

I don't think my experience with religion differs from my parents but I think my children's differs because the church started to change and as far as I am concerned they didn't make too many good changes. My parents had their processions in Ireland and I grew up with them and the Holy Days and the Communion and the First Fridays. So [it was] the same for me and my parents. It changed with my own children because [the church] took the processions away and as far as I was concerned as long as the child was in a procession the whole family went to see them and it brought them back into the church. I didn't like the changes from the Vatican. I learned the Latin mass and now the priest who used to stand with his back to us stands facing us. I didn't like what they did with the Holy Communion for a while. They were making the children at 6 receive first Holy Communion. That happened to my eldest daughter, she made her First Communion at 6 years of age and made her penance a year later. [Then] they switched it back.

I loved the processions; [they] gave a child a feeling of belonging for everyone. I don't see anything wrong with adoring Our Lord or Mary, and I loved the Latin and I don't think it should be in English. I think it is important for parents to be of the same faith because it makes it a lot easier on a child. I thoroughly believe that it is important for a child to be brought up in a particular faith. I was brought up to believe that Roman Catholic was *the* religion and all the rest were just following us around, but that's because, you know, it was my faith. I mean, I am a grown woman now and I see where they were coming from. It was pounded into us but how can you get away from your faith?

[My husband's] father did not believe any religion. He believed that as long as you were good and did good, that if there was a heaven up there you would be accepted in. I told him not to say that around my children, until they were old enough to understand. But when they were 5, 6, or 7, I told them they were Catholic and would go to Catholic school and that was it. So you might think it was a sort of a brain-washing technique. But you have your faith; when you are going to die or are very sick, in the end that's all you really have.

(Informant 134)

It's what you grew up with, it's what you will always be. I mean, sometimes I get awfully put out at the church for certain personal reasons but that has nothing to do with the faith. That's what you have.

(Informant 152)

I liked the old way because it seemed right. Priests were priests and nuns were nuns. You had Catholic schools.

(Informant 112)

Q: Would you say that your experience of religion is different from that of your parents' generation?

A: I think they were much stricter. My mother ... raised us very strict. But then, years later, my nephew, that's my sister's boy, married a Jewish girl. Ten years before he got married, [my mother] would never have gone to that wedding. But when he did get married she went and she was right up in the altar with the rabbi.

(Informant 141)

[In] 1961, my first cousin on my father's side (the only girl of two first cousins) married a Protestant in a ceremony performed by her husband's brother. I was told by the chaplain at school, Holy Names, that I could not be [a bridesmaid] in the wedding, and I could not attend. My father was deceased. My mother and I did not attend the wedding. I'm still sorry.

(Informant 67)

A: Our religion was stressed very, very strongly when I was growing up. Over here there is a priest by the name of Father Peyton who started something by the name of the block rosary, where families would gather and we were one of the host families. As a matter of fact my mother bought the statue of the Virgin that went from house to house. I don't know if it is Irish or it was just an old folk story but every time there was a thunderstorm my mother would light the blessed candle to protect the house from lightning and from damage. We would hang our rosaries out on the line to ensure we got good weather and say our novenas to St Ann.

Q: Would you say that your experience of religion differs much from your parents' generation?

A: I think the primary thing that has changed between the generations is not so much religion but the society in which we live. The parish in the 1920s and 1930s was the focal point, the centre of social activity for the family. The Holy Names Society for the men, the Rosary Society for the ladies, the Catholic youth organization for the kids, certain religious instruction, the Catholic school, and mass on Sundays. Because of the flight to the suburbs, the parish is no longer the centre of family life. [People are now involved in baseball,] golf and so on as opposed to the things in the parish. My generation—I am 38—grew up with the [second Vatican] council. I can remember serving mass as an altar boy in Latin, then half in Latin and half in English, and then all in English and nobody knew what the hell was going on. But we just did it because [the pastor] said we had to do it. It is the people in the middle that feel most alienated. They grew up with something that changed on them. They were looking for the security that their parents had and because the world around them was changing so rapidly they looked to the church for that security. The carpet was pulled out from under their feet.

(Informant 458)[11]

[In my family,] we all went to Catholic school. We went to church regularly and said the rosary regularly. It was very important. I can now identify that as being particularly Irish. I went to Catholic school but it was a German Catholic school where they spoke German; it was a German parish, but the faith came from home. The church has changed. For me it was very difficult to go to church because there was just my father and me, and he would [go out drinking on Saturday nights]. But I always got myself together and went to church. There was nobody to tell me to go to church for a lot of reasons, like that I was out late and didn't feel like going. It was so ingrained that I wouldn't miss mass. I found the changes in the sixties with Vatican II much better. I still go to church regularly, but the younger generation just don't attend, even my own kids.

(Informant 79)

Q: Would you associate your Catholic religion with your Irish ancestry?
A: I would associate the Catholic religion with Ireland but also with Germany too, I suppose, since I think my mother's family were Catholic too. My mother is still alive. She is 88 now and she brought us up to be religion-minded. I guess it is a really important part of my life. My father in fact did not go to mass on Sundays and then at Easter he would make a return, and go on Easter Sunday. He worked so hard, he worked six days a week. I was probably the most religious one in my family.

(Informant 240)

---

11 A Catholic parish priest.

Q: Would you associate your religion with your Irish background?
A: I don't, but I think that my parents did. I guess there is a difference between being Irish and being Catholic.
Q: Do you think they go together necessarily?
A: Well around here they do because that is the predominant mix: Irish-Catholic-Democrat. That is just the way that it has always been.

(Informant 14)

Albany's Catholicity makes it an unusual place, and probably less than wholly representative of America's smaller cities with large Irish-ancestry populations. Its Catholicity is largely the consequence of a historical coincidence: the existence of an Irish Catholic middle class since colonial times, and the arrival before the Great Famine of an ambitious young Catholic bishop. A set of Catholic institutions was already developing in Albany when the tide of immigrants from Ireland came. There was never an awkward gap, as there was in other cities, between the Catholic immigrants' arrival and the development of Catholic institutions; a gap in which these immigrants' faith was not institutionally regulated, and where to swim with the tide might mean marrying out, or ceasing to be a Catholic for reasons of social instrumentality.

IV

Church and party, each in its own way, succeeded in capturing the loyalty of the immigrants from Ireland and forging an ethos that transcended the social divisions of the old country. Something genuinely new was being created on American soil. Far from carrying their 'culture' from Ireland and reconstructing and reliving it in Albany, the everyday things that socially divided people in Ireland soon came to have no place in American life. The significance of rural class distinctions between farm servants, cottiers, tenant farmers, yeomen, shopkeepers, and landlords; and of local and interfamilial variation in language, dialect, religion, and piety; and of political differences among the plethora of possible positions on the land question and the Home Rule issue, fell away in the new country to be all but forgotten by the next generation, ultimately to be remembered and historicized only as truncated and essentializing myths. As the new, voluntary association between Irish immigrants and the American Catholic Church and Albany's political parties developed and gathered strength, people began to define themselves in new ways; not by the old loyalties engendered by their former social positions which had provoked most of them to emigrate, but by new, less-constraining ones that were more congenial to their search for better, more fruitful, and freer lives than they had known in Ireland.

A negative consequence of this process is that those Irish immigrants and their descendants who did not quite so readily fit this new definition were faced, as time went on, with the choice of abandoning either their ancestral connection with Ireland, or their confessional. The almost-perfect identity of Irish ancestry and Catholicism that exists today in Albany, and which is the bedrock of the notion of the Irish-Catholic-Democrat, has come at no personal cost to most people, but has been paid for by the historical disenfranchisement of others whose absence from the pages of this book is notable. Irish Anglicans, Methodists, Baptists, and Quakers gave up their faith, or redefined themselves as of English ancestry; Irish Presbyterians preferred to call themselves Scots, or when no Irish Catholics were nearby, Scots-Irish. Given Albany's developing reputation as a Catholic city, perhaps non-Catholic Irish immigrants chose not settle in Albany after the 1860s, or, feeling unwelcome, later moved away.

Paradigm types, ideal models, or generalizations based upon statistical frequencies, when they come to be believed as prototypes of selves or groups, have an unfortunate tendency to become reduced to simple stereotypes defining the qualities people feel must be displayed for any given individual to be accepted as a legitimate member of that group: *all* have to fit the model, not just the plurality in the middle of the statistical curve of frequency whose characteristics originally gave rise to the typification; those at either end of the continuum of normality are eliminated from the stereotype. For example, although the population of Ireland has been for centuries 20 to 25 per cent non-Catholic, some of our informants (who were otherwise blameless people who would be embarrassed to see their words quoted in this context and genuinely distressed to be thought of as bigots or as advocates of ethnic cleansing) questioned whether Protestants, Jews, or, nowadays, Muslims or Buddhists could be Irish, and a not insignificant number expressed the brutally sectarian opinion that there is not now, nor has there ever been, room for non-Catholics in Ireland or in the idea of Irishness. A handful went even further, and said that Ireland will not be truly free of the legacies of its melancholy past and troubled present until non-Catholics 'get out' of Ireland and 'go home'.

This is, emphatically, not to suggest that the majority of our informants held such views. Many were very tolerant and positively ecumenical in their feelings towards non-Catholics; and most people had no views at all on the subject, or refused to be drawn. But a minority *did* express such opinions. If these remarks are in any way indicative of a more wide-spread, if much milder and more muted mistrust of non-Catholics, especially those with claims upon Irish or mixed-Irish ancestry, then this goes a long way towards explaining why, in our sample of Albany-schooled informants of Irish ancestry, all of those who were of religiously mixed parentage were brought up as Catholics, and none was Protestant. Moreover, it helps to account for our finding that only 2.7 per cent of our sample of those born and raised in Albany and identifying themselves as of Irish descent said that they were not Catholic, while across the United States as a whole, between 55 and 61 per cent of those identifying themselves as of Irish ancestry are not Roman Catholic. Wherever one finds a strong definition of 'us', and what is 'normal', as in the cluster of attributes which make up the local stereotype of the Irish-Catholic-Democrat, one finds that others who do not quite fit the definition but do not fall readily into any other recognized category are socially marginalized as aberrant and abnormal. In Albany, to be 'Irish' is to be a Catholic and to be a Democrat. Clearly, most people have believed it to be more sensible to swim with the tide than against it, and have made decisions about their lives, and those of their children, in quite pragmatic ways. Just as most people choose to behave in ways that suggest that it still pays to be seen to be a Democrat, it also pays, if one is of Irish ancestry, to be a Catholic. This is the world that is (or was, until recently) most likely to be inhabited by one's relatives, friends, potential marriage partners, workmates, clients, patrons, and political allies. The shared confessional, perhaps rather more than the voting booth, is a common bond of experience and trust; it is proof of a we-relationship.

In the absence of any enduring ethnic neighbourhoods, and in the presence of constant, restless geographical movement and social and economic mobility within and over the generations, the organizing principle which tied together the Irish immigrants and their descendants and provided a sense of belonging and continuity was created by common adherence to the same church and the same party. People everywhere seem to have an emotional, if not rational, need for social association, of being clued in and being part of things, whatever shape these social and symbolic worlds might take, or whatever might be their content, criteria of association, or price of admission. Their shared origins or ancestral origins in Ireland, along with their membership of a single church and a single party, were the stigmata of belonging to one such world in Albany. In time, these three things came to reinforce and mutually define one another, giving the people who paid the price of admission by having or adopting all three attributes a powerful sense of belonging, and a powerful sense of who they were, even if others unwilling or unable to pay the full price were left, as outsiders, to negotiate their admission into other such worlds.

It would be easy to overemphasize the salience of this sense of belonging and the power of the notion of Irish-Catholic-Democrat to define 'culture' or 'community'. Max Weber reminds us that the existence of common qualities, a common situation, or common modes of behaviour does not imply the existence of communal social relationships.[12] In the pure case, communal social relationships are based mainly upon affective, emotional, or traditional ties (as within a family), and not mainly upon self-interest, rational calculation, instrumentality, or expediency (as in registering as a Democrat in Albany). The notion of Irish-Catholic-Democrat does not define an all-encompassing social or symbolic universe (a 'culture' or an *ethnie*); nor does it define a repository of firm and unchangeable attachments and values from which individuals are obliged to derive their identities *tout court*. Rather, it is but one partial and changeable stock of knowledge among many such partial and changeable stocks of knowledge held by individuals, whose intensity and salience may vary widely from one person to another, and over their lifetimes; in this instance, it is knowledge about the topography of a social landscape, a means of recognizing and classifying others within it: people in some ways like one's self, with whom one might, actually or potentially, have more life experiences and social acquaintanceships in common than with people who are not Irish, Catholics, and Democrats. At the level of social action, individuals may choose to associate with others *because* they share these attributes, or they may not. But no one has ever been *only* an Irish-Catholic-Democrat, and nothing else (a mother or a mechanic or a college student, for instance); nor, for most, has being an Irish-Catholic-Democrat been the most important thing in their lives; nor, for most, has it been the most determinative influence or constraint upon their life-chances.

This sense of belonging, not being based upon economic status but rather upon ancestral origin, religion, and a form of political attachment which was remarkably free of any commitment to ideological principles based on class interests, gave no hindrance to economic mobility and an individualistic pursuit of social honour through work, the accumulation

---

[12] Max Weber *The Theory of Social and Economic Organization*, Talcott Parsons (ed.) (New York, 1947), 136.

of capital, and material consumption, and thus to the eventual achievement of the American Dream. The climb up the socio-economic ladder from immigrant rags to middle-class respectability was not communal but individualistic: family by family, one rung at a time, each at its own rate. In the second and subsequent generations, the cost of belonging to this world, for most, was negligible or free: it came of being born into an Irish-Catholic-Democrat family, going to parochial school, marrying someone of similar background, and ensuring that one's children did the same. For others, the price of marrying someone outside the circle, or of rejecting one's religious upbringing, or of incurring the disfavour of the party, could be very high indeed.

Of course, Irish Catholics were not the only people in Albany who had a strong sense of themselves; there were a number of others—the Germans, Jews, Poles, and Italians, principally—but by virtue of their numbers, the timing of their arrival, and the fact that they were native English-speakers, Irish Catholics were not in direct competition with these other nineteenth-century European immigrants for jobs, housing, political spoils, or social status. Their main competitors for economic and political power and social honour were the Anglo-Dutch, the patrician Protestants who had been well established in Albany since colonial times. By the 1880s, small but gradually increasing numbers of Catholics of Irish ancestry, mainly the second and third generation whose forbears had arrived before the Famine, had succeeded in becoming business proprietors, owning factories, breweries, and newspapers. Irish-Catholic doctors, lawyers, judges, and members of Congress were appearing; and they were living in the best areas of the city. In economic and political power, they were beginning to rival the Anglo-Dutch, but the battle for social honour would take much longer. In *The Albany Blue Book* for 1906, the city's social register and self-styled 'elite family directory', only about thirty (2 per cent) of the 1,500 family names listed are unambiguously Irish Catholic. Apart from three or four prominent Irish-Catholic families, such as the Traceys, Farrells, and Delehantys, whose antecedents had founded St Mary's more than a century earlier, there were few if any recognizably Irish-Catholic names among the members of Albany's most exclusive clubs in 1906, including the Albany Country Club, the University Club, and the Fort Orange Club. By 1938–9, more than a generation later, Irish-Catholic names were scarcely more numerous; there were again about thirty such names out of approximately 1,300 listed. Full social acceptance by the Anglo-Dutch ascendancy would not occur until after the Second World War.

Nowadays, the Irish-Catholic-Democrat stereotype is a playful one, said half-jokingly by those who bear these attributes of social belonging. When used by others, however, it can be pejorative, a stigmatizing label characterizing its objects as assertive, manipulative, cunning, and clannish. Yet in some ways, the salience of the stereotype, whether friendly or not, is fading as the lived realities which created and nourished it have gradually melted away. Our informants saw the 'Irishness' of party politics, and the machine's power to command loyalty, as having largely disappeared. And they say that, unlike the strict religious practice of their parents' generation, they make up their own minds about churchgoing and their church's moral teachings on contraception, abortion, homosexuality, divorce, and mixed marriages, and fewer of our informants are sending their own children to parochial schools than in their parents' generation. They none the less have a warm, nostalgic regard for the old days, an admiration for Dan O'Connell's machine, which 'looked after the people', and good feelings about the way they were brought up by their parents to say the rosary together and to keep the faith as close-knit families. The institutional structures of this social landscape have, for many, vanished since the 1970s, as more and more people have moved to the anonymous suburbs beyond the city limits, where there are few Catholic parish churches and schools; where municipal government is more likely than not to be Republican; where two-thirds of one's neighbours are neither Catholic nor of Irish ancestry; and where every family is on its own. 'Irish-Catholic-Democrat' is becoming an ever-more abstract idea, a symbol of belonging which is losing its rootedness in the realities of everyday social experience, but which nevertheless remains a significant notion for most of our informants. Mary Waters, in *Ethnic Options: Choosing Identities in America*, has observed that:

Symbolic ethnicity is … not something that will easily or quickly disappear, while at the same time it does not need very much to sustain it. The choice itself—a community without cost and a specialness that comes to you just by virtue of being born—is a potent combination.[13]

The following chapter will go on to consider how 'being Irish', as a part of their senses of self, is structured and experienced by individuals, and Chapter 8 will look at the way that Irishness in Albany is symbolized and expressed in public arenas and rituals.

---

[13] M. C. Waters, *Ethnic Options: Choosing Identities in America* (Berkeley, 1990), 155.

7

The Importance of being Irish

I

Interviews with Phyllis[1]

You didn't have to think of who you were. Everyone around you was the same. We all went to mass together. We all went out on Monday night to a novena and had a Coca-Cola afterwards. Everybody you knew was Irish; everybody that you went to school with. We didn't know very many Protestants. And the old joke in our house, more than a joke, was if you went around with someone we asked, 'What does her father do?' and 'What is his name?' and 'Who are they?' They had to be a certain way or else you weren't supposed to go around with them. I had a few girlfriends that were Protestants but it never went too far. Mama found out that I once went with a girlfriend to St Peter's Episcopal church to some sort of function. She said, 'Well, you really don't have to go there again, do you?' This is how it was. You didn't go around with people who weren't your own kind.

Going to the high school was a big change for us coming from St Patrick's Catholic elementary school, where we were all the same. And even though Vincentian high school was Catholic too, the girls and boys came from all over. They came from St Casimir's, which was Polish; and the German school, Our Lady of Angels. There were children from even as far as Cohoes where it was all French at that time. And two or three of the girls I knew could only say their prayers in French. That is how they

---

[1] This account is edited from Brenda McAteer's interviews with Informant 152 (born 1922). The informant was happy to talk at length about her life and did not need much steering by the interviewer; her reminiscences about her ancestry, childhood, and adult life extend to nearly 27,000 words of typed transcript. Informant 152's narrative is not consistently patterned in its chronological thread and frequently interrupts one thought with another, sometimes returning later to the original point, sometimes not. This highly condensed version of her narrative rearranges some details and tidies up her grammar and syntax, as she would have wished, while attempting to preserve her style of expression. The names, places, and some other identifying details mentioned in this account have been altered to preserve her anonymity.

were up there in Cohoes. And some of my girlfriends from St Casimir's, the Polish school, they knew their prayers in Polish. But, of course, they knew them in English too, and they'd say, 'I hope I don't forget, and I hope I don't get up and cross myself and start saying it', because we said prayers so much. In French class, Sister Mary Francis was a devil. The other one, Sister Mary Joseph, was lovely and she would make you hold your nose so that you'd get a French accent. And everything had to be in French from the minute you went in. If we saw Sister Mary Francis outside of class, we would scatter, because she would stop you and she would immediately start speaking French, and if you didn't answer her in French you would be in trouble. We were petrified of her. She was very, very strict. If you got three pink slips you were thrown out of school, and she was known to give them.

When I left Vincentian, I went to the Albany Business College; two or three friends of mine went there too. The sisters were very disapproving of us taking commercial courses. They wanted us to take the college entrance which was really the humanities: languages, English, all that stuff. They didn't want us to study shorthand and typing. A few of my friends did because their mothers were widows, and the sisters probably thought well, they'll have to go to work. It was wartime, and we did. But it was hard to get used to, at first. Every time they rang the bell at the Albany Business College, we'd jump up and start to cross ourselves. It was a habit. At Vincentian there was a lot of prayer, at the beginning and end of every period: in your home room in the morning, and then when you went to another class; it went on like that all day. This was during the war. All of my friends who had steady boyfriends got married. Everyone was doing it, and so did I. I don't think my mother and father would have allowed it otherwise. I don't know why they did even then. I wasn't sure I wanted to get married. It was a terrible time. He was gone for a year after we were married. I didn't know where he was or what was happening and we didn't get much news. My husband had enlisted at 19. For a while I was living in a house with a German girl. She lived in the upstairs flat and said how terrible the Americans were to bomb Germany and everything, and I said how terrible it was that the Germans were bombing England.

When I was growing up, my mother never wanted me to help her doing anything around the house because she could do it quicker and better herself. I had five brothers. She was cooking for six men and she had no time to show me how to do anything. I couldn't even boil water when I got married. I was brought up in a houseful of men. Women were supposed to know their place. This is what I was taught. It's the way my husband felt, it's the way my brothers felt and my father. We'll take care of you as long as you know your place. I resented that terribly. I would do anything for anyone who asked me and gave me a reason, but just to be expected to wait on people is different. My oldest brother is just like my father was. If my brother's wife was outside in the yard when he came home at 4 o'clock, he would call her inside to start making his dinner, which had to be ready at 5.30 every evening. And every Friday my mother had to have creamed codfish because Papa wanted it, and then make about three or four other things which one of the other men wanted.

My mother's father insisted that my mother go through high school which girls in their neighbourhood didn't do very often then. He had these ideas that he never wanted her to work as a maid, like my grandmother, the girl he'd married. But most of the girls from Ireland were maids in those days. One of my mother's friends had worked for very rich people who owned a big department store, and she had gone back on a visit to Ireland, which nobody ever did. Maybe the people she worked for helped her. Boston was the worst place for the Irish to be put down. New England was the real bastion of the WASP society. The English and Scotch Protestants had the first chance at business, the first chance at everything. You know, they owned all the big mills. And if you were Irish you worked for them and that was it. Albany wasn't like that. There were a lot of lace-curtain Irish here. Pine Hills was full of them. Three of my grandparents had come over from Ireland in the 1870s, and my mother's mother about 1850. My mother's father had the brogue, and my mother would say all things her father had said. None of my friends had this Irish background, although they said they were Irish. My mother kept the brogue going and she used to say the things her father used to say and she had all kinds of expressions that would make us laugh. She'd talk about her father when he lived with us after grandma died and before I was born. My oldest brother had an awful temper and he'd throw himself down on the floor in fits of temper, and my grandfather would say, 'Ah the little mannyeen, he's having a terrible chitter' or something.

Mama would tell us stories about her side of the family. When I was little, I used to fall out of bed. She'd take me to bed with her, and Roy, my youngest brother, would lie on the end of the bed. Then she would tell us stories about her people, and we'd keep asking 'Why?' and 'Who was that?' and 'Where was that?' So I got to learn a lot more. My mother came from a small family. There were only three. Well, to go back a little. My mother's mother's name was Mary Catherine Flynn. She was born up in Washington County, just north of Albany. My great-grandparents were

Mary Ellen Murphy and James Flynn. I don't know where they came from in Ireland. They came up to Washington County because her brother John was already settled up there and had a farm. Evidently they worked for him, or rented some farm land from him; I can't remember which. They had three children: my grandmother, Mary Catherine, and two sons. James Flynn was conscripted into the Union Army in the Civil War. So I imagine they had to have come here in the 40s or 50s, 1850, about that. To have had three children they had to have been here a while. He came home wounded or sick, and he didn't live very long after he got back to the farm in Washington County. My great-grandmother then married a railroad man, William Simpson. An Englishman, as my mother always used to say. A fine man. But Mary Ellen died fairly young herself. My grandmother and her two brothers were put in an orphan asylum. My mother said that her mother said that Mr Simpson truly wanted to adopt them and take care of them, but that her mother had said no, probably because he wasn't Catholic. She wanted her brother John to have custody of her three children and bring them up properly. Maybe he couldn't look after them, or died or something. Well, a lot of people were orphaned very young then. My mother said that her mother told her that the worst thing the women had to do up there on the farms during the Civil War was to slaughter the pigs. There were no men around. But, of course, the Irish were all farm people anyway.

My grandmother Mary Catherine came to Albany to work as a maid for the priests in St Joseph's parish house. That's where she met my grandfather, Michael McMahon. My grandfather had studied to be a priest in Ireland, but he left the seminary. He wrote pamphlets or something and got into trouble over it and had to leave. He knew somebody here in America who got him a job. He went to work teaching in a school in Massachusetts. He didn't stay there long. He came to Albany, where he had some friends, and then he got a job as a teacher at the Albany Academy, a Protestant prep school for boys. And he used to say to his wife, 'Sure I married you Mary Catherine, I felt so sorry for you'. Well, she was a maid and had to run up and down stairs all the time. He died before I was born, but my mother says that he was always very friendly with the priests and at one time there was a bishop in Albany who came from some place near where grandfather McMahon had lived in Ireland. They were all very close and always had plenty to talk about and discuss. And he loved it, you know, he loved talking with them about Ireland. He used to take my mother with him down to the cathedral; he always went to mass at the cathedral, you know. She was spoiled because she was his only daughter. He would take her to the parish house because he ate dinner there on Sunday, which was a lovely affair, my mother said. Well, my mother couldn't eat with them because she was only a little girl, but the housekeeper would let her run and answer the door and things like that. Evidently she got fresh and her mother said she couldn't go there any more. My mother was like that. She probably went to the door and said, 'Well, I don't know if they're in', or something.

My father was a policeman. He wasn't interested in his background. It wasn't important to him at all, and he didn't talk about it much. His people forgot about everything in Ireland because they knew they'd never go back there again, I suppose. People didn't go back. Instead, people brought their relatives over: aunts, mothers, everybody brought some-body and kept on bringing them until there was nobody left over there. My husband wasn't interested in his background, either. It wasn't the thing then. Everybody wanted to be American. Our parents gave us American names: Richard, Philip, Edward, Charles, Roy, and Phyllis; no Patricks, Josephs, Colleens, or Marys. Two of my friends, if you went into their house, their mothers were sweet but they didn't speak English very well. They would start talking to the girls in Italian or Polish and my friends would say, 'Speak English, Ma, speak English'. They didn't like it; they felt it put them down. Most of the people that I recall only wanted to be American and the past didn't matter. Everybody was busy trying to get on. The Irish too, they were trying desperately to get on. My husband's mother and father were actually born in Italy. They came here as children and married here, probably very young. He came from a very big family; he had a lot of sisters. They were very good to the younger kids, and they worked hard to help. His older sisters quit school early and went to work in the family's fruit and vegetable business to pay for him to go to Vincentian. I don't think that he was terribly grateful or did ter-ribly well. Girls are more apt to do things like that, and say to themselves, 'Well I'm going to do well in high school and then try to better myself because my sisters are helping me'. But men take what they can get from women.

My brothers were tradesmen or policemen, things like that. My oldest brother was a master electrician. Some of the girls from Vincentian went to college, but in my family we didn't expect to. We had to go out and help earn money to help take care of ourselves. We didn't expect our parents to support us after 17 or so. Girls were expected to get married. There were matchmakers, you know; the women kept an eye out for somebody if they had daughters to marry off. It has always bothered me that men can be bachelors all their days, but if you are a woman there's something wrong if you are not married. In my father's family, there were six brothers, and they had sort of a history of being bachelors. Two of them never married. The Irish do this, you know. I remember a friend of mine from high school, a lovely girl. She and her boyfriend were high school sweethearts. He went into the army in the war and they married; they were 19 and 20. Perhaps they wouldn't have married if it hadn't been for the war. He came home and he told her he'd met someone else. She had a little baby, a little boy, an infant. Three or four years later a friend of mine— horrified, absolutely horrified, said to me, 'do you know that Ruth has got married again?' It was absolutely unheard of. How could she? We didn't think you could do things like that. But good for her that she did. She was only a young girl and she had a nice family, and her new husband was wonderful. That was fifty years ago, and that is how different it was. My mother was sort of like that girl Ruth. She was logical and philosophical, and I think her father talked to her about a lot of things that fathers didn't discuss with their daughters, like politics. She thought women got a terrible deal, and were terribly put down.

One of my daughters-in-law is Irish-German and my other daughter-in-law is of Polish descent. My sons met them in college; this is what most people do nowadays, while we married people we knew in high school. My older son, who married the Irish-German girl, lives in Pennsylvania and works for the state, and the younger one lives in Washington, DC, and has a job with the government. Both of them married Catholics. I've seen mixed marriages and I've seen wonderful mixed marriages. But I've seen marriages when everything was Catholic, there were three priests on the altar, and the couple never got along in all their married days. I've seen complete opposites be the happiest husband and wife you can imagine. I've had friends who have married Protestants, and they've got along just great. I have seen people brought up round the corner from each other go to churches that they've never been in. Religion has nothing to do with marriage. It's just that you think it does because that's the way you were brought up. My oldest brother was the only one in our family who married someone who wasn't a Catholic. That was back in the twenties, when marrying out wasn't the thing. My sister-in-law was a German Lutheran. But my brother saw to it that his three sons were brought up as good Catholics, and they are, although after the second son was born my sister-in-law wouldn't do anything about having him baptized as a Catholic. The baby was five months old, and they were visiting my mother one weekend. My mother told my brother, 'He has to be baptized right now and you'll have to do it'. So they went up to St Patrick's and my mother was the baby's godmother. People did that, you see. They're all good boys, their wives are Catholic, well, except for the last one that they didn't get around to having baptized. He married a girl in the Presbyterian church. That caused problems with our family because some wouldn't go to the wedding. He had been to a Catholic college but he couldn't get any of his friends to stand up for him, because they were all Catholics. They said, 'We can't go into a Presbyterian church and see you married by a minister. It's against the laws of the Church'. So another one of my brothers said, 'I'm going to go and stand up for you and watch while you're excommunicated'. But they aren't married any more. He has a second wife and they are very happy together. What's the difference, anyway? Times have changed. These days, if either of my sons were to say to me, 'I'm marrying so-and-so, Mother, but we're marrying in the city hall. We're going to have a civil marriage by a judge. We're very much in love. This is what we have decided', I'd say, 'Fine', and I'd go with them.

A Conversation with Helen and Joe[2]

Interviewer: Would you say that your feeling for your background differs from your parents?

Joe: Well, the first thing is [that] we did not have that strong identity with another country. When I was a kid, my mother corresponded with relatives in Germany, so we had that sort of identity. [But we had] no correspondence with [any] Irish relatives [on my father's side].

Helen: My father's family came [to America] I believe in the 1870s. My father's father was born here but his grandparents were both born in Ireland.

Interviewer [to Helen]:   Do you know what county or anything?

Helen: I was told that Doyle is a Wexford name, but I do not know if that is true.

Interviewer: What about the other side of your family?

---

[2]   This account is edited from the transcripts of Brenda McAteer's interviews with Informants 221 and 410, in their forties and of mixed Irish descent, both in terms of their European origins and generational distance from Ireland. Informant 221's mother was present during the first part of the interview, but had left the room by the time the conversation noted here was recorded. The house, in a lace-curtain part of Albany, was built by Informant 221's father before the Second World War, and has been the only house Informant 221 has ever lived in. As in Phyllis's account, given above, the names, places, and identifying details have been altered to protect the anonymity of the informants, and the grammar and syntax have been tidied up to make the conversation more readable.

Helen: My mother's family was a mixture. Her father was an immigrant
         from Wales. His name was David Thomas and her mother was
         half French Canadian and half English, so that makes me half
         Irish and 25 per cent Welsh and 25 per cent a kind of mixture.

Interviewer: Do you feel any particular attachment to any part of your
         background?

Joe: I don't know. I suppose there is kind of an Irish identity there.

Helen: With an Irish surname people automatically assume naturally
         that you are Irish; in fact you could only be a very small per cent
         Irish, really Irish descent. But both of us have Irish surnames.
         My father [put] much more of an emphasis on his ethnic back-
         ground than my mother. My mother did not emphasize it very
         much. She had no real family left. By the time I was born, her
         mother and father were both dead and she was an only child.
         She had a stepbrother and I still maintain contact with [him] and
         I consider [him] family, but in terms of blood relatives she did
         not have anybody on her side. She never really talked that much
         about it. [My father's side was Irish and] I grew up in an Irish
         neighbourhood with an Irish surname, so I more or less just
         identified with the Irish. My cousins all married Irish. [One of]
         my father's sisters married Italian, the other one married Irish.
         All [of us] kids went to St Patrick's school together. If someone
         were to ask what nationality I was I would say Irish even though
         my mother's family was not Irish. When she was young, French
         was [my mother's] first language. When she went to school, she
         had a lot of trouble. The kids made fun of her because she spoke
         English with an accent, which is why my mother would never
         speak French to us growing up. She could [still] speak French
         very, very well [when] we [went] to visit her family in New
         Hampshire; she would speak French like she had never been
         away from it, but she would not speak French to us at home
         because she thought that was not the thing to do. [To Joe:] Your
         mother did not speak German [in your] home, either.

Interviewer: As children, would you have been told any stories about
         Ireland or heard any legends?

Joe: About Ireland? From my father, no. He [had] never set foot in the
         place and nor had his father.

Helen: Mine wouldn't have [either], [even though] my father and his
         two sisters had very Irish names. My father was a hundred per
         cent Irish.

Joe: Irish first names have become very popular.

Helen: Well, names like Kelly and Casey, they don't really use those names much in Ireland do they? Our middle daughter's name is Kathleen. They were all named after people. My oldest daughter, her name is Eileen Margaret after my mother and her middle name is after Joe's mother. My second one, Patricia, is my mother's cousin and Kathleen, the middle one, is after my aunt. The little one [is] Colleen. When I had the two girls and they were babies I used to call [them] the colleens. It [was] a custom [in our family], because my father used to call us two girls the two colleens. He had two sisters and his father used to call them the colleens, so when I had the third girl I just thought well [we] may as well call her Colleen. Her middle name, Elizabeth, is after my aunt.

Interviewer: That's interesting about the colleens. Are there any more Irish expressions that have survived in your families?

Helen: My aunts always talked about buying the farm. It is an expression for when [you die]. I always think of that as an Irish expression, [but] I am not sure if it is.

Interviewer: What about any Gaelic words?

Helen: No.

Interviewer: Did you celebrate St Patrick's Day in your families?

Joe: Well, they celebrated it in Catholic school.

Helen: Both of us are products of Catholic school. On St Patrick's Day they had a parade and everybody had shamrocks and some people had green hats and shillelaghs. In college they put green food colouring in the beer. In high school on St Patrick's Day they had [green] cake. They still do that.

Interviewer: Would you celebrate it now?

Joe: We had a St Patrick's Day party here, once.

Helen: I think [one of our daughters] was about a year old [then]. She was born just before St Patrick's Day.

Interviewer: Speaking of schools and kids, what about your own children?

Helen: We are probably in the minority, in that you'll find our kids at Catholic school.

Interviewer: What made you decide to send them to Catholic school in preference to public school?

Joe: Well, a couple of things. The situation in Albany: in Albany many of the public schools are fine, [but] the middle schools are the first mixing point from all parts of the city and it makes for some fireworks. So having known some people who have been through this situation we figured one of the ways to avoid middle school is to use Catholic schools.

Helen: The Catholic schools go to eighth grade. The public schools only go to six. Which means [if you] use a Catholic school, you can send them up to eighth grade and [then] you can use the high school if you so choose, otherwise they finish in the grammar school at six and they have to go to middle school for seventh and eighth.

Joe: But that is not the only reason. We like the local Catholic school. It is a well-established parish and school. And also it has got a nice mix of people. It is a nice parish which is very cohesive.

Helen: I myself prefer the Catholic schools. The situation in Albany absolutely decides it, but I had very good experience in Catholic schools. I enjoyed it. Some people you talk to did not have such [a] good experience, and they say they would not want their children in Catholic school. [Our] oldest is going into third grade, my second one is going into first grade, and the little one is in nursery school. It is a small school, very family-oriented, we know the other people [and] you know who your kids are associating with. You can pretty much judge the experience they are going to get in the classroom. I don't call it religion, but I would call it values and morality. The values and morality you are taught as a child [stay with you].

Interviewer: Do you think is it important for a husband and wife to be of the same faith?

Helen: That you date somebody, marry somebody Catholic?

Joe: Absolutely. To my mother, absolutely. My father, he might have been more tolerant, but to my mother absolutely. Although it is ironic because two out of her three grandchildren are either married [to] or [are] announcing they're not marrying Catholics.

Helen: When my sister got married, she got married in a Catholic church but not with a mass. A Catholic service with a priest and a Catholic marriage, but of course he is not Catholic. She had to get some type of a dispensation ahead of time. [Joe's mother] has always been very nice to my sister and [her husband], [but then] one day [she said] to me something about her marrying a pagan. 'It's not a Christian religion you see,' [she said]. And I said to her very nicely [that] it would probably be better if you did not say that to my sister because I don't think she would particularly like being told that she was [married to] a pagan. I am sure that she did not mean it offensively but that is the way that she looks at it.

Joe: She asks us on Tuesday what mass we are going to on Sunday.

Helen: We are churchgoers, you know, but we don't start planning the mass schedule on Tuesday or Wednesday because we have other things on our minds. But that is her thing.

Joe: I would say that my mother ruled the family, [but] she would deny it.

Helen: We all get along well, the three generations [in this house], but we have to stand very firm on a lot of things. Over the years she has come around to it. Some things we go along with her if it does not make that much difference.

Joe: She would always profess that she wasn't calling the shots when in fact everybody knew that she was. My father would go along, go along, go along, and then all of a sudden explode.

Helen: He would get mad. He was probably mad all along and didn't have any way to express it.

Joe: And then for two days there would be a little minor change of course and then we would go back to it.

Helen: I would say that my father would profess that he was the head of [our] household. In many ways he was, but I would say that my mother was much more in charge of things. My family talked about everything. [We] might be loud and [we] might argue, [but] nobody would feel too uncomfortable. In [Joe's] household that was not the case: if you had a problem you did not discuss it. You went a couple of times around the beads, a few more decades, and you would somehow be inspired to know what the answer [was].

Interviewer: Does it ever happen that people ever comment on your ethnic background? Would anybody ever say anything?

Joe: What kind of thing? Would it be largely in response to your name, or ...

Helen: Yes. [We have] last names that are Irish. People will say, 'That is a really Irish name'.

Interviewer: Would you say that being Irish is important to you?

Joe: Yeah, yes it is.

Helen: I'll tell you something [that] I don't say too much about, but I was married once before when I was quite young. I had a church annulment. I was married to somebody who was Polish and I very much disliked having a Polish name. It bothered me when people would say to me, 'Oh, are you Polish', I would say, 'No, my husband is Polish, I am Irish'. It is a stupid thing, it doesn't necessarily make any big difference to anybody, but ...

Interviewer: It must be important to you.

Helen: Somehow it must be. I much prefer having O'Flaherty as a last name than a Polish or Italian name, because that's the same as my own maiden name, nationality-wise. I didn't pick him because his name was O'Flaherty, but I mean I know I never liked people [saying] to me you are Polish. I didn't like it.

Interviewer [to Joe]:   Is the Irish as important to you as the German?

Joe: I would say they are both just as important. If I were to look [at] the family, I would say the German side manifests itself in my brother being an engineer, and [on the Irish side] that I became a politician. The strongest point [of the Irish] was their politics and their literature and the Germans their scientific bent. Maybe I just attribute [these things] to those two backgrounds but I think I am right.

Helen: Well I know even in [our] own children [we] have one daughter, [the] oldest one, who is never going to be a scientist. She is probably going to be in the arts. I attribute a lot of that [to] my father's side of the family. My father's family on both sides were theatre people to a certain degree: musically inclined, dramatically inclined. Both my sister and I, when we were in high school, were in all the school shows, the musicals; we sang in most of those things. Joe's family on the Irish side were very musically inclined. His father played the violin in an orchestra. My father sang in a singing group, my mother was not at all musical, and his mother is not.

Joe: My mother is tone deaf.

Helen: [Being musical] comes from the Irish side: that gregarious, outgoing, performing type of quality comes I think more from that side of the family. Maybe it is just a stereotype, but when you think of the Irish and all the literature that comes from there, and the theatre and the drama I mean certainly that would be very much associated [with a] creative bent. I remember being very impressed when I went to Ireland and [saw the Liffey, and] everybody saying this is where James Joyce wrote all his stuff. When I was at school they [did] a lot of [Joyce's] plays. I could really relate to [them].

Interviewer: Can you think of times in your life when it has been more or less important to you to be of Irish background?

Helen: I know in my case when I was getting married [to Joe] and changing my name, I was very aware of going from one Irish name to another. And for my children to have Irish names it maintains that [connection].

Joe: I can't think of any one particular time when it was important [to me] to be ethnically identified.

Helen: Well, even being Catholic is part of our identity.

Joe: Yeah.

Helen: More than anything else probably, especially for [Joe]. I went all the way through [Catholic] high school, [but] he went to Catholic college [as well]. Both of us were very much raised in that kind of an environment. In our house we described [ourselves] as Irish Catholic. That is the term you would hear quite often. I don't know if that is common with everybody that you interview, but it was the case in our house. And yet my mother wasn't Irish and it always surprised me that my mother never talked all that much about her background.

Joe: Probably never had a chance to get a word in.

Helen: She never knew that much about it.

Interviewer: Would there be any specific times when you may feel that you have benefited from being Irish?

Joe: Well, from my perspective, Albany has a lot of Irish people [and] you can sort of fit in. I remember at my high school there was Irish, German, and Italian and Polish. That was the whole school. When I was going through school there was a much more [of a] Catholic identity. I guess that came from being Irish or being one of the five or six nationalities that were Catholic.

Interviewer: So when you were growing up, your Catholic identity would probably have been a lot more important to you than your ethnic identity?

Joe: Yes.

Interviewer: Would have felt closer to somebody who was, say, an Italian Catholic than an Irish Protestant?

Joe: Yes.

Helen: You rarely find Irish Protestants here. Maybe in this generation you would, but when I was growing up that wasn't the case. I hardly knew any Protestant people or Jewish people. You learned in school [that] there were different religions. They were not the true ones; we had the right one. They taught you that and I really didn't notice much of a difference, but I didn't really know that many people who weren't Catholic. In [the] neighbourhood [where I grew up] almost everybody was Catholic.

Joe: This neighbourhood was pretty mixed. It would probably [have been] 35 per cent [Catholic]. There were probably more Protestants than Catholics and a few Jewish.

Helen: Joe's neighbourhood had a much higher standard of living than the one that I grew up in. I grew up in a much lower socio-economic area than this is here.

Interviewer: Is there such a thing as an Irish-American character, do you think?

Joe: Oh, probably [something] out of a William Kennedy novel.

Helen: Gregarious, outgoing, colourful. But maybe that is stereotyping the Irish. That is what we do. But my family definitely was. If you compare my mother and my father's side of the family in terms of that quality definitely there was far more [on] my father's side, which was the Irish side.

Joe: I would say that they are more political. I think that they came into the system and networked it within a few generations. I sort of have a theory [that] a lot of the other groups that came in, like the Scandinavians, stayed in farming and stayed in enclaves but the Irish settled in the cities probably because they had been driven off the farms in Ireland. They settled in cities which was more natural for a social network getting into the political establishment.

Helen: It probably depends where you go in this country. There is a big Irish population here. [In] some [parts] of the country you don't hear the Irish names like you do here.

Interviewer: Would there be any times when being Irish is more important than being American to you?

Helen: I can't picture it. No.

Interviewer: What about your children? Do you think their backgrounds will be important to them?

Helen: [As for] marrying a different religion or marrying a different ethnic group for my own children I doubt that [it] would make a big difference to me. [But] I intend to raise my own children very much like the way I was raised, in a very traditional, close Irish Catholic [family].

Joe: I would [like] them [to] be aware of [their background].

Helen: They are bound to be aware of it. People will say, Colleen O'Flaherty, what an Irish name!

Interviewer: Do you have any interest in the history of Ireland?

Helen: We studied some of that in school. We had a lot of Irish-born nuns [at] St Patrick's when I was growing up. There was study time about County Armagh and the Book of Kells. They used to talk about the Potato Famine and emigration, those sorts of things.

Interviewer: Would you have done any reading on it yourself or watched documentaries or anything?

Helen: Yeah, they had a documentary on public television a few years back. I don't remember what it was called but we did watch that.

Interviewer: What about contemporary affairs in Ireland? If you saw something in the paper would you read it? Or would you go to a lecture on Irish affairs?

Helen: It would depend. I am not interested in the politics.

Joe: I personally don't endorse all this Irish Republican Army stuff. Some of the speaker circuit [is of] that type.

Helen: Yes, some of it is kind of political. We do not get into those causes. My philosophy has always been that we have quite enough of our own problems here without worrying about what is going on over there.

II

Most of Phyllis's childhood, during the 1920s and 1930s, was spent on Second Street in St Patrick's parish, an area that had enough people of Irish ancestry to allow her to think of everyone around her as the same. Even if the Irish were not in a majority, Phyllis saw it as a homogeneous social world of people like her and her family, a view coloured by her experience of school, where all the children were second- or third-generation Americans from Catholic families of much the same socio-economic level. Phyllis's father was not interested in his Irish origins and rarely spoke of them, leaving her with only a very sketchy knowledge of her ancestry on her father's side. Yet her mother spoke of her parents and grandparents frequently and with great warmth, giving Phyllis a feel for her Irish origins on her mother's side and a rich sense of the family's past. For Phyllis, a personal sense of Irishness came of repeatedly hearing her mother's anecdotes and Irish homilies and expressions, and her mother's love of reading about Ireland (Phyllis says that her mother sent her to all the libraries in the district to fetch books); it came of going to a school where Irish names were common and the children were taught by Irish nuns; it came of living in a place where many of the people nearby were of similar backgrounds, went to the same church, and had much the same kinds of experiences.

Phyllis's Irishness was a part of the fabric of her everyday life that she took for granted. While both of her parents were of unmixed Irish descent, they never ate any foods they regarded as especially Irish (even though other people might regard having creamed codfish on Fridays as Irish); nor was there any music in her house, although like almost everyone of her background and generation she knew the words of a few popular American songs with Irish associations. If Phyllis was secure in her sense of having an Irish background, she was also equally certain that she was not really Irish but American. Her parents strove to make their children fit in to American society and to be American, just like the families next door. Phyllis's parents made the conscious decision to give her and her brothers American names, not the Irish names which they associated with the menial jobs and low social status of the immigrant generation: Paddy the ditch-digger and Nora the maid. Much of what Phyllis regards as characteristically Irish qualities are, not surprisingly, derived from her world of personal experience: being Catholic, and thus religious, or at least concerned to make the correct observances; growing up in a working-class household where the women were expected to know their place, leading her to regard Irish families as typically patriarchal, yet viewing her mother as the strong figure in the family; seeing male bachelorhood as an Irish trait because two of her Irish uncles remained unmarried, while regarding it as an expectation that Irish women should marry and have children because that is what the women in her family did, and so on. For Phyllis, being part of a family of Irish background and growing up in what she perceived to be an Irish neighbourhood was an important influence in the development of a sense of Irishness that was still evident fifty years later. As with most other people, her intimate familiarity with a particular family and her feeling for her ancestry in a more general sense are inseparably intertwined; her perception of what it is to be Irish, quite naturally, was shaped by her own, first-hand social experience.

Helen and Joe, in contrast, are five generations removed from the generation of the Famine immigrants; they also have pedigrees that are mixed with other European origins. Their sixth-generation children, born in the 1980s, are half Irish, a quarter German, an eighth Welsh, a sixteenth French Canadian, and a sixteenth English. By any objective measure, Helen and Joe's claims upon being Irish were much weaker and more ambiguous than Phyllis's, yet they felt Irish none the less. Seldom were people of their generation able to articulate any better than Helen and Joe how this sense of Irishness was anchored, and why they felt Irish even though they could not point to much that they saw as especially Irish in their beliefs, practices, family traditions, or their own traits of character. In Helen and Joe's conversation with us, Helen acutely observes how important her surname was to her sense of being Irish; this is a common feeling not only for married women, but for men and women of mixed ancestry. People whose parents are of unmixed but different ancestral backgrounds are in principle half-and-half, but in practice our informants usually said that they felt closer to one side or the other; often this was their father's ancestry, because they inherited his surname.

> I have always heard it said about [my name] being a good Irish name. [It] is something I have heard my whole life long. It just seems to be a name [of which people say], 'What a fine Irish name!'
>
> (Informant 590)

> It's funny, but sometimes I wish I knew more about my Irish ancestors, [since] Albany is strongly Irish. I haven't made any effort. I guess not having an Irish name growing up meant my interest wasn't great.
>
> (Informant 598)

> I think it is your last name that kind of signifies who you are and you develop your identity to a large extent from that. People view you in a certain way, and even though I have probably got more German in me than I have Irish, there is a certain way people view you because of what your last name is.
>
> (Informant 583)

A change from one ancestral attachment to another was sometimes seen to occur during an individual's lifetime. One of our informants, a married woman whose maiden and married names were distinctively Irish, was none the less of three-quarters non-Irish descent. Somewhat reluctantly, she eventually came to emphasize the Irish part of her background, because of the repeated experience of having her name commented upon by other people:

> One time I was donating blood. I [gave] my name and [the nurse] said 'I would have guessed it, your face is a map of Ireland!', which

I don't think is true at all, but this woman was reacting to my name.
(Informant 256)

Several others mentioned their physical appearance as triggering a response in other people:

> A lot of people say, 'You must be Irish' because I have red hair. We get a lot of that because [there are] so many redheads in the family.
> (Informant 231)

Mixed ancestry is especially revealing of the way people think of their feelings towards their backgrounds. Some of our informants had more intense emotional feelings of belonging to their mothers' side but emphasized the ancestry on their fathers' side, or vice versa. Informant 106, who is German on his father's side and Irish on his mother's, leans toward his father's side in terms of emotional attachments. In his childhood, he had German grandparents and cousins in Albany, but no close relatives on his mother's side, yet he grew up in North Albany, an Irish neighbourhood, and described himself as Irish-German, rather than German-Irish, associating himself much more strongly with his mother's Irish ancestry, despite his German surname and his emotional attachments to the German side. Similarly, other informants stressed their Irish background over their German ancestry:

> My father always accused us of being pro-Irish and wanted to know where we got off with that. He said, after all you do have another side. But my mother always told better stories than my father could ever tell. I think myself that my mother was always very Irish. She just acted Irish, I mean her storytelling, her sense of humour: she was Irish. I think it annoyed my father that even [though I had a] German name I always preferred the Irish [side]. I think that I could identify more with the Irish because it was only two generations back and a lot of my friends were Irish too.
> (Informant 112)
>
> I would lean towards my mother's family, but I identify with the Irish and Catholic aspects on my father's side. My father had only one brother. They did not get along. We saw a lot more of my mother's relatives. [But] I don't go in for the German ancestry on my mother's side. I see myself as strictly Irish.
> (Informant 18)

In the words of one of our informants, Albany is 'a big Irish town'. Its perception as an Irish place, the currency of generally positive folk images of Irishness in Albany, and the toll taken by the two world wars on

German-American institutions and pride in Germanness is evident here, but not all the people we interviewed emphasized their Irishness over their Germanness:

> We had a very big sense of being Irish. It's funny, but I guess when I was a kid my mother never gave us any sense of being German. Her name was Mrs O'Brien and people always assumed that she was Irish and she never really encouraged our German[ness]. [Yet] I always think of myself as German-Irish. It was always more important to me than the rest of the family. I had a big, big thing about being German, particularly when I was a teenager. People would always say, 'Oh, O'Brien. Irish?' and I would say German-Irish. When I went to college I deliberately studied German. [Being German] was a bigger thing with me than it was with the rest of the family.
>
> (Informant 240)

Helen and Joe mention three of the most common factors which lead people to lean towards one ancestry or another: the geographical (and sometimes social) propinquity of relatives, the nature of the neighbourhood in which they grew up as children, and the social composition of the schools they attended (which are important pools of age-mates, potential friends, and possible marriage partners). Helen is only half Irish, yet all three factors combined to give her a strong sense of being Irish: the absence of her mother's (non-Irish) relatives and the presence of numerous Irish aunts, uncles, and cousins; the Irishness of her childhood neighbourhood, and going to a Catholic school with other children with Irish names, staffed by Irish nuns. In contrast, Joe, also half-Irish, identifies less strongly with his Irish side: he lived in a more heterogeneous neighbourhood where there were more Protestants and Jews than Irish Catholics, went to a less homogeneous (but still exclusively Catholic) school, and though it is not mentioned in this conversation, Joe had both Irish and German relatives living nearby. In fact, Joe regards his brother as German, as taking after his mother's side of the family, while he himself takes after his father's, Irish, side. We encountered a number of other cases where children of the same mixed-ancestry parentage were regarded as having different ancestral affinities, either by themselves expressing a preference, or being said to display features of physical appearance (such as hair colour) or traits of character which in their parent's estimation made them more or less Irish, German, or Italian, such that, as in Joe's case, one sibling could be regarded as Irish and another as German. Occasionally the preferences and views of parent and child were at variance:

My father tells me I have [more] German traits from my mother's
side in my personality than Irish, which I think is interesting. [But]
I never say [I am] German, English, and Scotch. I usually say I'm
Irish, and that's it.

(Informant 521)

This informant, in addition, strategically simplifies his pedigree in
what he usually says of it: he never mentions that he is a quarter English,
or that he has as much English ancestry as Irish. In Albany, English is the
second most common ancestry after German to be mixed with Irish, yet
it is mentioned much less often in our informants' oral accounts than its
frequency of occurrence in their genealogies would lead one to expect.
The essentializing myths, especially familiar to those who use their Irish
ancestry as a social resource (in Informant 521's case by being involved in
Irish folk music, whose lyrics usually draw upon mythological themes),
portray the English as primordial demons, the natural class enemies of
the Irish. The English are caricatured as venal landlords who enslaved the
Irish and starved them out of Ireland, and then contrived to keep them
down in America. Perhaps for this reason, some of our informants found
having English ancestry to be socially awkward (much more so than
having German ancestry) and, like Informant 521, were inclined to hide
or de-emphasize it, and to reinterpret and simplify their ancestral origins
in order to eliminate this source of embarrassment.[3]

There are circumstances in which it is not even necessary to have Irish
ancestry in order to be regarded as Irish, again demonstrating that being
Irish is, above all, a matter of social propinquity: we encountered at least
one case (and there are suggestions of others in our data) where adopted
children were held to have acquired Irish qualities through being brought
up by parents of Irish stock; in this instance, an Irish mother:

[Both] my kids are adopted. Christine is the one that step dances and
who would be out with the Irish and never come home. [The other]
I think identifies more American but she has that [Irish thing] about
the closeness of the family. You cannot be raised in an Irish household and have it not always be there.

(Informant 92)

Our informants' feelings of the importance of their Irishness could
also sometimes be seen to emerge from family traditions, which were

---

[3] Cf. S. Lieberson and M. Waters, *From Many Strands: Ethnic and Racial Groups in
Contemporary America* (New York, 1988), 258.

more marked in some families than others, and in the case of mixed-ancestry families, more accentuated on one side than the other. In Irish-German families, for example, as Joe's remarks suggest, it was often the case that in the wake of the two world wars, German was not spoken in Irish-German homes, nor were German traditions maintained, yet St Patrick's Day would often be marked in such households by green cupcakes and a Bing Crosby record, or a family meal of corned beef and cabbage. Irish music was a part of family life for many of our informants, who said that they listened to Irish music around St Patrick's Day, if at no other time of the year. Much of this music consisted of old favourites like 'Danny Boy', and 'When Irish Eyes Are Smiling'. In other families, music was a more important tradition. Indeed, Helen and Joe say that musicality is something that is typical of Irishness, but wonder if it is just a folk image. In our open-ended interviews and self-completion questionnaire, we made systematic enquiries about musicality to see how widespread it was as a tradition within Irish-American families, and to what degree it was being passed down from one generation to the next, as a way of gauging the strength of family traditions in general, which might serve as points of anchorage of our informants' attachments to their Irish ancestry.

We analysed the responses of a sample of 87 people of Irish background, brought up in Albany, to a series of questions in the self-completion questionnaire about their parents' musicality, their own musicality, and their children's musical tuition; these questions were designed to collect systematic information on topics which had frequently emerged in our earlier open-ended interviews. We asked our informants to indicate their degree of interest in, and knowledge of, music and music-making, ranging from occasional, passive listening to Irish tunes to their own active engagement in dancing, singing, or playing an instrument and teaching their children to do the same. We took these latter aspects of musicality—active engagement in dance, music-making, and teaching one's own children—to be diacritical of a family tradition, because they involve some sustained commitment and effort to maintain and pass down to the next generation. This contrasts with more passive involvements in music, which might involve nothing more than switching on the CD player, buying a ticket to a performance, going to an Irish bar, or purchasing a tin whistle and taking lessons from a professional teacher; these are expressions of musicality which anyone can enjoy or take up as a leisure interest that do not require a family tradition or, necessarily, much commitment to sustain, even though a taste for consuming these forms of music may have stemmed initially from a lively family interest in them.

We asked our informants about the nature of their parents' musicality. Twenty-four (27.5 per cent) reported that their fathers were musical in these active ways; and 26 people (31.0 per cent) said that their mothers were. Ten people (11.5 per cent) had fathers who played a musical instrument, and 6 (6.9 per cent) had mothers who did so. Twenty-two fathers (25.3 per cent) and 20 mothers (27.6 per cent) knew the words of some Irish songs and are remembered by their children as singing them. Three fathers (3.4 per cent) and 9 mothers (10.3 per cent) could dance Irish jigs or reels. Nine fathers (10.3 per cent) and 12 mothers (16.1 per cent) taught their children—our informants—how to play, sing, or dance. Twelve informants (13.8 per cent) had both fathers and mothers who were musical in these ways. Forty-nine (56.3 per cent), however, said that neither of their parents played any instrument, knew the words of any Irish ballads, or danced any Irish steps. A family tradition of musicality, if one had ever been present in the past, had already ended with these informants' parents. Those who had musical parents were in a minority. Of these, a quarter had two parents with active interests in Irish music; three-quarters had only one musically inclined parent, which was just as likely to be a mother as a father. Mothers and fathers were equally likely to sing; fathers were a little more likely to play an instrument; but mothers were somewhat more likely to dance and to spend time with their children teaching them how to play, sing, or dance.

Of those 38 people who had had musical parents, 11 (28.9 per cent of these 38) expressed no interest in music, and did not play, sing, or dance, despite their parents' example. Of the remaining 27, one person played an instrument, all 27 said they knew the words of some Irish songs, 12 people knew some Irish steps, and 8 people had taught their own children to play, sing, or dance. While 3 other people were sending their children to music or dancing lessons in preference to teaching them themselves, most of those who were teaching their own children were also sending them to lessons. However, 13 of the 38 musical people of musical parents with children of their own had neither sent their children to lessons nor taught them themselves, effectively bringing two or more generations of musicality to an end. Only 11 of the 38 people (28.9 per cent) had so far transmitted a musical tradition from their parents, through themselves, to their children. The other 27 were either without children (there were two or three who might still have children, however), or were not interested in playing, singing, or dancing; or, equally likely, their children were not interested in these pursuits.

Assuming all else remains equal, the proportion of people of Irish descent who have no musical tradition of this kind in their families will rise dramatically, from 56 per cent in the present grandparental generation to 89 per cent and beyond in their grandchildren's generation, since only 11 per cent of the current parental generation are passing it on. There is now little enough to give nourishment to the folk image of Irish families as especially musical; what musicality remains in the population is sustained largely by the experience of those people who came to maturity in the decades before television sets found their way into every American living room in the 1950s, replacing the upright piano. These were also the days before the widespread commodification of Irish and other ethnic music vastly increased its accessibility, while making its acquisition a simple, cheap marketplace transaction which obviated the need for any effort on the consumers' behalf to hear this kind of music by making it themselves. Most of the musical skills remaining among our sample population date from a time when playing the accordion and dancing a jig or a polka in the front room was a simple, unselfconscious part of normal American family life.

Apart from occasionally listening to recordings of Irish music, and now and again reading a book or watching a video of a Hollywood film set in Ireland, few of our informants were able to think of any everyday, domestic activities that they associated with their sense of Irishness. Most people, including those who said that their Irish ancestry and sense of being Irish was very important to them, could not think of any domestic activity or family tradition that they regarded as especially Irish, apart from those connected with the once-a-year St Patrick's Day season, when they might put on something green or have a special meal. Feeling Irish, it would seem, does not depend on doing uniquely Irish things.

We asked our informants of Irish ancestry if they could identify any attitudes which they thought were particular to people and families of Irish descent. A number said there were not, or said there were but beyond this were unable to say what they might be. Others tended to describe common American values which they often recognized were not exclusive to people of Irish ancestry, or mentioned characteristics of their own families which were then attributed significance as examples of Irish attitudes, again frequently recognizing that these were not necessarily shared by everyone of Irish background. There were four main values which were suggested as being Irish. They were religiosity, a close-knit family life and the love of one's parents and children, a belief in hard work, and an emphasis on the value of education. These responses came up again and again in the interviews. None the less, people became markedly less confident when we probed a little further as to whether or not the quality they had suggested was especially Irish. The response of Informant 17 is representative. She initially suggested strong religious devotion as an Irish-American value, but then decided that it was not exclusively Irish:

Q: Do you think there are such things as Irish family values?
A: Oh yes.
Q: What do they consist of, do you think?
A: Well, I think religion is the most important thing.
Q: Do you think that is different in any way from people of other ancestries?
A: Well, no, I don't think so. I think everybody should have the same values. It doesn't matter what nationality you are, really.

The point is made again in the responses of Informant 36. The initial reaction to the question was to say that there are Irish values, but then the respondent found it difficult to define what they might be:

Q: Do you think there are such things as Irish family values?
A: Yes, I think so.
Q: Could you explain what you think they are?
A: Mine are just the way we were brought up. That is what we must have had. But I don't think, now that I look back, that they are much different from anyone else's values.
Q: Could you explain what these values are?
A: I think just Catholic values is the main thing. As far as nationality is concerned, perhaps it doesn't make that much difference.

Informant 590, half Irish and half German, felt that there were specific Irish family values but then decided that they might be connected with Catholicism and the pursuit of the American Dream, and might not be peculiar to Irishness:

Q: Do you think there are such things as Irish family values?
A: Yes. [Well, actually] I don't know if it's exclusive to being Irish. I think there is to some degree an immigrant value system, a very strong work ethic and that you've got to do the right thing, a kind of effort to strive for success and achieve, but I'm not sure if that is exclusively Irish, or German for that matter. But yeah, I think there is a value system which is maybe Irish that's based partly on

Catholicism. The Catholic upbringing that we had was very closely associated with being Irish. The nuns in [elementary] school and the brothers in high school were Irish.

Some informants approached the matter by describing their own childhoods and, like Phyllis, attributed Irish qualities to the attitudes or behaviour of their parents and siblings. For Informant 215 it was Irish for men not to get married until late in life because her brothers did not get married until late in life. For Informant 521, siblings are closer in an Irish family because her siblings were close and her family was Irish. Informant 583 cited discipline and orderliness as Irish attitudes, because discipline and orderliness were important to his parents and grandparents. Informant 16 thought that a desire to be selfless and helpful towards others was an Irish characteristic, from what she had observed of her own family:

> Looking at my brothers and sisters, my brother was in the service, serving his country, my other two brothers are in the police doing police work. I have been in health care, you know. [We are] very much human services workers. Actually I have another two sisters who work for the State in mental health, again human services type of thing. So I see it as an Irish value.

Others saw their Irishness as emerging from their social roles or personalities. When asked if her children would feel closer to her husband's Italian background or to her own Irish background, Informant 215 answered by making a connection between her role as a mother and her ancestry:

> I think [they would lean towards] the Irish. They just do. We are extremely close. They tell me everything before they would tell their father if there was a problem.

When asked if this meant in fact that her children leaned towards her as individual rather than towards her Irish background, she continued:

> Probably me as an individual. It doesn't matter that I'm Irish. But you know, that's how Irish mothers are. I can just see that they will be home forever. They like it. They have a good deal, and of course that's kids today.

This suggests that Informant 215 saw her ancestry and personality as inextricably linked. But her attempt to explain the nature of this link through folk psychology soon caused her to become uncertain, and to confuse her persona (her social role as a mother) with her personality.

III

Is there an Irish-American personality? In the 1930s, the American anthropologists, Ruth Benedict and Margaret Mead, popularized the theory that cultures and personalities are connected; that individuals' personalities are formed by the cultural milieux in which they grow up. The mechanism by which personalities come to characterize cultures, and vice versa, they thought, was fundamentally sociological: people are alike because they are moulded, as creatures of culture, by those around them. This idea was derived from the work of other social theorists, and had had a long and distinguished pedigree by the time Benedict and Mead brought it to popular attention. The idea was further popularized by the psychoanalytic theorist Erik H. Erikson, who introduced the term 'identity' to the public twenty-five years later, in 1959. Personal identity, for Erikson, comes about through the unconscious responses individuals make to their social and cultural surroundings, as they mimic and develop personal variants of the modal types of personality that are available to them within the orbit of their historical time and social experience. In other words, as has been observed by many other social theorists before and since, how people are constituted as individuals is largely a matter of who they have associated with most closely over their lifetimes.

The idea that culture creates distinctive individual personalities has been largely abandoned in recent years in anthropology and sociology, mainly for methodological reasons connected with the difficulties of defining modal types of personality, and problems in dealing with the notion of the unconscious, which does not lend itself to readily testable propositions. Anthropologists and sociologists have mostly turned their attention away from personality as such, and now focus on the person as a site of agency within particular social and cultural settings; how individuals' cognitive worlds are constituted, and how what they say and what they do reflects, reproduces, creates, and changes the social and symbolic universes that they incorporate and inhabit. Nevertheless, typifications of an Irish-American character are ubiquitous in contemporary literature about the Irish in America, fictional and non-fictional, scholarly and non-scholarly. Such characterizations, however, owe more to literary imagination, ideological commitment, folk psychology, popular belief, and the wish to create difference or otherness than they do to persuasive evidence—or indeed any evidence at all—that people of Irish descent (or people of any other later-generation European ancestry, for that matter) are psychologically different from other Americans, and behave in different ways.

The propensity for writers on the Irish in America to see Irishness as culture, or to view Irish-Americans as an ethnic group, provokes the search for typicalities in order to validate the writer's initial assumption that they are culturally or socially distinct. For without such typicalities, the notions of 'culture' or 'ethnicity' cannot be sustained: the epistemological foundation of these concepts rests upon the possibility of generalization and its intellectual procedure: it demands the identification of a set of phenotypical traits by which the cultural species in question may be recognized and classified as distinct from all others in the museum collection. Under such pressure, the notion of typicality is not infrequently stretched beyond credulity. The term comes to mean something other than the middle part of a statistical curve of distribution: what most people say and do most of the time. Rather, it comes to rest on exampling, convenient illustration, anecdote, or so-called 'thick description'. Measurement is obscured or omitted, the pursuit of generality is abandoned, and any instance or episode of the phenomenon in question (whose typicality the reader is given no means of judging) may be used to justify the analyst's contention that these characteristics constitute distinctive *ethnies*, cultures, communities, symbolic and cognitive systems, or social identities.

In contemporary discussion, the term 'identity' has largely supplanted the earlier terms 'personality', 'mentality', and 'psyche'. This has made matters worse. Unless its meaning is clearly specified, 'identity' is an ambiguous term which creates more confusion than enlightenment. In its Eriksonian sense, the term refers to properties of uniqueness and individuality, a personal variant of a modal type, the essential differences making one person psychologically distinct from all others within a given cultural milieu; but the term may also refer to selfhood, personhood, or social persona in looser, less strictly psychological senses. In another, contrary meaning, 'identity' refers to qualities of sameness, in that persons may associate themselves, or be associated by others, with groups or categories on the basis of some salient common feature or set of features, as in 'ethnic identity'. In its sense of sameness, 'identity' refers to commonalities associated with groups or categories. The starting-point is taxonomic: the social and cultural world is held to be composed of a discontinuous set of named or labelled segments (for example, male, father, middle-class, middle-aged, college-educated, Catholic, white-collar worker, Irish, suburban, Democrat), membership in terms of which individuals must define themselves, or be defined by others. These groups and categories are accorded significant cognitive content 'of a type'. These may include evaluative or emotional contents from which the individual derives (or is held to derive) self-esteem, or a sense of knowing or belonging. These features are highly variable in intensity and importance, as are any associated normative expectations which may furnish individuals with guides to their social behaviour.

When the term is used loosely, one often does not know whether the people concerned have typified themselves in either of these ways, or whether they have been merely pigeon-holed by the writer and assigned a set of phenotypical characteristics which may or may not be based upon measurable (and measured) attributes. Moreover, even among careful scholars, these two senses of identity are frequently conflated as between individuals' categorical memberships and their individual dispositions, whether psychological, cultural, or sociological; self-identities are sometimes simply treated as the consequence of individuals' categorical memberships. Whatever is asserted about the categorical pigeon-holes in which they have been placed is held, *petitio principii*, to be evidential of their psychological qualities or social dispositions, although no other evidence about their self-identity may be offered to the reader. The ambiguity of the term, which tempts its users to make methodological mistakes and to beg crucial questions without even noticing that they have done so, makes a good deal of recent historical and anthropological writing on identity among nineteenth-century European immigrants and their descendants—and indeed ethnic groups of all kinds—difficult to interpret and next to impossible to use for comparative purposes.

Certain traits of personality, glossed as characteristic features of identity, are so often attributed to Irish-Americans that we looked for evidence of them. Our approach to the matter of establishing whether there were such traits, and what they might be, was to ask our informants, in a self-completion questionnaire, 'Are there any traits in your character or personality that you associate with your ethnic background?' We also asked them if there were such traits they could see in their mothers, fathers, wives, and husbands. In our open-ended interviews, we asked most of our 500 interviewees about their personal sense of Irishness, and in another series of interviews we went back to a sample of 40 people, chosen from among our original informants, to explore in greater depth their senses of themselves and how this connected with their Irish ancestry. Of the 252 respondents to the self-completion questionnaire, 143 people (56.7 per cent) said that they thought there were qualities of their personalities that they associated with their ancestry. Ninety-six people (38.1 per cent) said there were not, and 13 (5.2 per cent) did not reply to this question. Just over half, then, thought that some traits in their personalities were in some way connected with the cultural milieux from which their European ancestors had come. This sample included a number of people who were not of Irish descent, or who had recently moved to Albany as adults. To see if there was a more marked pattern, the sample was controlled for those identifying themselves as of Irish ancestry and who had been schooled in Albany. Of 88 cases, 46 (52.3 per cent) said that there were traits in their character that they regarded as Irish and were able to list at least one such trait; 30 (34.0 per cent) said there were not; and 12 (13.6 per cent) either said yes, but were unable to specify any particular trait they regarded as Irish; or did not reply to the question. The 46 people who listed such traits mentioned 82 qualities that they felt were Irish.

The lack of overlap was striking. Few people had exactly the same ideas about what constituted an Irish trait in themselves; the 46 people who identified such traits listed 122 items, only 40 of which overlapped. Three-quarters of the traits listed were mentioned only once. The most frequently mentioned characteristics were a sense of humour (9.0 per cent of all items listed); having a quick temper, being stubborn and argumentative (8.2 per cent); religiosity (8.2 per cent) sociability or friendliness (6.6 per cent); being good-hearted, good-natured, easy-going, or generous (5.7 per cent); being kind, tolerant, loving, caring, loyal, and patient (4.9 per cent); family-centredness (4.9 per cent); being moody, melancholy, pessimistic, or fatalistic (3.3 per cent); musicality (2.5 per cent) and, despite not being a trait of character or personality in a strict sense, physical characteristics such as being red-haired or Irish-looking were given five times. Table 7.1 gives a full listing of the traits our informants mentioned, together with the frequency of their occurrence.

We provided our informants with the opportunity to answer the question yes or no, and then gave them free rein to express any attribute that they wished; we made no a priori assumption that they saw themselves as having such attributes. We did not lead them by suggesting terms ourselves, nor ask them to agree or disagree with previously prepared statements about what might constitute an Irish trait, nor ask them to make their responses conform to pre-defined categories. Interviewing procedures that employ coded responses of this kind are common. They are computer-friendly and produce neat, compact results to which various statistical tests can be conveniently applied. Most such testing procedures

TABLE 7.1. Traits of personality attributed as Irish to selves, Albany-schooled (*n* = 88), in order of frequency

Traits	No.	Traits	No.
Humour/sense of humour/wit	11	Good-natured	1
Short-/quick-tempered	6	Good time	1
Generosity	4	Gregarious	1
Friendliness	3	Hair colour	1
Gift of gab/love to talk	3	Handsome	1
Love of music	3	Honesty	1
Religious	3	Irish-looking	1
Alcohol	2	Kindness	1
Commitment to/love of family	2	Light complexion	1
Good storyteller	2	Literate	1
Hard worker/work ethic	2	Love of dance	1
Love of beauty	2	Love of history	1
Love of language	2	Love of outdoors	1
Love of people	2	Love of poetry	1
Love of religion/faith	2	Love of stories	1
Loving	2	Love of the arts	1
Loyalty	2	Melancholic	1
Religious	2	Moodiness	1
Religion/religious belief	2	Outspoken	1
Stubborn	2	Patience	1
Tolerance	2	Perseverance	1
Affable	1	Pessimism	1
Appearance	1	Poetic	1
Argumentative	1	Pride	1
Bad temper	1	Religious belief	1
Caring	1	Sense of family	1
Charm over substance	1	Sensitivity	1
Close family ties	1	Sentimental	1
Close-knit family	1	Sharing	1
Commitment	1	Sincerity	1
Compatibility	1	Sociable	1
Easy-going	1	Spontaneous	1
Emotional	1	Temperament	1
Family values	1	Quick wit	1
Fatalism	1	Vengeful	1
Frugality	1	Zest for life	1
Good-hearted	1		

are designed rigorously and their outputs are carefully scrutinized for statistical validity. None the less, they are not entirely without problems on the input side. If, unintentionally, interviewees are in any way led to think that they ought to have such traits, and if these traits are identified for them, the result may be an exaggerated set of positive or negative responses. For example, if we had suggested that the Irish traits that our informants might see in themselves were good-humouredness, sociability, and sentimentality, and had they been asked to scale their responses between 'agree strongly' and 'disagree strongly', a substantial majority of our sample would probably have agreed with our suggestions, as indeed they did on other questions which were designed in this way. Our more open procedure on this question, however, reveals that most of our informants would not spontaneously have used such terms to describe their traits of character, nor would the frequency of positive association have been as high.

Those of our informants who saw themselves as having Irish traits in their character listed 122 responses; some, as mentioned above, were mentioned by more than one informant. A little over a third of these responses (46) referred to what could broadly be called interactional qualities: how people saw themselves as relating socially to others. These qualities included a sense of humour, talkativeness or garrulity, affability or friendliness, loyalty, generosity, sincerity, honesty, and kindness; qualities which, overall, predominated. These qualities were, however, offset by a handful of negative traits which included a propensity to drink too much, a tendency to be argumentative, vengeful, and shallow ('charm over substance', as one of our informants put it). About a fifth of the responses (26) were connected, broadly speaking, with our informants' views of their emotional characteristics. Here the overall picture was about half-and-half good and bad. People saw the Irish qualities in themselves as, on the negative side, expressed in their quick tempers, stubbornness, fatalism, pessimism, moodiness, melancholia, and bad-temperedness. Contrarily, other people saw far more positive traits in themselves which they likewise attributed to their Irish backgrounds: being loving, good-natured, easy-going, good-hearted, spontaneous, good-tempered, sensitive, and having a patient, caring, and sharing nature. A quarter of the responses (31) approached the question by mentioning attachments to things as qualities that our informants perceived as Irish. Listed here were religiosity, a propensity for hard work, the centrality of family values, and the love of music, literature, language, history, beauty, and landscape. The remaining 19 responses consisted of items that were ambiguous or unclear, or referred to physical appearance, or did not comfortably fit into any of the three main categories mentioned above.

If we turn to our informants' responses to the same question with respect to their fathers, mothers, husbands, and wives—people whom we can presume our informants know nearly as well as themselves, and in whom they might see qualities that they regard as connected with these persons' Irish ancestry—a not dissimilar picture emerges. The question, 'Are there any traits in your father's personality that you associate with his ancestral or ethnic background?', yielded 65 usable replies; most of the others had fathers who were not of Irish ancestry. Forty (61.5 per cent) answered yes, and 25 (38.5 per cent) indicated, by answering no, that they did not associate anything they regarded as an Irish trait with their father's character. Overall, the 40 people who said yes listed 71 traits. Half of these traits (35) referred to interactional qualities, and included a sense of humour or wittiness (12.7 per cent of all traits listed), gift of the gab (8.5 per cent), sociability or gregariousness (5.6 per cent), and generosity (4.2 per cent); but there were also 6 mentions of a tendency towards alcoholism. Sixteen of the traits listed (22.5 per cent) were emotional qualities. Here, only 2 traits were mentioned more than once: stubbornness (4.2 per cent) and a quick temper (5.6 per cent); the other traits included having a loving or sharing nature, being moody, sensitive, pessimistic, easy-going, emotional, strong, and logical. There were 20 traits associated with an attachment to things: religion (7.0 per cent), family (5.6 per cent), a work ethic (5.6 per cent), and music (4.2 per cent).

When asked the same question about their mothers, slightly fewer saw what they perceived as Irish traits: 27 of the 59 people (45.8 per cent) reported that their mothers had such traits; and 32 (54.2 per cent) said that they did not. Those who responded positively again emphasized interactional qualities as connected with their mothers' Irishness. Of the 57 traits mentioned, 28 (49.1 per cent) were of this kind: a sense of humour or wittiness occurred 5 times (8.7 per cent of all traits listed), talkativeness (5.3 per cent); friendliness, warmth, and honesty each occurred twice (3.5 per cent each). Twelve of the traits listed concerned emotional qualities; only one, having a temper, occurred more than once (3 times). The other emotional qualities included a loving, easy-going, cheerful or whimsical nature, stubbornness, fatalism, having strong resolve, and being in control or independent. Seventeen traits concerned their mothers' attachments to things: nearly half (8 occurrences; 14.0 per cent of all traits listed) identified their religiosity; family-centredness was mentioned 4 times, and a work ethic twice.

Considering our informants' views of the Irish qualities of their mothers and fathers together, there is a close correspondence in the way the distribution of these traits breaks down: in interactional qualities, 49.3 per cent for fathers and 49.1 per cent for mothers; for emotional qualities, 28.2 per cent for fathers and 29.8 per cent for mothers; for devotional qualities, 28.2 per cent for fathers and 29.8 per cent for mothers. On balance, our informants gave a somewhat warmer view of the Irish qualities of their mothers: seeing them as nurturing, religious, and independent but just as inclined to be as stubborn and quick-tempered as their fathers. None the less, to keep these figures in perspective, only 8 of the 65 people (12.3 per cent) having mothers of Irish descent in our sample mentioned the single most frequently listed characteristic, religiosity: 88 per cent either did not have mothers who were especially religious, or did not connect their mothers' religiosity with their Irish backgrounds. Similarly, the most frequently mentioned Irish characteristic of their fathers, a sense of humour, was reported by only 9 of the 65 informants having Irish fathers: 86 per cent either had fathers who were not particularly witty, or their fathers' sense of humour was not regarded by our informants as associated with their Irish descent.

Largely because of the high degree of intermarriage which now prevails in Albany (discussed in Chapter 5), there were many fewer usable responses to similar questions about husbands and wives among our controlled sample of 88 locally schooled people of Irish ancestry. Only 14 women (15.9 per cent) and 20 men (22.7 per cent) had spouses of single or mixed Irish ancestry. The remainder of our informants were unmarried, married to people of non-Irish backgrounds, or were widowed or divorced and declined to give any information about their deceased or former spouses. With such small numbers, any analysis is of questionable validity if our goal is to establish what is typical. None the less, for what it may be worth, 8, or 57.1 per cent of wives perceived their husbands as having traits that they perceived as Irish, and 6 (42.9 per cent) did not. Altogether, 19 traits were mentioned. Under interactional qualities were sociability (mentioned twice), a sense of humour, frugality, fairness, and a concern for others (all mentioned once). Husbands' emotional traits were stubbornness (listed 3 times) and a quick temper (once). Their devotional qualities were an attachment to religion (mentioned 3 times); a work ethic, a sense of family, and a love of landscape. If our sample is indicative, husbands had a markedly lower propensity to attribute Irish traits to their wives than vice versa. Of the 20 cases, 7 men (35.0 per cent) thought their wives had traits they regarded as Irish, and 13 (65.0 per cent) did not. A total of only 10 traits was listed, none more than once. These included being a good companion, empathetic, independent, conscientious, temperamental, stubborn, being hard-working, appreciating literature, and taking pride in being Irish. Notably, while religiosity had been the most frequently mentioned Irish trait in their mothers, none of the husbands connected their wives' religiosity with their Irish backgrounds. Similarly, only one woman identified in her husband the most common Irish trait that our informants saw in their fathers, a sense of humour.

This suggests a generational shift, which a larger sample is likely to confirm. If we accept the conventional wisdom that how people are constituted as individuals, and, consequently, what they see in others is largely a matter of who they have associated with most closely over their lifetimes, then this is no more than we might expect to see in the data. A hundred years have now passed since most of our informants' immigrant ancestors came to Albany. Those of our Albany-schooled informants who had (or have) Irish-born parents or grandparents are relatively few in number and becoming ever fewer as the years pass. Those who had never known an Irish-born parent, whose traits of character might have influenced them in childhood, comprised 87.2 per cent of our informants; and 68.3 per cent of our sample had never known an Irish-born grandparent, being more than three generations distant from any Irish immigrant in their ancestries, however late-arriving. Thus notions of an 'Irish' trait of character or behaviour have come within the orbit of their experience only at one, two, or more generational removes, at second, third, or fourth hand. If social surroundings mould personalities, then what happened in Ireland a century or a century and a half ago, to people they have never known, cannot have had a direct effect upon them. For half of our informants, a connection between personality and Irish ancestry was completely absent, or they were unable to mention anything beyond an otherwise-undefinable feeling of having Irish traits of character. For the other half, what now may be perceived as an Irish trait can be impossible to distinguish from a trait of character that someone of, say, Italian descent might list; indeed, some of our informants mentioned exactly the same traits for parents and spouses who were not of Irish descent. In other respects, some traits associated with Irishness have entered into folklore and have become familiar stereotypes that people might apply to themselves and others when it seems apt to do so: traits such as sociability, the gift of the gab, stubbornness, religiosity, musicality, a quick temper, and a tendency to drink too much.

Is it possible to construct a modal Irish-American personality from these findings? To begin, let us recall that nearly half of our informants, in both the larger sample of 252 people and the smaller controlled sample of 88 individuals, either reported that they did not perceive themselves as having any traits that they associated with the Irishness of their back-grounds, or were unable to list anything specific. Thirty-two people in the controlled sample, or 36.4 per cent, mentioned their sociability, friendli-ness, and talkativeness as being attributable to their Irish backgrounds. Seventeen people, or 19.3 per cent, reported emotional qualities that they connected with their Irishness. Nineteen people, or 21.6 per cent, said that their attachment to things such as religion and family values was an attribute of their Irishness. Put another way, 64 per cent of our Albany-born sample of people who identified themselves as Irish did not connect their own Irishness with being gregarious, outgoing, or witty: either they did not consider themselves as having these qualities, or they did not see these traits as being particularly Irish. About 80 per cent did not regard themselves as having any emotional qualities they viewed as especially Irish, and about the same proportion, 80 per cent, did not make any direct connection between their own attachment to their religion or families and their Irish ancestry. Our informants' perceptions of the Irish traits in their fathers, mothers, husbands, and wives confirm this general pattern, and, if anything, bring it into even sharper relief. Gregariousness and being outgoing and witty were not regarded as Irish traits in 71 per cent of fathers or 83 per cent of mothers; in 79 per cent of husbands or 95 per cent of wives. Stubbornness and a quick temper were not seen in 91 per cent of fathers or 93 per cent of mothers, 71 per cent of husbands or 90 per cent of wives. Religiosity and family-centredness were not regarded as Irish traits in 86 per cent of fathers or 80 per cent of mothers; or in 71 per cent of husbands, and received no mention at all as qualities of our informants' wives.

Remarkably, none of our informants spontaneously mentioned a specific inclination for politics, or homesickness for Ireland, or anglopho-bia, or a sense of being part of an oppressed minority as traits of their own characters, nor did they attribute any of these qualities to their fathers, mothers, husbands, or wives. Nor, despite their propensity to connect their Catholicism with their Irishness in other contexts, did this emerge strongly here. What they say about the historical experience of the Irish *in general* might well bring up these matters, and they might attribute these qualities to a folkloric Irish psyche or mentality *in the abstract*, but the absence of these qualities in our informants' senses of themselves and those close to them is surely highly significant. This raises an important point about the nature of different data-collection methods and the results they are likely to produce. Had we asked our informants to scale their responses to the question, 'Would you say that a penchant for politics (or a dislike of the English, or a sentimental attachment to Ireland) is an attribute of your character?' we would have led them to compare their own characters to a stereotypical image of Irishness with which most of them were familiar. At least some of our informants are likely to have been tempted to agree with this statement, first because the idea had been suggested to them, and secondly because they may have felt that they ought to agree with it if a sense of being Irish was at all important to them.

Were we, on the basis of these findings, to attempt to map out a modal—that is, typical—Irish-American personality, we would first have to accept that at least eight-tenths of the topography is blank, featureless, and unnamed terrain; the measurable evidence for any typicality at all is extremely weak. Perhaps to the consternation of those who hold these traits to be the 'natural' attributes of 'the Irish-American character', there would be no waypoints or features on this map marked homesick, anglo-phobic, oppressed, or political. The high ground would be marked gift of the gab, sociable, funny, patient, good-hearted, family-centred, religious, hard-working, musical, generous, loyal, and so forth. The valleys and ravines, here and there, would be marked stubborn, fatalistic, easily angered, argumentative, hard-drinking, and so on. This is probably about as much as we could plot on the map without putting words in our informants' mouths, going beyond what is measurable, or abandoning the search for typicality and retreating behind the smokescreen of anecdote, convenient illustration, 'thick description', and unverifiable assertions about the unconscious.

Any attempt to delineate 'the' Irish or Irish-American character, as it might be typified now or at any time in the past, is a perilous undertaking, full of methodological pitfalls. One of the most telling criticisms of the personality and culture tradition in American anthropology has concerned the hypothesis that a single personality type, or modal personality, can give rise to, or be created by, any given society or cultural institution. Empirical investigations have confirmed what ordinary common sense tells us, that people and their lives are far more than just the sum of their psychological characteristics and predispositions propelling them through cultural and social space over their lifetimes. To try to derive a modal personality from the abstract generalities of culture, or vice versa, is doomed to hen-and-egg circularity. There is no sound evidence of such modal personalities in any society, large or small, past or present. There are simply no methodologically rigorous grounds upon which the idea of a modal Irish-American or Irish personality can be supported. In the end, any such proposition can be based on nothing more than the author's wish to persuade us of something that cannot be empirically demonstrated, and his or her artfulness in attempting to do so.

None the less, there is still much that we can say on the basis of the evidence and findings presented in this chapter, to which we shall return in Chapters 8 and 9.

8

The Wearing of the Green

I

While Irish immigrants, and their descendants, have formed a large part of Albany's population since the mid-nineteenth century, the St Patrick's Day parade is a recent civic invention dating only from 1951. Since then, the parade has become one of the city's biggest annual events. Several hundred people march in the parade, and thousands more line the streets to watch the spectacle and celebrate the day in the city's Irish bars and social clubs. Tens of thousands of other people in Albany and other towns and cities in upstate New York participate vicariously in the festivities by watching the event on television in their local Irish bar, or at home with friends. The day is one of intense sociality. The normally deserted winter streets are filled with people 'wearing the green'; throughout the day and late into the evening, the city's bars, clubs, and restaurants are thronged with people drinking, dancing to Irish tunes, eating Irish food, and having a riotously good time. Most of the people of Irish ancestry taking part will have driven into Albany from the suburbs, since few of them still live in the old city-centre neighbourhoods.

The day begins with a solemn mass in St Patrick's parish church on lower Central Avenue, built in 1858 and the focal point of one of the neighbourhoods where people of Irish ancestry once lived. The parade route, a little short of 2 miles long, starts at the junction of Quail Street and Central Avenue near St Patrick's church and the Hibernians' Hall, and joins Washington Avenue at Lark Street, continuing down Washington Avenue past the City Hall. Crowds congregate along the route to watch the spectacle, and the local television station relays the event with live commentary. Vendors stroll along the route selling green balloons, green hats, badges proclaiming 'Irish for a Day', and 'Kiss Me, I'm Irish'.

There are eight divisions in the parade, which correspond to the organizations or main groups of marchers who regularly take part. These include the Albany Fire Department, the South End Irish, the Colonie

Irish, the Watervliet chapter of the Ancient Order of Hibernians, Capital District Irish Northern Aid, the North Albany Irish, the Menands Irish, and the Albany chapter of the Hibernians. The parade order is rotated every year so that each of the eight divisions will have a turn to lead the parade. The mayor always serves as the Honorary Grand Marshal, who heads the parade along with the Grand Marshal. The Grand Marshal dresses in a frock-coat with a top hat and a sash in the Irish national colours. Following the Grand Marshal are the fifty or so marching units. The units include Miss Teen Albany, floats sponsored by local businesses and organizations, the Albany Police Department pipe band, and a number of high school bands preceded by pompom girls, baton-twirlers, and drum majors. Also represented are the Veterans of Foreign Wars, the Boy Scouts and Girl Scouts, and a number of other civic organizations in the city and the surrounding area. A number of well-known Albany politicians march in the parade.

The choice of Grand Marshal in 1993 was controversial. It was the turn of Capital District Irish Northern Aid (Noraid) to lead the parade, and Paul Murray, national chairman of the organization and an Albany resident, was chosen as Grand Marshal. Not until a series of editorials in the local daily newspaper, the *Times-Union*, questioned the wisdom of having the INA national chairman as Grand Marshal did it become a matter of concern to the parade committee and to the public at large. Before the editorials appeared, the Hibernians in Albany (the traditional custodians of the parade) had been chiefly preoccupied with the New York parade and the matter of gay and lesbian participation, and were preparing themselves for a similar development in Albany. The *Times-Union* criticized the hypocrisy of the Ancient Order of Hibernians for their preparedness to discriminate against a 'peace-loving' Irish gay group by refusing them permission to march in New York, while failing to object to the fact that Irish Northern Aid (who were accused of supporting those who 'blow up women and children in bus stations') were leading the parade in Albany. Over the next two weeks, six letters of rejoinder were printed which claimed that the *Times-Union* had a grudge against those in favour of the unification of Ireland. The *Times-Union* stated again that it was not questioning the personal integrity of Paul Murray; rather, it was Noraid's declared support for the IRA which was the source of the difficulty. The publicity was an embarrassment to the parade committee, since the official policy of the Hibernians on the issue of Irish unification was, and is, neutrality; the committee was now very concerned that the INA was exploiting their leadership of the parade to politicize it with their concerns about Northern Ireland, thus risking the alienation of large numbers of people from an event which was intended to be of broad public appeal and a celebration of civic pride. As the day of the parade approached, there was speculation that the mayor might not march. The parade committee feared that Mayor Whalen might be concerned that his presence at the head of the parade, alongside Murray, could be construed by the public as implying support for Noraid, and so for the IRA's bomb-and-bullet tactics in Ireland.

As it turned out, the city, the Democratic Party, and the mayor were providentially saved major political embarrassment by a heavy snowfall which forced the cancellation of the parade at the eleventh hour. When the committee met on the following Monday to decide whether the parade should be staged on the next Saturday, a couple of members suggested that it should be abandoned that year. A decision was nevertheless made to go ahead. The mayor sent apologies that he was unable to attend, citing previous obligations. There was no television crew available that day. The parade was considerably smaller than usual and there were many fewer spectators. Irish Northern Aid, however, was very well represented, and did not deviate from their normal practice of wearing black armbands and carrying banners advocating a British withdrawal from Northern Ireland ('England Out').

The 1993 parade in Albany thus evoked and might have repeated what happened in New York City on St Patrick's Day ten years earlier in 1983, not long after the hunger strikes in the Maze Prison which led to the death of Bobby Sands. Michael Flannery, an 81-year-old Irish Republican, veteran of the Irish Civil War, and founder of Irish Northern Aid in the United States, was chosen as the Grand Marshal of the parade. Only months before, Flannery had faced charges in a US federal court for running guns to the IRA. There was deep consternation about his appointment to lead the parade. New York's mayor Ed Koch did nevertheless turn up, and so did Governor Cuomo, but Senator Daniel Patrick Moynihan and former Governor Hugh Carey, both prominent Irish-Americans who usually marched in the parade, did not. Washington forbade the US Army, Navy, and Air Force from taking part, more than a dozen high school bands refused to march, and the Roman Catholic Cardinal of New York, who traditionally reviews the parade, did not emerge from St Patrick's Cathedral until after Flannery had passed. Aer Lingus, the Irish national airline, withdrew its long-standing sponsorship of the television coverage of the parade. And, the then Prime Minister of Ireland, Garret Fitzgerald, condemned the choice of Flannery as Grand

Marshal with the words, 'Why is a supporter of these terrorists leading the parade?'

As it turned out, no permanent damage was done to the parade as an institution, and in the following year things were back to normal. However, by 1991, the New York parade organizers were confronted by a new problem: what to do about the Irish Lesbian and Gay Organization (ILGO). According to the organizers, ILGO was one of about forty would-be groups on the reserve list, waiting for an official place in the parade. According to ILGO, they had been consistently discriminated against by the parade's organizers, the Ancient Order of Hibernians, and were being denied 'the right' to march. Controversy raged while New York's lawyers and judges tried to decide what kind of thing the parade was in law, whether anyone had any entitlement under the law to representation in the parade, and thus whether anyone could either be held accountable for discrimination or could claim any civil rights in respect of it. At the last moment, Mayor Dinkins forced the parade's organizing committee into an accommodation. The mayor's city hall lieutenants had arranged the agreement of Hibernians' Division 7, one of the groups marching in the parade, to issue an invitation for ILGO's 200 members to march along with them, provided that they did not march separately, carry an ILGO banner, or wear identifying T-shirts or hats. ILGO accepted this compromise, and the parade committee were left with no grounds upon which they could object. To show his solidarity with ILGO, and his annoyance with the Hibernians' leadership, Dinkins decided to march with Division 7, instead of in the Honorary Grand Marshal's traditional place at the head of the parade.

On the day, feelings ran high. Public disapprobation was more intense and far more vocal than it had been ten years earlier. Dinkins and Division 7 were booed for miles. There were placards on the sidewalks which said, 'Gay Sex, No Way' and 'Dinkins the Catholic-Basher', references, of course, to the Catholic Church's strong disapproval of homosexuality. There were shouts of 'You're finished, Dinkins!' and chants of 'One-term mayor!'; raw eggs were thrown, and at one point two half-full beer cans were hurled at the mayor from the hostile crowd. The parade was stopped temporarily while the police used umbrellas to shield him from further missiles. There was more drama when Division 7 reached St Patrick's Cathedral. Cardinal O'Connor pointedly did not descend the steps to greet the mayor, as was traditional, and Dinkins was forced to climb the steps himself. Later, when Mayor Dinkins and Division 7 reached the reviewing stand filled with officials of the Hibernians, a number of them turned their backs until the contingent had passed.

In Boston, resistance to gay and lesbian demands was responsible for the cancellation, in 1994, of one of the biggest St Patrick's Day events in the country. Its organizers, the South Boston Allied War Veterans' Council, took the extraordinary step of cancelling the parade rather than comply with a state superior court's decision which would have forced them to allow the Irish-American Gay, Lesbian, and Bisexual Group of Boston to march under a banner proclaiming their sexual orientation. The Boston parade committee was reviled by journalists as representative only of blue-collar ethnics, living in the past, who had not yet awakened to the multicultural, postmodern age. For example, the authors of a series of *New York Times* editorials and articles described the parade organizers (and by implication, the parades' participants and supporters generally) as divisive, exclusionary, intolerant, bigoted, racist, without conscience, and as staining the character of their city.[1] The civil rights issues raised by the gay and lesbian challenge to the Boston parade were fought all the way up to the to the United States Supreme Court, which eventually delivered a decision in June 1995.[2]

II

Religious processions were once a part of American civic life in many places, just as they were in Europe. Few have survived or have been successfully reintroduced; those which have, like the Albany St Patrick's Day parade, have gradually and unintentionally accumulated all the accretions of modern American life, including waltzing high school bands in outlandish uniforms, pompom girls, and scantily clad beauty queens woodenly waving from their perches on Oldsmobile convertibles, as well as the posturing politicians who can be seen in virtually any big-city or

---

[1] See, among a number of examples, 'Parading the Wrong Message', 15 Mar. 1994; 'Black Flags in Boston Protest Gay Group', 20 Mar. 1995; 'The Right to March in Bigotry', 20 June 1995.

[2] The Supreme Court decided, in a unanimous opinion, that the parades were private events which expressed the opinions of their organizers. The court held that the parade organizers' right to free expression, guaranteed under the Constitution, would be compromised if they were forced to allow people to march under banners or otherwise proclaim sentiments of which the parade organizers did not approve. The parade organizers' right to remain silent on the issue of homosexuality, or any other such issue, was also held to be inviolate.

small-town parade, Irish or not. 'Everybody loves a parade' is a traditional American expression. If there had been no Second World War, and the Italians or Germans had established the tradition of an annual civic parade rather than the Irish, people in Albany today might instead wear, once a year, badges which say 'Swabian for a Day' or 'Kiss Me, I'm Neapolitan'.

In some ways, the absence of the tradition of an old-country language and the lack of nucleated neighbourhoods meant, at times, that the Irish were less visible in Albany's cultural landscape than other nineteenth-century European immigrants. The Germans, for instance, by virtue of their regional and religious differences and their initial linguistic isolation from the anglophone mainstream of Albany society, developed a large and distinctive set of old-country associations and public festivals. Before the First World War there were more than forty German societies, lodges, provident associations, choral groups, and glee clubs in Albany, most of which would have conducted their affairs through the medium of *Hochdeutsch*, *Plattdeutsch* dialects, or Yiddish. This is not to count societies directly associated with three German Catholic congregations, and one Evangelical German, four Evangelical Lutheran, one German Evangelical Protestant, and two Jewish congregations. Three German-language newspapers were published in Albany; and German saints' days and other religious and secular holidays were celebrated with processions, parades, and festivals.

By contrast, Irish old-country associations in Albany were never anything like as numerous. The city directories listed only five or six in the half-century from 1887 to 1936, only two of which survived much beyond 1900.[3] That the Irish were English-speaking greatly accelerated their integration into Albany society, even if it meant at the same time that their cultural distinctiveness had largely melted away by the second generation. At the turn of the century, there were still enough Irish-born people in the population and sufficient interest in maintaining an attachment to the old country to sustain four men's divisions of the Hibernians, each with its own set of officers, meeting twice a month on alternate Tuesdays or Thursdays at Hibernia Hall, as it was then called. By the late 1920s, however, its membership had dwindled along with the number of Irish-born, and supported only one men's division and a ladies' auxiliary. The location of Hibernia Hall was itself reflective of the fluidity and lack

---

[3] While these lists are almost certainly incomplete, there is no reason to believe that they were any less complete for Irish associations than for German associations. The relative difference in numbers of organizations is the salient point.

of nucleation of Irish immigrant settlement in Albany, having had several different addresses over the last hundred years; in 1887 Hibernia Hall was on South Pearl Street in the South End; by 1900 it had moved north and west to Sherman Street, between Clinton and Central, and since then it has occupied various premises in and around St Patrick's parish, seemingly at least as much for its symbolic associations with the patron saint of Ireland as for reasons of any particular concentration of people of Irish ancestry in the locality.

Our interview responses generally indicate that old-country associations have not played a significant role in the lives of most people of Irish ancestry for quite some time. Few of our informants were members of any organizations associated with their ancestry, and most people said that no one in their family ever had been. The largest Irish old-country organization in Albany, and the one to which people are most likely to belong, is the Ancient Order of Hibernians, which has 550 members; we collected questionnaires from 50. Given that the 1990 Census showed that there were approximately 90,000 people of Irish descent aged over 18 in Albany County, the participation rate is roughly 0.6 per cent of its potential recruitment base. Put another way, 99.4 per cent of Albany County's Irish-ancestry adults are not members of the AOH. Of the Hibernians' members, of whom about 150 are women, only a relatively small number are active in the organization. Some attend functions regularly, but many others merely pay their dues, taking no part in the AOH's activities from one year to the next. The members' bar is frequented by a few middle-aged regulars, who meet with their friends and quietly sip glasses of Budweiser; the small room is usually more empty than full. Most of our informants were familiar with the hall only on St Patrick's Day, when spirits are high, the hall is packed with people, and Guinness is being spilt all over the floors by colliding and sometimes rather unsteady revellers.

The Ancient Order of Hibernians is the largest Irish-American organization in the United States. It was founded in New York in 1836 and from there spread back to Ireland, although its origin myth claims that it had its beginnings in Ireland during penal times as an underground brotherhood whose purpose was to defend Catholicism. In America, the Ancient Order of Hibernians developed in the nineteenth century as a provident association devoted to the advancement of the interests and welfare of Irish immigrants. Its organization in the form of a semi-secret men's society followed much the same pattern as many other such societies formed in the United States during the nineteenth century, including the Shriners, Foresters, Odd Fellows, and a number of others; and also, undoubtedly, drew on the tradition of Irish secret societies. At the local lodge level, the AOH actively assisted its immigrant members to become established in America by various practical means. At the national level, the organization worked to counteract the pamphleteering Know-Nothings who sought an end to Irish Catholic immigration. The AOH aims 'to perpetuate in America the spirit of our Catholic ancestors'. The criteria for membership are that one must be Irish, or have a parent or grandparent born in Ireland, and be a practising Catholic. Today, as with many other old-country associations, the Ancient Order of Hibernians is suffering a gradual decline in membership, although it has not yet become moribund (as, for example, has the Orange Lodge in Canada, which is now virtually extinct). As immigration from Ireland has slowed to a trickle, and few new Irish immigrants any longer settle in places like Albany, little new blood has come into the local chapter in recent years. The upkeep of the building, which the members own, is financed mainly by Friday-night bingo sessions. The bar makes a profit only in the St Patrick's Day season when the club is packed with people celebrating their Irishness.

The AOH's charter states that one of its aims is to promote 'unity among the men of the race, regardless of sectional differences or political preferences'. This aim is conventionally held to refer to the unification of the Irish nation, but the AOH's charter objectives are silent on the matter of *how* Irish unity is to be achieved. Within the AOH this is a highly contentious matter. In Albany, some AOH members are also members of Irish Northern Aid, but support for the INA is seen by the majority of Hibernians as being indistinguishable from support for the methods adopted by the Provisional IRA to expel the British from Ireland, methods which they deplore. The relationship between Noraid and the Hibernians in Albany is therefore an uneasy one. The organizations need one another; the Hibernians cannot afford to do without those of its members who belong to the INA, and Noraid recruits from the AOH membership as well as needing to use the facilities of the Hibernians' Hall to stage its public events, since it has no premises of its own. Tension is sometimes openly expressed on these occasions: when the INA invites guest speakers, an anti-IRA reaction by AOH members is usually provoked; on other occasions, moderate nationalist speakers invited by the Hibernians have been heckled by Noraid supporters.

Another aim of the Hibernians is that of 'cultivating the history and traditions of the Irish race'. The hall is the venue for a number of self-consciously Irish activities: step-dancing classes, with an enrolment of approximately forty children and a dozen adults; Irish language classes, sponsored by the Irish-American Cultural Institute, with around fifteen students; the Albany Police Pipe Band hold their rehearsals in the hall; and occasional concerts are staged by well-known Irish-American musicians and bands. Those who participate in these activities are not necessarily members of the AOH. Only a couple of the members of the police band are Hibernians. The step-dancing group draws some of its membership from the children of Hibernians, but most have parents who are not connected with the AOH. None of those enrolled in the Irish language classes at the time of our fieldwork were Hibernians.

Symbols of Irishness are ubiquitous in the images the AOH creates of itself. Their functions are accompanied by Irish music, newsletters and programmes are printed in green ink and decorated with Celtic crosses and the Irish tricolour, photographs of Irish heroes and celebrities are displayed in the members' bar, and AOH ritual is replete with Irish imagery. None the less, the membership encompasses a wide range of experience of what it is to be Irish. Hibernians may be first-generation, Irish-born immigrants; or the fourth- or fifth-generation mixed-pedigree descendants of nineteenth-century immigrants. They may have been raised in one of Albany's old city-centre neighbourhoods and have attended a Catholic parochial school; or they might have been brought up in the suburbs and have gone to a public school along with non-Catholics. They might still have relatives in Ireland whom they regularly visit; or they might no longer have the means of discovering who their Irish ancestors were and have never visited the ancestral country. Hibernians are, however, also Catholic, and the Catholicism of the organization is, in practice, at least as important as its Irishness. Catholicism permeates every aspect of the Hibernian ethos. The AOH actively supports Catholic Action, campaigns against abortion, seeks the restoration of prayer in schools, works to retain 'In God We Trust' as an official motto of the United States, endows a chair of American Catholicism at the University of Notre Dame, and resists the secularization of St Patrick's Day. Hibernians are expected to remain in good standing with the church and may not be divorced. In public, they must be seen to uphold the ordinances of the church.

In contrast, the other main organization in Albany based on old-country ties, the Capital District Irish Northern Aid Committee, is not interested in its members' religion, but only in their support for Irish unification. While the Ancient Order of Hibernians is very careful about the Irish political issues it will back, Noraid has chosen to make the political situation in the Northern Ireland its central concern, and to identify itself closely with one of the most extreme varieties of Irish nationalism. Noraid members tend not to interpret the American public's disapproval of them as connected with the organization's apparent endorsement of the methods employed by the Provisional IRA, which are also disapproved of by the two largest political parties in the Republic of Ireland, Fine Gael and Fianna Fail, as well as by the mainly-Catholic Social Democratic and Labour Party in the north of Ireland. Rather, Noraid sees its unpopular image as attributable to the power of the British government to manipulate American newspaper and television coverage of their organization. The Capital District INA branch publishes a bimonthly newsletter and holds monthly meetings which are open to the public. A well-publicized field day is held each year to raise funds for the organization; Noraid organizes a big annual Irish Benefit Concert in aid of West Belfast and Derry charities at Albany's Convention Centre; INA stalls selling republican political literature and 'IRA All the Way' T-shirts are set up at every Irish event in the Albany area; and, of course, a prominent Noraid contingent marches in the Albany St Patrick's Day parade. Although the number of Noraid members in our sample was very small, it was none the less a significantly greater number than belonged to any other organization with specifically Irish associations, apart from the Hibernians.

III

Q: Do you belong to any ethnic organizations or clubs?

A: I belong to Irish Northern Aid. I work with the Children's Fund and I have been with that since the beginning. I think that is probably the one [organization] I feel most connected to. The Children's Fund started from nothing [with a Wolfe Tones concert at] Bishop McGinn High School, 3,000 dollars and a hall and we ended up making 1,500. That night we sold 800 dollars' worth of 50-cent wine and beer. And I thought the people would bring the place down, they loved them so much. The following year we moved [the benefit concert] to the Convention Centre and it has been growing ever since.

I joined [Ladies'] Division One [of the Hibernians] when I was in High School. At that point they had no interest [in] a young kid. I dropped out. And then they started Division Two because ... they could not [get along with each other in] Division One and they asked me to join and I said yes. [Later] I fell away. I send in my dues [but] I don't go to meetings … any longer. They were a fine group, but something changed.

Q: What about your parents: would they have been members of any ethnic organizations or clubs?

A: My mother was in several church organizations. My mother was in the Daughters of Erin and my father was in the AOH. My brother is in the AOH and he supports Noraid too.

(Informant 92)

A: We belong to the AOH. I used to go to Irish dances, and I used to march in the St Patrick's Day parade. My father always was in the St Patrick's Day parade. He was very, very Irish, my father. He was one of those Irishmen who had a beautiful baritone. All my uncles too, they all sang in all the shows and minstrels and in church things. They were very Irish, even though they were born in America. Albany was a very Irish city [then]. I mean, Dan O'Connell was Irish. He ran the city, so Irish was definitely [the] thing to be in Albany.

Q: Were there any other things apart from songs in your family which were associated with being of Irish descent?

A: They were very Catholic and went to mass all the time. They made Easter Duty. My father [belonged to] the Catholic Union and all that stuff. It was all very Irish at that time.

(Informant 215)

Q: How did your parents feel about their Irish background?

A: They met in the Hibernian Hall. My grandmother used to take my uncle and mother to dances when they were kids. In those days you didn't get sitters; you would bring the kids with you and the kids would bring their pillows and they would go under the tables and they would all go to sleep. My mother remembers that [the children were] hustled into a corner when a fight started because there was always a fight, and that is one of the reasons my grandmother stopped going. [My grandmother] was not into heavy drinking and had no tolerance for people that drank to a great excess and lost control. She was never as [far as] I know involved with the Daughters of Erin or the [AOH] auxiliary or anything like that. She was never a member. Her niece was a member of the Daughters of Erin, and also the [AOH] auxiliary, and my mother became involved when she was old enough.

(Informant 242)

My father did not belong to the AOH. I [asked him about this] and it seems that he did at one time belong, but [he] felt that it was more of a drinking thing. My dad did drink, so it is not that he was an abstainer or anything like that, but evidently the answer to my question was, well, all they do is stand around and drink or whatever. Because of what my father said about the AOH, I never joined [laughs]. My brother joined. My brother is a member of the AOH. He likes to drink.

(Informant 217)

Q: When you were growing up did you consider yourself ethnic at all?
A: Yes.
Q: How did your parents feel about their ethnic background?
A: Stay with your own kind.
Q: Did they talk about Ireland often?
A: All the time.
Q: Did they belong to any ethnic organizations or clubs?
A: Just the AOH.

(Informant 134)

Q: Do you belong to any ethnic organizations or clubs?
A: Yeah, I am a joiner.
Q: What do you belong to?
A: The AOH.
Q: And what is it that they do there?
A: Oh, they have dances and meetings and things which I am not very active in, I must say. And the K of C, of course. That is Irish here, but it is not really an Irish organization, or is it?

(Informant 243)

My grandfather was a member of the AOH, probably the Friendly Sons of St Patrick, too. My father, my uncle, and my cousins were members of the Knights of Columbus, which was a Catholic, not necessarily an Irish Catholic, organization, but Albany being Albany it was heavily Irish. The women were not in anything. My family [weren't] really joiners.

(Informant 72)

Q: Was anyone in your family a member of any organization connected with your Irish ancestry?
A: Religious really, the Knights of Columbus. But it turned out to be ethnic. There were a lot of Irish people in the Knights of Columbus. It was a hard thing to separate, the religious from the ethnic.

(Informant 14)

Q: Did either of [your parents] belong to any organizations or clubs connected with their Irish ancestry?

A: My father more so than my mother. My mother was a lifetime member of [the] PTA [and the] Ladies' Auxiliary at the American Legion post. My father belonged to the Knights of Columbus, the Elks, [and] the American Legion.

(Informant 18)

Q: How did your parents feel about their Irish background?

A: Well, my parents taught us that we were Irish and that we came from Ireland, but they were always proud that they were American.

Q: Did they talk about being Irish much or about their ancestry?

A: My mother's mother, my grandmother, was born in Ireland. She told us stories about Ireland. Saying our night prayers, she would say them in Gaelic, I can remember. My father never really said much, but when he did he would talk about his grandparents from Ireland.

Q: Did your parents belong to any organizations or clubs connected with their background?

A: Not when I was growing up, no.

(Informant 130)

The people [in the neighbourhood] were a whole mixture. Irish, Italian, Jewish. The only time anything was ever mentioned about ethnic ties was on St Patrick's Day.

(Informant 242)

Q: Can you think of any times in your life when it has been more or less important to you to acknowledge your Irish background?

A: I am not sure I know what you mean.

Q: Can you think of any occasions when you were really proud to be Irish or when it meant an awful lot to you to acknowledge your Irish background?

A: On St Patrick's Day! [Laughs.] Isn't that awful?

(Informant 217)

Q: Was there much emphasis on your Irish background when you were growing up?

A: No. We might have corned beef and cabbage on St Patrick's Day, but that was it.

(Informant 600)

Q: Do you celebrate St Patrick's Day?

A: Oh, sure. Everybody has to be Irish, even if they are Italian!

(Informant 227)

I would just wear green. You would go to work and wear a green tie. Everyone becomes Irish in America. When I was growing up, there were big celebrations on St Patrick's Day. I remember them saying [that] everyone was Irish on St Patrick's Day.

(Informant 591)

I celebrate St Patrick's Day occasionally. Sometimes I forget all about it. If I am aware of it, I wear a green tie.

(Informant 150)

[On St Patrick's Day] they have an annual black tie affair here, for men, called the Friendly Sons of St Patrick. It's six or seven hundred. It's just a nice party, dinner, drink, speakers. You get to know a lot of people. Albany's a small town. The people who go to it aren't necessarily Irish. Jewish, Italian, everybody goes.

(Informant 55)

All the politicians and lawyers and professional people in the area [go to the Friendly Sons dinner]. It is not [only] Irish people who go. Probably as many of my Jewish friends go as my Irish friends.

(Informant 33)

I am very much a part of the good-time Irish. I am proud of my name, proud of my heritage, love the St Patrick's Day celebrations, the happy part of being Irish. I don't want to hear about Irish politics, raising money for guns, all that.

(Informant 18)

On St Patrick's Day I would be wakened by the smell of corned beef and cabbage, which is more American, I guess, than Irish. My mother would have green cup-cakes and green this and green that. We had green pancakes. We got dressed in our best clothes. We have a family heirloom, a shillelagh. My father went to the [VFW] post to help get things ready for the parade. The parade was always on the Saturday before St Patrick's Day. We would go to one of the pubs and they would be singing Irish songs. As a young boy, for a special treat, my father would let me have a shot of Irish whiskey.

(Informant 18)

I [used to celebrate St Patrick's Day] in the past by going to mass and then we would march in the North Albany parade and the one downtown. We would go out and celebrate with everyone else and have a good time.

(Informant 326)

We have a favourite bar that we go to. It isn't Irish, but we like it because there is no one else there and we can sort of take it over. I would say about forty or fifty of us go and we wear everything green and we have a few Irish glasses before the parade and then we watch the parade and enjoy that.

(Informant 391)

We [used to go] to the parade and wear green. We would have corned beef and cabbage. [We] used to drink green beer and go to the Irish Hall, but I don't drink any more, so I don't go.

(Informant 231)

We always went to the parade as children. Then, as we got older, my brothers and sisters [and I] would go downtown and get drunk. We would go into all the bars.

(Informant 565)

Now I don't do anything. Back then it was basically partying and drinking. Basically it is a day to go drink green beer and if you want to you can go get slap happy drunk.

(Informant 139)

I don't go out on St Patrick's Day because I think it is ridiculous the way people go out and get drunk and make fools of themselves. I think it is a silly idea.

(Informant 521)

There is a whole tradition among Americans starting with green beer and making an ass out of yourself in public, corned beef and cabbage and wearing something green. I always thought that was generally repulsive. Everyone knows that we are Irish, and we do not have to prove anything.

(Informant 29)

[People] would come up to me and say, 'Why don't you have your green on?' I don't need green. I am Irish all the year around.

(Informant 92)

My father ... didn't feel it was necessary to wear green clothes on St Patrick's Day and to march in the parades and whatever. He always believed that there were two [kinds of] people in the world—those who were Irish and those who wanted to be, and that [was] the extent of it and that's what I grew up with. He never joined the Hibernians, he was never involved in any of that.

(Informant 44)

Q: Do you celebrate St Patrick's Day?

A: Not particularly. Everybody here is Irish on St Patrick's Day. It doesn't interest me at all.

(Informant 157)

My mother and father were not attached to their Irish heritage. Growing up and going to Catholic schools and living in a mostly Catholic area, we had basic St Patrick's Day Irish [but that's] about all [there] was.

(Informant 130)

On St Patrick's Day I always loved to raise my hand [at school] and say my father is from Ireland [but] it never got me anywhere; nobody ever asked me to sing a song or tell a joke.

(Informant 217)

Q: Would you say you lean towards one side of the family more? Would you identify with the German over the Irish, or the Irish over the German?

A: I don't know whether the war had anything to do with it; maybe it did. I always tell people I [am] half Irish. On St Patrick's Day I always wore the green. We always got along pretty well, the [two] families. Probably I was a little closer to my German relatives because they lived a little closer and they had some children that were more my age.

(Informant 106)

Then when my youngest son was born, I said what about a German name to go with [our last name, so we named him] Konrad. On St Patrick's Day when he was in fourth grade, he was the only one [who] wanted to get all dressed in green and the teacher made fun of him because his name was [so German]. And I felt so sorry for him. He came home in tears, [saying] 'She does not believe I am Irish!' Who would?

(Informant 149)

Seventy per cent of our informants of Irish ancestry told us that they celebrated St Patrick's Day in some way, or had done so at some stage in their lives. This consisted, for over 90 per cent, of wearing something green. Seventy per cent had gone to see the parade at least once in their lives, although far fewer (less than 20 per cent) had done so regularly, and an even smaller number had actually marched in it. If St Patrick's Day fell on a weekday, people went to work as usual, and some said they had St Patrick's parties at their workplaces. About half might have occasionally played some Irish music, which could have been anything from Bing Crosby to the latest Irish bands. Fourteen per cent had a special meal of corned beef and cabbage at home; 7 per cent went out for a 'St Patrick's Special' at a local restaurant; a few of our informants reported having entertained friends, having gone to a neighbourhood drinks party, or a dance. About a quarter of our sample said that they had at one time or another gone to church on St Patrick's Day, or had visited the Hibernians' Hall on the Saturday of the parade.

Put another way, 80 per cent said that they did not regularly go to see the parade or celebrate in a bar or the Hibernians' Hall. Eighty per cent said that they did not have a special meal at home or at a restaurant. Eighty-five per cent said that they did not normally watch the Albany parade on television. Fifty per cent had never listened to any Irish music. The one thing that nearly everyone did was also the most token: wearing the green. When we asked our informants about other kinds of Irish activities and associations, a similar picture emerged. Less than half of our non-random sample of people who identified themselves as Irish but who were not members of the AOH, Noraid, or any other self-consciously Irish group reported having attended an 'Irish' function or event of any kind in the preceding two years.[4] Of those who had, 80 per cent said this was a concert of Irish music. All other 'Irish' events had attracted very few of our informants: 16 per cent of this sample had attended a lecture with an Irish theme, an event at the Hibernians' Hall, or the Governor Dongan Féis, which is an annual festival of Irish music, dancing, needlework, soda-bread-baking contests, and Irish language competitions; but 84 per cent had not attended any of these events. Twelve per cent had been to the Irish-American Heritage Museum at East Durham in the previous two years, but 88 per cent had not; 3.4 per cent had attended a Noraid event, but 96.6 per cent had not.

These figures, together with those for AOH and INA membership, do not suggest that people of Irish ancestry are conspicuous joiners of old-country associations, or are very concerned about the public display of their ancestry. Ninety-nine per cent of the Irish-ancestry population do not belong to the AOH, and 84 per cent of our sample had not made an effort to attend any Irish event except, perhaps, a concert. There are

---

[4] This figure is none the less a good deal higher than we would have expected, given trends elsewhere in the data. A possible explanation is that in their responses, our informants may not have adhered closely to the qualification in the question relating to their participation *in the previous two years*.

number of factors which might contribute to an explanation of this. The first is that people of Irish ancestry are a large plurality of people in Albany; they are not a beleaguered minority who need to assert themselves through public displays, or to reassure themselves of their sense of belonging by actively participating in ritual behaviour or in activities which bring them together. Church group membership and party political activism bring like-minded people together in settings where the dominant ancestry is more likely than not to be Irish in any case. Thus some of our informants, when asked whether they belonged to any organizations they associated with their ancestry, replied by mentioning the Knights of Columbus, the Rosary Society, Catholic charities, or the Democratic Party. This is not to say that our informants believed the Democratic Party or the Knights of Columbus to be exclusively Irish, but it is certainly evident that they strongly associated Irish descent with membership of church and party.

Merely having had some part of one's ancestral origin in the same European country 150 years ago is, it would seem, a tenuous indication of like-mindedness. A century ago, this may not have been much different. First-generation Irish immigrants had a wide spectrum of social, economic, religious, and political characteristics: they were not all of the same social class, nor did they all speak the same language or dialect, nor were they of the same confessional. Nor were their political views identical: the issues of land reform and Irish independence did not unite all Irish men and women even then. In New York City, and for a time in Albany during the nineteenth century, there was a variety of factions and splinter groups on Irish political concerns, whose members were no more agreed on what political ideals to pursue, how to rank them, and how to pursue them than they are today. Whatever differences Irish immigrants brought with them were soon compounded and eventually supplanted by home-grown differences in America, as the Irish and their descendants began to climb the social and economic ladder. That they were English-speaking or bilingual immediately led to their residential dispersal in Albany; thus they lacked a powerful incentive to cling together, and in consequence they lacked a focal point in space. While this hindered the development of the kind of old-country associations, communal activities, and public rituals possessed by the Germans, for example, it greatly speeded the assimilation of the Irish into American society. Although we did not specifically ask them, a significant number of our informants spontaneously said that they perceived a class dimension in belonging to the AOH and Noraid; middle-class professional people diffidently observed (not wanting to appear snobbish to the interviewers) that such memberships were definitely 'not for us'.

IV

Ninety-nine per cent of those of Irish ancestry in Albany did not belong to any old-country associations. Seventy per cent of our sample publicly expressed their Irishness on only one day of the year, and then, for most, only in the most token way, by 'wearing the green'; the other 30 per cent did not mark St Patrick's Day at all. Yet some felt so strongly Irish that they regarded doing self-consciously Irish things as superficial and frivolous: as merely playing at being Irish. None the less, it is one thing for people to believe themselves to be Irish, and to feel Irish, however these beliefs and feelings might be anchored in their ancestry and individual experience, and quite another thing to presume those who identify themselves as Irish to be an organic social or cultural collectivity. As Max Weber reminds us, ethnic membership does not constitute a group in and of itself whose members necessarily share concrete social action, distinctive attributes, or ways of seeing the world: ethnic identification merely facilitates the formation of groups of other kinds based upon the presumption of a tie of common origin.[5] By this criterion, participation in old-country associations and public gatherings is a critical measure of the strength of ethnic commitment in everyday life. By expressing an affinity with Irishness, which may be metaphorical or actual, public or private—as through 'wearing the green' on St Patrick's Day, or simply knowing one's self to be of Irish descent, those who do so are claiming membership of a group based upon an identity of common origin. They meet the primary qualification for admission into the realms of ethnic Irishness, but this alone does not make them ethnic in the sense of being a part of an organic social or cultural collectivity, from which they might then be presumed to derive some part of their social personae or senses of being in the world. Their affinity with Irishness is merely a ticket of admission which they may choose to use, or not, to join collectivities— groups of *other* kinds—based upon the primordial tie. For some, these collectivities may come into being on only one day of the year, and consist in gatherings of friends who get together to celebrate their Irishness by

---

[5] M. Weber, *Economy and Society*, G. Roth, and C. Wittisch (eds.) (Berkeley, 1978), i. 389–95.

marching in the parade or drinking green beer: if this is the extent of the social practice of their Irishness, they are most certainly socially and culturally ethnic by Weber's criterion, but they are ethnic in these ways only on St Patrick's Day.

Weber also points to the centrality of shared political memory or religion in the constitution of ethnicity:

Whenever the memory of the origin of a community by peaceful succession or emigration ... from a mother community remains for some reason alive, there undoubtedly exists a very specific and often extremely powerful sense of ethnic identity, which is determined by several factors: shared political memories or, even more importantly in early times, persistent ties with the old cult, or the strengthening of kinship and other groups, both in the old and new community, or other persistent relationships. Where these ties are lacking, or once they cease to exist, the sense of ethnic group membership is absent, regardless of how close the kinship may be.[6]

Our informants expressed the feeling that Ireland has had a difficult past and a few related these difficulties to the reasons why their forebears originally emigrated to the United States, even if they were not certain of the specific reason. An informant might remark that, say, a grandmother had come from Ireland as a direct result of the Great Famine, even though the dates might show that the grandmother came to the United States as a girl in the 1890s, fifty years after the Famine, quite certainly as an economic migrant rather than as a refugee escaping fever or starvation. If our informants did not actually know about the circumstances of their ancestors' emigration, or their points of origin in Ireland, they often attempted to fill in the gaps in their knowledge on the basis of what they had heard or read about Irish political history. When they guessed about the places in Ireland from which their ancestors came, the west—that area of the country most redolent of tradition and most heavily promoted by the tourist agencies as the 'real' Ireland, and also that part of the country which suffered the greatest poverty and devastation consequent upon the Famine and its aftermath—was chosen with striking frequency, to the virtual exclusion of any other part of Ireland except the south, despite being the region from which the fewest nineteenth-century immigrants actually came.[7] Leon Uris's novel *Trinity*, a fictional account of events in

---

[6] Ibid.

[7] For the USA as a whole, 17.1 per cent of emigrants from Ireland came from Connaught, 17.4 per cent from Leitrim, 29.6 per cent from Ulster, and 35.7 per cent from Munster during the years 1851 to 1899. See P. J. Blessing, *The Irish in America: A Guide to the Literature and the Manuscript Collections* (Washington, 1992), 328–9.

Ireland from the 1840s to the Irish Civil War, was reported to have been read, remarkably, by fully half of our informants, who said that the book had helped them to put Irish history in perspective. The book appeared in 1976, at a time when the concern of Irish-Americans with the Troubles of the 1970s was at its height.

In contrast to the reasons—where known—that they gave for their ancestors' emigration, which were largely economic, with a minority giving political reasons, their understanding of Irish history in general reversed this emphasis. Of those who offered any sentiment at all, roughly half expressed ideas about Irish history which were predominantly political in character, connected with British colonialism, hostility towards the English, the national struggle, and the Catholic–Protestant problem in the north of the country as the last remnant of the British presence in Ireland. Only about a quarter of our informants described their understandings of Ireland's past in terms of the economic and social conditions which prevailed at the time of their ancestors' departure from Ireland, ascribing their emigration to the Famine, rural poverty, or lack of opportunity or choice in their employment or marriage prospects, rather than to the political events of later decades. For those who expressed a sentiment, the general feeling associated with Irish history was that Ireland's past was marked by tragedy and sadness, and that Ireland had suffered a metaphorical fall from grace since the mythical golden age of the pre-conquest millennium. A deeply Catholic world-view is joined with nineteenth-century nation-building rhetoric which sought to transform the people of the island of Ireland into the Irish nation, and is leavened with a dash of American republicanism. It is little related to the actual circumstances of their ancestors' decisions to emigrate or their reasons for settling in Albany. That there is a difference between these two domains of knowledge does not mean that one must be real and the other 'imagined' or created. The one—family history—is a private discourse; the other, the enduring legacy of Irish history, is a public discourse. Part of this public discourse may have been manufactured initially in the cause of Irish nationalism, and some of its symbols are nowadays nourished and perpetuated by a commodified popular culture of Ireland in America, but it is far from arbitrary. Our informants' views of the past are rooted in Irish Catholicism and in a plausible (if simplified) interpretation of history in Ireland and America. Significantly, this two-nation version of history shares the same demons, British colonialism and Anglo-Saxon Protestantism. The anti-British sentiments of Irish nationalism are reinforced by the ideals of American patriotism that also derive from having broken free of British domination. These are powerful symbols for those to whom a sense of Irishness matters. For some of our informants, who for whatever reason have taken an interest in their origins, this interpretation of history, which has as its main theme the demonization of the English, has had a powerful effect in shaping an understanding of the past and a sense of self; a history and a biography that is simultaneously defined by having one's origins in the British Isles but being emphatically not Anglo-Saxon but rather a member of a different, purer, nobler, and more primordial 'race', the Celts.[8]

In the United States, there are 40 million potential consumers of Irish-American popular culture. In Albany, bookshops sell a wide range of books on Ireland, mostly of the glossy coffee-table variety, filled with romantic photographs. One can also choose from hundreds of books of Irish names, jokes, sayings, and stories; cookbooks; novels; panegyric popular histories of Ireland, and accounts of the Irish in America. One can buy videos of Hollywood films and television series set in Ireland; records, tapes, and CDs of Irish folk music; Irish linens, pottery, and glass; and wall-plaques, door-knockers, and other curios decorated with shamrock motifs. On St Patrick's Day, people wear green T-shirts and wave Irish flags, drink Irish beer and whiskey, and eat corned beef sandwiches in bars and restaurants decorated for the season with shamrocks and green balloons. One can visit the Irish museum and theme park in East Durham, purchase the services of a genealogist, and buy a wide range of package tours of Ireland from any travel agent. For people interested in highbrow culture, subscriptions to Irish-American cultural clubs and heritage societies will purchase admission to recitals of Irish poetry and music, and lectures on Irish literature, history, and politics. Lessons in the Irish language, traditional step-dancing, and playing the Irish harp can also be bought locally. Theme days in Albany, such as the Governor Dongan Féis, held every summer, sell Irish wares and celebrate Irishness with crafts displays and dancing and musical competitions performed by elaborately (and expensively) costumed children and adults. Irishness is a part of a heritage industry that is well developed in Albany; it is a commodity that can be bought and sold, and some of our informants appeared to identify their sense of Irishness almost entirely with their consumption of commodities with Irish associations. For many people, it is the only way they are still able to express their sense of Irishness.

---

[8] See M. Chapman, *The Celts: The Construction of a Myth* (London, 1992).

Sunday, May 26 1991[9]

Today Eamonn and I went to East Durham to check out the Irish festival. We drove through the hamlet a couple of times to see how many people were about. The street was largely quiet. Most people seemed to be gathered around the marquee in the field behind the museum. We parked beside the small amusement park on the main road where another crowd was gathered. Looking around the tourist goods on sale, I saw some people sitting in the back room: they were speaking very loudly and it was obvious that they were Irish. We got something to eat and sat at a table in the back room near them. The room looked out onto a go-kart track which belonged to the complex. The three women were chatting about some friend. Occasionally they would look out the window and squeal. Their husbands were on the go-karts. Talk when the men returned revolved around their hotels and the food. They were talking about which pub to meet up in that night.

There were a couple of stalls set up on the roadside selling T-shirts and bumper stickers. People on the roads were walking between the marquee and the pubs. We then went up to the marquee. As we were going in we met some friends. They were just leaving to go to a Latin mass a few miles away. They asked us to accompany them. Mass was held at a convent. I had to be kitted out with a skirt and veil for my head before I was allowed into the church. About thirty people were at mass, which was a comfortable number since the place was so small. Some of the crowd present obviously knew one another. There was handshaking and talk. Mass was an experience. The priest kept his back to the people. The six nuns present sang throughout. The nuns were young girls in their twenties, who had decided to follow the Tridentine faith. The priest gave a homily on the Latin mass and explained how the post-Vatican mass was more like the Protestant version than its own original form. He also explained that as first-timers at this mass we were not permitted to receive communion because in their eyes we had not yet received First Holy Communion properly. Also if we wished to embrace the Latin form we had to go to confession and start anew.

Back to the happenings in East Durham. We paid to go into the area where the two marquees were located. In the large marquee was a stage for the groups to play. I think that over thirty groups were playing over the weekend. Stalls were set up all around around the walls of the marquee. There would have been over twenty of them. They were all selling Irish goods, Irish music, T-shirts with Irish slogans, family crests, some Irish candy bars and soft drinks. Noraid had the largest booth there: they were selling T-shirts with 'Brits Out of Ireland' slogans and there was a lot of hunger striker memorabilia. There were leather belts with the hunger strikers' names, mugs, etc. The type of music that was on sale was stuff like the Clancy Brothers and Wolfe Tones which was very popular in all the stalls.

[9] This vignette is edited from Brenda McAteer's field diary.

There was a lot of Irish-American music. Also popular were tapes of '100 Irish Pub Songs', and '100 Irish Ballads'. Not a lot of modern Irish music was on sale; the most modern stuff there were Christy Moore LPs. There was no U2 material; one tape by Sinead O'Connor. Soda bread was on sale. Budweiser and Guinness had tents selling beer at highly inflated prices. Almost everyone in the tent was squiffy to say the least. There was a dance floor in front of the stage. A lot of middle-aged couples were waltzing. A couple of people were trying to do Irish dancing. Outside the marquee there were trailers selling food. One was selling corned beef and cabbage burgers. The others were selling ordinary burgers and some Mexican food. In the second tent people were selling paintings and leather stuff. Every money-making opportunity possible was being exploited. A couple of stalls were selling books about the hunger strikers and folk histories of Ireland. Most people were browsing like myself without buying a lot. There was seating for a couple of hundred people in the marquee and there would have been the same outside also. Seated inside were a lot of older people and families. Outside were all the students. I heard a lot of Irish voices. There were Belfast and Dublin accents. The probability is that they were down from New York. I did not see anyone that I knew from Albany, apart from the people we met at the gate and went to mass with. The whole place reminded me of Bundoran or something like that, touristy, exploiting patriotic feelings, but mainly a watering hole. The marquee was set up just for the festival. Normally all the entertainment is in the pubs. The museum was shut by 4.00 pm, which I think was very early, especially when there was such a large crowd down this weekend. The majority of people were here for the drinking. There was not much of a family atmosphere; it was more of a weekend for friends to hang out together.

V

As each succeeding generation has become more American and less Irish, and personal accounts of the nineteenth-century immigrant experience handed down through families have dimmed and disappeared, perceptions of what is Irish have become increasingly informed by an American popular culture of Irishness. Its symbols have now settled into rigid, iconic shapes. They are ubiquitous, simple, easy to grasp, and good to play with. Every Irish-American—indeed, virtually any American—recognizes them, and can deploy them in the appropriate contexts: the 'wearing of the green', shamrocks, Jameson's whiskey, 'Danny Boy', leprechauns, and 'England Out'. Unlike the Germans, the Irish have never fallen out of favour this century. They share the historical experience with earlier generations of Americans settlers in having broken free of British colonialism. Their oppression-to-freedom and rags-to-respectability experience of

America is paradigmatic of that claimed by a version of American history and by millions of people of other immigrant origins who have also successfully assimilated into American society. The Irish have (it is said) the gift of the gab; they are outgoing and boisterous; yet they are also pious, family-centred, tough-minded, and industrious people who make solid, public-spirited citizens like schoolteachers and police officers. They have earned a reputation as model Americans, and they have achieved the American Dream of the split-level suburban ranch house with two cars in the driveway, money in the bank, and kids in college. There are millions of people of other ancestral backgrounds like them. In some ways, the Irish have become a metaphor for all the other immigrant peoples in the United States who have also succeeded in melting into the mainstream. Indeed, any American, whether white or black, Irish, German, Italian, Polish, Catholic, Protestant, or Jewish, can assert a claim to membership of this fully assimilated majority by 'wearing the green' on St Patrick's Day.

The middle-American majority, who are Irish for only a day, are not especially interested in foreign political squabbles, gay rights, or in what, according to some interpretations of contemporary Irish nationalist politics, Irishness might or might not be really about. On the only day on which most people are 'Irish', being 'Irish' is about wearing something green, and perhaps watching the parade on television or listening to a Chieftains record while munching corned beef sandwiches, having a few drinks with friends, and feeling good about being a part of the comfortable majority. St Patrick's Day is not about sectional interests, whether these are ethnic politics or gay rights. It is, rather, melting-pot day with a dash of Catholicism: it is about the middle-American values of accommodating to the mainstream, not standing apart from it.

'Irish', as a category to which people say they belong on the basis of their ancestry, does not nowadays stand in opposition to any other categories in any marked degree. While it might once have done so, a generation or two ago in relation to the Italians or WASPs (say), there is no hint in our material that by identifying themselves as Irish they are currently distancing themselves from anything in particular, or are reacting to a perceived threat of marginalization by others. Moreover, as the generations have passed, the categorical boundaries of ethnic membership have become blurred. Few of our informants, after the passage of several generations and a great deal of intermarriage, were unambiguously 'Irish', but most were of mixed Irish, English, German, and Italian descent. They were not always certain about their categorical memberships. The same persons may sometimes think of themselves as Irish—or

German, or English, or Italian—depending upon the social setting. It is becoming increasingly clear that what now constitutes a sense of ethnic identity among Americans who are the descendants of nineteenth-century immigrants is highly variable from one individual to another, and is pre-eminently a matter of biographical experience. There are no longer any recognizable symbolic practices that belong exclusively to people of Irish descent. After five or six generations of assimilation, few people still possess any ethnic family traditions. The remaining icons of Irishness have largely passed out of the exclusive proprietorship of Irish-American families and some of them, overstylized and oversimplified, have entered into the common repository of popular, mainstream American cultural artefacts. These icons now belong to everyone, and anyone is free to play with these public symbols of Irishness, whether they have several Irish ancestors, just one or two, or even none at all. In Albany, the great-grand-children of English, German, Italian, Polish, and Lithuanian immigrants are now just as likely as the descendants of Irish immigrants to bear such names as Patrick or Colleen, and, dressed in green or costumed as leprechauns, to march down Washington Avenue on St Patrick's Day to the tune of 'It's a Long Way to Tipperary'.

The St Patrick's Day parade has become a secular ritual[10] (even if it retains a substratum of Catholicism) which presents a certain view of the lived-in world,[11] recreating, reinforcing, and organizing a vernacular and largely inarticulable interpretation of citizenship, history, and society, what it means and how it works.

In this sense, such ritual plays, as Durkheim argued, a cognitive role, rendering intelligible society and social relationships, serving to organize people's knowledge of the past and present and their capacity to imagine the future. In other words, it helps us to define as authoritative certain ways of seeing society: it serves to specify what in society is of special significance, it draws people's attention to certain forms of relationships and activity—and at the same time, therefore, it deflects their attention from other forms, since every way of seeing it is also a way of not seeing.[12]

Most of the parade's participants and their audiences are 'Irish' only on St Patrick's Day. On that day, for those whose day it is, the normally dispersed and fragmented are brought together and everyday complexity

---

[10] S. F. Moore and B. Myerhoff, *Secular Ritual* (Assen, 1977).
[11] A. Schutz and T. Luckmann, *The Structures of the Life-World* (London, 1974); D. Handelman, *Models and Mirrors: Towards an Anthropology of Public Events* (Cambridge, 1990).
[12] S. Lukes, 'Political Ritual and Social Integration', *Sociology*, 9 (1975), 301.

and uncertainty are banished in the 'wearing of the green'. As the fast-nesses of ethnicity have disappeared, as people have lost touch with the experiences of their ancestors, and as they have become hybridized through intermarriage and Americanized through assimilation, their categorical identities in a society in which everyone is none the less assumed to have a distinct ethnic or categorical identity have become increasingly ambiguous.[13] For people whose ancestry is complicated or indeterminate, Irishness, with its generally positive cultural associations, is a kind of generic ethnic identity that can be assumed when the occasion demands it: when the census-taker on the doorstep demands to know one's ancestry in not more than one or two words, or on St Patrick's Day.

People drive in to Albany from the affluent suburbs, or watch the parade on television as it passes through the old city-centre neighbour-hoods once occupied by the Irish and Germans, then Italians and Poles, and now African-Americans and Hispanic-Americans. It does not matter whether the paraders and their supporters are of mixed ancestry or might not have any Irish ancestors at all, or whether one is middle class or work-ing class, white or black, a Catholic, a Protestant, a Jew, a Democrat, or a homosexual. No one asks, and no one wants to know. All that matters is what is displayed, and that what is displayed is iconic of the *représentation collective*, those objects of thought and feeling which the paraders invest with special significance.[14] For the paraders, the American Dream is a reality, a moral landscape, and a lived-in world. The oversimplified popu-lar icons of Irishness displayed on St Patrick's Day have come to stand for that reality: for the American middle majority, for their unexceptionable moral conventionality. These icons are not readily renegotiable. The Irish-American Gay, Lesbian, and Bisexual Group of Boston failed in their attempt to march under a green banner proclaiming their sexual orientation, and to secure for their movement the legitimacy that would have been conferred by their association with an established source of social acceptability. The parade's organizers, however, saw the gays' attempt to call attention to themselves not only as a challenge to Catholic teachings, but also as special pleading for a sectional interest, and thus contemptuous of the inclusive, assimilative moral world for which sham-rocks stand. Events in Albany which threatened to give heightened public prominence to a radical, minority political position on Irish unification also provoked much consternation. If the icons were readily negotiable,

---

[13] Cf. Z. Bauman, *Modernity and Ambivalence* (Cambridge, 1991).
[14] Lukes, 'Political Ritual', 301.

and came to signify other things, the ritual of St Patrick's Day would eventually become what it has not yet become: a programmatic tableau seeking to transform the moral and social order of middle America, or a carnival of inversions and self-parody.

There is no a priori reason to believe that what is symbolized by the St Patrick's Day parade is different in Albany than it is elsewhere. St Patrick's Day parades are now to be found far and wide across the United States, in places which have never been especially connected with the Irish: Fairbanks, Albuquerque, Honolulu, Palm Beach, and two hundred others. In the last ten years, fifty new parades have started up, in the suburbs, in the sunbelt, in the western prairies. As the everyday milieux of ethnic life have gradually disappeared, and as the Irish have melted into the American mainstream, so St Patrick's Day has become revitalized and has grown in popularity across the country. It has become a quintes-sentially American institution celebrating a nostalgic attachment to one European immigrant tradition that stands as a metaphor for all others now also largely vanished.

Clearly, the parade strikes a chord in the sentiments of the American people. It is a day when its participants, who are nowadays mostly of mixed ancestry and several generations removed from their nineteenth-century immigrant origins, can still celebrate what their country is to them—a nation of immigrants who by their own efforts have succeeded in becoming respectable, middle-class citizens—a day when they all know what that means, and what sacrifices their great-grandparents made to learn English, educate their children in American ways, and climb the social and economic ladder out of the old urban immigrant neighbour-hoods to become a part of the modern, suburban American Dream. The St Patrick's Day parade is no longer a celebration just of Irishness, but of Americanness. So thoroughly assimilated have the descendants of Irish immigrants become, and so completely have the remaining icons of Irishness been absorbed into the mainstream of American public culture, that the 'Irish'—six generations on—have come to be truly paradigmatic Americans. Nothing could be more American than to be a little 'Irish', especially on St Patrick's Day.

9

A Socioscape of Irish America

I

Albany is a very Irish place in a very Irish part of the country, yet its qualities seem rather different from those which have been reported as characterizing the few remaining Irish ethnic enclaves in New York City, Philadelphia, or Boston. These big-city, traditional neighbourhoods have provided the setting for generations of scholarship on Irish America. There is a long tradition of immigration and ethnic studies which has focused on these initial places of urban settlement by the Irish, the Italians, the Jews, and others. And, studies such as Glazer and Moynihan's *Beyond the Melting Pot*,[1] which have emphasized the vibrant and enduring nature of ethnicity in these places, have had a deep influence on our views, both scholarly and popular, of the character of European ethnicity in contemporary America.

For the Irish, there has been a succession of studies of first-generation immigrants in these nineteenth-century cities and the social institutions they created or of which they were a part; and some have attempted to bring our knowledge up to date by considering the experience of the second and third generations.[2] Most of these studies have been sound and well-executed pieces of research. None the less, through repetition, a weight of knowledge derived from a limited range of urban settings has accumulated which, for the Irish, is now heavily out of balance with the broader demographic picture. Eighty-five per cent of those Irish immigrants who landed at the Port of New York in the peak years of immigration in the immediate aftermath of the Famine did not settle in the city's urban ethnic neighbourhoods, but went straight on to other places across the country. Yet much of our knowledge about Irish immigrant life and culture comes from those 15 per cent, and their descendants, who

---

[1] N. Glazer and D. P. Moynihan, *Beyond the Melting Pot: The Negroes, Puerto Ricans, Jews, Italians and Irish of New York City* (Cambridge Mass., 1963); *Ethnicity* (Cambridge, Mass., 1974).
[2] See Bibliography.

went no farther. Our ideas about the Irish in America, then, may be coloured by the experience of a small minority. This minority lived in places where people of Irish ancestry would have been concentrated in space to an unusually high degree; where, in consequence, their social, political, and other local institutions would have been unusually highly developed; and where the pool of potential marriage partners would have been great enough to have encouraged unusually high rates of in-marriage. They would have retained their ethnic characteristics in more pronounced form for longer, and thus would have been more distinctively Irish, than those who settled in smaller cities, towns, villages, and rural areas in other parts of the country where their concentration in space was insufficient for ethnic institutions to have come into being or to have survived for very long, and where there were too few co-ethnics to form a pool of potential marriage partners and hence to sustain in-marriage over the generations: predictably, under these latter conditions, their ethnic distinctiveness would have melted away much more rapidly.

That most of our knowledge of the Irish is derived from studies set in the nation's largest industrial cities would appear to have far-reaching implications about the way we understand the immigrant experience, what is characteristic of Irishness, and the place occupied by the Irish in American society. There are, arguably, things about big-city ghetto life that make it different from life elsewhere. The most important of these is inter-ethnic competition. Immigrant newcomers queue up and jostle with one another for decent jobs and housing within urban structures and spaces which are strongly defended by earlier arrivals with prior claims upon them. Large numbers make it virtually inevitable that they will be perceived by their competitors as blocs rather than seen as individuals, and indeed they may further their own deindividualization by pursuing political aims whose success demands that they present a united, collective front towards those against whom they are pitted in their struggle to make their way up the ladder. Their economic position thus comes to be politicized as a class phenomenon. Pulling the whole class up the ladder by political means is a long and arduous process; those individuals and families who manage to ensure their own social mobility and escape to the suburbs are pejoratively described as lace-curtain, while those who lag behind in the struggle or who never make it suffer lives—perhaps generations—of discrimination and alienation.

The Irish had this kind of experience in the big eastern cities, just as many other immigrant groups did, and still do. Their slow and painful struggle for social acceptance in these places, however accurately portrayed, may be a reflection not of the generality of their experience across the country, but of the conditions of ethnic competition which tended to be found in their most acute form in these cities. In the absence of much information about the places where the other 85 per cent of Irish immigrants settled, their protracted struggle to succeed in these cities is extended as a general view of the immigrant condition everywhere. This view has been applied to Albany, and places like it, where the nature of ethnic competition was different; places which do not deserve to have it said of them that the Irish were alienated from American society, had reason to resent the way they were treated, or that they were forced to adopt ways that were alien to them. Such a view treats the Irish as ineffectual victims of circumstance, and gives no credit to the hopes and triumphs of all those millions who succeeded in finding better lives than they had known in the old country. Such a view disparages all those who had no wish to cling to the past, but *intended* their children to be unethnic Americans; it also demeans the generosity and extraordinary openness of all those millions of Americans in thousands of places across the country who readily accepted the Irish as their neighbours and workmates, husbands and wives, and sons- and daughters-in-law.

The scholarly focus on the immigrant ghetto, while unrepresentative of the broader picture of the dynamics of Irish immigrant settlement, is nevertheless understandable. For a historian, many more fragments of the past remain in such places, compared with those where Irish immigrants were thinner on the ground. Urban nucleations often encouraged the development of occupational specializations, forms of political activism, old-country associations, and other kinds of social groupings; and they provided the conditions for the continuation of musical and linguistic traditions, varieties of religious practice, and many other things about which historical evidence can be recovered, analysed, reconstructed, and presented as case studies illustrative of the nineteenth-century immigrant experience. For anthropologists and sociologists, ethnographic studies of Irishness likewise require that they be situated in space. There are obvious practical advantages in choosing sites where people of Irish ancestry are concentrated; where there are local institutions which the fieldworker can describe; where there are possibilities for participant observation; and where evidence of culturally distinctive beliefs and social practices might still be discovered. The focus on these urban enclaves seems largely to be the consequence of such scholarly convenience. What scholars have found interesting and significant about the Irish-Americans who live in them, however, may be of questionable value in our attempt to understand what is typical of Irish America in general. We may have been led to hold ideas about Irish-Americans that tend to exaggerate or misrepresent their characteristics, and thus we may have inadvertently reinforced the essentializing myths and stereotypical images of popular belief rather than submitting them to the kind and degree of critical scrutiny that would otherwise have been much more probable. Both popular stereotype and the findings of scholarly studies have had a propensity to exaggerate Irishness, and so have mutually supported and merged into one another in a confusing jumble of folklore and fact (or if not fact, at least those provisional assertions which derive from inductive methods, substantiated by evidence). Some of these ideas may look alike, but their epistemological status is very different: only some of them are grounded in the sorts of evidence which would withstand close inspection by a careful scholar.

To take one example: that scholarly studies set in these urban neighbourhoods have generally emphasized their Catholicism or the centrality of local-level Catholic institutions has reinforced and fused with the partisan popular myth that all Irish-Americans, properly so-called, are Catholic: a folk essentialism that is accepted as if it were a fact in some recent scholarly treatments of Irish-Americans, despite the objective circumstance that only 33 per cent of Americans of Irish ancestry across the United States are Catholic.[3] To take another example: the scholarly finding that the main nineteenth-century ethnic competitors of the Irish in the big cities were the English (or, more accurately, people predominantly of mixed British, Dutch, and other northern European stocks who had arrived and taken their place in the urban ethnic queue a generation or more earlier), has merged with the nation-building myth that the English are not only the natural class enemies of the Irish but also that the Irish, as 'Celts', are racially distinct, despite the objective circumstance that millions of Irish immigrants and their descendants married and are still marrying English people or their descendants in Britain, Canada, the United States, Australia, and New Zealand—which is strong evidence of ethnic propinquity rather than ethnic distance. Nevertheless, in recent scholarly accounts of the Irish in America one can find references to the popular belief that Irish people are inherently anglophobic, reported not merely as a folk view but stated as if it were an

---

[3] G. Gallup and J. Castelli, *The People's Religion: American Faith in the 90s* (New York, 1989), 119–22; B. Kosmin and S. Lachman, 'Research Report: The National Survey of Religious Identification, 1989–90: Selected Tabulations', (City University of New York Graduate Center, 1991), 14.

accepted scholarly opinion based on a body of sound sociological or historical evidence.

Sociologists tell us that ethnic characteristics are much more likely to persist in ethnic enclaves than elsewhere. By one view, as soon as people are able to improve their social and economic situations, they move out of such places, leaving behind those who are less able or less motivated to compete in the wider world beyond the ghetto. Some, like William Foote Whyte's college boys,[4] are more interested in personal achievement (and family honour, if this is what the family's ideals of honour involve) than in being ethnic; while others, like his corner boys, are happy to follow in their parents' footsteps, staying in the ghetto, maintaining their school-days friendships, marrying a co-ethnic, speaking the old-country language at home, and taking whatever work is available locally that does not require them to move out of their natal neighbourhood. According to this theory, as the most ambitious and successful move out, they leave behind the least motivated. Those who stay remain more ethnic, but the old neighbourhood withers and eventually dies as its conditions of existence are gradually outmoded by general demographic and socio-economic shifts which render it obsolete and incapable of being defended against incursions by newer waves of immigrants competing for living space and jobs. Meanwhile, those who have moved out to the suburbs mix in with people of a wide variety of other backgrounds, converting their upward educational and economic mobility into assimilation as they form social associations with people who are not co-ethnics, and as they, and their children, marry them. Recent empirical studies of changes in the residential patterns of white ethnics generally support this theory.[5]

This view is disputed by a competing interpretation, associated particularly with Glazer and Moynihan, which argues that the decline of ethnic enclaves is not an inevitable consequence of social mobility, which leaves behind only those who have been unable or unwilling to climb the ladder out of the ghetto. According to this theory, such communities can survive, and indeed be strengthened, by social mobility as the neighbourhood is remade by successive generations who pull the entire community up the socio-economic ladder; such neighbourhoods can also be created anew in other parts of the city or in its suburbs where co-ethnics coalesce and establish new institutional structures.

---

[4] W. F. Whyte, *Street Corner Society: The Social Structure of an Italian Slum*, 3rd edn. (Chicago, 1981).

[5] R. D. Alba, J. Logan, and K. Crowder, 'White Ethnic Neighborhoods and Assimilation: The Greater New York Region, 1980–1990', *Social Forces*, 75 (1997), 884.

In New York City, there is evidence for both points of view. The number and size of white ethnic enclaves have indeed shown gradual decline. As the socially mobile have moved out, their places have not been taken by a balancing inflow of new immigrants from the old country; the territorial integrity of such neighbourhoods has therefore often become very problematic, causing many to crumble and vanish, sometimes with astonishing rapidity. But, in contrast, there are still some white city-centre ethnic areas which have moved with the times, are still strong, and show no signs of disappearing. New white ethnic neighbourhoods have also been created in the city's suburbs.

Yet, of all New York's white ethnic neighbourhoods, the steepest rate of decline between 1980 and 1990 was among the Irish. The number of Irish city-centre neighbourhoods (defined as those areas where 40 per cent or more of the residents were of unmixed Irish ancestry) fell from ten to eight; in 1990, these enclaves accounted for 97,676 of the 574,009 people of Irish ancestry living in New York's central city areas, or 5.9 per cent of the Irish population of the metropolitan region. Seventy-five per cent of New York's Irish-ancestry population lived in the suburbs. Those suburban areas where people of Irish descent were concentrated in something approaching a suburban ethnic enclave declined from thirteen to ten from 1980, in 1990 accounting for 85,764 of the 1,808,327 people of Irish ancestry who lived in the suburbs, or 3.6 per cent of the total Irish-ancestry population in the New York metropolitan region.[6] It would thus appear that the Irish are increasingly becoming of mixed ancestry and are slowly drifting away from both the city-centre and suburban ethnic neighbourhoods. Their numbers are decreasing and they are becoming more dispersed residentially as they continue to intermarry, to move up the socio-economic ladder, to have smaller families, and to merge into a broad category of middle-class European-Americans who no longer have strongly marked ethnic characteristics associated with their old-country backgrounds. Where city-centre Irish ethnic enclaves can still be identified, however, there are significant, measurable socio-economic differences when compared to the suburban population. The people who remain in the old city-centre neighbourhoods are almost 80 per cent more likely to be of unmixed Irish ancestry than those who live in the suburbs; while 61.0 per cent of the urban Irish were of unmixed ancestry, only 34.3 per cent of the suburban Irish were. This is probably the result of the

---

[6] Ibid. 890, 893. The total Irish-ancestry population of the New York metropolitan region in 1990 was 2,382,336.

presence of networks of religious and other institutions which are concentrated in the old city-centre enclaves and so continue to foster the sorts of social propinquity that classically favour in-marriage. In the city-centre neighbourhoods, 41.5 per cent of those aged over 25 had had some post-high-school education, compared with 51.7 per cent in the suburbs. A little over half (56.5 per cent) of those in the central city neighbourhoods were owner-occupiers, while over three-quarters of the suburbanites were. Median household income in the city-centre neighbourhoods was $39,500 as against $51,700 in the suburbs. On the whole, then, those who live in New York's old Irish enclaves are substantially less likely to have married non-Irish people, and somewhat more likely to be blue-collar than those who live in the suburbs.

Two things stand out about these findings for our purpose: first, those who live in these ethnic enclaves have measurably different sociographic characteristics from those who do not; secondly, their relative numbers are so small as to be, today, almost insignificant. Ninety-four per cent of New York City's Irish-Americans do *not* live in such neighbourhoods. It seems self-evident that any scholarly study which aims to discover what is truly typical of contemporary Irish-Americanness is unlikely to find it in any of the few surviving big-city ethnic enclaves. Rather, the typical experience of Irishness is, and has always been, to be found in the ordinary, non-ethnic city streets, suburbs, and small towns across the United States. This carries important implications for our historical understandings of the Irish immigrant experience, if thus far they have been based mainly on studies of urban ethnic neighbourhoods which have had measurably different sociographic attributes, and have represented only a relatively minor proportion of the whole immigrant flow into and across America.

II

A sociographic profile of the Irish in America more than a century after the peak years of immigration can be sketched from the 1980 US Census, which for the first time asked people to identify their ancestry. Stanley Lieberson and Mary Waters, in their book, *From Many Strands*,[7] used this data and material from previous censuses and surveys to analyse the ethnic and racial composition of the population, ethnic spatial patterns

---

[7] S. Lieberson and M. Waters, *From Many Strands: Ethnic and Racial Groups in Contemporary America* (New York, 1988).

and cultural differences, and the dynamics of intermarriage. In 1980, the three most common ancestries in the American population were English and German (both with about 50 million, and each representing about 22 per cent of the population), Irish (40 million, or about 18 per cent), and Black (27 million, or about 12 per cent). No other single category was even half as large as the last of these four. However, it is important to remember, as we noted in Chapter 5, that these three European-ancestry categories do not represent distinct groups of people: we cannot add them up and say that there are 140 million people of these three ancestries, because each category contains persons of mixed as well as unmixed ancestries: thus the same mixed-ancestry individual can be counted in two or even all three of these most common European-ancestry categories.

With a couple of changes of fortune between the Germans and the Irish in second or third place, the dominance of these three ancestries— English, German, and Irish—has held since the beginnings of the American republic. The figures given by the US Bureau of the Census for the ancestral origins of the population in 1790, which were based on a set of estimates produced by the American Council of Learned Societies in 1931, are not altogether without problems, however. In their attempt to deal with the Irish fraction of the population, they commit the staggering solecisms of dividing Irish immigrants between those originating from Ulster and the 'Free State' even though the Free State did not come into being until 1921, and until then Ulster consisted of nine counties, not six; and of attempting to distinguish between the quasi-racial categories 'Celtic-Irish', 'English-Irish', and 'Scots-Irish'. These distinctions seem to have been used as euphemisms for Catholic, Anglican, and Presbyterian, and appear to have relied on a primordialist interpretation of social difference: the idea that kinship, religious cult, and community are tied together; a notion which merges race and culture, and takes it as axiomatic that through being born into a group, one genetically inherits its cultural substance. Yet the American Council of Learned Societies did not, apparently, consider it necessary to try to distinguish between the Catholic, Protestant, and Jewish fractions of the English and German populations, which were also mixed. Their reasons for doing so for the Irish alone were purely political, and stemmed from the requirement that their findings should be useful to the United States immigration authorities who needed this information in order to set a quota for the post-partition twenty-six counties of Ireland (which were presumed, to all intents and purposes, to be Catholic), following the 1924 Immigration Act which provided that the flow of immigrants was to be restricted to the national origins of the existing American population. Since there was no official or any other reliable record of the confessionals of the Irish immigrants arriving in the United States, the American Council of Learned Societies proceeded by attempting to classify the 1790 population on the basis of their surnames. Yet religion was no more the unalterable consequence of the patrilineal transmission of the family name among eighteenth- or nineteenth-century Irish immigrants, much less a quasi-genetic trait, than it is with anyone else today. Religious adherence is not a matter of racial inheritance but a matter of the most readily demonstrable Weberian sociology. One's confessional is a sociological phenomenon of the purest kind: it is a matter of upbringing, sometimes personal belief, sometimes practical convenience, occasionally all three. Large numbers of people converted to Anglicanism in Ireland for reasons of economic and political self-interest, just as, over the years, many Irish Catholic immigrants to the United States, or their descendants, became Protestants. While the estimates of Irish historians differ, it is clear that there were at least three, and perhaps six times as many Anglicans as Presbyterians in Ireland in the nineteenth century; that the majority of Irish Anglicans were likely to have been of native Irish, not English stock; that they were widely distributed throughout Ireland; and that they were not under any obligation to change their names when they changed their confessional and usually did not. Conversely, in Albany, one-third of our Irish Catholic informants had common British surnames which gave no clue to their bearers' Irishness, Catholicism, or putative Celtic racial inheritance; virtually all brought these names with them from Ireland, rather than having acquired them through intermarriage with British-stock people subsequent to their arrival in America. Anyone who has lived in the north of Ireland, where religious mixing is greatest, will know that attempting to judge a stranger's Catholicism or Protestanism on the basis of his or her surname alone is unlikely to be very accurate: one needs a given name and the name of the person's elementary or secondary school or place of residence to be reasonably confident of a correct guess; even then one is very unlikely to be able to tell, if that person does not seem to be a Catholic, whether he or she is an Anglican, a Presbyterian, a Methodist, a Baptist, a Quaker, a Christian Scientist, a Mormon, a member of any of a number of other non-Catholic denominations and sects, or professes no religion at all.

All we can say for certain is that the total number of immigrants from all parts of Ireland, whatever their religion might have been, was second only to people of English origin in 1790. This number marginally exceeded the German-speakers who might themselves have come from settlements east of the Vistula or the Danube as well as from the German-speaking heartlands, who might have been Catholic or Jewish or Protestant, and who might also have changed their confessional once or twice along the way. In 1790, there were as many Irish as Germans in New York State, and more Irish than Germans in every other state in the Union except Pennsylvania. Two centuries later, in 1980, more than 90 per cent of all three ancestries had been resident in the United States for three generations or more, meaning that the census respondents' grand-parents had been born in America; no measurement beyond this was attempted by the census. About three-quarters of those of English and Irish ancestry were of mixed origins, with parents or grandparents who had intermarried. The Germans were a little less likely to be of mixed ancestry.

Lieberson and Waters note some telling discrepancies in the data for people reporting these old-stock, mixed European backgrounds: those in the same household sometimes identified themselves differently from one population survey to the next; indeed, it is suspected that the same individuals may have done so. Depending on the complexity of the respondent's ancestry, or who is doing the reporting for the other members of the household, or how the ancestry questions were put, the answers could vary from one year to the next: for example, all else held constant, there was a 6 per cent difference in the number reporting themselves as Irish from 1979 to 1980. The authors point out that as individuals' ancestries become more complex, there is a certain tendency to simplify one's pedigree, or to respond situationally to questions about one's ancestral background: one might be Irish-German-English today but English or Irish or German tomorrow. As people's pedigrees become more complicated, they also become less fixed. As, for the Irish, Germans, and English, an unknown but very large proportion have been resident in the United States for longer than three generations (for the English ten or more is possible; for the Irish and Germans, seven or more), the odds favouring intermixing and further ancestral complexity increase with each generation, but so too—if Lieberson and Waters are right—does the likelihood that people will quote their pedigrees selec-tively, meaning that the true complexity of their ancestries will not show up in the census data, and may even decline over the generations as ancestries become tiresomely complicated and people simply lose track of them. If, instead of saying that they are English-German-Greek-Irish-Italian-Lithuanian-Polish-Swedish, having had parents who each had four different but equal ancestries, they merely say that they are Irish because they happen to live in a place like Albany where being Irish has especially positive cultural associations, this datum will appear in the census as unmixed—100 per cent—Irish ancestry, instead of its true 12.5 per cent, so distorting the figures. There are suspicions that, for the old ancestries like the Irish, this is already occurring on a significant scale.

As the Irish in America are often believed to be an inherently urban people, the historical demographics of Irish settlement in America, as summarized by Lieberson and Waters, help to put this in perspective. By 1850, people born in Ireland (not those descended from earlier generations of Irish-ancestry immigrants, who are thought less likely to have been Catholic) were among the two largest immigrant groups, along with either the Germans or the English, in virtually every part of the country: in New England, the mid-Atlantic states, the north central states, the south Atlantic states, and the south central states. In only two regions, the mountain and Pacific states, were the Irish proportionately fewer: in the former they were the third-largest group, in the latter the fourth. These simple statistics are filled with meaning if we look at them for their human significance, and there is much that we can infer from them. In 1850, little of the country was urbanized, which meant that those 85 per cent of Irish immigrants who were passing straight through the Port of New York without pausing for long, if at all, were making their way west as far as the Mississippi River and beyond.

The Irish, like millions of other nineteenth-century European immigrants to the United States, came from rural backgrounds; many had been tenant farmers displaced by the waves of social and economic change which advanced across Europe in the eighteenth and nineteenth centuries; others were the younger sons and daughters of farmers who were unlikely to inherit or could not find land to farm in their localities. Because of plentiful and cheap land, America offered the opportunity for people to continue ways of life to which they were accustomed and to better themselves and their families in ways that were not readily available to them in their countries of origin. For generations before industrialization began to take hold in earnest, rural labour, farm work, and small-scale family farming remained the first rung on the ladder of assimilation into American society. Farm work could accommodate the whole family and make profitable use of their labour; it was a way of life familiar to the European immigrants; and some European immigrants could join fellow countrymen and co-religionists who had already settled in well-defined rural communities with their own mutual-aid networks, churches, schools, farm-service businesses, and cooperative institutions. Some of those who had enough capital or a family who could supply the necessary labour went immediately into farming. Others may have worked initially as farm hands or in any available labouring jobs while they gathered together the resources necessary to farm. Even after the United States began to industrialize on a broad scale, farming and rural work remained an attractive alternative to the urban ghetto.

Our informants' family histories make numerous references to farming, farm work, and rural labour among the immigrant generation from Ireland. In some cases, settlement in the cities was intended to be only temporary; a means to make enough money to set up in farming, a goal that some of them realized. In other cases, an association with farming or rural labour lasted less than a generation, as the immigrants' initial choice of a way of life suited to the skills they brought with them from Ireland later gave way to a preference for city life as they, or their children, acquired additional skills and learned about other ways of making a living, and as the prospects for urban employment increased and became more highly differentiated as the country industrialized. While, by 1870, roughly two-thirds of the Irish-born in the United States were already living in urban centres, more than 36 per cent were still resident in rural areas.[8] By 1900, as Lieberson and Waters note, only 14 per cent of the Irish-born were still employed in agriculture. We must, however, qualify this with the observation that the Irish-born were by this time a much smaller proportion of the Irish-ancestry population as a whole, which was now mainly second or third generation. Counting the children and grandchildren of those who had arrived at mid-century would yield a larger number of Irish-ancestry people still employed in farming.

The majority of those Irish immigrants arriving during and following the Famine years did not, however, go into farming. Those who had relatives who were already established in the nation's rapidly developing cities, or who were young and single, went straight into the urban labour markets and were among the vanguard of a new pattern of incorporation into the American economic order, as industrial work began to supplant small-scale farming as the first rung on the American socio-economic ladder.[9] Immigrants from all parts of Europe arriving after 1880 had less

---

[8]   D. N. Doyle, 'The Irish as Urban Pioneers in the United States, 1850–1870', *Journal of American Ethnic History* (fall–winter 1990–1), 49. These proportions were determined by enumerating the Irish-born in the rural counties of the twenty states with significant Irish-born populations in 1870.
[9]   Ibid.

opportunity or desire to establish themselves as farmers, bypassing farming and rural labour and going directly into the lower ranks of industrial employment in the expanding cities. By the closing decades of the nineteenth century, industrial employment was increasing dramatically, and the cities to the west of the Mississippi were growing. These newer waves of immigrants from Ireland, Germany, England, Italy, Norway, Russia, Sweden, Poland, and other countries were joined by the children and grandchildren of earlier waves of European immigrants who were escaping the increasingly limiting economic possibilities of small-scale farming and were moving into these dynamic new places where there were greater prospects of better jobs, better housing, and better lives.

The widespread distribution of nineteenth-century Irish immigrants' destinations across the United States, which was already well established in 1850, and their early gravitation to urban areas as part of a more general pattern of rural to urban migration over the following century had resulted, by 1980, in people of Irish ancestry being among the most uniformly spread across urban America and displaying one of the least distinctive patterns of spatial distribution of any ancestral category. Table 9.1 gives Lieberson and Waters's figures on the distribution of Irish ancestry in selected American cities, which we have extracted from their tables showing all the main ancestral categories. These figures need to be interpreted with care, however. Only relativities are shown: while it will be seen that in Boston nearly twice as many people report Irish ancestry as in New York, in terms of actual numbers there are about three and a half times as many people reporting Irish ancestry living in New York's central cities as there are in the city of Boston; and while Albany is second only to Boston in relative rank among those cities listed, Boston's number of Irish-ancestry people is roughly six times greater. Moreover, it should be noted that this is not a complete listing of American cities, but is intended only to illustrate the spatial distributions of various ancestries; and it should also be noted that these percentages do not necessarily correspond to numbers of individuals, because they include people of mixed ancestry who are counted more than once. None the less, despite these caveats, the rank-order produces some surprising and, for our purpose, highly significant results. Oklahoma City, Kansas City, and St Louis rival Philadelphia and Pittsburgh in the proportion of the population reporting Irish ancestry, with Dallas-Fort Worth, Denver, and Portland not far behind. The west coast cities of Seattle, San Diego, Oxnard-Ventura, San Bernardino, San Jose, and San Francisco-Oakland all exceed New York and Chicago, and Houston is just as Irish as either

TABLE 9.1. Distribution of Irish ancestry in selected urban areas, 1980

City	Percentage	Rank in city
Boston	29.8	First
Albany	25.2	First
Oklahoma City	23.4	Second
Kansas City	23.1	Third
Pittsburgh	23.1	Second
Philadelphia	22.7	Second
St Louis	21.3	Second
Dallas-Fort Worth	20.2	Second
Denver	20.2	Third
Portland (Oregon)	20.2	Third
Cincinnati	19.3	Third
Seattle	19.1	Third
Indianapolis	18.4	Fourth
San Diego	17.9	Third
Minneapolis-St Paul	17.8	Second
Oxnard-Ventura (California)	17.7	Fourth
Buffalo	17.7	Third
Baltimore	17.4	Third
Atlanta	16.6	Third
San Bernardino	16.6	Fourth
San Jose	16.6	Third
Washington, DC	16.3	Fourth
San Francisco-Oakland	15.9	Third
Detroit	15.5	Fourth
New York	15.2	Third
Houston	15.1	Fourth
Chicago	14.5	Third
Cleveland	14.2	Third
New Orleans	13.0	Fourth
Los Angeles-Long Beach	12.9	Fourth
Milwaukee	12.9	Third
San Antonio	11.6	Fourth
Salt Lake City	10.8	Third
Miami	7.9	Fourth

Note: After S. Lieberson and M. Waters, *From Many Strands: Ethnic and Racial Groups in Contemporary America* (New York, 1988), 84–9, with the addition of Albany as a comparator.

by this measure. While Irish is the largest ancestral category in only two of the cities listed (Boston and Albany), it is second in six, third in sixteen, and fourth in ten. Irish is the second or third most common ancestry in nearly 65 per cent of these cities, and the third or fourth most common in over 75 per cent. These findings confirm what we might have suspected by comparing the number of Irish immigrants arriving at Boston, New York, and Philadelphia with the number of Irish-born resident in these cities during the peak years of immigration. That they were spreading themselves across the country and taking part in full measure in the expansion of social and economic opportunity created by the nation's growth and industrialization, and were succeeding as well as any other ancestral category in climbing the ladder of the American Dream, now seems indisputable. Myths notwithstanding, they were not left behind, stuck in the ghettos, and stereotyped and despised. Or at least not most of them, and not for long.

The sociographic profile of people of Irish ancestry drawn by Lieberson and Waters, comparing a number of variables against those of other ancestral categories, demonstrates a marked pattern of convergence in the characteristics of European old-stock ancestries across the country over the last century. By 1980, there were virtually no detectable or significant differences between those reporting Irish and English ancestry in educational levels, in the nature of the occupations in which they were employed, or in the relationship between education and occupation. There was very little difference between men of English and Irish descent in employment in executive, managerial, and administrative positions (both 16 per cent), professional specialities (15 per cent for English, 13 per cent for Irish), technical jobs (3 per cent for each), sales (10 per cent for each), craftsmen (21 per cent for English, 22 per cent for Irish), or production workers (18 per cent for English, 19 per cent for Irish). More significantly, when occupations were analysed as a function of educational qualifications, no differences could be detected in the rates of their success in securing the kinds of jobs for which they were qualified by reason of their educational credentials: this means that no structural biases acting to discriminate against people of Irish descent, as compared with English, could be seen in the data. The picture is very much the same for women: exactly the same percentages of women of Irish ancestry and English descent held executive, managerial, and administrative positions at the apex of the occupational hierarchy, and, as with their male counterparts, they were employed in the same proportions or within a percentage point or two of one another in every other occupational category. There was also no detectable difference in expected income levels between people of English and Irish ancestry, whether men or women.

Lieberson and Waters go on to demonstrate high rates of intermarriage between the three European ancestries which are most numerous and widespread across the country. Along with the economic convergence of the English, Germans, and Irish, a marked tendency to merge socially is demonstrated by the most intimate measure that is available to us, their propensity to marry one another. The conditions classically governing intermarriage have to do with the availability of co-ethnics, and the frequency of contact and perceived social distance between groups. As we might have expected from their spatial distribution—all three are widespread, and the same three ancestries have dominated the social landscape almost everywhere in America for two centuries—these three ancestral groups display relatively high rates of intermarriage and, by comparison with other ancestral categories, their propensities for in-marriage are measurably less marked. That is, people of Irish ancestry (as well as English and German) have a lower tendency to marry other persons of the same ancestry and a greater tendency to marry people of other ancestries.

If we take these three ancestries together and treat them for the moment as a single field, Lieberson and Waters's figures show, for the cohort born between 1946 and 1955, that 89.7 per cent of single-ancestry English women have husbands of either unmixed or mixed English, German, or Irish ancestry; as do 77.5 per cent of single-ancestry German women; and 81.5 per cent of single-ancestry Irish women. For those women of the same age cohort reporting *mixed* English, German, or Irish ancestry, limitations on the published tabulations prevent a breakdown into precise percentages; none the less, rates of marriage within this field are likely to be at least as high as for single-ancestry women.[10] Looking more closely at those Irish women born between 1946 and 1955, of those of single ancestry, 18.0 per cent married men of single or mixed English descent, 24.5 per cent married men of German descent, and 38.1 per cent married men of Irish background. Beyond this field, the most frequent choices for these Irish single-ancestry women were Italian, with 8.5 per cent, French (5.5 per cent), and Scottish (4.5 per cent). For mixed-ancestry Irish women, the most frequent marriages were with men of German

---

[10] This is because some of those mixed-ancestry individuals enumerated were present in more than one of these categories; for example, the same Irish-German woman is counted twice, once as Irish and again as German, making the figures, when added together, total more than 100 per cent.

descent (37.2 per cent), Irish background (35.6 per cent), and English ancestry (28.3 per cent); beyond this, the most frequent choices were Scottish (9.2 per cent), French (8.0 per cent), and Italian (7.6 per cent). Overall, then, Irish women in this age cohort had a very high propensity to marry out of their own ancestral group, but within these two adjacent ancestries. Single-ancestry Irish women chose English- or German-ancestry husbands marginally more frequently than Irish (42 versus 38 per cent). Mixed-ancestry Irish women, however, chose English or German husbands with a much greater degree of frequency than Irish husbands (65.5 as against 35.6 per cent). Only about a third of this age cohort were marrying men of the same ancestral background, but the great majority of the other two-thirds were not going beyond English or German, or mixtures involving these ancestries.

Some interesting patterns can be seen in these statistics. Our familiarity with Albany will suggest to us the obvious connections between Irish, German, French, and Italian, in as much as Albany is—unusually—a very Catholic place. But the connections with English and Scottish may not be quite as apparent from our Albany-centred viewpoint, and we might be tempted to jump to the conclusion that we are seeing two patterns in the data: a Catholic one and a Protestant one, with the mainly Protestant Irish who arrived in the eighteenth century and settled in the south marrying the English and Scots, and the later arrivals, the Catholic Irish, marrying the Germans, French, and Italians. As Lieberson and Waters note, the picture for the Irish ancestral category across the nation is obscured by the absence of information about religion in the US Census. They raise the question of whether these rates would be different if we were able to distinguish between Catholics and Protestants (the same question arises in the case of the Germans, who might be Catholic, Protestant, or Jewish). There are clues, however. A rigorously constructed random sample of Catholic Americans compiled by the National Opinion Research Center (NORC) in Chicago, enumerating over 2,000 people, was analysed by Richard Alba and Ronald Kessler for the indications it could give on inter-ethnic marriage patterns.[11] The conclusions we might draw from their analysis do not support the idea that subtracting the Protestant fraction from the Irish-ancestry category would necessarily produce a radically different pattern of relativities for the remaining Catholics. Alba and Kessler found that Irish Catholics were marrying

---

[11] R. D. Alba and R. C. Kessler, 'Patterns of Interethnic Marriage among American Catholics', *Social Forces*, 57 (1979).

people of English background at more than 8 per cent *above* the expected rate, while they married people of German, Italian, and Polish ancestry with a frequency of about 3 per cent *below* the mathematically modelled expected rate. As a whole, Irish Catholics were selecting *against* the Germans, Italians, and Poles, who are predominantly fellow Catholics, and selecting *for* the predominantly Protestant English. Alba and Kessler express the view that 'Irish Catholics are drawn toward marriage to others from the British Isles, whether Catholic or Protestant'.[12] This would include, of course, the Scots.

The NORC sample indicates that while 50 per cent have spouses of unmixed Irish ancestry, 16 per cent marry people of unmixed English descent, and 13 per cent have husbands or wives of unmixed German ancestry, compared with the next-most-frequent choice, the 8 per cent who have have spouses of Italian background. This pattern is consonant with that for the whole Irish-ancestry category: among Catholics, the English and Germans are preferred to all other ancestries by a wide margin. Further substantiation comes from Ruby Jo Reeves Kennedy's classic notes on marriage patterns in New Haven over the years from 1870 to 1950. She found that the Irish, who as in Albany were overwhelmingly Catholic, preferred British-stock partners (who were overwhelmingly Protestant) over the more numerous—and Catholic—Germans, Italians, and Poles; and that people of Scots ancestry, though few in number, none the less figured in the list of preferred marriage partners.[13] If anything, these studies by Kennedy, and Alba and Kessler, suggest an even stronger preference among Irish Catholics for English-ancestry spouses than the aggregated choices for all people of Irish ancestry given by Lieberson and Waters. In other words, if we were able to subtract the Protestants from their figures, we would be likely to get an Irish-English pattern of preference that is *more* marked, not less.

What we are seeing is social propinquity as it is expressed in the most intimate of all social relationships, and by the most significant sociographic measure that is available to us. Language never divided the English and the Irish in America, and after a century or two of intermixing on more or less equal social levels in most parts of the country, whatever cultural differences there were have very largely melted away. Clearly, not even religion matters very much to large numbers of

---

[12] Ibid. 1137.

[13] R. J. R. Kennedy, 'Single or Triple Melting Pot? Intermarriage in New Haven, 1870–1940', *American Journal of Sociology*, 49 (1944); 'Single or Triple Melting Pot? Intermarriage in New Haven, 1870–1950', *American Journal of Sociology*, 58 (1952).

Catholics of Irish ancestry, at least as far as their relationships with people of British backgrounds are concerned, and Kennedy's findings suggest that it might never have done so in places that were less self-consciously Irish than Albany, or less self-consciously English than places that are, or were, Albany's ethnic mirror image. Across America, at least a million Irish Catholics in the current generations have husbands or wives of English or mixed-English ancestry, despite the pervasive American myth that the English and the Irish are as different as chalk and cheese.

III

The nature of Albany's Irishness today is intimately intertwined with its history, and with recent developments in the way people have come to think of the past and thus of themselves. While it was still a Dutch manorial estate, at least one of Van Rensselaer's settlers is said to have been from Dublin, and after Albany became a British possession and assumed importance as a garrison town, Irish soldiers were billeted there. Britain's colonial claims were extensive, her wars taxing upon her resources, and her need for troops, labourers, and settlers was great. No one looked closely at the religion of those young Irishmen who volunteered to take the King's shilling for service in the British Army or found their way to America as farmers and canal-diggers. By the end of the eighteenth century, an extensive pattern of emigration from the old world to the new was beginning to develop in earnest as the Irish, along with people from other parts of the British Isles and north-western Europe, sought better lives for themselves and their families in North America. In 1845, the year before the Famine struck, the annual rate of migration from Ireland to the United States had reached a level of more than 40,000.

The Famine provoked a huge surge in immigration between 1847 and 1854, and then reverted to its pre-Famine level. Twenty per cent of all nineteenth-century Irish emigrants to America arrived during those seven fateful years. Thousands of refugees came directly to Albany or soon gravitated there, for not only were they welcomed and helped by the religious and civic authorities, but at that time Albany was industrializing rapidly and could absorb all the people who came its way. As English-speakers and natives of the British Isles, the Irish were not handicapped by an initial inability to cope linguistically and culturally in their new surroundings, and they moved straight into the mainstream of the local labour and housing markets, spreading themselves throughout the city and the lower ranks of the urban economy. Their large and growing numbers had a significant effect on the way they were treated; those local institutions which were prepared to accept the immigrants and to harness their labour, voting power, and religion were greatly strengthened and their rise to unrivalled and enduring dominance in Albany's affairs followed as a direct consequence. Church, party, and people derived mutual benefit from the relationship. With the support and patronage of powerful local institutions, the Irish rapidly began to climb the ladder from immigrant rags to lace-curtain respectability. Family by family, one rung at a time, in Albany they succeeded as well as any contemporaneous emigrants to America in realizing their aspirations of better lives than they could have hoped for in the old country.

Five generations have passed since then. Their descendants are now thoroughly assimilated Americans. In their everyday private lives, few traces remain of their Irish immigrant great-great-grandparentage. For most, and for 90 per cent of the fifth generation, their connections with the Famine refugees of the mid-nineteenth century have become increasingly distant and uncertain, as their own and previous generations married people of other European ancestries, and as they married the descendants of Irish immigrants who had arrived in America before 1847 or after 1854. Many of our informants had lost touch, through their genealogical knowledge, with that fateful moment in history a century and a half ago; and how, if at all, they were connected to it. Two-thirds had an incomplete knowledge of the basic details of their grandparents' biographies which took them back to the beginning of the twentieth century or the end of the nineteenth, and fewer still were able to account for their great-grandparents and great-great-grandparents a half-century earlier, knowing when their Irish ancestors left the old country, and why. Until recently, this kind of backward-looking knowledge was clearly unimportant to most people. The previous generations were not especially interested in where their ancestors had come from, or when, but rather in making lives for themselves and investing in the future through their children. There was nothing to be gained by looking back, and there was no practical use to which such knowledge could be put.

None the less, most of our informants were conscious of being of Irish ancestry, and there were occasions when they still felt Irish, displayed their Irishness, and did self-consciously Irish things even if this was only to wear something green on St Patrick's Day. Much of this was related to the particular social milieu of Albany, where being of Irish descent and being a Catholic are so common that they are firmly tied together in the popular imagination. While the conjuncture of these two things, along with being a Democrat, is the consequence of local historical circumstance, the ideas people had about themselves were not necessarily backward-looking, and usually were not. For the majority of our informants, it was enough to know that being of Irish ancestry made one normal, like most other people, a part of the fully-assimilated, old-stock European majority in Albany society, and signified little more than this.

Until the 1924 Immigration Act required the census bureau and the immigration service to set quotas related to the American population as it was then constituted, little effort had been made to determine the ancestral composition of the American population. No question on place of birth was asked until the Census of 1850. The second generation, whatever their parents' origins, were merely recorded as native-born until 1880, when they were asked whether they had foreign-born parents and if so where they had been born. No question would be asked about the grandparentage of the third generation for another century, by which time the older-stock ancestries who had arrived by 1850 were already into the fifth or sixth generation and beyond. And, no question on religion was ever asked, or would be asked in a US Census. When the American Council of Learned Societies (ACLS) was commissioned to prepare its report on the US population in 1790, it was required to differentiate within the immigrant flow from Ireland. The only possible motive there could have been for this requirement was to distinguish between Irish Catholics (who were presumed to have come from Leinster, Munster, and Connaught) and Irish Protestants (who were presumed to have come from Ulster). There being no direct evidence about this, the ACLS had to use indirect evidence; but in order to determine how to proceed, it had to have a working definition of what we would nowadays call 'ethnicity'. The ACLS used the notion of 'national character', commonplace at the time, which did not distinguish between race and culture, but treated loyalty to faith and custom as facts of nature inherent in bonds of blood and descent from common origins, as if they were inherited traits of the same order as skin colour or hair texture. In accepting the report, the United States government thus endorsed as authoritative a definition of 'ethnicity' based upon primordialism—that membership of an ethnic community is the consequence of the facts of birth—and in so doing entered the arena of modern American ethnic

politics extraordinarily ill-equipped to perceive its sociological realities.[14]

The civil rights debates of the 1950s and 1960s, since they eventually
became reduced to skin colour—an inherited physical trait—as the defining characteristic of those suffering the most grievous political disadvan-
tage and social alienation from the American Dream, was so easily
accommodated within the primordialist interpretation of ethnicity
already accepted by the federal authorities that it appeared to confirm its
validity as a general principle and to justify its extension into other realms
of American life. The essentializing idea that ethnicity is unambiguously
and unalterably fixed by ancestry eventually came to underpin official
policies on multiculturalism and equal opportunities. Thus one can read
in a contemporary American manual on hiring practices:

For the purposes of this discussion we will define *primary dimensions of diversity*
as those immutable human differences that are inborn and/or that exert an important impact on our early socialization and an ongoing impact throughout our lives.
… Listed in alphabetical order, they are: (1) Age. (2) Ethnicity. (3) Gender. (4)
Physical abilities/qualities. (5) Race. (6) Sexual/affectional orientation.[15]

Ethnicity, thus defined, is concerned only with the category itself and
the criterion of belonging to it, and not—at least initially—with its
content. The categorical boundary may be imposed from the top down,
as a matter of official policy; if so, it is not a matter of self-definition by
the group or, necessarily, the product of negotiation with its members
(for no such category may have existed as a coherent social group in
advance of its official definition). The boundary encloses all those who
are perceived to have inherited membership of it through birth. This
definition allows only one way in and no way out. Ethnicity, thus understood as an ascriptive phenomenon which merges genetics and culture,

---

[14] Anthropologists and sociologists have repeatedly demonstrated that 'culture' and
'ethnicity' are learnt, not inherited; none the less, theories of 'race', 'ethnicity', 'culture',
and 'nation' which are founded upon folk essentialisms of shared substance are commonplace occurrences in social life, and have been interpreted in a variety of ways by social
scientists. See Bibliography, esp. B. Anderson, *Imagined Communities* (London, 1991);
E. Gellner, *Nations and Nationalism* (Oxford, 1983); C. Geertz, *The Interpretation of
Cultures* (New York, 1973); J. Hutchinson and A. D. Smith, *Ethnicity* (Oxford, 1996);
R. Jenkins, *Rethinking Ethnicity: Arguments and Explorations* (London, 1997); and A. D.
Smith, *Nations and Nationalism in a Global Era* (Cambridge, 1995).

[15] M. Loden and J. B. Rosener, quoted in K. Verdery, 'Ethnicity, Nationalism, and
State-making: "Ethnic Groups and Boundaries": Past and Future', in H. Vermeulen and C.
Govers (eds.), *The Anthropology of Ethnicity: Beyond 'Ethnic Groups and Boundaries'* (The
Hague, 1996), 53.

cannot cope comfortably with the problems of ambiguity, choice, or denial. It is an astonishing reversal of ideology that the country which regarded itself as a melting-pot, and which for generations encouraged its citizens to slough off their attachments to their foreign origins and to become unethnic Americans, should now require its citizens to belong, at least nominally, to a set of officially defined, primordial, quasi-racial *ethnies*. Nowadays, in the interests of even-handed, egalitarian multiculturalism, American schoolteachers not uncommonly ask children to say what they 'are' (not merely to say what their immigrant ancestors' origins were a century ago), forcing them to identify with an *ethnie*, no matter how irrelevant such a question might be to the child's circumstances or how complicated or indeterminate their ancestry. Teachers rely on manuals and textbooks to tell the children about 'their traditions' and 'their history' which they are presumed to have inherited along with their skin and hair colour, books which are authorized for use in publicly funded classrooms by state legislatures and local school boards. These interpretations of 'culture', and 'history' are, then, subject to political definition and surveillance.

Arguably, contemporary ethnic politics has had the effect, intended or not, of creating cleavages and deepening differences in the American social fabric. New *ethnies* have been defined which would have been scarcely recognizable to the ancestors of most present-day generations of Americans, since more often than not they are based on boundaries of inclusion and exclusion that are not congruent with those which had significance for the first generations of immigrants to America, one, two, or three centuries ago; and in any event, for a large part of the European-ancestry population, have become obscured and all but erased by subsequent generations of intermarriage. Once the boundaries encompassing these new *ethnies* came to be defined by the continent, region, or the modern nation-state encompassing the place of one's ancestors' birth, the void thus created within these boundaries demanded to be filled with cultural stuff; with moral content; with stories.

Multiculturalism tends to become a form of identity politics, in which the concept of *culture* becomes merged with that of ethnic identity. From an anthropological standpoint, this move, at least in its more simplistic ideological forms, is fraught with dangers both theoretical and practical. It risks essentializing the idea of culture as the property of an ethnic group or race; it risks reifying cultures as separate entities by overemphasizing their boundedness and mutual distinctness; it risks overemphasizing the internal homogeneity of cultures in terms that potentially legitimate repressive demands for communal conformity.[16]

There is another risk. The politics of multiculturalism encourages competition between *ethnies*: in practice, as the game has been played, those who can sustain their claims to have endured the most suffering and injustice by presenting the most persuasive stories through their ethnic advocates have won the contests for recognition and special treatment. The success of some claims has not been lost on all those other players seeking to advance their interests or even just to avoid losing ground relative to the rest. There are points to be scored for being a wronged and exploited minority, but none for being part of the lace-curtain majority. Political expediency thus influences what stories come to fill the space within the ethnic boundaries.

Five generations is a long time, long enough for most people to have lost touch with distantly removed branches of their families in the United States, let alone with even more distant relatives in Ireland, if any still remain. For many of our informants, a knowledge of who their Irish ancestors were, where they lived, whether they were the landless poor from the rocky Atlantic shores of Donegal or Mayo or the middle ranks of the yeomanry from the rich fields and pastures of Down or Wexford; whether they were Famine refugees escaping poverty and pestilence; or whether they were surplus daughters their fathers were shipping off to New York to avoid paying a dowry or the social embarrassment of a 'wrong' marriage, or sons impatient with the prospect of remaining unmarried and having to work as unpaid farm hands until their forties or fifties when their fathers chose to retire and hand over the house and farm; or whether they were simply seeking the promise of the American Dream like so many other European immigrants of the time, is knowledge which is now lost to their descendants. Our informants' understandings of the past may or may not have had much relationship to the stories their ancestors might have told. These understandings varied from one informant to the next; they were a jumble of the particular and the general, of fragments of actual events in Irish history and the nation-building rhetoric of the nineteenth century, together with ideas drawn from panegyric popular histories, fiction, film, television, schoolroom

---

[16] T. Turner, 'Anthropology and Multiculturalism: What is Anthropology that Multiculturalists should be Mindful of it?' *Cultural Anthropology*, 8 (1993), 411–12, quoted in G. Baumann, *Contesting Culture: Discourses of Identity in Multi-ethnic London* (Cambridge, 1996), 20.

projects, museum displays, and theme days. Contemporary public debate about multiculturalism in North America has given a great deal of impetus to the creation and revitalization of folk images and scholarly interpretations of Irishness: and especially to certain kinds of images and interpretations.

For people of Irish ancestry, simply being an American and climbing the ladder of success, that which their great-grandparents strove for and achieved by putting a stony, no-hope farm in County Clare behind them, are today no longer enough, it seems. Since the 1970s, with public debates about multiculturalism, everyone has come to be regarded as needing 'an ethnic identity'. Compared with previous generations, consciousness of ancestry has become heightened and people have been goaded into taking an interest in their ethnic heritage: the cultural stuff of being Irish. As a consequence of this awakening of interest, as well as creating demand through its own dynamics, an entire industry has developed which supplies a surfeit of ready-made, off-the-shelf stories and pictures of the past, among which the consumer may browse, and that satisfy the curiosity that anyone of Irish ancestry might have about the immigrant experience, about what happened in Ireland, and about Irish traditions. Like written-to-a-formula airport novels, some of these stories sell rather better than others. Those which contrive to pluck at the emotional heartstrings are always among the best-sellers.

For the Irish, the cultural space newly authorized by multiculturalism was quickly filled. The materials already existed to transform Irish ancestry into Irish ethnicity. A useful, if dated, model of ethnic Irishness was close at hand, and so was its cultural stuff. The waves of religious, linguistic, economic, and political transformation reached Ireland in her island fastness on the western edge of Europe after they had swept across the rest of the continent, arriving late enough for the traumas of modernization to be entering their most painful and politically difficult phase when a new idea, that of the nation, appeared in Europe at the end of the eighteenth century. Irish society had already become complex and highly differentiated, but the main thing most of the population still had in common that was distinctively different from the English, and eventually came to form the cultural foundation of a new nation, was their religion. The notion of Celticness, a racial metaphor, came to embody the sectarian division of Ireland into those who saw themselves as the natural inheritors of her history and native traditions, and those who were seen as invaders and despoilers. The idea of an Irish *ethnie*, based upon primordial attachments, had been forged in the crucible of Irish nationalism by more than a hundred years of political persuasion and intellectual industry.

The battle for Irish independence was won in 1920; a half-century later these ideas were beginning to gather dust when the need for a primordial Irish *ethnie*, pictured as a wronged and exploited underclass, arose again in the United States in the 1970s. The sectarian, quasi-racial, nineteenth-century nation-building image of the Irish as Celts, Catholics, and children of the Famine was dusted off and resurrected as the definition of 'true' Irishness, and its stories—written for a particular political purpose in another country in another century—were likewise dusted off and supplemented by home-grown tales of the hardships and homesickness of the first generation of Irish Catholic immigrants in America's big-city enclaves.

In much the same way that ethnic advocates have found that pleading past suffering and injustice wins political points, heritage-industry entrepreneurs have discovered that adversity and tragedy, like romance, is a winning formula for selling stories to a public presumed to be hungry for knowledge of who they are in this multicultural world, a world in which everyone must now have 'a history', 'a culture', and 'an ethnic identity', however and by whomever contrived, and from whatever motives. Ethnic politicians and heritage-industry businesspeople alike have an interest in raking over the past and turning over the mossiest of stones to find winning stories which have clear moral messages. Under one of these mossy stones was John Mitchel's hyperbolic dramatization of the Famine,[17] the tale of a cruel and calculating tyrant (Britannia) and an innocent and pitiable victim (Erin): a story that succeeds brilliantly in anthropomorphizing and embellishing historical contingency, and in transforming impersonal, unintended, and unconnected events into a seamless moral epic: a just-so story with all the makings of a modern myth.

That 10 per cent of Ireland's population was lost in the fearful and fateful calamity of the Famine which it was the misfortune of Ireland to bear with such severity, and that some Irish immigrants to America were maltreated just as the Italians who followed them were maltreated by earlier arrivals in America (including the Irish themselves) are facts that are beyond question. But it is equally indisputable that 90 per cent survived the Famine, and that most of those who came to America as wholly unremarkable economic migrants—who formed 80 per cent of

---

[17] See Ch. 3, 56.

the immigrant flow from Ireland to America in the nineteenth century[18]—found what they were looking for, succeeded as well as any, made more rapid gains than non-English-speakers arriving at the same time from Germany, Italy, Poland, and elsewhere, and over the generations have merged completely into the lace-curtain American ascendancy. The Irish historian Mary Daly has observed that:

The Great Famine is arguably the only event in modern Irish history to have achieved widespread international recognition. The steady sales of Cecil Woodham-Smith's *The Great Hunger*, which has been in print for more than thirty years, testify to a continuing wish to be informed about this crisis. The more recent runaway success of the spurious *Famine Diary*—allegedly the diary of school teacher Gerald Keegan who emigrated with his wife to Canada on a 'coffin ship' where both died of fever—and its continuing sales despite being revealed as a piece of late nineteenth-century Canadian-Irish fiction—suggest a strong desire to wallow in its emotional horrors, perhaps at the cost of a wider understanding. For some U. S. and Canadian citizens of Irish descent the Famine is in danger of becoming their answer to the Jewish Holocaust: evidence that the Irish too are a nation of victims, a causal explanation for mass emigration and a symbol of national unity. With the sesquicentennial of the Famine in 1995 and the promises of Famine walks, Famine museums and the commemoration of Famine-era graveyards the Famine seems set to become a part of the Irish heritage industry.[19]

The anthropomorphic interpretation of the Famine, as the event that is popularly believed to have caused the Irish diaspora, has assumed mythic status and now informs most people's understandings of the 'immigrant experience'. Like other myths, its relationship to history and social organization is problematic: it is only partly related to reality. It is an allegory that invites us to consider how something that does not exist except as a nominal abstraction and might never have existed in the other America beyond the first-generation big-city immigrant ghetto—an Irish-American *ethnie*—can be represented in our imagination. It is a

---

[18] According to Blessing's figures, 3,785,222 immigrants from Ireland arrived in the United States from 1820 up to and including 1899. Those arriving during the Famine and its immediate aftermath, from 1847 through 1854, totalled 1,186,928. One must, however, subtract from this the number of immigrants who might reasonably have been expected to arrive had it not been for the Famine. This is estimated at 50,000 per year, which was the level seen immediately before the Famine, and which followed from 1855 onwards. See P. J. Blessing, *The Irish in America: A Guide to the Literature and the Manuscript Collections* (Washington, 1992), 289.

[19] M. E. Daly, 'Revisionism and Irish History: The Great Famine', in D. G. Boyce and A. O'Day (eds.), *The Making of Modern Irish History: Revisionism and the Revisionist Controversy* (London, 1996), 71.

means by which we can begin to understand how people whose repertoire of social practices from one year to the next is in their own estimations in no way Irish, who are several generations removed from anyone who ever lived in Ireland, and whose genealogies might reveal them to be mostly German or English, can none the less feel the emotional tug of being Irish for an hour, a day, or a lifetime. That the arresting imagery of this picture is the very opposite of social and historical reality, and stands in a dialectical relationship to it, adds to its power to command our attention.

It is conventional, but probably an anthropological conceit, to say that everyone need myths. It may be that people need ideals, things to believe in, and stories about the worlds they inhabit that provide more or less satisfying explanations, but these do not necessarily have to be culturally specific parables which reach back into the past. Our informants' parents and grandparents looked to the future, to the day their children and grandchildren would attain the American Dream. The dream may have turned to dust for some Americans, but for millions of descendants of European immigrants there was suburban middle-class respectability at the end of the rainbow and the melting-pot was, and is, most certainly *not* a myth but the everyday moral project of past and current generations. Multiculturalism has brought about a new kind of project and has opened up a bourgeoning market in politicized and manufactured heritage: both have produced essentializing myths. In place of the variety of views of the world as their ancestors actually experienced it, as it was related to their time, place, and individual social circumstances, we now have 'a diasporic culture': mass-produced, standardized, pre-packaged, one size fits all.

Myths fill a need. That need should not be ridiculed or disparaged. But we might question why some myths take the form they do, and wonder why they have done so, and in whose political or economic interest it is to create or perpetuate certain kinds of stories. There is another mythology of the Irish in America waiting to be written and popularized; another story to pluck at the heartstrings that does not seek to exclude people because of their religion or to mobilize tears of bitterness and anger at past injustices, but instead instils pride in the achievements and triumphs of the 85 per cent in the other America beyond the big-city ghettos; which gives their histories back to those 80 per cent who came to America before the Famine, or later; and restores the dignity that is rightfully theirs, as Irish-born men and women, to *all* the people who came to America from Ireland. As scholars, we have a duty to distinguish between those ideas whose epistemological status derives from serious scholarship and demonstrable and measurable evidence; and those which merely reify hackneyed, essentializing myths.

It is ironic that as Irishness has dimmed and disappeared in everyday social practice, it should now be reinvented as 'social memory', 'shared identity', and 'collective self-image'. Tradition needs to be preserved in a condition of post-traditionality, or it fades away. As traditions are no longer nourished in families, they no longer have a life of their own except through their inscription in best-selling stories and their embodiment in museum displays and theme days. Most of the people we interviewed knew something about Ireland and Irishness, and a very large proportion of our informants had made visits to their ancestors' homeland. The evidence of a shared social memory of the immigrant experience in our informants' accounts, as something that binds them together as a collectivity is, however, exceedingly equivocal, and raises searching methodological questions about what counts as social memory or self-image and how one establishes that these things are shared to the extent that one can speak of them as 'collective'. There was wide variation among our informants in their accounts of their Irishness. Which of them should we have chosen as paradigmatic, had we decided to proceed by ignoring the sociological questions of who and in what degree, giving the reader only convenient illustration, or 'thick description'? Their accounts were differently structured; some derived from personal experience, others from the experiences of other people they knew, still others from abstractions and beliefs not rooted in the experience of anyone whom they knew but which were none the less taken to be evidence of something significant, real, and true. Much the same can be said of their social practices. How is such wide variation to be regarded as evidence of 'a shared culture'? Or as informing 'the ethnic identity' of individuals? One suspects that it is simply because, as the storytellers, we say so. We have taken it as our task to discover what lies within the space bounded by the idea of 'Irish-American ethnicity'. But if we do not question the legitimacy of the category by critically examining the nature of its boundaries, how they have been defined, by whom and for what purpose, and what happens at the boundary-zone and beyond, we merely create that which we are looking for as a consequence of our scholarly practice.

Only a handful of our informants were sufficiently interested in their ancestry or ethnicity that one might have said that their 'identity' as Irish-Americans had some everyday importance to them. There were so few that they have scarcely merited mention in this book. The assumption that everyone is interested in their ethnic identity, or that, despite the strident demands of multiculturalism, they have the wish, or the means, to assign themselves to a single *ethnie* is not unambiguously borne out by our findings in Albany. That we were a research team from Ireland interested in their Irish connections and their sense of Irishness undoubtedly influenced what our informants told us. There is no reason to think that someone half Irish and half German might not have said very different things had we been a research team from Germany.

What is now understood to be Irish-American ethnicity is a creolization of Irish and American history and popular culture produced in the rough and tumble of American pluralism and multiculturalism, and has probably taken different twists and turns in different places across the country over the last century and a half. We are now in danger of losing all this richness of variety as understandings about 'Irish ethnicity' and 'the immigrant experience' settle into rigid, iconic shapes which canalize and constrain the way that Irish-Americanness is represented, authorizing—even sacralizing—some ideas and interpretations and condemning others as 'revisionism'. What has been said about life in the ghetto now informs how people can know themselves, and people in Albany have come to believe there was a time when signs saying 'No Irish Need Apply' were to be seen everywhere. The commonplace, increasingly standardized and essentialized stereotypes of Irishness held by Americans, including their interpretations of the Famine, have been exported across the Atlantic along with bagels, baseball, and St Patrick's Day parades (complete with cheer-leaders and marching bands) and are now repackaged and sold back to Americans as 'heritage' when they visit Ireland. Providing for American and Canadian tourists is one of Ireland's biggest and most important industries and sources of dollar revenue. Nothing is left to chance: the national tourist board and private entrepreneurs in Ireland do highly professional market research and know what North Americans want to see and hear, which stories and pictures are acceptable and saleable and which are not; a brief package tour of Ireland is therefore much less likely to disturb North American preconceptions than to reinforce them.

Although Albany is as Irish a place as one might expect to find outside the big-city enclaves, in many respects it is less markedly Irish than one might have anticipated from the way Irish-Americanness is portrayed in much of the scholarly literature. This study set out to discover in what senses and in what degrees the descendants of nineteenth-century Irish immigrants still possessed distinctive social practices and ways of seeing the world, a goal which influenced the research methods that were used, what pieces of evidence have been included in this book, and how they have been interpreted. We have aimed to achieve a balanced analysis by attempting to measure the distribution and degree of our informants' Irishness, emphasizing the middle of the spectrum at the expense of the extremes. A view of Irishness from the vantage point of Murphy's Tavern, the folk music scene, or the Hibernians' Hall, as seen through the eyes of people who were especially conscious of their Irishness and were involved in Irish-American affairs, would have been very different. Had we limited our horizons in this way, it would not have been difficult to have sustained a plausible argument that Irishness was undimmed by a century and a half of social change, though its contemporary manifestations might perhaps have taken different forms. We collected a great deal of material of this kind, through many months of patient participant observation, material which is not included in this book because it would have exaggerated its representativeness. The world of the self-conscious Irishness of the few would not have been the world of the many: the other 90 per cent of Albany's residents, who have an equal—or even stronger—claim upon descent from the Famine-era immigrants who made Albany into such an Irish place in 1855, but soon left their Irishness behind as they began to succeed in climbing the ladder of the American Dream, never to look back. Our core sample of 252 people, 86.5 per cent of whom had Irish ancestry, had sociographic characteristics which showed them to be markedly middle-class. Seventy-three per cent of this sample had college degrees, compared with 40 per cent for the whole European-ancestry population of the city of Albany in 1990. And, their median family income was $55,000, as compared with $35,000 for the whole population of European descent in the city of Albany.

If a degree of Irishness can be detected, however variably and indistinctly, among people who are so comfortably a part of the middle-American mainstream, it is unlikely to disappear without trace or merge completely into a generalized white European ethnic category, at least not in places like Albany, and not for a long time. In places less Irish than Albany, a semblance of Irishness will be kept alive by the demand which multiculturalism imposes, that every American ought really to be something else that is more primordial—unrealistic and artificial as this may be in the case of later-generation Americans of complex ancestries. After the passage of five or six generations of assimilation and intermarriage, Irishness, for most, is already a virtual ethnicity, no longer a lived reality: a composed and constructed one consisting of a contrived categorical boundary containing idiosyncratic individual collections of bits and pieces, highly variable in provenance, quality, and quantity. Like a reversible T-shirt saying 'Irish for a Day' on one side and 'Kuβ mich, ich bin Schwabe' on the other that one can keep in a bottom drawer, and put on when the mood takes one, or as the occasion warrants, such manifestations of ethnicity are not very demanding to maintain, take up very little space in one's wardrobe, and might still come in useful now and again.

BIBLIOGRAPHY

ABRAMSON, H., *Ethnic Diversity in Catholic America* (New York, 1973).

AKENSON, D., 'Why the Accepted Estimates of the Ethnicity of the American People, 1790, are Unacceptable', *William and Mary Quarterly*, 41 (1984), 102–18.

—— 'The Historiography of the Irish in the United States', in P. O'Sullivan (ed.), *The Irish World Wide*, ii, *The Irish in the New Communities* (Leicester, 1992).

—— *The Irish Diaspora: A Primer* (Streetsville, Ontario, 1993).

ALBA, R. D., 'Social Assimilation among American Catholic National Origin Groups', *American Sociological Review*, 41 (1978), 1030–46.

—— *Italian Americans: Into the Twilight of Ethnicity* (Englewood Cliffs, NJ, 1985).

—— 'The Twilight of Ethnicity among Americans of European Ancestry: The Case of Italians', *Ethnic and Racial Studies*, 8 (1985), 134–59.

—— *Ethnicity and Race in the U.S.A.: Toward the Twenty-First Century* (London, 1988).

—— *Ethnic Identity: The Transformation of White America* (New Haven, 1990).

—— 'Assimilation's Quiet Tide', *The Public Interest*, 119 (spring 1995), 3–18.

—— and CHAMLIN, M., 'A Preliminary Examination of Ethnic Identity among Whites', *American Sociological Review*, 48 (1983), 240–7.

—— and GOLDEN, R., 'Patterns of Ethnic Marriage in the United States', *Social Forces*, 65 (1986), 202–23.

—— and KESSLER, R. G., 'Patterns of Interethnic Marriage among Catholic Americans', *Social Forces*, 57 (1979), 124–40.

—— and LOGAN, J., 'Variations on Two Themes: Racial and Ethnic Patterns in the Attainment of Suburban Residence', *Demography*, 28 (1991), 431–53.

—— —— and CROWDER, K., 'White Ethnic Neighborhoods and Assimilation: The Greater New York Region, 1980–1990', *Social Forces*, 75 (1997), 883–909.

—— and MOORE, G., 'Ethnicity in the American Elite', *American Sociological Review*, 47 (1982), 373–83.

ANDERSON, B., *Imagined Communities* (London, 1991).

BAUMAN, Z., *Modernity and Ambivalence* (Cambridge, 1991).

BAUMANN, G., *Contesting Culture: Discourses of Identity in Multi-ethnic London* (Cambridge, 1996).

BAX, M., *Harpstrings and Confessions: Machine-Style Politics in the Irish Republic* (Assen, 1976).

BECKER, M. J., 'A History of Catholic Life in the Diocese of Albany, 1609–1864', Ph.D. thesis (Fordham University, 1973).

BEEBE, R. T., *Albany Medical College and Albany Hospital: A History, 1839–1982* (Albany, NY, 1983).

BEILINSKI, S., 'A Middling Sort: Artisans and Tradesmen in Colonial Albany', *New York History*, 83 (1992), 260–90.

BIEVER, B., *Religion, Culture, and Values: A Cross-Cultural Analysis of Motivational Factors in Native Irish and Irish-American Catholicism* (New York, 1976).

BIRR, K., 'The American Religious Experience', in A. Roberts and M. Cockrell (eds.), *Historic Albany: Its Churches and Synagogues* (Albany, 1986).

—— 'Merchants, Manufacturers and Bureaucrats', in A. Roberts and J. Van Dyk (eds.), *Experiencing Albany: Perspectives on a Grand City's Past* (Albany, NY, 1986).

BLESSING, C. W., *Albany Schools and Colleges Yesterday and Today* (Albany, NY, 1936).

BLESSING, P. J., *The Irish in America: A Guide to the Literature and the Manuscript Collections* (Washington, 1992).

BOTTIGHEIMER, K., *Ireland and the Irish: A Short History* (New York, 1982).

BOURKE, P. M. A., *'The Visitation of God'? The Potato and the Great Irish Famine*, J. Hill and C. Ó Gráda (eds.) (Dublin, 1993).

BOWERS, V., *The Texture of a Neighborhood: Albany's South End, 1880–1940* (Albany, NY, 1991).

BOYCE, D. G., *Nationalism in Ireland* (London, 1982).

—— *Nineteenth-Century Ireland: The Search for Stability* (Dublin, 1990).

—— and O'DAY, A. (eds.), *The Making of Modern Irish History: Revisionism and the Revisionist Controversy* (London, 1996).

BROWN, T., *Irish-American Nationalism* (New York, 1966).

BURKE, T. F., *Mohawk Frontier: The Dutch Community of Schenectady, New York, 1661–1710* (Ithaca, NY, 1991).

CHAPMAN, M., *The Celts: The Construction of a Myth* (London, 1992).

CLARK, D., *The Irish in Philadelphia: Ten Generations of Urban Experience* (Philadelphia, 1974).

—— *Irish Blood: Northern Ireland and the American Conscience* (Port Washington, NY, 1976).

—— *The Irish Relations: Trials of an Immigrant Tradition* (Rutherford, NJ, 1982).

—— *Hibernia America: The Irish and Regional Cultures* (Westport, Conn., 1986).

—— *Erin's Heirs: Irish Bonds of Community* (Lexington, Ky., 1991).

CLARK, T. N., 'The Irish Ethic and the Spirit of Patronage', *Ethnicity*, 2 (1975), 305–59.

CLARKSON, L. A., 'Conclusion: Famine and Irish History', in E. M. Crawford (ed.), *Famine: The Irish Experience 900–1900* (Edinburgh, 1989).

—— and CRAWFORD, E. M., 'Dietary Directions: A Topographical Survey of the Irish Diet, 1836', in R. Mitchison and P. Roebuck (eds.), *Economy and Society in Scotland and Ireland, 1500–1939* (Edinburgh, 1988).

COHEN, A. P., *The Symbolic Construction of Community* (London, 1985).

—— 'Boundaries of Consciousness, Consciousness of Boundaries', in H. Vermeulen and C. Govers (eds.), *The Anthropology of Ethnicity: Beyond 'Ethnic Groups and Boundaries'* (The Hague, 1996).

COHEN, D. S., 'How Dutch were the Dutch of New Netherland?', *New York History*, 62 (1981), 43–60.

COLEMAN, T., *Passage to America: A History of Emigrants from Great Britain and Ireland to America in the Mid-Nineteenth Century* (London, 1972).

CONDON, T. J., *New York Beginnings: The Commercial Origins of New Netherland* (New York, 1968).

CONNELL, K. H., *The Population of Ireland, 1750–1845* (Oxford, 1950).

CONNERS, M. E., 'Their Own Kind: Family and Community Life in Albany, New York, 1850–1915', Ph.D. thesis (Harvard University, 1975).

CONNERTON, P., *How Societies Remember* (Cambridge, 1989).

CONNERY, D., *The Irish* (New York, 1970).

CORISH, P. (ed.), *A History of Irish Catholicism*, vi. 2, *The United States of America* (Dublin, 1970).

CORRIGAN, K. P., ' "I gcuntas Dé múin Béarla do na leanbháin': eisimirce agus an Ghaeilige sa naoú aois déag" ', in P. O'Sullivan (ed.), *The Irish World Wide*, ii, *The Irish in the New Communities* (Leicester, 1992).

CRAWFORD, E. M. (ed.), *Famine: The Irish Experience 900–1900* (Edinburgh, 1989).

—— 'Subsistence Crises and Famine in Ireland: A Nutritionist's View', in E. M. Crawford (ed.), *Famine: The Irish Experience 900–1900* (Edinburgh, 1989).

DALY, M. E., *The Famine in Ireland* (Dublin, 1986).

—— 'Revisionism and Irish History: The Great Famine', in D. G. Boyce and A. O'Day (eds.), *The Making of Modern Irish History: Revisionism and the Revisionist Controversy* (London, 1996).

DAVIDSON, S., and PASSMORE, R., *Human Nutrition and Dietetics* (Baltimore, 1963).

DAVIS, G., *The Irish in Britain, 1815–1914* (Dublin, 1991).

DILLON, J. J., *The Historic Story of St. Mary's, Albany, N.Y.: First-Second-Third Church* (New York, 1933).

DIMAGGIO, P., and MOHR, J., 1985. 'Cultural Capital, Educational Attainment and Marital Selection', *American Journal of Sociology*, 90 (1985), 1231–61.

DINER, H., *Erin's Daughters in America: Irish Immigrant Women in the Nineteenth Century* (Baltimore, 1983).

—— ' "The Most Irish City in the Union": The Era of the Great Migration, 1844–1877', in R. H. Bayor and T. J. Meagher (eds.), *The New York Irish* (Baltimore, 1996).

DONNELLY, J. S., 'Famine and Government Response, 1845–46', in W. E. Vaughan (ed.), *A New History of Ireland*, v, *Ireland under the Union, I, 1801–70* (Oxford, 1989).

—— 'The Administration of Relief, 1847–51', in W. E. Vaughan (ed.), *A New History of Ireland*, v, *Ireland under the Union, I, 1801–70* (Oxford, 1989).

DONNELLY, J. S., 'The Soup Kitchens', in W. E. Vaughan (ed.), *A New History of Ireland*, v, *Ireland under the Union, I, 1801–70* (Oxford, 1989).

—— 'Excess Mortality and Emigration', in W. E. Vaughan (ed.), *A New History of Ireland*, v, *Ireland under the Union, I, 1801–70* (Oxford, 1989).

DOYLE, D. N., 'The Regional Bibliography of Irish America, 1800–1930: A Review and Addendum', *Irish Historical Studies*, 23 (1983), 254–83.

—— 'The Irish in North America, 1776–1845', in W. E. Vaughan (ed.), *A New History of Ireland*, v, *Ireland under the Union, I, 1801–70* (Oxford, 1989).

—— 'The Irish as Urban Pioneers in the United States, 1850–1870', *Journal of American Ethnic History* (fall–winter 1990–1), 36–61.

—— 'The Re-making of Irish-America, 1845–80', in W. E. Vaughan (ed.), *A New History of Ireland*, vi, *Ireland under the Union, II, 1870–1921* (Oxford, 1996).

—— and EDWARDS, O. D., *America and Ireland, 1776–1976: The American Identity and the Irish Connection* (Westport, Conn., 1980).

DRUDY, P. J. (ed.), *The Irish in America: Emigration, Assimilation and Impact* (Cambridge, 1985).

DUFF, J., *The Irish in the United States* (Belmont, Calif., 1971).

ERIE, S. P., *Rainbow's End: Irish-Americans and the Dilemmas of Urban Machine Politics, 1840–1985* (Berkeley, 1988).

ERIKSEN, T. H., *Ethnicity and Nationalism: Anthropological Perspectives* (London, 1993).

ERIKSON, E. R., *Identity and the Life-Cycle* (New York, 1959).

EYLER, A., and GARRATT, R. (eds.), *The Uses of the Past: Essays on Irish Culture* (Newark, Del., 1988).

FALLOWS, M., *Irish Americans: Identity and Assimilation* (Englewood Cliffs, NJ, 1979).

FISHMAN, J., NAHIRNY, V., HOFFMAN, J., and HAYDEN, R., *Language Loyalty in the United States* (The Hague, 1966).

FITZPATRICK, D., 'Irish Emigration in the Later Nineteenth Century', *Irish Historical Studies*, 22 (1980–1), 126–41.

—— 'Emigration, 1801–70', in W. E. Vaughan (ed.), *A New History of Ireland*, v, *Ireland under the Union, I, 1801–70* (Oxford, 1989).

—— 'Emigration, 1871–1921', in W. E. Vaughan (ed.), *A New History of Ireland*, vi, *Ireland under the Union, II, 1870–1921* (Oxford, 1996).

FLANAGAN, T., *Tenant of Time* (New York, 1988).

FREEMAN, T. W., 'Land and People, c.1841', in W. E. Vaughan (ed.), *A New History of Ireland*, v, *Ireland under the Union, I, 1801–70* (Oxford, 1989).

FROGGATT, P., 'The Response of the Medical Profession to the Great Famine', in M. E. Crawford (ed.), *Famine: The Irish Experience, 900–1900* (Edinburgh, 1989).

FUNCHION, M., *Chicago's Irish Nationalists, 1881–1890* (New York, 1976).

GALLUP, G., and CASTELLI, J., *The People's Religion: American Faith in the 90s* (New York, 1989).

GANS, H., 'Symbolic Ethnicity: The Future of Ethnic Groups and Cultures in America', *Ethnic and Racial Studies*, 2 (1979), 1–20.

—— *The Urban Villagers: Group and Class in the Life of Italian-Americans*, rev. edn., (New York, 1982).

—— *Middle American Individualism* (New York, 1988).

GEERTZ, C., *The Interpretation of Cultures* (New York, 1973).

GELLNER, E., *Nations and Nationalism* (Oxford, 1983).

—— *Nationalism* (London, 1997).

GLAZER, N., and MOYNIHAN, D. P., *Beyond the Melting Pot: The Negroes, Puerto Ricans, Jews, Italians and Irish of New York City* (Cambridge, Mass., 1963).

—— *Ethnicity* (Cambridge, Mass., 1974).

GORDON, M., *Assimilation in American Life* (New York, 1964).

GOTSCH, C., 'The Albany Workingmen's Party and the Rise of Popular Politics', Ph.D. thesis (State University of New York at Albany, 1976).

GREELEY, A., *Why Can't They Be Like Us? America's White Ethnic Groups* (New York, 1971).

—— *That Most Distressful Nation: The Taming of the American Irish* (Chicago, 1972).

—— *Ethnicity in the United States: A Preliminary Reconnaisance* (New York, 1974).

—— *The Irish Americans* (New York, 1981).

—— 'The Success and Assimilation of Irish Protestants and Irish Catholics in the United States', *Sociology and Social Research*, 72 (1988), 229–37.

—— and ROSSI, P., *The Education of Catholic Americans* (Chicago, 1966).

GREENBERG, B., *Worker and Community: Response to Industrialization in a Nineteenth-Century American City, Albany, New York, 1850–1884* (Albany, NY, 1985).

GRIFFEN, C., and GRIFFEN, S., *Natives and Newcomers: The Ordering of Opportunity in Mid-Nineteenth Century Poughkeepsie* (Cambridge, Mass., 1978).

GRIFFIN, W., *The Irish in America 550–1972: A Chronology and Fact Book* (Dobbs Ferry, NY, 1973).

HACHEY, T., *A Portrait of the Irish in America* (New York, 1981).

—— *The Irish Experience* (Englewood Cliffs, NJ, 1989).

—— and MCCAFFREY, L., *Perspectives on Irish Nationalism* (Lexington, Ky., 1989).

HANDELMAN, D., *Models and Mirrors: Towards an Anthropology of Public Events* (Cambridge, 1990).

HANNERZ, U., *Cultural Complexity* (New York, 1992).

HANSEN, M. L., *The Atlantic Migration 1607–1860: A History of the Continuing Settlement of the United States* (New York, 1940).

HIRSCH, S. E., *Roots of the American Working Class: The Industrialization of Crafts in Newark, 1800–1860* (Philadelphia, 1978).

HISLOP, C., *Albany: Dutch, English and American* (Albany, NY, 1936).

HOUT, M., and GOLDSTEIN, J., 'How 4.5 Million Irish Immigrants became 40 Million Irish Americans: Demographic and Subjective Aspects of the Ethnic Composition of White Americans', *American Sociological Review*, 59 (1994), 64–82.

HUTCHINSON, J., and SMITH, A. D. (eds.), *Ethnicity* (Oxford, 1996).

IHDE, T., *The Irish Language in the United States: A Historical, Sociolinguistic, and Applied Linguistic Survey* (Westport, Conn., 1994).

JAMESON, J. F., *Narratives of New Netherland, 1609–1664* (New York, 1909).

JENKINS, R., *Rethinking Ethnicity: Arguments and Explorations* (London, 1997).

KANE, E., 'Man and Kin in Donegal: A Study of Kinship Functions in a Rural Irish and an Irish-American Community', *Ethnology*, 7 (1968), 245–58.

KENNEDY, L., and CLARKSON, L. A., 'Birth, Death and Exile: Irish Population History, 1700–1921', in B. J. Graham and L. J. Proudfoot (eds.), *An Historical Geography of Ireland* (London, 1993).

KENNEDY, R., *The Irish: Emigration, Marriage and Fertility* (Berkeley, 1973).

KENNEDY, R. J. R., 'Single or Triple Melting Pot: Intermarriage in New Haven, 1870–1940', *American Journal of Sociology*, 49 (1944), 331–9.

—— 'Single or Triple Melting Pot? Intermarriage in New Haven, 1870–1950', *American Journal of Sociology*, 58 (1952), 56–9.

KENNEDY, W., *O Albany!* (New York, 1983).

KENNEY, A. P., 'The Transformation of the Albany Patricians, 1778–1860', *New York History*, 68 (1987), 151–73.

KINEALY, C., 'The Poor Law During the Great Famine: An Administration in Crisis', in E. M Crawford (ed.), *Famine: The Irish Experience 900–1900* (Edinburgh, 1989).

—— *This Great Calamity: The Irish Famine, 1845–52* (Dublin, 1994).

KOSMIN, B. and LACHMAN, S., 'Research Report: The National Survey of Religious Identification, 1989–90: Selected Tabulations' (City University of New York Graduate Center, 1991).

LEARY, M. A., *The History of Catholic Education in the Diocese of Albany* (Washington, 1957).

LIEBERSON, S., *Ethnic Patterns in American Cities* (New York, 1963).

—— *A Piece of the Pie: Blacks and White Immigrants since 1880* (Berkeley, 1980).

—— 'Unhyphenated Whites in the United States', *Ethnic and Racial Studies*, 8 (1985), 159–80.

—— and BELL, E., 'Children's First Names: An Empirical Study of Social Taste', *American Journal of Sociology*, 98 (1992), 511–54.

—— and WATERS, M., 'Ethnic Mixtures in the United States', *Sociology and Social Research*, 70 (1985), 567–76.

—— *From Many Strands: Ethnic and Racial Groups in Contemporary America* (New York, 1988).

LODEN, M., and ROSENER, J. B., *Workforce America! Managing Employee Diversity as a Vital Resource* (Homewood, Ill., 1991).

LOUDEN, M. J. (ed.), *Catholic Albany* (Albany, NY, 1895).

LUCAS, H. S., *Netherlanders in America: Dutch Immigration to the United States and Canada, 1789–1950* (Ann Arbor, 1955).

LUKES, S., 'Political Ritual and Social Integration', *Sociology*, 9 (1975), 289–308.

McCAFFREY, L., 'The Conservative Image of Irish America', *Ethnicity*, 2 (1975), 271–80.

—— *Irish Nationalism and the American Contribution* (New York, 1976).

—— *The Irish Diaspora in America* (Bloomington, Ind., 1984).

—— *The Irish in Chicago* (Urbana, Ill., 1987).

McDONALD, F., and McWHINEY, C., 'The Celtic South', *History Today*, 30 (1980), 11–15.

MACDONOUGH, O., *States of Mind: A Study of the Anglo-Irish Conflict, 1780–1980* (London, 1983).

McENENY, J. J., *Albany: Capital City on the Hudson* (Woodland Hills, Calif., 1981).

MEAGHER, T., ' "Irish All the Time": Ethnic Consciousness among the Irish in Worcester, Massachusetts, 1880–1905', *Journal of Social History*, 19 (1985), 273–303.

—— *From Paddy to Studs: Irish-American Communities in the Turn-of-the-Century Era, 1880 to 1920* (New York, 1986).

MERWICK, D., *Possessing Albany, 1630–1710: The Dutch and English Experiences* (Cambridge, 1990).

METRESS, S. P., *The Irish-American Experience: A Guide to the Literature* (Washington, 1981).

MILLER, K., *Emigrants and Exiles: Ireland and the Irish Exodus to North America* (New York, 1985).

—— 'Paddy's Paradox: Emigration to America in Irish Imagination and Rhetoric', in D. Hoerder and H. Rössler (eds.), *Distant Magnets: Expectations and Realities in the Immigrant Experience, 1840–1930* (New York, 1993).

—— BOLING, B., and DOYLE, D. N., 'Emigrants and Exiles: Irish Cultures and Irish Emigration to North America', *Irish Historical Studies*, 22 (1980), 97–125.

MILLER, N., *The Enterprise of a Free People: Aspects of Economic Development in New York State during the Canal Period, 1792–1838* (Ithaca, NY, 1962).

MOKYR, J., *Why Ireland Starved: A Quantitative and Analytical History of the Irish Economy, 1800–1850* (London, 1983).

MONAHAN, K., 'The Irish Hour: An Expression of the Musical Taste and the Cultural Values of the Pittsburgh Irish Community', *Ethnicity*, 4 (1977), 201–15.

MOORE, S. F., and MYERHOFF, B., *Secular Ritual* (Assen, 1977).

MORAWSKA, E., 'The Sociology and Historiography of Immigration', in V. Yans-McLaughlin (ed.), *Immigration Reconsidered: History, Sociology, and Politics* (New York, 1990).

NAHIRNY, V., and FISHMAN, J. A., 'American Immigrant Groups: Ethnic Identification and the Problem of Generations', *Sociological Review*, 13 (1965), 311–26.

NEIDERT, L. J., and FARLEY, R., 'Assimilation in the United States: An Analysis of Ethnic and Generation Differences in Status and Achievement', *American Sociological Review*, 50 (1985), 840–50.

NISSENSON, S., *The Patroon's Domain* (New York, 1937).

O'CALLAGHAN, E. B. (ed.), *Documents Relative to the Colonial History of the State of New York*, 13 vols. (Albany, NY, 1853–87).

Ó GRÁDA, C., 'Irish Emigration to the United States in the Nineteenth Century', in D. N. Doyle and O. D. Edwards (eds.), *America and Ireland, 1776–1976: The American Identity and the Irish Connection* (Westport, Conn., 1980).

—— *Ireland before and after the Famine: Explorations in Economic History, 1800–1925* (Manchester, 1988).

—— *The Great Irish Famine* (Dublin, 1989).

—— 'Poverty, Population and Agriculture, 1801–45', in W. E. Vaughan (ed.), *A New History of Ireland*, v, *Ireland under the Union, I, 1801–70* (Oxford, 1989).

O'GRADY, J., *How the Irish Became Americans* (New York, 1973).

OKAMURA, J., 'Situational Ethnicity', *Ethnic and Racial Studies*, 4 (1981), 452–65.

PADDOCK, W. H., *History of the Police Service of Albany* (Albany, NY, 1902).

PARKER, A. J. (ed.), *Landmarks of Albany County, New York* (Syracuse, NY, 1897).

POUND, A. C., *Johnson of the Mohawks* (New York, 1930).

—— *The Golden Earth* (New York, 1935).

—— *Lake Ontario* (Indianapolis, 1945).

PURVIS, T. L., 'The National Origins of New Yorkers in 1790', *New York History*, 67 (1986), 133–53.

RINK, O. A., 'The People of New Netherland: Notes on Non-English Immigration to New York in the Seventeenth Century', *New York History*, 62 (1981), 5–42.

—— *Holland on the Hudson: An Economic and Social History of Dutch New York* (Ithaca, NY, 1986).

ROBERTS, A., and VAN DYK, J. (eds.), *Experiencing Albany: Perspectives on a Grand City's Past* (Albany, NY, 1986).

ROBINSON, F. S., *Albany's O'Connell Machine: An American Political Relic* (Albany, NY, 1973).

ROOSENS, E., 'The Primordial Nature of Origins in Migrant Ethnicity', in H. Vermeulen and C. Govers (eds.), *The Anthropology of Ethnicity: Beyond 'Ethnic Groups and Boundaries'* (The Hague, 1996).

ROWLEY, W. A., 'Albany: A Tale of Two Cities, 1820–1880', Ph.D. thesis (Harvard University, 1967).

—— 'The Irish Aristocracy of Albany, 1798–1878', *New York History*, 52 (1971), 275–304.

SCHUTZ, A., and LUCKMANN, T., *The Structures of the Life-World* (London, 1974).

SHANNON, W., *The American Irish: A Political and Social Portrait* (New York, 1966).

SHAW, R. E., *Erie Water West: A History of the Erie Canal, 1792–1854* (Lexington, Ky., 1966).

SHILS, E. A., *Tradition* (London, 1981).

SMITH, A. D., *Nations and Nationalism in a Global Era* (Cambridge, 1995).

SMITH, W. B., 'Wage Rates on the Erie Canal, 1828–1881', *Journal of Economic History*, 23 (1963), 298–311.

SOLAR, P., 'The Great Famine was no Ordinary Subsistence Crisis', in E. M. Crawford (ed.), *Famine: The Irish Experience, 900–1900* (Edinburgh, 1989).

THERNSTROM, S., *Poverty and Progress: Social Mobility in a Nineteenth Century City* (Cambridge, Mass., 1964).

—— *The Other Bostonians: Poverty and Progress in the American Metropolis* (Cambridge, Mass., 1973).

—— (ed.), *The Harvard Encyclopedia of American Ethnic Groups* (Cambridge, Mass., 1980).

—— and SENNETT, R. (eds.), *Nineteenth-Century Cities: Essays in the New Urban History* (New Haven, 1969).

TOMASKOVIC-DEVEY, B., and TOMASKOVIC-DEVEY, D., 'The Social Structural Determinants of Ethnic Group Behavior: Single Ancestry Rates among Four White American Groups', *American Sociological Review*, 53 (1988), 650–9.

TRELEASE, A. W., *Indian Affairs in Colonial New York: The Seventeenth Century* (Ithaca, NY, 1960).

TURNER, T., 'Anthropology and Multiculturalism: What Is Anthropology that Multiculturalists should be Mindful of it?' *Cultural Anthropology*, 8 (1993), 411–29.

URIS, L., *Trinity* (New York, 1976).

VAN DER DONCK, A., *A Description of the New Netherlands*, T. F. O'Donnell (ed.) (Syracuse, NY, 1968).

VERDERY, K., 'Ethnicity, Nationalism and State-making: "Ethnic Groups and Boundaries": Past and Future', in H. Vermeulen and C. Govers (eds.), *The Anthropology of Ethnicity: Beyond 'Ethnic Groups and Boundaries'* (The Hague, 1996).

WALSH, J. (ed.), *The San Francisco Irish, 1850–1976* (San Francisco, 1978).

WATERS, M. C., *Ethnic Options: Choosing Identities in America* (Berkeley, 1990).

WEBER, M., *The Theory of Social and Economic Organization*, T. Parsons (ed.) (New York, 1947).

—— *From Max Weber: Essays in Sociology*, H. H. Gerth and C. Wright Mills (eds.) (London, 1948).

—— *Economy and Society*, 2 vols., G. Roth and C. Wittisch (eds.) (Berkeley, 1978).

WEISE, A., *The History of the City of Albany, New York* (Albany, NY, 1884).

WEISZ, H., 'Irish-American Attitudes and the Americanization of English-Language Parochial Schools', *New York History*, 53 (1972), 157–76.

WHYTE, W. F., *Street Corner Society: The Social Structure of an Italian Slum*, 3rd edn. (Chicago, 1981).

WILCOXEN, C., *Seventeenth Century Albany: A Dutch Profile* (Albany, NY, 1981).

WILENTZ, R. S., 'Industrializing America and the Irish: Towards the New Departure', *Labor History*, 20 (1979), 579–95.

WINSBERG, M., 'Irish Settlement in the United States, 1850–1980', *Eire-Ireland*, 20 (1985), 7–14.

WINSTANLEY, M., *Ireland and the Land Question, 1800–1922* (London, 1984).

WITTKE, C., *The Irish in America* (New York, 1970).

WOODHAM SMITH, C., *The Great Hunger* (New York, 1962).

YINGER, J. M., 'Towards a Theory of Assimilation and Dissimilation', *Ethnic and Racial Studies*, 4 (1981), 249–64.

INDEX